The Best Season - The First Ninety Games

Bob May

Halo
PUBLISHING
INTERNATIONAL

ISBN: 978-1-61244-899-2

PUBLISHING
INTERNATIONAL

Halo Publishing International, LLC
8000 W Interstate 10, Suite 600
San Antonio, Texas 78230
www.halopublishing.com

Printed and bound in the United States

Table of Contents

This book is dedicated to my loving parents –

As a child I was blessed. My parents let me be me. I loved baseball from as early as I can remember. Summers I would be at the playground baseball diamond all day except for lunch and supper.

When Dad was home, we often played catch. Dad took me to Fenway Park (Ted Williams and Joe DiMaggio) and Braves Field (Warren Spahn vs. Robin Roberts).

At age nine, I made the Green Sox Little League team as an outfielder. Dad was an assistant coach. As a teenager I realized I could not hit the fast ball very well and began to play baseball board games. My parents used to worry about me. However, they let me enjoy my hobby.

Just as I want to honor the players from the Black Ball Era, I also want to honor my wonderful parents who let me be a kid and pursue my passion, baseball.

Thanks for your unconditional love.
Bob

What would Joe DiMaggio have done hitting against Satchel Paige? How many home runs would Josh Gibson have hit off Sandy Koufax? These are the kinds of questions that many of us ask as baseball fans and researchers. We wish we could answer questions like these. Well, author Bob May has tried to give us some answers in *The Best Season-The First 90 Games*. Through a baseball simulation board game May has brought to life the careers of twenty-one black ball stars, giving them the opportunity they never got in their playing days. He has had them play a full season against Major League stars to bring to life their stats. By following their day to day exploits on the diamond readers will finally get a chance to see what might have been if some of the Negro League's greatest players had been given a chance in the Major Leagues.

Bob May has been working with baseball board games for many years (President of Pursue the Pennant from 1989 to 1995). He brings experience and expertise to this effort. He has also interviewed me and a number of Negro League players to be able to better tell their story. As a result, not only does he provide the stats but he also tells a story. This book and the second volume to follow is Bob May's way of paying tribute to the Negro Leagues. It is a way to honor what they did and what they were not able to do because of America's segregationist policies. The gentleman's agreement in baseball denied so many young men the chance to test their skills against Major League players. As a result their play was never as widely recognized no matter how many home runs Gibson hit or strikeouts Satchel Paige had.

Bob May's simulated games give voice and numbers to what could have been. He wants to give these men the honor and recognition they never got while they toiled in the Negro Leagues. As you read the stories and follow the games readers will get a glimpse into what the game of baseball might have looked like if everyone had been able to play on the same diamonds. Thanks to Bob May's efforts recognition and respect is being paid to the talents and accomplishments of some of baseball's greatest stars. Read and enjoy the games that follow. You will learn a great deal about what should have been a part of baseball's history and be able to answer some of those great what if questions all baseball fans love.

Leslie Heaphy
Assoc. Professor, history

How many of you saw the baseball classic *Field of Dreams*[1] starring Kevin Costner? How many of you cried? I bawled my eyes out when Kevin asked his dad to play catch. It was always special for me to play catch with my dad

I remember the time he took me to my first Red Sox game during that special summer of 1949 to see the Yankees. I was 7 years old. As we walked up the ramp to our seats behind first base, I saw (1) the famous Green Monster, (2) the greenest grass I'd ever seen, (3) Ted Williams and his Boston Red Sox teammates Dom DiMaggio, Johnny Pesky, and Bobby Doerr, and finally, of course, (4) the great New York Yankees, featuring Dom's more famous brother, Joe. In 1949 the Yankees celebrated the first of five straight World Series championships.

When I decided in the late summer of 2010 to use a board game, Pursue the Pennant, to play a tournament with 21 black ball stars vs. the Major League stars from the 1880s through 1970s, I broke them down into 3-game series by decade. But I had no plan to write about it. When I finished the tournament, the black ball stars dominated, and I wanted to share the outcome with other baseball fans.

About 10-12 years ago I was in Kansas City, and I visited the Negro League Baseball Museum, where I met Dr. Ray Doswell, the acting Executive Director. He showed me around the museum. I put all his information into my address book.

More recently, I called the NLBM in October or November of 2010 to see if Dr. Doswell was still there. I believe now that God helped me to recall Dr. Doswell. When I reached Dr. Doswell, I refreshed his memory about our meeting about a decade ago. I told him why I was calling him to share the results of the board game tournament and to see if it might honor these great players and Black Ball (Negro Leagues) if I wrote about this tournament, as well as the background behind it. He asked me to send him some information, which I did. He thought it was an interesting idea.

Dr. Doswell gave me Dr. Leslie Heaphy's email. Dr. Heaphy is the Detail Editor for *Black Ball: A Negro Leagues Journal*, and Dr. Doswell is on the Editorial Board. They encouraged me to send them a manuscript, including all the background and data on Pursue the Pennant, the baseball game simulation behind the tournament. I owned the company that produced that board game from 1989 through 1995.

On January 18, 2011, I sent them a 44-page manuscript that included the background behind the tournament, the decision in 1993 to create the 400+ Hall of Fame/All Star Player Card Set (including 21 black ball stars), the write-up of the first four 3-game series (decades 1880, 1970, 1890, and 1960), a

1

Pursue the Pennant baseball board game Fact Sheet, the 12-game box scores, and rosters/stats for all five teams (including black ball stars).

I believed this could be a *Field of Dreams* moment. What if we could create the excitement of putting black ball stars (mostly Hall of Famers) and a season's worth of baseball game simulations (165 games plus playoffs) against 375 other great players (250 career greats, mostly Hall of Famers and 125 short-time All-Stars)? It could include daily box scores, game reporting, analysis, stat leaders, editorials, simulated radio broadcasts, debates, everything a baseball fan could want. Even Win Shares, which are discussed in the next section. The purpose of this two book series is to honor these 21 Black Ball Era stars with a full documented season of baseball (165 game season plus a post season six team playoff) against 375 great Major League ballplayers from the 1880s to the 1980s!

I have a nine-year-old grandson who has played some of these black ball game simulations with his grampa. He rolls the dice and is amazed at how good these black ball stars are, as well as the other greatest players of all time. He appreciates the skills of black ball stars such as Josh Gibson, Oscar Charleston, and Satchel Paige, as well as Ted Williams, Mickey Mantle, and Walter Johnson. And when we play, he chooses the black ball stars.

Win Shares - How many of you are familiar with the baseball writings of Bill James, currently Sr. Vice President with the Boston Red Sox? Two of my favorite baseball resource books have his name on them. *Win Shares*[2] was written with Jim Henzler of Stats Inc. (2002); *The New Bill James Historical Baseball Abstract*[3] was published in 2001.. All of these books have been used in some way on this black ball baseball writing project.

In the Win Shares system, whatever is accomplished by the team is credited to the players. Win Shares, a revolutionary system that allows for player evaluation across positions, teams, and eras, measures the total sum of player contributions in one groundbreaking number. According to the back cover of *Win Shares*, James' latest advancement in the world of statistical analysis is the next big stepping stone in the "greatest players of all time" debate.

How does the Win Share system help evaluate the black ball stars who are not part of Major League baseball statistics? It does not help directly, but it does help indirectly.

Mark Armour, author of many baseball bios, wrote *MLB Integration, 1947 to 1986*[4] an article about the impact of integration on the playing field using Win Share player data that showed how the black star players improved the quality of play between the lines.

In the 1950s and 1960s, the National League (NL) had more star black ball players than the American League (AL), and it showed up in the All-Star Classics. The National League was the more dominant league. When Frank

Robinson was traded from the Reds (NL) to the Orioles (AL), Robinson won the Triple Crown in 1966.

Armour says near the end of his article, "There were players like Willie Mays and Frank Robinson playing in the 1930s, the theory goes, and they should be honored just as their successors were."

For some anecdotal evidence, Bill James has a section in *The New Bill James Historical Baseball Abstract* (published in 2001 by Free Press, a division of Simon and Schuster, Inc.) called The 100 Greatest Players of All Time (pages 358 to 368[5]).

Below is a list from back to front (100 down to 1) of the black ball stars he has in the Top 100. Those with an asterisk (*) are included in the 21 Negro League stars we created at Pursue the Pennant, the focus of all this research and writing.

Rank	Player	Position	Pursue the Pennant
96	Martin Dihigo	All	*Pitcher
86	Willie Wells	SS	*
76	Cool Papa Bell	OF	*
67	Cristobal Torriente	OF	*
65	Buck Leonard	1B	*
52	Joe Williams	P	
43	Mule Suttles	OF-1B	*
27	Pop Lloyd	SS	*
25	Turkey Stearnes	OF	*
17	Satchel Paige	P	*
9	Josh Gibson	C	*
4	Oscar Charleston	OF	*

Note: Josh Gibson is the first catcher on the entire list, and Satchel Paige is the second pitcher, while Walter Johnson is the first pitcher. As I write this section of my book, Satchel Paige faces Walter Johnson for the third time (Game Nine of the BB Stars vs. the Senators/Twins series). To find out whether Number 1 outpitches Number 2, keep reading.

In 1993 when we created the card set, we did not include Joe Williams. He was one of many great Negro League players we overlooked. Remember, there was limited box scores and score sheets for the games played in the Negro Leagues. Our information was very limited.

The Best Season Tournament is the second part of a project to honor the great black ball stars who did not have the opportunity to play in the Major

Leagues, with two exceptions, Satchel Paige and Monte Irvin. Hopefully this project will honor everyone connected with black ball, including family members and friends.

This will be a two-book series. This is the first book, *The Best Season – The First Ninety Games,* and the second book will be *The Best Season – The Challenging Finish.* This two-book series will honor 21 black ball stars from the Negro Leagues through baseball board game simulation. It will feature

1) Fifteen nine-game series vs. the 16 original post-1900 teams. The Braves and Pirates will combine to be one of the 15 teams.
2) Two special fifteen-game All-Star Series.
3) Post-season six-team playoff from the 15 nine-game series.

Note: To balance the 25-man rosters/by position, free agents will be included from 19th century teams (over 40 players), other major league teams like the Astros, Brewers, Rangers, Mets, and Royals, and extra players from surpluses of Yankees, Giants, Cardinals, and Dodgers. The Black Ball Stars 25-man roster has four free agent Major League black pitchers (Newcombe-1956 Dodgers; Tiant-1968 Indians; Richard-1979 Astros; Moore-1985 Angels.

In the summer of 2011, God made it clear why I was supposed to write these books. In July I had the honor to take one of my grandsons to meet Monte Irvin. He played for the Newark Eagles of the Negro Leagues and the New York Giants of the National League. Monte participated in two World Series, 1951 and 1954. The Giants were the World Champions in 1954 when they swept the powerful Cleveland Indians (111-43, .721).

Monte was 92 years old. He was so gracious with Caleb, my 9-year-old grandson. He gave Caleb an autographed picture, signed a baseball, and let me take a picture of the two of them. For the next 10-15 minutes, I asked Monte to share with Caleb about his experiences in the Negro Leagues. Monte kept repeating, "We just loved to play ball." He shared stories about the bus rides, including sleeping on the bus. He said, "I could sleep better on the bus than in a hotel!" We thanked him for a wonderful visit. As I look back on that visit, I will always remember the look in Monte's eyes when he said, "We just loved to play ball."

At the July 2011 Lester Malloy Negro League Baseball Conference, attended by over 100 baseball historians, I also met two other former Negro League players. One of these was Jumping Johnny Wilson, better known for his basketball prowess. He was one of the great basketball players from the Hoosier State, Indiana. He was one of the star players on the Harlem Globetrotters. The other was Alvin Spearman, former Chicago American Giants star pitcher. Al called me in August 2011, and we talked for over an hour. He sent me an article *"Finishing What He Started"* written by Kevin Czerwinski (MLB.com) in September 2006. Al Spearman was very proud of this accomplishment - he completed 33 consecutive games as a pitcher in the minor leagues. In fact, over two years, he completed 48 out of 50 games. His great career had a sad ending, however, as he quit baseball in 1959 because of racism. I was touched by Al's comment at the bottom of the copy of the article he sent me. He thanked me for our wonderful conversation.

Finally, but not least, in October 2011 I met 90-year-old Bill Blair, publisher of *The Elite* weekly newspaper in the Dallas/Ft. Worth metro area. He pitched for the Indianapolis Clowns from 1946-1951. In September 2011, Bill had a baseball stadium named for him in Dallas. I contacted him when I realized he was referred to as "The Legend" when it came to black baseball (the Negro Leagues) in the Dallas area.

Bill was instrumental in getting me on "Talking Sports" with Roger B. Brown, including a 30-minute segment for me to talk about my project for honoring Black Ball through baseball board game simulation. The project includes writing (articles, books, FaceBook page, blog), and speaking (directly about baseball or indirectly about honor, respect, and going for your dream). The project includes a website and will eventually include radio broadcasts/CDs of the simulated games.

I have a question in my brochure about honoring Black Ball. "How would the stars of the black ball era like to be honored? I believe they would like to have more recognition and visibility. I also believe they would agree with this statement 100%: "Let us put on the spikes for one more complete season of baseball competition (160+ games with a playoff) against the greatest players of all time, and let us show you what we can do! Document our complete season through writing, such as articles/books; discussions, including sports talk shows; radio broadcasts and CDs."

This first book, *The Best Season (The First 90 Games)* is your box seat behind the BB Stars team dugout in all the great baseball parks/stadiums of the twentieth century. I hope you enjoy reading this book as much as I did researching (playing/managing the games) and writing (mostly as a pseudo baseball reporter).

Remember, a second book will complete the season, *The Best Season – The Challenging Finish*. A third book is under consideration, *The Pennant Race*. The first two books focus primarily on the BB Stars (100% participation in the 165 games). In *The Pennant Race*, the BB Stars become the eighth National League team in a 28-game pennant race. (Remember that the Braves and Pirates franchises were combined). The BB Stars will use Milwaukee County Stadium as their home park. The eight American League teams (franchises) do not have to play the BB Stars unless the BB Stars win the National League pennant race. The World Series will be the 100-Year World Series

(1880 – 1980). Which of these 16 franchises will come out on top? Can these great forgotten heroes, the black ball stars, win it all?

Before we go any further, I was asked how was a ball player defined as "black" and therefore kept out of organized baseball. In the nineteenth century, there were black ball players in organized baseball. Then in 1887, there was an unwritten secret agreement among the white owners of baseball clubs barring the Negroes from professional baseball (source - First Inning, pages 2-3, Kadir Nelson *"We Are The Ship" The story of Negro League Baseball* [7].)

However, these owners were always looking for an edge. If there was a very talented ball player from Cuba or somewhere in Latin America, who may have been black but had light skin, the owner who signed him, pretended he was white but Latino. Therefore, "black" depended on the eye of the beholder. Other owners soon complained and the player was released. Essentially, the Negro ballplayer was banned from Major League Baseball for sixty years.

Chapter 1

Black Ball - Player Biographies/Roster

THERE ARE TWENTY ONE BIOGRAPHIES[1] for the players from the "Black Ball Era" or the Negro Leagues. For the four "free agent" pitchers that augment the Black Ball Stars roster, there is a highlight of their pitching accomplishments during their "Best Season" in the Major Leagues. Many great biography sources are available. I am going to keep my black ball bios focused on a few areas for these twenty-one Black Ball Era players.

1. Where ranked in the Top 100 ballplayers (source – Bill James' *Historical Baseball Abstract* [2], 2001) -
2. Years played and years managed (source – National Baseball Hall of Fame website)
3. Primary Negro League teams
4. Two or three interesting facts about the player

Listed below are the best ballplayers of all time at each position, based on Bill James' *Historical Baseball Abstract*, 2001, and their rank in the Top 100. This list will consist of the best players by position (includes two pitchers).

- **Outfielders (OF)** – Babe Ruth (1); Willie Mays (3); *Oscar Charleston (4)*
- **Shortstop (SS)** – Honus Wagner (2)
- **Third Base (3B)** – Mike Schmidt (21)

- **Second Base (2B)** – Joe Morgan (15)
- **First Base (1B)** – Lou Gehrig (14)
- **Catcher** – *Josh Gibson (9)*
- **Pitchers** – Walter Johnson (8) and *Satchel Paige (17)*

As you can see, three of the ten players listed above are from the Negro Leagues (30%). The bios of the 21 black ball stars will start with the Negro League players in the *Top 100 Players of Baseball History,* per baseball historian Bill James.

Eleven of the twenty one Black Ball Stars are in the Top 100 ranking.

The Black Ball Stars 25 man roster is near the end of the Biography section (Chart 1-1 on page 17). The players statistical data is based on a 162 game season (comparable with today's Major League schedule).

Oscar Charleston Rank – 4 DOB – October 4, 1896 **Died** – October 6, 1954

   Years Played – 1920-1942 **Years Managed** – 1924-1954 (some years)
   Position – OF
   Primary Teams – Indianapolis ABCs; Harrisburg Giants; Pittsburgh Crawfords
   Notes – Charleston was inducted into the Baseball Hall of Fame (HOF) in 1976. He is recognized by most baseball historians as the greatest all-around player in Negro League history. He was a great left-handed power hitter. He had great speed and was a very good base stealer and a great defensive outfielder with a very good throwing arm. He was known to have a mean streak. In fact, Charleston was a factor in the race riots in Indiana during the 1920s. After a disputed call, Charleston punched a white umpire in the face. The KKK had a strong presence in the state of Indiana during the 1920s.

Josh Gibson Rank – 9 DOB – December 21, 1911 **Died** – January 20, 1947

   Years Played – 1930-1946 **Years Managed** – None **Position** – Catcher
   Primary Teams – Homestead Grays; Pittsburgh Crawfords
   Notes - Gibson was inducted into the Baseball HOF in 1972. Baseball historian Bill James ranks Gibson as the greatest catcher in baseball history. He was a right-handed hitter and had tremendous power. He hit over 900 home runs. It is believed he is the only player to ever hit a home run over the roof and out of Yankee Stadium. Gibson died prematurely. Gibson died (thirty-five years old) from a suspected brain tumor.

Leroy "Satchel" Paige   Rank – 17   DOB – July 7, 1906   **Died** – June 8, 1982

> **Years Played** – 1926-1948   **Years Managed** – None   **Position** – Pitcher
>
> **Primary Teams** – Pittsburgh Crawfords; Kansas City Monarchs
>
> **Notes** - Paige was inducted into the Baseball HOF in 1971. He is recognized by most baseball historians as the premier pitcher in Negro League history. According to baseball historian Bill James, Walter "Big Train" Johnson was the only pitcher better than Paige. He was considered the first free agent in baseball history. Paige had no problem leaving his team for a weekend, weeks, or months if he could make more money. He drove his teammates, manager, owner, and fans crazy with his free spirit. In 1948, at the age of 42, he was signed by the Cleveland Indians in July. He posted a 6-1 record to help the Indians clinch the American League title and proceed to the World Series. This was the last World Series the Indians won.

Norman "Turkey" Stearnes   Rank – 25   DOB – May 8, 1901   **Died** – September 4, 1979

> **Years Played** – 1921-1940   **Years Managed** – None   **Position** – OF
>
> **Primary Teams** – Detroit Stars; Chicago American Giants; Philadelphia Stars
>
> **Notes** - Stearnes was inducted into the Baseball HOF in 2002. He won four batting titles in the 1920s. He was a left-handed power hitter. He was also an excellent outfielder, with great range and a strong arm. When he was with the Chicago American Giants, he was selected to four East-West All-Star Games. Turkey had an odd batting stance whereby he looked off balance, but pitchers had a hard time throwing the ball past him.

John "Pop" Lloyd   Rank – 27   DOB – April 25, 1884   **Died** – March 19, 1965

> **Years Played** – 1906-1932   **Years Managed** – Ten years   **Position** – SS
>
> **Primary Teams** – Cuban X Giants; New York Lincoln Giants
>
> **Notes** – Lloyd was inducted into the Baseball HOF in 1977. He was the best SS of his era and the top run producer. He had a consistently high on-base-percentage. A keen strategist, he was excellent on the bases and was among the top managers in black baseball.
>
> **"I am honored to have John Lloyd called the Black Wagner. It is a privilege to have been compared to him." Honus Wagner quote[3].**

George "Mule" Suttles Rank – 43 DOB – March 2, 1901 **Died** – July 9, 1966

> **Years Played** – 1923-1944 **Years Managed** – 1943-1944 **Position** – 1B, OF
>
> **Primary Teams** – St. Louis Stars; Newark Eagles
>
> **Notes** – Suttles was inducted into the Baseball HOF in 2006 and played in five East-West All-Star contests. With his great range and strong arm, he was a great defensive player (1B, OF). He was one of the most feared right-handed sluggers in Negro League history.

Walter "Buck" Leonard Rank – 65 DOB – September 8, 1907 **Died** – November 27, 1997

> **Years Played** – 1923-1948 **Years Managed** – None **Position** – 1B
>
> **Primary Teams** – Homestead Grays
>
> **Notes** – Leonard was inducted into the Baseball HOF in 1972. Josh Gibson and the left-handed hitting Buck Leonard formed the most feared batting twosome in Negro League history. The Grays won the Negro National League pennant nine years in a row (1937-1945). He was a smooth-fielding first baseman.

Cristobal Torriente Rank – 67 DOB – November 16, 1893 **Died** – April 11, 1938

> **Years Played** – 1913-1932 **Years Managed** – None **Position** – OF
>
> **Primary Team** – Chicago American Giants
>
> **Notes** – Torriente was inducted into the Baseball HOF in 2006 and led the Chicago American Giants to three NNL Championships in a row (1920-1922). His clutch home run won the deciding game in the 1921 Championship. The notorious bad-ball hitting left-handed hitter excelled in the field, and he had an excellent throwing arm.

James "Cool Papa" Bell Rank – 76 DOB – May 17, 1903 **Died** – March 7, 1991

> **Years Played** – 1922-1946 **Years Managed** – None **Position** – OF
>
> **Primary Teams** – St. Louis Stars; Pittsburgh Crawfords; Homestead Grays
>
> **Notes** – Bell was inducted into the Baseball HOF in 1974. A switch hitter, he was noted for his speed on the base paths. He had great ability as a lead-off hitter, and his defensive skills in the outfield were superb. Satchel Paige said, "Bell was so fast that he could shut the light off in the hotel room and be in bed before the light was out!" [4]

Willie Wells   Rank – 86   DOB – August 10, 1905   **Died** – January 22, 1989

> **Years Played** – 1924-1954   **Years Managed** – 1942, '45, '47, '54.
> **Position** – SS
> **Primary Teams** – St. Louis Stars; Newark Eagles
> **Notes** – Wells was inducted into the Baseball HOF in 1997. Willie Wells hit right-handed, and he was the first shortstop to show dazzling skills in the field combined with home run power. He had great success in the Mexican League. As a manager, he was a great teacher and helped Monte Irvin and Don Newcombe when they were young players in the Negro Leagues.

Martin Dihigo   Rank – 96   DOB – May 24, 1905   **Died** – May 20, 1971

> **Years Played** – 1923-1936   **Years Managed** – 1935   **Position** – All
> **Primary Teams** – Cuban Stars; New York Cubans
> **Notes** – Dihigo was inducted into the Baseball HOF in 1977. A native Cuban, Dihigo embarked upon his baseball career with the Cuban Stars in 1923. For thirteen years he remained one of black baseball's stars, proving himself to be not only competent but exceptional at every position on the field. In the Best Season competition, Dihigo is a pitcher. Dihigo spent the off-season playing winter ball in his native Cuba. In his later years, he played ball all over Latin America.

Leon Day   DOB – October 30, 1916   **Died** – March 13, 1995

> **Years Played** – 1934-1950   **Years Managed** – None   **Position** – Pitcher
> **Primary Team** – Newark Eagles
> **Notes** – Day was inducted into the Baseball HOF in 1995. Day was a right-handed pitcher. Day had a great fast ball and a wicked curve ball. In 1937, his won and loss record with the Eagles was 13-0.

William Foster   DOB – June 12, 1904   **Died** – September 16, 1978

> **Years Played** – 1923-1937   **Years Managed** – None   **Position** – Pitcher
> **Primary Team** – Chicago American Giants
> **Notes** – Foster was inducted into the Baseball HOF in 1996. The side-armed left-hander had a great fastball, a devastating curve ball, and pin-point control. His winning percentage in the Negro Leagues was over .700. In competition against Major League players, such as barnstorming exhibitions, his winning percentage was over .600. He led the Chicago American Giants to four Negro League World Series.

Wilber "Bullet Joe" Rogan   DOB – July 28, 1889   **Died** – March 4, 1967
   Years Played – 1917-1938   **Years Managed** – None   **Position** –
   Pitcher
   Primary Team – Kansas City Monarchs
   Notes – Rogan was inducted into the Baseball HOF in 1998. Though
   the right-handed Rogan was a small man, he threw a blazing fast ball and
   an assortment of other pitches, such as fork balls, palm balls, curves, and
   a spitter. He threw all these pitches from a quick, no wind-up delivery.
   He led the Kansas City Monarchs to four Negro League Titles.

Hilton Smith   DOB – February 27, 1912   **Died** – November 18, 1983
   Years Played – 1932-1948   **Years Managed** – None   **Position** –
   Pitcher
   Primary Team – Kansas City Monarchs
   Notes – Smith was inducted into the Baseball HOF in 2001. He was a
   stand-out right-handed pitcher who won twenty or more games for
   twelve years with the Monarchs, including an imposing record of 93-11
   (1939-1942). He had a great fast ball and a sweeping curve ball. He
   played in six consecutive East-West All-Star Games (1937-1942) and
   was a member of seven Monarch pennant-winners and one World Series
   Championship team.

Raleigh "Biz" Mackey   DOB – July 27, 1897   **Died** – September 22, 1965
   Years Played – 1920-1947   **Years Managed** – 1941, 1946-1947   **Position** – Catcher
   Primary Teams – Hilldale Daisies; Philadelphia Stars: Newark Eagles
   Notes – Mackey was inducted into the Baseball HOF in 2006. A switch
   hitter, he hit line drives all over the ball park. He was a mentor for Roy
   Campanella while Campy was in the Negro Leagues. A great leader and
   successful manager, he was also probably the best defensive catcher in
   Negro League history.

Judy Johnson   DOB – October 26, 1899   **Died** – June 15, 1989
   Years Played – 1918-1936   **Years Managed** – None   **Position** – 3B
   Primary Teams – Hilldale Daisies; Pittsburgh Crawfords
   Notes – Johnson was inducted into the Baseball HOF in 1975. He was
   a sure-gloved third baseman and a dependable .300 hitter with little
   power. He played in the first Negro League World Series in 1924.

Ray Dandridge   DOB – August 31, 1913   **Died** – February 12, 1994
   Years Played – 1933-1949   **Years Managed** – 1949   **Position** – 3B
   Primary Team – Newark Eagles

Notes – Dandridge was inducted into the Baseball HOF in 1987. He was a very good defensive third baseman. A right-handed contact hitter, he consistently hit over .300.

Monte Irvin DOB – February 25, 1919 **Home** – Houston Texas
Years Played – 1937-1948 **Years Managed** – None **Position – OF**
Primary Team – Newark Eagles
Notes – Irvin was inducted into the Baseball HOF in 1973. He was a high average right-handed hitter with good power, an above-average outfielder with a very good throwing arm, and a very successful Major League player with the New York Giants. He played in two World Series. He was the Giants hitting star (.458 average) in a losing cause (1951) and played on the World Championship team in 1954. In July 2011, my grandson, Caleb and I had the honor of spending 20-25 minutes with Monte Irvin. He is a very gracious and humble man

Newt Allen DOB – May 19, 1901 **Died** – June 11, 1988
Years Played – 1922-1942 **Years Managed** – 1937 **Position** – 2B
Primary Team – Kansas City Monarchs
Notes – The diminutive 5'7" Allen was a great second baseman. He was a switch hitter who could bunt and slap the ball to all fields. A successful base-stealer, he had great speed. He was a team leader who guided the Monarchs in their dominating years (1937-1942).

Frankie Warfield DOB – 1895 **Died** – July 24, 1932
Years Played – 1915-1932 **Years Managed** – 1924-1925, 1929 **Position** – 2B
Primary Teams – Detroit Stars; Hilldale Daisies; Baltimore Elite Giants
Notes – A contact hitter, the right-handed Warfield was a great second baseman.

Special Note - In 1993 when our Pursue the Pennant Hall of Fame/All Star Card Set was created, nine of the above twenty-one players were in the National Baseball Hall of Fame. We created twenty-one Negro League player cards in the set to provide the minimum number of players that could provide a team with enough players by position. We wanted our customers to be able to play these black ball stars in competition as a team, if they so desired. Nineteen of these twenty-one players are now in the National Baseball HOF. The two second basemen, Newt Allen and Frankie Warfield are not in the National Baseball HOF. As of 2011, I believe there are now thirty-nine players from the Negro Leagues who are enshrined in the National Baseball HOF.

Below are notes on four free agent pitchers, which increases the black ball roster to 25 players. The data is from *Total Baseball* (1993 edition)[5].

Don Newcombe   Free Agent – Pitcher   Best Season – 1956 Dodgers
Notes – Newcombe led the league in wins (27); winning percentage (.794); and opponents batting average (.221). He also led in Total Pitching Index (3.9).   Newcombe began his baseball career in the Negro Leagues.

Luis Tiant   Free Agent – Pitcher   Best Season – 1968 Indians
Notes – Tiant led the league in shutouts (9); fewest hits/game (5.3); opponents batting average (.168); and ERA (1.60).   He was third in Total Pitching Index (4.0).   Tiant's dad, Lefty Tiant, had a 10-0 record on the 1947 New York Cubans, the Negro League champs.

J. R. Richard   Free Agent – Pitcher   Best Season – 1979 Astros
Notes – Richard led the league in fewest hits/game (6.77); strikeouts (313); strikeouts/game (9.64); opponents batting average (.209); and ERA (2.71).   He was second in Total Pitching Index (2.7).   Richard's career was cut short because of heart problems.

Donnie Moore   Free Agent – Pitcher   Best Season – 1985 Angels
Notes – Moore led the league in Relief Ranking (51.9), and he was third in Saves (31).   Moore committed suicide one year after retiring from Major League Baseball.

Roster Review - Below is a Roster Review for the Black Ball Stars team. Through out the book I will use BB Stars (team name). The purpose of the Roster Review is to highlight the best offensive and defensive players as well as key pitching information for all of the teams for their specific series. I choose to do the BB Stars just once (in Chapter One). See the complete BB Star Roster, Chart 1-1 on page 17.

Appendix One – Baseball Definitions - explains all of the columns in the various baseball charts in this book including the chart of Offensive Leaders below.

Offensive Leaders (Black Ball Stars) Ranked by OPS

Player	OBP	SPct	OPS	R	+ RBI -	HR =	NR
J. Gibson	.412	.684	1.097	122	154	44	232
O. Charleston	.412	.601	1.012	83	107	30	160
M. Suttles	.395	.612	1.007	97	123	35	185
T. Stearnes	.380	.626	1.006	117	131	33	215
M. Irvin	.396	.529	.925	97	108	21	184
W. Wells	.395	.522	.917	99	112	22	189
B. Leonard	.356	.545	.901	101	113	30	184
C. Torriente	.404	.495	.899	97	68	13	152
P. Lloyd	.412	.475	.887	121	65	9	177
C. P. Bell	.395	.460	.856	95	78	10	163

The following players would be base-stealing threats: Bell 31, Charleston 30, and Warfield 22 (numbers listed are their projected stolen bases totals for 162 game season.)

Fielding Leaders	Pos	Range	Error	Throwing
C. P. Bell	CF	AA	8	-1
C. Torriente	OF	A	6	-1
O. Charleston	LF	A	5	-1
T. Stearnes	OF	A	5	-1
M. Irvin	OF	B	6	-2

For outfielders, range (AA is best, D is poor) and throwing (-4 is exceptional, -3 is excellent, -2 is very good, -1 is above average, 0 is average, + 1 is below average and + 2 is poor) are most important. Error rating (10 is best, 1 is poor) is not as critical as for infielders, because outfielders normally do not make as many errors.

W. Wells	SS	AA	7	-
P. Lloyd	SS	A	7	-
J. Johnson	3B	A	7	-
N. Allen	2B	A	7	-
M. Suttles	1B	A	7	-

Black Ball Roster - Best Season Series

Pos.	E	R	TH	PB	Hitters	G	AB	R	H	RBI	2B	3B	HR	TB	W	HB	SO	SF	SH	SB	B.AVG.	OBP	S.PCT.	OPS
LF	5	A	-1		Charleston	162	601	83	211	107	36	12	30	361	60	2	60	-	-	30	0.351	0.412	0.601	1.012
CF	8	AA	-1		CP Bell	162	706	95	235	78	36	12	10	325	70	3	56	-	-	31	0.333	0.395	0.460	0.856
OF	5	A	-1		Stearnes	162	615	117	212	131	36	19	33	385	33	2	65	-	-	17	0.345	0.380	0.626	1.006
OF	6	B	-2		M Irvin	162	569	97	193	108	33	6	21	301	53	1	50	-	-	16	0.339	0.396	0.529	0.925
OF	6	A	-1		Torriente	162	572	97	187	68	31	13	13	283	73	1	52	-	-	16	0.327	0.404	0.495	0.899
SS	7	A			P Lloyd	162	613	121	221	65	31	6	9	291	53	1	49	-	-	19	0.361	0.412	0.475	0.887
SS	7	AA			W Wells	162	624	99	204	112	38	9	22	326	67	3	45	-	-	16	0.327	0.395	0.522	0.917
3B	7	A			J Johnson	162	609	89	182	56	28	10	4	242	63	3	67	-	-	11	0.299	0.367	0.397	0.765
3B	6	B			Dandridge	162	595	76	196	43	28	9	3	249	37	1	65	-	-	1	0.329	0.370	0.418	0.788
2B	7	A			N Allen	162	675	83	197	42	28	9	4	255	63	3	46	-	-	19	0.292	0.355	0.378	0.733
2B	7	A			F Warfield	162	614	89	158	45	22	22	3	235	73	1	41	-	-	22	0.257	0.337	0.383	0.720
1B	7	A			Suttles	162	587	97	197	123	33	12	35	359	53	5	53	-	-	7	0.336	0.395	0.612	1.007
1B	8	B			B Leonard	162	682	101	218	113	36	14	30	372	35	3	62	-	-	4	0.320	0.356	0.545	0.901
C	7	A	-2	Fr	J Gibson	162	580	122	202	154	35	14	44	397	60	3	71	-	-	5	0.348	0.412	0.684	1.097
C	6	B	-2	Av	B Mackey	162	598	75	189	77	23	9	13	269	35	3	69	-	-	10	0.316	0.357	0.450	0.807

Fat.	H	WP	E	R	Pitchers	G	GS	QS	CG	S	W	L	IP	H	SO	BB	HB	HR	R	ER	ERA
10/L	Vg	N	9	B	BJ Rogan	44	33	-	-	4	26	10	309	254	156	71	-	15	-	-	2.21
9/L	Ex	R	7	B	B Foster	45	33	-	-	2	23	11	281	165	124	63	-	10	-	-	1.86
10/L	Vg	NL	8	B	L Day	43	35	-	-	0	26	11	280	186	108	60	-	11	-	-	1.29
10/L	Av	NL	7	B	M Dihigo	46	31	-	-	0	25	19	286	218	117	56	-	13	-	-	1.67
8/L	Md	R	8	C	S Paige	45	33	-	-	1	20	13	256	185	190	39	-	11	-	-	1.44
L/9	Vg	R	8	A	H Smith	59	23	-	-	7	29	13	320	237	144	56	-	14	-	-	1.60
9/L	Av	R	9	A	Newcombe	38	36	-	-	0	27	7	268	219	139	46	-	33	-	-	3.06
10/L	Ex	NL	8	D	L Tiant	34	32			0	21	9	258	152	264	73	-	16	-	-	1.60
9/L	Av	N	5	C	J R Richard	38	38			0	18	13	292	220	313	98	-	13	-	-	2.70
Long	Md	NL	4	B	D Moore	65	0			31	8	8	103	91	72	21	-	9	-	-	1.92

Chart 1-1 – Black Ball Roster

For infielders, range (AA is best), + rating increases probability of turning double plays because of excellent pivot capability for this shortstop (SS) or second baseman (2B). The error rating is as important as range for an infielder (10 is excellent, 1 is poor).

Catcher Throwing – Gibson and Mackey. are very good (-2).

Pitcher Hold Rating – Foster and Tiant are excellent, which will result in fewer successful steal attempts. Rogan. Day and Smith are very good. Dihigo, Newcombe and Richard are average. Paige and Moore are mediocre which will result in more stealing attempts and successes.

Pitching – Paige, Foster (only left handed pitcher on staff) and Tiant will be the aces of the staff and will primarily be starting pitchers. Smith and Richard will be the key relief specialists.

Chapter 2

Parameters for the Best Season

BEFORE I PLAYED THE BEST Season Tournament with the Pursue the Pennant game (165 games plus playoffs), I played a 30-game tournament with the BB Stars playing 250 great players broken down more by decade (1880-1970). The 30-game tournament was called The Decades Tournament.

In the Decades Tournament, the Major League players' stats were their average career stats. In the Best Season Tournament, the Major League players' stats are their Best Season stats. These stats are based on the opinion of the staff at the Pursue the Pennant Game Company, 1993. See Appendix Two for the Creation of the Card Set. For example, Ted Williams' career statistics player card (career batting average of .345) was used for Ted Williams in the Decades Tournament (1940 decade); Ted Williams best season (1941) statistics player card (.406 batting average) was used for the Red Sox Best Season players/team. The 15 teams have a total roster of 375 players (125 additional to the 250 career players in Decades Tournament). The additional players are mostly players that had a great season but a short career, such as Mark Fidrych, '76 Tigers. There are a few other career players.

1. The Decades Tournament favored the BB Stars because their 21 best players were matched against 250 Major League players (25 players/decade). In other words, the two best black ball catchers (Gibson and Mackey) went up against 20 great catchers (based on career averages) over ten decades. Advantage BB Stars.

2. Another difference is that in the Best Season Tournament, the competition is against franchised teams, the original sixteen post-1900 teams. Remember that two teams are combined, the Braves and Pirates. This gives a regional flavor to the competition.

3. The Decades Tournament was a ten 3-game series, for a total of 30 games. In the Best Season Tournament, it was a 15 nine-game series, for a total of 135 games.

4. In the Decades Tournament, the BB Stars were always the road team. In the Best Seasons Tournament, the BB Stars were home team for four or five games per nine-game series. The BB Stars used various Major League ball parks as their home park, using the Barnstorming concept.

5. In the Decades Tournament, the BB Stars had a roster of 21 players; six were pitchers. For the first five games of the initial Best Season nine-game series (Braves/Pirates), they continued with the 21-man roster with 6 pitchers. I decided to expand their roster to 25 players (10 pitchers) for the balance of the Best Season Tournament. The four free agent pitchers added to their roster were Don Newcombe (1956 Dodgers), Luis Tiant (1968 Indians), J. R. Richard (1979 Astros), and Donnie Moore (1985 Angels).

6. In the Decades Tournament, injuries affected only the 3-game series against each decade team. In the Best Season Tournament, injuries would not be limited. If a player was injured for more than two games, his spot could be filled by free agents not currently being used. About 25 players were not assigned to a specific roster.

7. There is no designated hitter (DH) in either tournament.

In the Introduction to this book, I included a section on Win Shares. To help you understand the competitive difference from the Decades Tournament, just below is a comparison of the win shares for two great pitchers. This example compares their career average Win Shares with their best season Win Shares.

Player	WS for Career (avg/year)	WS for Best Season
Bob Feller	18	32 (1946 Indians)
Walter Johnson	28	54 (1913 Senators)

Remember that the Decades Tournament is not part of this book. This was the initial research that led to this book. I like to look at the Decades Tournament as Spring Training or Preseason Exhibition Games.

Chapter 3

Highlights of BB Stars vs. 1880-1970 Decade All-Stars

Ten Game Projection Unbelievably Accurate!

THE BB STARS WERE 7-3 through ten games, which projects to a 21-9 record (.700 winning percentage), which is exactly where they ended up. As shown below, the other statistical data is also amazingly close.

Games	Runs	Hits	HR	Avg	OBP	Slg.	OPS	ERA	RD*
10 Gs Proj. 30	216	402	33	.341	.392	.529	.921	3.45	+108
30 Gs Actual	215	392	39	.330	.374	.541	.915	3.50	+110

* Run differential - It is the difference of runs scored between the teams. The +110 run differential in the thirty games (actual) means the BB Stars outscored their opponents by 110 runs.

Definition of other terms – HR is home run; .Avg is Batting Average; OBP is on base percentage: Slg. Is slugging percentage; OPS is on base percentage + slugging percentage; ERA is Earned Run Average. For example, the BB Stars pitching staff in the thirty games actual, gave up 3.50 earned runs/nine inning game. See Appendix One – Baseball Definitions.

I want to emphasize that I was not surprised by the results of this 30-game tournament. I projected that the BB Stars would finish, 20-10, .667. If the 21 BB Stars played the 21 best Major Leaguers (not 250 best), it would have been a very competitive series. Another factor to consider is that the stats we are using for the BB Stars are incomplete, and the overall competition level may have been more like AAA ball. I would say the stats we are using for the BB Stars would equate to their prime years if they had played Major League ball.

Preseason - Black Ball All-Stars – Highlights vs. Decade All-Stars

Player	AB	R	H	RBI	2B	3B	HR	TB	B. AVG
Stearnes	85	17	36	19	3	7*	4	65	.424*
Suttles	84	17	35	21	8	3	6	67*	.417
Irvin	69	14	27	17	4	4	4	51	.391
Johnson	62	8	24	4	5	0	0	29	.387
Charleston	101*	23*	37*	20	7	0	7	65	.366
C P Bell	95	16	34	8	5	2	2	49	.358
Wells	68	12	23	10	6	1	1	34	.338
Gibson	84	20	28	24*	9*	2	8*	65	.333
Lloyd	92	19	29	13	4	3	2	45	.315
Mackey	54	9	17	12	2	2	2	29	.315

The above players were the .300+ hitters.
The asterisked (*) players were category leaders.

Below are the OPS leaders:

Player	OBP	Slg.Pct.	OPS
Suttles	.473*	.798*	1.271*
Stearnes	.449	.765	1.214
Gibson	.417	.774	1.191
Irvin	.425	.739	1.164
Charleston	.396	.644	1.040

* category leaders

In other categories, Gibson led in walks (12), Suttles hit by pitch (3), Bell sac flies (2), pitcher Bill Foster sac bunts (2), Torriente and Lloyd tied with stolen bases (2). Bell and Lloyd led with strikeouts (14).

Below are key pitching stats:

Pitcher	G	CG	Saves	W-L	IP	H	SO	W-hb	HR	ERA
S. Paige	14	2	2	3-1	48.3	32	31*	9	2	1.86*
H. Smith	15*	1	4*	4-2	40.7	39	11	11	2	2.66
B. Foster	12	2	0	4-1*	45.0	36	14	10	2	3.00
L. Day	11	3*	1	3-2	44.3	40	18	9	3	3.86
BJ Rogan	9	0	0	4-1*	54.7	60*	19	14-1	3	3.95
M. Dihigo	9	1	0	3-2	37.3	43	20	18*	5*	6.03
Totals	**30**	**9**	**7**	**21-9**	**270.3**	**253**	**116**	**81-1**	**17**	**3.50**

* **category leaders**

The Best Season Projections for the BB Stars

This should be very competitive baseball with the BB Stars playing .500 to .550 ball in this 15 nine-game series (135 games), which equates to 68 to 75 wins. In the 2 fifteen-game All-Star Series, I see them winning 13-16 games, and at the high end a 91-74 .552 to a low end 81-84 .491. for the 165 games. Splitting the difference, the BB Stars will end up at 86-79, .521 (results would be total for Book One and Book Two).

Chapter 4

Match Ups and Managerial Tendencies

EARLIER, WE REVIEWED THE BB Stars' biographies and 25-man roster. The ten-man pitching staff has nine right-handed pitchers. Satchel Paige and Luis Tiant (free agent, 1968 Indians) are the dominant right-handers and will primarily be starting pitchers. Bullet Joe Rogan, Leon Day, and Don Newcombe (free agent, 1956 Dodgers) will see time as starters and relievers. Hilton Smith, J. R. Richard (free agent, 1979 Astros), Donnie Moore (free agent, 1985 Angels), and Martin Dihigo will be primarily used in the bullpen.

This is a very strong right-handed pitching staff. Add to this staff the great left-hander Bill Foster, who had the highest winning percentage in the Negro Leagues against Major League competition and this staff is very strong.

The great Major League right-handed power hitters who do not have an exceptional On Base Percentage (OBP) of .430 and up are at a major disadvantage hitting against this Black Ball pitching staff. The left-handed Foster is almost as tough against right-handed hitters as he is against left-handed hitters.

Some great right-handed power hitters like Johnny Bench, Mike Schmidt, Willie Mays, Hank Aaron, and Frank Robinson, will be challenged in this competition. Their power will not be diminished too much, but their ability to get on base (OBP) will be.

Right-handed power hitters with higher OBP like Jimmy Foxx, .455 OBP (1932 Athletics) and Rogers Hornsby, .503 OBP (1924 Cardinals), will do fine. Hugh Duffy, .513 OBP from the nineteenth century, will be a strong right-handed hitter as a free agent for the Dodgers.

The offense of the BB Stars is excellent. Casey Stengel, the great platoon-oriented manager of the powerful Yankees (1949-1953 World Champs for five consecutive years and a power house team for over a decade) would have loved to manage this black ball squad. This team has a great balance of right- and left-handed hitters, including three great switch hitters, Biz Mackey (catcher), Newt Allen (second baseman), and Cool Papa Bell (center fielder).

The power is from both sides (lefty and righty). Below are listed the projected home runs over a 162 game schedule (current Major League schedule) for seven BB Stars.

1.	Josh Gibson – R	44
2.	Mule Suttles – R	36
3.	Turkey Stearnes – L	33
4.	Oscar Charleston – L	30
5.	Buck Leonard – L	30
6.	Willie Wells – R	22
7.	Monte Irvin – R	21

The BB Stars are always explosive. They often eat up left-handed pitching. They do a pretty good job on right-handed pitching, also. With no one on base and two outs, they can put up three or more runs quite easily.

The best way to beat the BB Stars is with a lot of base runners and as many 3-run home runs as possible. To do that, you need a team with left-handed power and players with a high OBP. You'd need players like Ted Williams, Babe Ruth, Lou Gehrig, Ty Cobb, Stan Musial, Shoeless Joe Jackson, George Sisler, and Micky Mantle.

As an opponent, if you do not score five runs or more, the BB Stars are tough to beat. In the first 90 games, teams that score four runs or fewer had a winning percentage of .191 (9 wins, 38 losses) vs. the BB Stars.

As a manager, playing for one run before the eighth inning against the BB Stars is probably a mistake. The game is never over until the last out.

Chapter 5

Best Season Nine-Game Series 1 –
BB Stars vs. Braves/Pirates

Braves/Pirates Roster Review

SIXTY PERCENT OF THE ROSTER are from the Pittsburgh Pirates. Thirty-two percent of the roster are from Boston, Milwaukee, and the Atlanta Braves. Eight percent of the roster are free agents. See the Braves/Pirates Roster (Chart 5-1 on page 27.).

Offensive Leaders (Braves/Pirates) Ranked by OPS

Player	OBP	SPct	OPS	R +	RBI -	HR =	NR
A. Vaughn	.491	.607	1.098	108	99	19	188
R. Kiner	.432	.658	1.090	116	127	54	189
W. Stargell	.395	.646	1.041	106	119	44	181
E. Mathews	.406	.627	1.033	110	135	47	198
K. Cuyler	.423	.598	1.021	144	102	18	228
P. Waner	.437	.549	.986	114	131	9	236
H. Aaron	.395	.586	.981	121	130	44	207
D. Evans	.405	.556	.961	114	124	41	197
R. Clemente	.399	.554	.953	103	110	23	190
H. Wagner	.424	.505	.929	114	101	6	209

Braves/PiratesRoster Best Season Series vs. BB All-Stars

Team	Year	WS Hitters	G	AB	R	H	RBI	2B	3B	HR	TB	W	HB	SO	SF	SH	SB	B.AVG.	OBP	S.PCT.	OPS
Milwaukee	1963	41 H Aaron	139	631	121	201	130	29	4	44	370	78	2	94	-	-	31	0.319	0.395	0.586	0.982
Pittsburgh	1925	26 Carey	133	542	109	186	44	39	13	5	266	66	4	19	-	-	46	0.343	0.418	0.491	0.909
Pittsburgh	1929	27 L Waner	151	662	134	234	74	28	20	5	317	37	1	20	-	-	6	0.353	0.389	0.479	0.867
Pittsburgh	1927	36 P Waner	155	623	114	237	131	42	18	9	342	60	3	14	-	-	5	0.380	0.437	0.549	0.986
Pittsburgh	1925	34 Cuyler	153	617	144	220	102	43	26	18	369	58	13	56	-	-	41	0.357	0.423	0.598	1.021
Pittsburgh	1967	35 Clemente	147	585	103	209	110	26	10	23	324	41	0	103	-	-	9	0.357	0.399	0.554	0.953
Pittsburgh	1949	37 Kiner	152	549	116	170	127	19	5	54	361	117	1	61	-	-	6	0.310	0.432	0.658	1.089
Pittsburgh	1905	46 H Wagner	147	548	114	199	101	32	14	6	277	54	4	41	-	-	57	0.363	0.424	0.505	0.930
Pittsburgh	1935	39 A Vaughn	137	499	108	192	99	34	10	19	303	97	7	18	-	-	4	0.385	0.491	0.607	1.098
Milwaukee	1953	39 E Mathews	157	579	110	175	135	31	8	47	363	99	2	83	-	-	1	0.302	0.406	0.627	1.033
Pittsburgh	1923	28 Traynor	153	616	108	208	101	19	19	12	301	34	5	19	-	-	28	0.338	0.377	0.489	0.866
Pittsburgh	1960	21 Mazeroski	151	538	58	147	64	21	5	11	211	40	1	50	-	-	4	0.273	0.325	0.392	0.717
Boston (N)	1936	23 Cuccinello	150	565	68	174	86	26	3	7	227	58	0	49	-	-	1	0.308	0.372	0.402	0.774
Pittsburgh	1973	36 Stargell	148	522	106	156	119	43	3	44	337	80	3	129	-	-	0	0.299	0.395	0.646	1.041
Atlanta	1973	31 D Evans	161	595	114	167	124	25	8	41	331	124	0	104	-	-	6	0.281	0.405	0.556	0.961
New York A	1973	25 Munson	147	519	80	156	74	29	4	20	253	48	3	64	-	-	4	0.301	0.363	0.487	0.851
Cleveland N	1895	17 C Zimmer	88	315	60	107	56	21	2	5	147	33	0	30	-	-	14	0.340	0.402	0.467	0.869

Team	Year	WS Pitchers	G	GS	QS	CG	S	W	L	IP	H	SO	BB	HR	R	ER	ERA
Milwaukee	1953	31 Spahn	35	32	-	24	3	23	7	265	211	148	70	14	-	-	2.10
Boston (N)	1948	28 Sain	42	39	-	28	1	24	15	315	297	137	83	19	-	-	2.60
Pittsburgh	1902	24 Tannehill	26	24	-	23	0	20	6	231	203	100	25	0	-	-	1.95
Atlanta	1974	28 P Niekro	41	39	-	18	1	20	13	302	249	195	88	19	-	-	2.38
Pittsburgh	1922	27 W Cooper	41	37	-	27	0	23	14	295	330	129	61	13	-	-	3.18
Pittsburgh	1979	20 Tekulve	94	0	-	-	31	10	8	134	109	75	49	5	-	-	2.75
Pittsburgh	1962	20 Face	63	0	-	-	28	8	7	91	74	45	18	7	-	-	1.88
Atlanta	1982	19 Garber	69	0	-	-	30	8	10	119	100	68	32	4	-	-	2.34
New York A	1939	22 Ruffing	28	28	-	22	0	21	7	233	211	95	75	15	-	-	2.93

Chart 5-1 – Braves/Pirates Best Season Roster

The following players would be base-stealing threats: Wagner 57, Carey 46, Cuyler 41, Aaron 31, Traynor 28 (numbers listed are their stolen bases totals for their best season).

Fielding Leaders	Pos	Range	Error	Throwing
Lloyd Waner	CF	AA	9	-2
Roberto Clemente	RF	AA	4	-4
Max Carey	OF	AA	3	-4

For outfielders, range (AA is best) and throwing (-4 is exceptional, -3 is excellent) are most important. Error rating (10 is best, 1 is poor) is not as critical as for infielders, because outfielders normally do not make as many errors.

Bill Mazeroski	2B	AA+	9	-
Tony Cuccinello	2B	AA+	5	-
Honus Wagner	SS	AA	4	-

For infielders, range (AA is best) + rating increases probability of turning double plays because of excellent pivot capability for this shortstop (SS) or second baseman (2B). The error rating is as important as range for an infielder (10 is excellent, 1 is poor).

Catcher Throwing - Munson is -2 (very good); Zimmer is 0 (average).

Pitcher Hold Rating - Spahn, Tannehill, and Ruffing are excellent, which will result in fewer successful steal attempts. Garber is mediocre. Niekro and Tekulve are poor, which will result in more stealing attempts and successes.

Pitching - Lefty starters Spahn (23-7, 2.10) and Tannehill (20-6, 1.95) and right-hander Face (8-7, 28 saves, 1.88) in the pen lead the Braves/Pirates staff.

Game One, Monday April 26, Forbes Field (Pittsburgh), 1 pm (Paige vs. Spahn)

It is a hot, cloudy day. The Braves/Pirates are the home team for Games One and Two. The BB Stars put pressure on Warren Spahn (Milwaukee Braves 1953) right away. Cool Papa Bell doubles to the gap in right center. Charleston and Wells walk to load the bases for Josh Gibson. Spahn gets Gibson to hit a high fly ball to short center, and Max Carey (-4 throwing arm) makes the catch. With Carey and Clemente in center and right field, respectively, the BB Stars' speed on the bases will be diminished significantly. Suttles hits a slow grounder to Honus Wagner at short, and he is thrown out (two outs) as Bell scores the first run (1-0). Irvin grounds out to end the inning. Spahn recovers nicely. **BB Stars 1, Braves/Pirates 0.**

In the top of the second, Judy Johnson homers over the wall in left. **BB Stars 2, Braves/Pirates 0.**

In the top of the third, the BB Stars strike again. With one out, Gibson singles to center, Suttles walks, and Irvin doubles into the left field corner, scoring Gibson, **BB Stars 3, Braves/Pirates 0.**

In the sixth inning, Spahn's last inning, Johnson leads off with a walk, Warfield triples (4-0), and Paige lays down a perfect squeeze bunt to make it **BB Stars 5, Braves/Pirates 0.** Spahn's stats are 6 IP, 8 H, 5 R, 1 HR, 0 K, 4 BB.

Through eight innings, Paige has blanked the Braves/Pirates on 5 hits, and he has fanned nine while walking none. The Braves/Pirates finally score their lone run in the bottom of the ninth.

	R	H	E	LOB
BB Stars	5	9	0	8
Braves/Pirates	1	7	0	6

Winning Pitcher – Paige   Losing Pitcher – Spahn
BB Stars lead the series 1-0.

Game Two, Tuesday April 27, Forbes Field (Pittsburgh), 1 pm (Foster vs. Sain)

It is a hot, partly cloudy day. In the bottom of the first, Kiki Cuyler leads off with a triple over Bell's head in center. Wagner singles him in. **Braves/Pirates 1, BB Stars 0.**

In the bottom of the third, the Braves/Pirates add to their lead. Cuccinello (Boston Braves, 1936) leads off with a single. Sain (Boston Braves, 1948) singles to right, with Cuccinello stopping at second. Cuyler flies out to Charleston on the warning track in left, with Cuccinello moving to third. Wagner bounces out to Leonard, with Foster covering first. Cuccinello scores (2-0). Sain goes to second. Kiner lines a single to left center, with Sain sliding in ahead of Charleston's throw (3-0).

In the fourth, Turkey Stearnes hits a long home run to center field (3-1). In the bottom of the fourth, Thurmon Munson (Yankees 1973) hits a 2-run home run to left. **Braves/Pirates 5, BB Stars 1.**

Dihigo replaces Foster in the bottom of the fifth inning. In the top of the sixth, Pops Lloyd doubles to left center, and Cool Papa Bell launches a 2-run home run over the wall in right. **Braves/Pirates 5, BB Stars 3.**

After Sain gives up a lead-off double to Dandridge to lead-off the seventh, Elroy Face (Pirates ace closer, 1962, 1.88 ERA and 28 saves) pitches a three-inning save (3 IP, 2 H, 0 R, 3 K, 0 BB). The series is tied, 1-1.

	R	H	E	LOB
BB Stars	3	7	0	5
Braves/Pirates	5	11	0	6

Winning Pitcher – Sain   Save – Face   Losing Pitcher – Foster
Series is tied 1-1.

Game Three, Wednesday April 28, Yankee Stadium, 1 pm (Tannehill vs. Rogan)

The Braves/Pirates score in the second inning on Tannehill's successful squeeze bunt scoring Lloyd Waner. **Braves/Pirates 1, BB Stars 0.**

In the bottom of the second with two outs, Johnson is on second (single, advanced on a groundout). Rogan helps himself with a sharp single to right, scoring Johnson (1-1). Bell and Wells get back-to-back triples. **BB Stars 3, Braves/Pirates 1.**

In the bottom of the third, the BB Stars chase Tannehill. Gibson lines out to Mathews at third base (one out). Suttles homers into the lower deck in left field (4-1). Torriente singles to right, and Johnson follows with a bloop single to right with Torriente scampering around to third. Warfield walks to load the bases.   Ruffing (free agent Yankees, 1939) is warming up for the Braves/Pirates. Rogan taps one between third and short that Mathews cuts off and throws out Rogan as the runners advance (5-1). Rogan has his second RBI. Bell lines a base hit to left center as both runners score (7-1). Ruffing is now pitching. **BB Stars 7, Braves/Pirates 1.**

In the bottom of the fourth, Torriente hits 2-run home run into the upper deck to close out the scoring. **BB Stars 9, Braves/Pirates 1.** Bullet Joe Rogan retires the last 21 batters he faced (9 IP, 4 H, 1 R, 0 HR, 4 K, 1 BB). BB Stars lead the series, 2-1.

	R	H	E	LOB
Braves/Pirates	1	4	1	4
BB Stars	9	15	0	10

Winning Pitcher – Rogan   Losing Pitcher - Tannehill
BB Stars lead series 2-1.

Game Four, Thursday April 29, Yankee Stadium, 1 pm (Niekro vs. Day)

It is a cool, partly cloudy day. Max Carey leads off and reaches second base on shortstop Lloyd's 2-base throwing error. Wagner walks (first and second). With the hit-and-run on, Paul Waner swings and misses, and Mackey throws Wagner out at second with Lloyd covering (one out). On the next pitch, Waner singles to center, scoring Carey (1-0). Mathews triples over Stearnes' head in deep center (2-0). Day escapes without any further scoring. **Braves/Pirates 2, BB Stars 0.**

In the top of the third inning, Day walks Max Carey. Wagner drives a ball off the wall in left, and Carey scores from first. **Braves/Pirates 3, BB Stars 0.**

In the top of the fourth, Lloyd Waner leads off with a triple to deep center. Munson follows with an RBI single to center. **Braves/Pirates 4, BB Stars 0.**

Through five innings, the score remains 4-0. Niekro's knuckleballs are keeping the BB hitters off balance. He is in only one jam, when bases are loaded in the first inning. In the fifth inning, Niekro has retired 13 men in a row (first through two outs in fifth). Allen singles but Day strikes out, ending the inning. **Braves/Pirates 4, BB Stars 0.**

With one out in the top of the sixth, Munson triples to left center. Cuccinello hits a fly ball to Stearnes in right center, deep enough to score Munson with the fifth run (sac fly for Cuccinello). **Braves/Pirates 5, BB Stars 0.**

In the sixth, Niekro gets in trouble. These BB Stars can change a game quickly. Cristobal Torriente opens with a single to right. Lloyd bloops a single to left. Torriente, with the ball in front of him, never hesitates at second and slides safely into third (first and third, none out). Niekro walks Charleston on four pitches to load the bases (none out). Stearnes lifts a fly to center field, trailing 5-0, and Max Carey's great throwing arm (-4). Torriente stays at third (one out). Leonard grounds a base hit past the lunging Cuccinello (2B) into right field, scoring two runs. Charleston stops at second (5-2).

Cooper (L) and Tekulve (R) begin to throw in the bullpen. Biz Mackey is coming up. Niekro steps off the mound to gather his thoughts. Mackey knows what is coming, a knuckleball. Mackey swings, the ball dips as it hits the bat, and it is a one-hopper to Cuccinello at second. He flips to Wagner as he comes across the bag (two outs); Wagner fires a strike to Stargell for an inning-ending double play. **Braves/Pirates 5, BB Stars 2.**

In the bottom of the eighth, Wilbur Cooper (L) has replaced Niekro (7 IP, 7 H, 2 R, 5 K, 1 BB). Lloyd singles to center. With two outs, Suttles is announced to bat for Leonard. Tekulve, the right-hander, replaces Cooper. Suttles bloops a single to center; Lloyd stops at second out of respect for Lloyd Waner's arm (-2). Josh Gibson pinch hits for Mackey. A home run will tie the game. Gibson lines a single to left that Max Carey fields quickly and fires to Munson as Lloyd takes the turn at third and holds. With the bases loaded, Johnson lofts an easy fly ball to Carey to end the inning. The Braves/Pirate's outfield has played a major role in keeping the BB Stars offense in check. **Braves/Pirates 5, BB Stars 2.**

Hilton Smith is pitching his second inning in relief of Leon Day (7 IP, 9 H, 5 R, 4 ER, 3 K, 2 BB). The Braves/Pirates add two more runs. **Braves/Pirates 7, BB Stars 2.**

Tekulve closes the door on the BB Stars in the ninth. The Braves/Pirates played solid baseball, clutch hitting, and excellent defense with great pitching. This series is now even (2-2).

	R	H	E	LOB
Braves/Pirates	7	14	0	8
BB Stars	2	11	2	8

Winning Pitcher – Niekro   Losing Pitcher - Day

The series is tied 2-2.

Game Five, Saturday, May 1, Forbes Field (Pittsburgh), 1 pm (Paige vs. Spahn)

It is a warm, cloudy day, but rain is not expected. This has been a great series, very evenly matched.

After four and one-half innings, the Braves/Pirates lead 1-0 on Willie Stargell's bases empty home run to right in the second inning off Satchel Paige. In the bottom of the fifth, Paige is hurt again by the long ball. After Munson's lead-off single to left, Mazeroski homers to left (3-0). Spahn doubles into the right field corner, and Clemente hits a home run inside the foul pole in left field. The Braves/Pirates have taken a 5-0 lead with none out in the fifth. Paige retires the next three batters. He is done for the day (5 IP, 6 H, 5 R, 3 HR, 7 K 1 BB). **Braves/Pirates 5, BB Stars 0.**

Through five innings, Spahn has blanked the BB Stars on three singles. However, he never completes the sixth inning. When he leaves, he has faced nine batters in the inning. He retired two (long fly outs near the warning track). He gave up seven hits (one out HR to Suttles and six singles). He left the game with the bases loaded and a 5-4 lead. Bell greeted Red Ruffing with a 2-run single to left before Suttles (eleventh batter in the inning) lined out to Mazeroski to end the inning. The final line on Spahn is 5.7 IP, 10 H, 6 R, 1 HR, 3 K, 0 BB. **BB Stars 6, Braves/Pirates 5.**

Dihigo pitches in the bottom of the sixth, and Braves/Pirates do not score.

Ruffing, a very good hitting pitcher, leads off the bottom of the seventh with a single to left off Dihigo. Bill Foster (L) is warming up. Clemente singles to right, and Ruffing stops at second. Dihigo uncorks a wild pitch, and runners move to second and third with none out. Wagner flies out to Bell in center, and the runners hold with one out. Eddie Mathews is intentionally walked, loading the bases, to set up the double play with the dangerous right–handed hitting Hank Aaron coming to the plate.. Pitching too carefully, Dihigo walks Aaron (6-6), and Rolfe scores. Bill Foster (L) is brought in to face Evans (L). Ralph Kiner is going to pinch hit, and the Pittsburgh crowd goes crazy. In this series, Kiner has had to learn to play first base so that the great defensive outfielders are in the field. Kiner takes a called third strike, for two outs. Carey bats for Stargell and flies out to center, leaving the bases loaded. **Braves/Pirates 6, BB Stars 6.**

Defensive changes occur for the Braves/Pirates in the top of the eighth. Kiner is at first base, Carey is in center field, and Aaron moves from center to left field. Ruffing strikes out Dandridge, for one out. Warfield singles to left. Stearnes bats for Foster, and Cooper replaces Ruffing. Cooper gets Stearnes to take a called third strike with a great curve ball for two outs. Charleston flies out to Aaron in left to end the inning. **Braves/Pirates 6, BB Stars 6.**

The BB Stars do a double switch. Stearnes stays in the game and replaces Charleston in left field. Hilton Smith replaces Foster in the bottom of the eighth. With two outs, Arky Vaughn pinch hits for Cooper. Vaughn waits on Smith's 2-2 pitch, times his swing perfectly, and crack! The ball explodes off Vaughn's bat. It is headed deep to right center, and everything appears in slow motion. Cool Papa Bell (CF) is off at the crack of the bat, watching the ball, glancing toward the wall, moving at full speed.

As Vaughn makes the turn at first, he believes he has hit a tie-breaking home run. But Bell times his leap perfectly. He reaches up and over the fence and falls in a heap on the warning track. Did he catch it? As the second base umpire runs toward the fallen player, Cool Papa Bell raises his glove with the white ball stuck in the web. What a catch! Vaughn cannot believe it, and neither can the sellout crowd. As Bell starts to trot toward the infield, the crescendo from the crowd begins. They are all standing and honoring this great player for a once-in-a-lifetime catch that becomes the turning point in this classic series. **Braves/Pirates 6, BB Stars 6.**

The information below shows what happened after the seventh inning for the next eleven innings.

Innings 8-18	R	H	E	LOB
BB Stars (use two pitchers)	0	6	0	7
Braves/Pirates (use five pitchers)	0	2	0	5

Smith (three innings) and Rogan (eight innings) held the Braves/Pirates to two hits over eleven innings. Rolfe (one and two-thirds innings, includes seventh), Cooper (two-thirds of an inning), Face (three innings), Tekulve (three innings), and Niekro (four innings) held the BB Stars to 6 hits over those eleven innings.

In the top of the nineteenth inning, Niekro retires the first two batters, then faces Josh Gibson. Niekro throws his knuckleball, but there is little movement. Niekro is in his twelfth inning in three days. Josh Gibson jumps on it and hits it about 450 feet to left field, home run. Hank Aaron never turns around to look. Wells strikes out. **BB Stars 7, Braves/Pirates 6.**

Rogan is beginning his ninth inning in relief; he has been brilliant. Paul Waner singles to right. He had pinched hit for Face in the eleventh and replaced Clemente in a double switch when Tekulve came in to pitch. Lloyd Waner bats for Niekro and bounces out to first while advancing his brother, Paul to second, leaving one out. Wagner bounces out to Dandridge for two outs, while Waner holds at second base. Rogan walks Mathews. Leon Day replaces Rogan. The Braves/Pirates fans give Rogan a standing ovation, and he tips his cap to the crowd. This has been an epic ball game. Leon Day faces Hank Aaron. The crowd wants one thing, a score: a walk-off double, triple, or home run. Aaron hits a hard line drive, but it is right at Dandridge. Game over! **BB Stars 7, Braves/Pirates 6.**

19 Innings	R	H	E	LOB	Pitchers
BB Stars	7	18	1	13	6 (entire staff)
Braves/Pirates	6	11	2	13	6
Winning Pitcher – Rogan	Save – Day			Losing Pitcher – Niekro	

The BB Stars lead the series, 3-2.

This game led to some changes for the Best Season tournament. The Braves/Pirates roster was changed. Clarke (extra outfielder) was replaced by Gene Garber (Braves reliever); Chief Zimmer was added as a second catcher, while Phil Niekro was inactivated for Games Six through Eight. Four free agent pitchers were added to the BB Stars roster, Newcombe, Tiant, J. R. Richard, and Donnie Moore.

Game Six, Sunday May 2, Forbes Field (Pittsburgh), 1 pm (Foster vs. Sain)

With each team exhausted, they catch a break; more rain, no game on Sunday.

Game Six, Monday May 3, Forbes Field (Pittsburgh), 1 pm (Foster vs. Sain)

It is a cool, partly cloudy day. The crowd is still buzzing over the unbelievable nineteen-inning classic of two days ago. The BB Stars lead the series

3-2. They waste no time vs. Johnny Sain. Lloyd triples, followed by a Torriente double into the gap in right center (1-0). Sain gets Bell, Stearnes, and Leonard to fly out. **BB Stars 1, Braves/Pirates 0.**

With one out, the Braves/Pirates get a break when Turkey Stearnes (RF) misplays Wagner's fly ball for a two-base error. Kiner walks (runners at first and second, one out). Aaron hits a slow roller to Dandridge, who barehands the ball, throwing out Aaron as runners advance (two outs). Clemente hits a smash down the third base line. Dandridge dives and knocks it down. While on his knees, he tries to throw out Clemente and throws the ball into the dugout as two runs score (credit Clemente with a single, RBI and he goes to second on the error). Traynor pops out to Wagner. **Braves/Pirates 2, BB Stars 1.**

In the top of the fourth with one out, Leonard lines a home run over the right field wall. **BB Stars 2, Braves/Pirates 2.**

In the top of the fifth, the BB Stars score two more runs off of Sain. A Zimmer throwing error is a factor, but Cuyler's great throw nails Torriente at the plate, saving a run. **BB Stars 4, Braves/Pirates 2.**

The Braves do nothing off Foster in the bottom of the fifth. Carey stays in the game after pinch hitting for Sain. He replaces Cuyler in center field. Cooper (L) replaces Sain in the top of the sixth. The BB Stars widen the lead in the seventh with four more runs (Stearnes two run home run). **BB Stars 8, Braves/Pirates 2.**

Munson enters the game in the eighth, in a double switch replacing Zimmer, while Garber replaces Cooper on the mound. BB Stars do not score. In the bottom of the eighth, Foster retires the first two batters (sixteen retired in a row). He has only given up two singles and two unearned runs in the first. The Braves/Pirates come to life. Munson singles to center, and Wagner walks. Hilton Smith is warming up. Ralph Kiner wakes up the crowd with a home run to deep left, and it is now 8-5. Hank Aaron triples to center. Smith replaces Foster and strikes out Clemente, looking. The final line on Bill Foster is 7.7 IP, 5 H, 5 R, 3 ER, 1 HR, 2 K, 2 BB. **BB Stars 8, Braves/Pirates 5.**

In the top of the ninth, Garber retires the side in order. In the bottom of the ninth, Paul Waner pinch hits for Traynor and doubles into the right-field corner. No one is warming up for the BB Stars. They are going with Hilton Smith all the way. Lloyd Waner pinch hits for Garber, and he singles to center. His brother Paul stops at third. Cuccinello bloops a single in front of Bell. Paul Waner scores (8-6), and brother Lloyd stops at second (still none out). Carey hits a drive to deep center. Bell leaps, but it is off the wall. Both runners score to tie the game (8-8). Casey is safe at third with a triple. The crowd is going crazy. The BB Stars move the infield and outfield in. Munson bounces the ball to short, and Carey fakes a dash for the plate, but Lloyd looks him back as he throws out Munson (one out). Wagner smashes the ball up the middle past Smith into center field for a walk-off, game-winning hit, scoring Carey. **Braves/Pirates 9, BB Stars 8.** A great comeback win that evens the series again, 3-3.

	R	H	E	LOB
BB Stars	8	16	2	6
Braves/Pirates	9	10	1	4

Winning Pitcher – Garber   Losing Pitcher – Smith
The series is tied, 3-3.

Game Seven, Tuesday May 4, Yankee Stadium, 1 pm (Tannehill vs. Dihigo)

Evans hits a 3-run home run off Dihigo in the first. **Braves/Pirates 3, BB Stars 0.**

In the fourth inning, the Braves/Pirates chase Dihigo. An Arky Vaughn 3-run home run is a key blow. Dihigo is replaced by J. R. Richard. Dihigo's final line is 3.7 IP, 5 H, 7 R, 2 HR, 1 SO, 4 BB. **Braves/Pirates 7, BB Stars 0.**

The Braves hold on to take a one-game lead in the series, 4-3.

	R	H	E	LOB
Braves/Pirates	9	9	1	5
BB Stars	4	9	1	7

Winning Pitcher – Tannehill   Losing Pitcher – Dihigo
The Braves lead the series, 4-3.

Game Eight, Wednesday May 5, Yankee Stadium, 1 pm (Spahn vs. Paige)

The BB Stars need to win the final two games to win the first Best Season series. In the bottom of the third inning, Wells crushes Spahn's 2-2 pitch over the fence in deep right center (1-0). **BB Stars 1, Braves/Pirates 0.**

In the top of the fifth, the Braves use speed and an error to tie the game. Clemente singles to left and steals second; Gibson throws the ball into center field, sending Clemente to third. Clemente scores the unearned run when Cuccinello grounds out to Wells (deep short). **Braves/Pirates 1, BB Stars 1.**

In the top of the sixth, the Braves/Pirates get a second unearned run off Paige (a walk, one out error and Traynor single). **Braves/Pirates 2, BB Stars 1.**

In the bottom of the sixth, Suttles leads off with a single lined into center field. Stearnes hits a high drive to right field that curves toward the foul pole and hits it about 10 feet above the fence for a 2-run home run (3-2). In most other ball parks, that would have been an out. Spahn cannot believe his bad luck.

He kicks the dirt and slams down the resin bag in disgust. Spahn strikes out Johnson with a curve catching the outside corner. Allen bounces out to Wagner (two outs). Paige takes three straight strikes, inning over. Spahn is still talking to himself as he heads for the dugout. **BB Stars 3, Braves/Pirates 2.**

Paige breezes through the seventh. In the bottom of the seventh, with one out, Wells lines a home run into the lower deck in left field, his second home run of the game (4-2). Spahn gets Charleston to fly to center. Tekulve is brought in to face Josh Gibson. Spahn gets a good hand as he dejectedly walks off the mound (6.7 IP, 10 H, 4 R, 3 HR, 6 K, O BB). The long ball hurt Spahnie today. Tekulve strikes out Gibson. **BB Stars 4, Braves/Pirates 2.**

There is no further scoring. Satchel Paige pitches a 5-hitter for the win to even the series, 4-4. The final line for Satchel is – 9 IP, 5 H, 2 R, 0 ER, 0 HR, 7 K, 1 BB.

	R	H	E	LOB
Braves/Pirates	2	5	0	4
BB Stars	4	11	2	7

Winning Pitcher – Paige   Losing Pitcher – Spahn
The series is tied, 4-4.

Game Nine, Thursday May 6, Forbes Field (Pittsburgh), 1 pm (Day vs. Niekro)

No matter who wins Game Nine and the first Best Season series, this has been vintage, exciting baseball, played by some of the greatest players of all time. The most effective starter and long reliever for the Braves/Pirates, Phil Niekro, will be matched against Leon Day, who was the losing starting pitcher in Game Four, where Niekro was the winner. Day got the save in Game Five (the nineteen-inning classic that Niekro lost in relief on Gibson's HR). Which one will get the job done today?

After three innings, there has been one hit, a Lloyd single in first. Niekro and Day both look sharp. **BB Stars 0, Braves/Pirates 0.**

With one out in the top of the fourth, Niekro walks Torriente. Josh Gibson steps to the plate. Niekro does not want a repeat of the nineteenth inning from Game Five, also played at Forbes Field. Niekro falls behind 2-0 and tries to sneak a fast ball low in the strike zone. But Gibson is ready. As soon as it leaves the bat, there is no doubt. It's high and majestic over the left field fence (2-0). The Braves/Pirates outfield throws out another BB Stars base runner to quell the threat. **BB Stars 2, Braves/Pirates 0.**

Leon Day is sharp as he retires the side in order. He has faced the minimum 12 batters (walking one, erased in a double play). In the top of the fifth,

Niekro continues to struggle. With one out, Day singles to right field. Bell goes the opposite way and grounds one between Mathews (3B) and Vaughn (SS) for a single; Day stops at second. Vaughn's range could have been a factor. Wagner may have been able to make the play (AA range vs. C). Torriente hits a line drive over Mazeroski (2B) for a run-scoring single (3-0). Gibson takes a called third strike. **BB Stars 3, Braves/Pirates 0.**

In the top of the sixth, Niekro retires the side in order. His pitching is done for the day (6 IP, 7 H, 3 R, 1 HR, 3 K, 1 BB). **BB Stars 3, Braves/Pirates 0.**

In the bottom of the sixth, the Braves/Pirates know they are down to their final 12 outs and are three runs behind. They must put some pressure on Day. Cuccinello bats for Mazeroski and goes in defensively at second base. He flies to right. Lloyd Waner bats for Niekro. Waner bloops one over Lloyd's head into short left field for the first hit off of Day. Carey flies out to Bell in center (two outs). Paul Waner singles to right; his brother stops at second. Vaughn takes a called third strike. **BB Stars 3, Braves/Pirates 0.**

In the top of the seventh, Ruffing replaces Niekro. Wagner replaces Vaughn at shortstop, and Cuccinello is playing second. Ruffing retires the first two batters before Bell singles. Ruffing strikes out Lloyd (looking). **BB Stars 3, Braves/Pirates 0.**

In the bottom of the seventh, Kiner walks. Darrel Evans runs for him and plays first base. Mathews strikes out (one out). Cuyler lines one into the gap in left center, but Bell runs it down (two outs). Munson strikes out. **BB Stars 3, Braves/Pirates 0.**

Ruffing retires the first two batters in the eighth (Torriente strikes out swinging, Gibson grounds out to SS). Stearnes doubles off the wall in right, his second hit. Leonard is walked intentionally; Suttles pinch runs and will be a defensive upgrade at first base (A vs. B range). Judy Johnson (replaced Dandridge in sixth, A vs. B range) strikes out. **BB Stars 3, Braves/Pirates 0.**

Leon Day has six outs to go. Cuccinello bounces out to Lloyd (SS) for the first out in the bottom of the eighth. Traynor singles to right, pinch hitting for Ruffing (two shut out innings). Carey hits a slow roller to second and Warfield throws him out as Traynor moves to second. Paul Waner walks. Wagner represents the tying run stepping to the plate. He lifts a lazy fly ball to straight away center, and the dependable Bell makes the catch, ending the threat. **BB Stars 3, Braves/Pirates 0.**

In the top of the ninth, Elroy Face, who had a superb series out of the pen, retires the BB Stars in order. **BB Stars 3, Braves/Pirates 0.**

Leon Day has pitched a great game. Hilton Smith is loosening up in the bullpen, just in case. Day strikes out Evans looking with a great curve on the outside corner (one out). Mathews hits a fly ball to Bell (two outs). Cuyler lines a base hit into center field (only the fourth hit, all singles). Chief Zimmer is sent up to pinch hit for Munson. He slaps a one-hopper to Johnson (3B), who fires to Suttles, game and series over. The BB Stars take Game Nine and the series (5-4) behind Leon Day's masterful 4-hit shutout (9 IP, 4 H, 0 R, 6 K, 4 BB) and Josh Gibson's fourth inning 2-run homer to beat the Braves/Pirates 3-0.

	R	H	E	LOB
BB Stars	3	9	0	7
Braves/Pirates	0	4	0	7

Winning Pitcher – Day   Losing Pitcher – Niekro
The BB Stars win the series 5-4.

Recap of Best Season Series 1 (BB Stars vs. Braves/Pirates)

If all 15 Best Season series are as good as this first one, we are in for some great baseball played by the best players of all time from the 1880s-1980s. Chart 5-2 on page 40 has BB Stars individual/team statistics for this series. Chart 5-3 on page 41 has Braves/Pirates individual/team statistics for this series.

The turning point of the series was in Game Five, eighth inning, when Cool Papa Bell robbed Arky Vaughn of a sure HR. Eleven innings later, Josh Gibson hits a HR in the 19th inning off Phil Niekro to win the game. See Chart 5-2 (BB series results) and Chart 5-3 (Braves/Pirates results) for a statistical summary by players/teams.

The Most Valuable Player of the Series is Bullet Joe Rogan (3 G, 1 CG, 2 W, 0 L, 19.7 IP, 1 ER, 0.46 ERA). His 8.7 innings in relief (3 H, O R) in the nineteen-inning win was spectacular (winning pitcher), and he also started, completed, and won Game Three (9-1), allowing 4 hits and 1 run.

The Clutch Performer of the series is Josh Gibson. He had a relatively quiet series batting .250 with only 3 RBIs. However, his 3 RBIs were on game-winning HRs (nineteenth inning, Game Five and 2-run HR, fourth inning, Game Nine).

The best efforts on the losing side (Braves/Pirates)

1. **Outfield Defense** - The strong arms and very good range neutralized the BB Stars' aggressive base running, which made a difference in Games Four through Six (two wins and the loss in the epic nineteen-inning Game Five).

2. **Bullpen** - While the Brave/Pirate starters struggled (37 ER, 11 HR, 6.36 ERA), Niekro was an exception (SP ERA – 3.46; RP ERA – 1.80). The bullpen (7 ER, 5 HR, 1.72 ERA) was excellent (Face and Tekulve 16 IP, 0.00 ERA).

Black Ball Roster - Best Season Series

BB Stars Results vs. Braves/Pirates 5-4, .556

Pos.	E	R	TH	PB	Hitters	G	AB	R	H	RBI	2B	3B	HR	TB	W	HB	SO	SF	SH	SB	B.AVG.	OBP	S.PCT.	OPS
LF	5	A	-1		Charleston	6	23	0	5	0	1	0	0	6	0	0	2	0	0	0	0.217	0.217	0.261	0.478
CF	8	AA	-1		CP Bell	7	40	3	12	9	1	1	1	18	2	0	5	0	1	0	0.300	0.333	0.450	0.783
OF	5	A	-1		Stearnes	6	26	3	7	7	1	1	3	19	1	0	4	0	0	0	0.269	0.296	0.731	1.027
OF	6	B	-2		M Irvin	4	20	0	5	1	1	0	0	6	0	0	3	0	0	0	0.250	0.250	0.300	0.550
OF	6	A			Torriente	5	18	4	8	4	4	0	1	15	1	0	3	0	0	0	0.444	0.474	0.833	1.307
SS	7	A			P Lloyd	5	16	6	9	1	1	1	0	12	2	0	1	0	0	0	0.563	0.611	0.750	1.361
SS	7	AA			W Wells	5	27	4	9	4	1	2	2	20	1	0	5	0	0	0	0.333	0.357	0.741	1.098
3B	7	A			J Johnson	5	19	5	5	1	1	0	1	9	2	0	6	0	0	0	0.263	0.333	0.474	0.807
3B	6	B			Dandridge	6	21	1	5	2	1	0	0	6	0	0	4	0	0	1	0.238	0.238	0.286	0.524
2B	7	A			N Allen	4	16	1	5	0	1	0	0	6	0	0	3	0	0	1	0.313	0.313	0.375	0.688
2B	7	A			F Warfield	5	19	3	5	1	0	1	0	7	2	0	2	0	0	0	0.263	0.333	0.368	0.702
1B	8	A			Suttles	8	27	5	8	3	1	0	2	15	1	0	2	0	0	0	0.296	0.321	0.556	0.877
1B	8	B			B Leonard	5	15	2	3	3	1	0	1	7	0	0	1	0	0	0	0.200	0.200	0.467	0.667
C	7	A	-2	Fr	J Gibson	7	32	2	8	0	0	0	2	14	0	0	8	0	0	0	0.250	0.250	0.438	0.688
C	6	B	-2	Aw	B Mackey	4	12	3	2	3	0	0	0	2	0	0	3	0	0	0	0.167	0.167	0.167	0.333
					pitchers	9	26	3	8	4	1	0	0	9	0	0	5	0	3	2	0.308	0.308	0.346	0.654
					TOTAL	9	357	45	104	43	16	6	13	171	14	0	57	0	3	4	0.291	0.318	0.479	0.797

Fat.	H	WP	E	R	Pitchers	G	GS	QS	CG	S	W	L	IP	H	SO	BB	HB	HR	R	ER	ERA
10/L	Vg	N	9	B	BJ Rogan	3	3	1	1	1	0	2	19.7	8	5	4	0	0	2	1	0.46
9/L	Ex	R	7	B	B Foster	3	3	2	1	1	0	0	12.3	13	4	3	0	2	10	8	5.84
10/L	Vg	NL	8	B	L Day	3	3	1	1	0	1	1	16.3	13	9	6	0	0	5	4	2.20
10/L	Av	NL	7	B	M Dihigo	3	3	1	0	0	1	0	7	7	6	7	0	2	8	8	10.29
8/L	Md	R	8	C	S Paige	4	1	0	0	2	0	2	23	18	24	2	0	3	8	6	2.35
L/9	Vg	R	8	A	H Smith	3	0	0	0	2	0	0	7.7	11	4	2	0	0	6	5	5.84
9/L	Aw	NL	9	A	Newcombe	0	0	0	0	0	0	0	0	0	0	0	0	0	0	0	
10/L	Ex	NL	8	D	L Tiant	0	0	0	0	0	0	0	0	0	0	0	0	0	0	0	
9	Aw	N	5	C	JR Richard	1	1	0	0	0	0	0	1.3	0	0	1	0	0	0	0	0.00
Long	Md	NL	4	B	D Moore	1	0	0	0	0	0	0	2	2	1	1	1	1	1	1	4.50
					TOTAL	21	9	5	4	5	1	5	89.3	75	53	25	0	8	40	33	3.32

Chart 5.2 – BB Stars Statistics for this series

Braves/Pirates Best Season Series vs. BB All-Stars 4-5, .444

Team	Year	WS Hitters	G	AB	R	H	RBI	2B	3B	HR	TB	W	HB	SO	SF	SH	SB	B.AVG.	OBP	S.PCT.	OPS
Milwaukee	1963	41 H Aaron	5	22	0	4	3	0	1	0	6	2	0	3	0	0	0	0.182	0.250	0.273	0.523
Pittsburgh	1925	26 Carey	7	23	4	4	2	0	1	0	6	2	0	2	0	0	1	0.174	0.240	0.261	0.501
Pittsburgh	1929	27 L Waner	7	16	4	8	0	0	1	0	10	0	0	0	0	0	0	0.500	0.500	0.625	1.125
Pittsburgh	1927	36 P Waner	7	22	5	7	3	2	0	0	9	6	0	0	1	0	0	0.318	0.464	0.409	0.873
Pittsburgh	1925	34 Cuyler	4	11	1	2	0	0	1	0	4	0	0	3	0	0	1	0.182	0.182	0.364	0.545
Pittsburgh	1967	35 Clemente	5	21	2	5	3	0	0	1	8	1	0	4	0	0	0	0.238	0.273	0.381	0.654
Pittsburgh	1949	37 Kiner	5	17	3	6	4	0	0	1	9	3	0	2	0	0	0	0.353	0.450	0.529	0.979
Pittsburgh	1905	46 H Wagner	7	31	3	7	4	1	0	0	8	2	0	8	0	0	0	0.226	0.273	0.258	0.531
Pittsburgh	1935	39 A Vaughn	6	14	1	3	3	1	0	1	7	0	0	1	0	0	0	0.214	0.214	0.500	0.714
Milwaukee	1953	39 E Mathews	7	28	2	5	2	1	1	1	11	5	0	5	0	0	0	0.179	0.303	0.393	0.696
Pittsburgh	1923	28 Traynor	7	11	0	5	1	0	0	0	5	0	0	2	0	0	0	0.455	0.455	0.455	0.909
Pittsburgh	1960	21 Mazeroski	5	10	1	2	2	0	0	1	5	0	0	3	0	0	0	0.200	0.200	0.500	0.700
Boston (N)	1936	23 Cuccinello	7	24	3	4	3	1	0	0	5	0	0	3	1	0	0	0.167	0.167	0.208	0.375
Pittsburgh	1973	36 Stargell	5	19	1	1	1	0	0	1	4	0	0	1	0	0	0	0.053	0.053	0.211	0.263
Atlanta	1973	31 D Evans	6	10	1	1	1	0	0	1	4	2	0	2	0	0	0	0.100	0.250	0.400	0.650
New York A	1973	25 Munson	8	30	4	7	3	1	1	1	13	1	0	5	0	0	0	0.233	0.258	0.433	0.691
Cleveland N	1895	17 C Zimmer	4	8	1	0	0	0	0	0	0	1	0	1	0	0	0	0.000	0.111	0.000	0.111
		pitchers	9	18	3	5	2	1	0	0	6	0	0	8	1	3	0	0.278	0.278	0.333	0.611
		TOTAL	9	335	39	76	37	8	6	8	120	25	0	53	2	3	2	0.227	0.281	0.358	0.639

Team	Year	WS Pitchers	G	GS	QS	CG	S	W	L	IP	H	SO	BB	HB	HR	R	ER	ERA
Milwaukee	1953	31 Spahn	3	3	0	0	0	0	0	18.3	28	9	4	2	5	15	15	7.36
Boston (N)	1948	28 Sain	2	2	1	1	0	0	1	11	13	4	2	0	3	7	7	5.73
Pittsburgh	1902	24 Tannehill	2	2	1	0	0	0	1	10	15	4	3	0	2	11	10	9.00
Atlanta	1974	28 P Niekro	3	3	2	1	0	0	2	18	17	12	3	0	2	6	6	3.00
Pittsburgh	1922	27 W Cooper	4	2	0	0	0	1	0	4.3	5	4	0	0	0	4	4	8.31
Pittsburgh	1979	20 Tekulve	4	0	0	0	1	0	0	7.7	7	9	1	0	1	0	0	0.00
Pittsburgh	1962	20 Face	5	0	0	0	1	0	0	8.3	7	7	2	0	0	0	0	0.00
Atlanta	1982	19 Garber	1	0	0	0	0	0	0	1.7	2	2	3	0	0	0	0	0.00
New York A	1939	22 Ruffing	4	4	0	1	0	0	0	9.7	10	11	3	0	0	2	2	2.79
		TOTAL	29							89	105	56	16		13	45	44	4.45

Chart 5-3 – Braves/Pirates Statistics for this series

1. **Offense** – The Waner brothers (38 AB, 9 R, 12 H, 3 RBI, 6 W, .909 OPS) and Ralph Kiner (17 AB, 3 R, 6 H, 4 RBI, 1 HR, 3 W, .979 OPS) were the offensive stars in the losing cause.

2. **Best Comeback** - After losing Game Five, the nineteen-inning game where Bell robbed Vaughn of a HR and Gibson the game-winning HR, the comeback in Game Six by the Braves/Pirates was outstanding. Trailing 8-2, with two out and no one on base in the eighth inning, was a miracle. To have Ralph Kiner, one of the great home run hitters, hit the 3-run HR in the eighth to initiate the comeback was appropriate. Consider the park he played in; Forbes Field will never be confused with Fenway Park for a right-handed hitter. In the ninth, the Waner brothers started the rally with singles as pinch-hitters and a great series. Cuccinello (.167 batting average for the series) got a clutch hit and RBI. Carey (.174 BA for series) got his only extra base hit (2-run triple). The game-winning hit was made by Mr. Pirate, Honus Wagner (.226 BA for series).

Chapter 6

Best Season Nine-Game Series 2 — BB Stars vs. Browns/Orioles

Browns/Orioles Roster Review

THIRTY-TWO PERCENT OF THE ROSTER are made up of St. Louis Browns. Twenty-four percent of the roster are made up of Baltimore Orioles. Forty-four percent of the roster are free agents. See the Browns/Orioles Roster (Chart 6-1 on page 45).

Offensive Leaders (Browns/Orioles) Ranked by OPS

Player	OBP	SPct	OPS	R +	RBI -	HR =	NR
G. Sisler	.449	.632	1.082	137	122	19	240
K. Williams	.439	.623	1.062	106	91	29	168
F. Robinson	.412	.637	1.049	122	122	49	195
H. Manush	.415	.575	.991	104	108	13	199
H. Clift	.414	.546	.960	103	118	29	192
B. Powell	.388	.559.	.947	83	121	37	167
K. Singleton	.409	.533	.942	93	111	35	169
G. Stone	.412	.501	.913	91	71	6	156
H. Jennings	.424	.488	.912	125	121	0	246
D. Porter	.423	.484	.907	101	112	20	193

The following players will be base stealing threats: Jennings 70, Sisler 42, Stone 35, Pratt 26. Numbers listed SB for their best season.

Fielding Leaders	Pos	Range	Error	Throwing
Ken Williams	CF	B	5	-2

For outfielders, range (AA is best) and throwing (-4 is exceptional, -3 is excellent) are most important. Error rating (10 is best, 1 is poor) is not as critical as for infielders, because outfielders normally do not make as many errors.

Hugh Jennings	SS	AA+	5	-
Bobby Wallace	SS	AA	4	-
Brooks Robinson	3B	AA	10	-
Harland Clift	3B	AA	8	-
Del Pratt	2B	AA	4	-
George Sisler	1B	AA	8	-

For infielders, range (AA is best), + increase in DPs because of excellent pivot, error rating is as important as range (10 is excellent, 1 is poor).

Catcher Throwing - Mcguire is -2 (very good); Porter is -1 (above average).

Pitcher Hold Rating - Radbourn, Griffith, and Shocker are excellent (less successful steal attempts); Smith is mediocre.

Pitching - Radbourne (59-12, 1.38), Palmer (23-11, 2.09), and Hendrix (29-10, 1.69) lead a very good staff (seven free agents, including two from the 1914 Federal League, Hendrix and Falkenberg).

Browns/Orioles Roster Best Season Series vs. BB All-Stars

Team	Year	WS	Hitters	G	AB	R	H	RBI	2B	3B	HR	TB	W	HB	SO	SF	SH	SB	B.AVG.	OBP	S.PCT.	OPS
Baltimore	1966	41	F Robinson	155	576	122	182	122	34	2	49	367	87	7	90	-	-	8	0.316	0.412	0.637	1.049
St. Louis (A)	1923	29	K Williams	147	555	106	198	91	37	12	29	346	79	2	32	-	-	18	0.357	0.439	0.623	1.062
St. Louis (A)	1905	27	G Stone	154	581	91	208	71	25	20	6	291	52	2	22	-	-	35	0.358	0.413	0.501	0.913
St. Louis (A)	1928	35	H Manush	154	638	104	241	108	47	20	13	367	39	2	14	-	-	17	0.378	0.415	0.575	0.991
Baltimore	1979	32	K Singleton	159	570	93	168	111	29	1	35	304	109	1	118	-	-	3	0.295	0.409	0.533	0.942
Baltimore	1896	36	H Jennings	130	521	125	209	121	27	9	0	254	19	2	11	-	-	70	0.401	0.424	0.488	0.912
St. Louis (N)	1901	26	B Wallace	134	550	69	178	91	34	15	2	248	20	2	25	-	-	15	0.324	0.350	0.451	0.801
St. Louis (A)	1937	23	H Clift	155	571	103	175	118	36	7	29	312	98	6	80	-	-	8	0.306	0.413	0.546	0.960
Baltimore	1967	24	B Robinson	158	610	88	164	77	25	5	22	265	54	4	54	-	-	1	0.269	0.332	0.434	0.767
Baltimore	1978	27	D DeCinces	142	511	72	146	80	37	1	28	269	46	2	81	-	-	7	0.286	0.347	0.526	0.873
St. Louis (A)	1916	24	D Pratt	158	596	84	159	103	35	12	5	233	54	3	56	-	-	26	0.267	0.331	0.391	0.722
St. Louis (A)	1920	33	G Sisler	154	631	137	257	122	49	18	19	399	46	2	19	-	-	42	0.407	0.449	0.632	1.082
Baltimore	1969	27	B Powell	152	533	83	162	121	25	0	37	298	72	1	76	-	-	1	0.304	0.388	0.559	0.947
Kansas City	1979	31	D Porter	157	533	101	155	112	23	10	20	258	121	1	65	-	-	3	0.291	0.423	0.484	0.907
Washington	1895	17	D McGuire	132	533	89	179	97	30	8	10	255	40	3	18	-	-	15	0.336	0.385	0.478	0.864

Team	Year	WS	Pitchers	G	GS	OS	CG	S	W	L	IP	H	SO	BB	HB	HR	R	ER	ERA
Providence	1884	89	O Radbourn	75	73	-	73	-	59	12	679	528	441	98	-	18	-	-	1.38
Baltimore	1975	31	J Palmer	39	38	-	25	1	23	11	323	253	193	80	-	20	-	-	2.09
Chicago (F)	1914	37	C Hendrix	49	37	-	34	5	29	10	362	262	189	77	-	6	-	-	1.69
Chicago (N)	1898	32	C Griffith	38	38	-	36	0	24	10	326	305	97	64	-	1	-	-	1.88
St. Louis	1985	27	J Tudor	36	36	-	14	0	21	8	275	209	169	49	-	14	-	-	1.93
St. Louis (A)	1922	29	U Shocker	48	38	-	29	3	24	17	348	365	149	57	-	22	-	-	2.97
St. Louis (A)	1950	25	N Garver	37	31	-	22	0	13	18	260	264	85	108	-	18	-	-	3.39
St. Louis (N)	1953	27	H Haddix	36	33		19	1	20	9	253	220	163	69	-	24	-	-	3.06
Indianapolis	1914	34	F Falkenberg	49	43		33	3	25	16	377	332	236	89	-	5	-	-	2.22
Houston	1987	15	D Smith	50	0		0	24	2	3	60	39	73	21	-	0	-	-	1.65

Chart 6-1 – Browns/Orioles Best Season Roster

Game One, Friday May 7, County Stadium (Milwaukee), 1 pm (Radbourn vs. Paige)

The BB Stars will use pitcher-friendly Milwaukee County Stadium as their home park for this series.

It is a cool, clear, windy day (blowing toward the right field fence). In the bottom of the second inning, the BB Stars initiate scoring vs. Old Hoss Radbourn. Gibson triples over Ken Williams' (CF) head to start the inning. With one out, Suttles drills the ball off the wall in deep center, and it bounces away from Williams. Suttles goes into third with a stand-up triple as Gibson scores the first run. **BB Stars 1, Browns/Orioles 0.**

In the top of the fifth inning, the Browns/Orioles capitalize on a costly error by Allen (2B). With one out, Allen bobbles a ground ball, and the speedy George Stone beats the throw. Porter triples to left center, scoring Stone (1-1). Pratt lays down a good bunt in front of the plate. Gibson can only make the play at first as Porter slides in with the second run (both runs unearned). Radbourn fans. **Browns/Orioles 2, BB Stars 1.**

In the bottom of the fifth, the BB Stars threaten again. Suttles doubles into the gap in left center (Suttles has a triple and a double). Johnson tops one down the third base line. Clift bare hands the ball and throws out Johnson as Suttles moves to third. Radbourn walks Allen. Paige pushes a bunt to the left of the mound. Radbourn sees he cannot get Suttles and throws Paige out at first with Pratt (2B) covering (2-2, two outs). Allen is now on second. Radbourn hits Bell on the shoulder, now runners are on first and second. Lloyd takes a called third strike. **BB Stars 2, Browns/Orioles 2.**

In the bottom of the sixth, Charleston singles to right. Gibson singles to left, Charleston stops at second. The veteran Radbourn (59-game winner, Providence, 1884) then strikes out Stearnes (swinging), Suttles (swinging), and Johnson (called strike three at the knees). With two outs in the top of the seventh, Stone (not a HR hitter) takes Satchel deep over the fence in right. Porter strikes out, looking. **Browns/Orioles 3, BB Stars 2.**

With one out in the bottom of the seventh, Torriente comes out of the dugout to bat for Paige (7 IP, 3 H, 3 R, 1 ER, 1 HR, 7K, 0 BB). Paige pitched superbly. Torriente tries hard to even the score. He lifts a high fly ball to deep right. The wind is helping to blow it toward the fence, but Frank Robinson catches the ball on the warning track with his back to the wall. Radbourn throws both his arms into the air (two outs). Bell flies out to Williams. **Browns/Orioles 3, BB Stars 2.**

Hilton Smith replaces Paige and retires the side in order. In the bottom of the eighth, Radbourn gets in trouble quickly. Lloyd doubles into the right field corner. Charleston singles to left. Stone grabs it with a one-hop and throws a one-hop strike to Porter. Lloyd holds at third. Radbourn now faces

Josh Gibson (none out). Gibson has a triple and a single in three at-bats with a run scored. Gibson hits a ground ball that Clift (3B) cuts off and throws to second for the force, but Charleston's hard slide takes out Pratt (2B). Lloyd has scored the tying run (Gibson RBI). **BB Stars 3, Browns/Orioles 3.**

In the top of the ninth, Hilton Smith gives up a lead-off triple to Sisler. The infield is in. Smith gets Frank Robinson with a called third strike (one out). Williams is walked intentionally. The infield is in at the corners and medium deep at short and second (hoping for DP). Clift chops one to Lloyd at short; he flips it to Allen (second out), but Allen's relay to Suttles is not in time. Sisler crosses the plate with the go-ahead run (4-3). Stone hits one up the middle into center field. Clift stops at second. Porter lines a base hit into right center. Clift scores a big insurance run, and Stone advances to third. Pratt lines to short. **Browns/Orioles 5, BB Stars 3.**

That is all Old Hoss Radbourn needs. Johnson lines out to Jennings (one out). Allen takes a called third strike (two outs). Mackey bats for Smith and pops out to Jennings (SS). Radbourn has a complete game win in the opener (9 IP, 8 H, 3 R, 0 HR, 6 K, 1 BB, 1HB).

	R	H	E	LOB
Browns/Orioles	5	6	0	3
BB Stars	3	8	2	6

Winning Pitcher – Radbourn   Losing Pitcher – Paige
The Browns/Orioles lead the series, 1-0.

Game Two, Saturday May 8, County Stadium (Milwaukee), 1 pm (Palmer vs. Rogan)

It is a beautiful day for baseball (warm, clear, no wind). The Browns/Orioles score with two outs in the first. Jennings is on second (single, advanced on ground out). Williams bloops one to center that drops in for a hit as Jennings scores. **Browns/Orioles 1, BB Stars 0.**

With two outs and no one on base in the third, Rogan walks Sisler. With Sisler running, Robinson slugs one off the wall in left field for a double; Sisler scores (2-0). Rogan walks Williams. Clift pops out to Lloyd. **Browns/Orioles 2, BB Stars 0.**

In the bottom of the third with one out, Allen singles to right, and then he steals second. Rogan singles to left, and Allen beats the throw to score the first run for the BB Stars. **Browns/Orioles 2, BB Stars 1.**

In the top of the fourth, Stone singles to left. Porter lines it over the fence in right (just inside the foul pole, 4-1). **Browns/Orioles 4, BB Stars 1.**

With two outs and no one on in the fifth, Rogan's day is about over. Williams homers to right (5-1). Clift doubles off the wall in left center. Stone singles to right, scoring Clift (6-1). Rogan heads for the showers. Newcombe (27-7, 1956 Dodgers) replaces him. On the hit-and-run, Porter doubles into the right field corner, Stone scores from first (7-1). Rogan's line is complete (4.7 IP, 8 H, 7 R, 2 HR, 0 K, 2 BB). Pratt singles to right, and Porter comes around to score.. **Browns/Orioles 8, BB Stars 1.**

In the top of the seventh, Newcombe is chased. He walks Williams. Clift doubles to right center; Williams stops at third. Stone doubles off the wall in center as Williams and Clift score (10-1). J. R. Richard (18-13 1979 Astros) replaces Newcombe. The hard throwing right-hander strikes out Porter (looking, one out). Pratt singles to center, scoring Stone (11-1). Palmer and Jennings go down swinging (Richard strikes out the side). **Browns/Orioles 11, BB Stars 1.**

In the eighth and ninth, the Browns/Orioles add two more runs, and the BB Stars get to Palmer for one run in the ninth. **Browns/Orioles 13, BB Stars 2.**

	R	H	E	LOB
Browns/Orioles	13	18	0	8
BB Stars	2	7	0	5

Winning Pitcher – Palmer   Losing Pitcher – Rogan
The Browns/Orioles lead the series, 2-0.

Game Three, Sunday May 9, Memorial Stadium (Baltimore), 1 pm (Foster vs. Tudor)

It is a warm, cloudy day in Baltimore. In the bottom of the second, the Browns/Orioles scratch out a run vs. the lefty, Bill Foster. Decinces and McGuire single, and Wallace has an RBI ground out. **Browns/Orioles 1, BB Stars 0.**

Suttles' home run in fourth ties the game, 1-1. With one out in the bottom of the fifth, Manush doubles to right; Sisler singles (his third single of the game) to drive in Manush. **Browns/Orioles 2, BB Stars 1.**

Through five innings, Tudor has given up 2 hits, 1 run, and 1 walk and has three strikeouts. With one out in the sixth, it all changes. Bell doubles, and Suttles singles to right, scoring Bell (2-2). Gibson singles, Suttles stops at second. Irvin smashes a 3-run home run to left (5-2). Shocker is warming up quickly. Wells singles to center. Shocker is now pitching. Johnson doubles to left center with Wells stopping at third (sixth hit in a row). Allen pinch hits for Warfield and doubles into the gap in right center, scoring two runs (seventh hit in a row, 7-2).

Shocker retires the ninth and tenth batters of the inning. The final line on Tudor is 5.3 IP, 7 H, 6 R, 2 HR, 2 K, 1 BB. **BB Stars 7, Browns/Orioles 2.**

This was the final score. Foster's final line is 8 IP, 9 H, 2 R, 0 HR, 6 K, 1 BB. Hilton Smith pitched the ninth.

	R	H	E	LOB
BB Stars	7	10	0	4
Browns/Orioles	2	9	0	7

Winning Pitcher – Foster,   Losing Pitcher – Tudor
The Browns/Orioles lead the series, 2-1.

Game Four, Monday May 10, Memorial Stadium (Baltimore), 1 pm (Day vs. Hendrix)

It is a warm, cloudy day with possible showers later in the day. Hendrix (29-10, Chicago, Federal League, 1914) strikes out Torriente. He walks Bell, who steals second. Charleston lines out to Pratt, who makes a great catch diving to his right. Pratt then steps on second, doubling up Bell who thought it was going to be a single to center. In the bottom of the first, with one out, Stone doubles off the wall in right. Williams singles to center, scoring Stone (1-0). Frank Robinson walks. Powell flies out to deep right. Williams tags at second and goes to third (two outs). Clift doubles into the corner in left; Williams scores. Robinson is thrown out trying to score from first (Torriente to Lloyd to Mackey). **Browns/Orioles 2, BB Stars 0.**

In the fourth, the Browns/Orioles score without benefit of a hit. Day walks Robinson (second time). Powell tops the ball to the right of the mound. Day slips just as he goes to throw the ball, and the ball sails down the right field line (two-base error). Clift bounces out to Lloyd, and Robinson scores (3-0). **Browns/Orioles 3, BB Stars 0.**

Through five innings, Hendrix has held the BB Stars to just two hits. In the sixth Day, who is also pitching well, helps himself with a single to left. Pratt bobbles Torriente's grounder. It would have at least forced Day at second. Instead there are runners on first and second (none out). On Hendrix's first pitch to Bell, the ball bounces off Porter's catcher's mitt (passed ball) and goes to the back stop. The runners advance to second and third, still none out. Bell grounds out to deep first, Day scores, and Torriente moves to third, with an RBI for Bell (3-1). Charleston hits one to Powell's right. Powell makes a good play and throws to Hendrix, covering first as Torriente scores the second run (Charleston RBI). Both runs are unearned. Stearnes triples to center. Lloyd grounds out, Powell to Day. **Browns/Orioles 3, BB Stars 2.**

There is no further scoring. Day's pitching line is 7 IP, 5 H, 3 R, 2 ER, 0 HR, 3 K, 3 BB. Richard pitches a scoreless eighth. Hendrix' final line is 9 IP, 5 H, 2 R, 0 ER, 0 HR, 4 K, 2 BB.

	R	H	E	LOB
BB Stars	2	5	1	5
Browns/Orioles	3	5	1	5

Winning Pitcher – Hendrix   Losing Pitcher – Day

The Browns/Orioles lead the series, 3-1.

Game Five, Wednesday May 12, Milwaukee County Stadium, 1 pm (Radbourn vs. Paige)

It is a warm, cloudy day, with no wind. With two outs in the first, Sisler hits a home run to right field. Robinson flies out. **Browns/Orioles 1, BB Stars 0.**

In the top of the fourth, the Browns/Orioles add to their lead. Sisler singles to left. He steals second. After Robinson pops out to Dandridge (3B) in foul territory (one out), Williams singles to center. Sisler is determined to score and beats Bell's throw with a head-first slide. He reaches out his hand to tag home plate. Williams takes second on the throw home (2-0). Paige strikes out Clift looking (two outs). However, Porter doubles into the gap in left center to score Williams. Pratt flies to Stearnes in right. **Browns/Orioles 3, BB Stars 0.**

In the top of the fifth, with one out, Manush hits one up the middle and through for a base hit. Jennings hits a high chopper back to Paige, who throws him out with Manush moving into scoring position (two outs). Sisler gets his third hit slapping the ball over shortstop Lloyd's head into left center. Manush races around to score their fourth run (4-0). Robinson bounces out to first. **Browns/Orioles 4, BB Stars 0.**

Radbourn strikes out the side, in the fifth. He has faced one batter over the minimum (Allen double in the third). With the way he is pitching and the Browns/Orioles aggressive offense, the BB Stars could find themselves down four games to one in the series.

In the bottom of the sixth, Radbourn shows the first sign of weakness. Allen leads off by lining a single to center. Torriente pinch hits for Paige (6 IP, 6 H, 4 R, 1 HR, 3 K, 1 BB). With Allen running on the pitch, Torriente smashes the ball between first and second into right field as Allen steams into third (none out). Bell lifts a fly ball to center. Williams comes in to make the catch, and then he fires a strike to Porter. Allen bluffs a move toward home to draw the throw (one out). Lloyd singles to left. Allen scores; Torriente stops at second (4-1). Charleston flies out to Robinson (RF) for the second out; runners hold. Gibson lines a rope just fair into the left field corner, scoring Torriente. Lloyd goes through the stop sign by the third base coach. The Browns/Orioles execute perfectly, Williams to Jennings to Porter, just beating Lloyd for the final out of the inning. **Browns/Orioles 4, BB Stars 2.**

Hilton Smith replaces Paige and retires the side in order. In the bottom of the seventh, Radbourn fans Stearnes (swinging). Suttles singles to center before Radbourn fools Leonard (batting for Dandridge) for his second strike-out in the inning. Newt Allen steps up to the plate. Radbourn seems to have regained his confidence. He tries to sneak a fast ball on the inside corner, but Newt is waiting for it and lines it over the fence in right to tie the game (4-4). With hands on his hips, Radbourn kicks the dirt and begins muttering to himself. Allen is not the guy you expect to beat you with the long ball. Allen has owned Radbourn today (double, single, HR, 2 R, 2 RBI). **Browns/Orioles 4, BB Stars 4.**

In the top of the eighth, the Browns/Orioles put their first two batters on base. Jennings singles to center. Sisler has a hit and run a single to right, sending Jennings to third (Sisler is 4 for 4). There is no one out. Frank Robinson lines Smith's first pitch to center. It looks like it will drop in, but Bell makes a sliding catch. With his movement sliding forward, Bell jumps up and throws the ball on the fly to Gibson, who blocks the plate and tags Jennings for a big double play. Williams hits a routine groundball to Lloyd, who flips to Allen. Sisler slides in (third out). Sisler is slow to get up. He limps off the field. Powell replaces him in the bottom of the eighth. **Browns/Orioles 4, BB Stars 4.**

As Radbourn takes the mound, the Browns/Orioles have warm-up action in the pen. The left-hander is Harvey Haddix (1953 Cardinals), and the right-hander is Cy Falkenberg (Indianapolis, 1914 Federal League). Bell pops one up into shallow right field; Pratt (2B) races to the ball, lunges at the last second, and makes a great catch (one out). Lloyd lines a single to center. Haddix replaces Radbourn to pitch to Charleston. Charleston singles to right; Lloyd races to third and beats the throw from Robinson, and Charleston goes to second on the throw. Haddix walks Gibson (intentional), loading the bases. Stearnes lofts a fly ball toward the right field line, not very deep. Robinson positions himself to make the catch and throw in one motion. Lloyd is standing on third, anticipating the catch. Robinson catches the ball (two outs), and Lloyd breaks for home. It is another bang-bang play at the plate (ball and runner simultaneously arrive). With the slide, the umpire is slow to make the call. His arm goes up, the runner is out. Lloyd has been thrown out at home twice in the last three innings. **Browns/Orioles 4, BB Stars 4.** Radbourn's final line is 7.3 IP, 8 H, 4 R, 1 HR, 5 K, 0 BB.

In the top of the ninth inning, Hilton retires the side in order (2 Ks). The final out is pinch hitter Singleton striking out swinging (batting for Pratt). The Browns/Orioles do a double switch (DeCinces replaces Pratt at second base and will bat ninth; Falkenberg replaces Haddix, batting eighth). Hilton has pitched three shutout innings in relief. Suttles greets Falkenberg with a double off the wall in left center. Johnson (eighth inning replaced Dandridge at 3B) strikes out (one out). Allen walks (on base all four times); Mackey comes out to bat for Smith. Suttles leads off second, Allen takes his lead at first and the 2-2 pitch is ripped to deep center. Williams leaps but it is over his head, bouncing off the wall. Suttles comes in to score the winning run as Mackey is mobbed at second base with a walk-off double. The BB Stars come back from a 4-0 deficit to win Game Five, 5-4.

	R	H	E	LOB
Browns/Orioles	4	8	0	4
BB Stars	5	11	0	6

Winning Pitcher – Smith   Losing Pitcher – Falkenberg
The Browns/Orioles lead the series, 3-2.

Game Six, Thursday May 13, Milwaukee County Stadium, 7 pm (Griffith vs. Tiant)

It is a cold, partly cloudy day; wind is blowing in. Jennings opens with a single to center off Luis Tiant (Cleveland Indians, 1968). On the hit-and-run, Sisler bounces out to Lloyd (SS). Jennings slides into second. Williams lines a base hit to right, scoring Jennings (1-0). Frank Robinson hits a deep drive to left; it is going, going, caught at the fence by Charleston. The wind becomes a literal wall, and the ball dies (two outs). Manush hits into a force play (Lloyd to Warfield). **Browns/Orioles 1, BB Stars 0.**

In the top of the second, despite the wind, Clift lines one over the fence, just fair in left field. **Browns/Orioles 2, BB Stars 0.**

Stearnes hits Griffith's first pitch of the second inning and crushes it for a home run to right field (2-1). Griffith retires the next three hitters. **Browns/Orioles 2, BB Stars 1.**

In the top of the fourth, Manush leads off with a single to right. On the hit-and-run, Clift singles up the middle with Manush moving over to third (no out). Tiant has his work cut out for him. Porter hits a ball to the right side; Warfield fields it and fires to Lloyd, just beating Clift (one out), while Manush scores (3-1). **Browns/Orioles 3, BB Stars 1.**

As we enter the bottom of the seventh, Griffith has held the BB Stars to five hits, no walks. Suttles leads off with a triple off the wall in center.

Johnson singles to left, scoring Suttles (3-2). Dave Smith is warming up for the Browns/Orioles. Allen pinch hits for Warfield and flies out to Williams in shallow center (one out). Torriente bats for Tiant (7 IP, 8 H, 3 R, 1 HR, 8 K, O BB). Torriente bloops a single into shallow center; Johnson stops at second. Dave Smith replaces Griffith. Bell hits the ball in the gap (left-center), and it rolls to the wall. Both runners will score, and Bell's head-first slide into third beats the throw. The final numbers for Griffith are 6.1 IP, 8 H, 4 R, 1 HR, 4 K, 0 BB. The BB Stars have their first lead of the game, 4-3. Dave Smith gets Lloyd to pop out to DeCinces (sixth inning replacement after Powell pinched hit for Pratt). Charleston flies out to Manush in left. **BB Stars 4, Browns/Orioles 3.**

Rogan and Dave Smith retire the sides in order in the eighth. In the top of the ninth, Rogan retires Clift (pop to shortstop), and Porter is robbed of a hit by Warfield, who throws him out after a diving stop in the hole (two outs). Rogan has retired five in a row. Decinces singles to center. Singleton is coming up to bat for Smith. Rogan falls behind 3-1 and tries to jam Singleton with a fast ball, but it drifts too much over the plate. Singleton crushes the ball to deep right and it is gone, home run. The Browns/Orioles have regained the lead, 5-4. Foster is ready in the bullpen. Jennings singles to right, and Foster is on to pitch to Sisler. Foster's 2-2 slow curve just catches the outside corner, strike three. **Browns/Orioles 5, BB Stars 4.**

Falkenberg (Indianapolis, 1914 Federal League) is on to protect the lead. He starts well, getting Johnson to fly out to Robinson (one out). Allen singles to left. Batting for Foster, Leonard doubles to left center, but Williams gets the ball in quickly, and Allen is held at third.

The corner infielders are in on the grass; short and second are back. Falkenberg is pitching carefully to Bell. He finally walks him. Shocker replaces Falkenberg. The bases are loaded, one out. Shocker's 1-1 pitch is hit to straight away center, not too deep. Williams has a good arm (-2). Allen is tagging; he is headed home. Williams throw is up the first base line 2-3 feet, and Porter does a good job of keeping the ball in front of him as Allen scores the tying run (Lloyd – sac fly). The other runners also advance. Charleston hits one to Sisler, who throws to Shocker covering, to end the inning. **BB Stars 5, Browns/Orioles 5.** We are going into extra innings.

Hilton Smith is now pitching. Kenny Williams singles up the middle. In the first inning, Frank Robinson thought he had a home run, but the wind (still blowing in from left), held it up, and Charleston caught it in front of the fence. Charleston is playing deep and toward the line. Robinson hits Smith's first pitch to deep left, toward the line. Charleston runs back to the warning track as another Robinson drive falls short, and Charleston makes the catch and throws it in to keep the runner from moving to second. Manush fouls out to Gibson (two outs). Clift lines a single to right, and Williams goes into third standing. Porter flies out to Stearnes in right to end the inning. **BB Stars 5, Browns/Orioles 5.**

In the bottom of the tenth, Gibson hits Shocker's first pitch over second base into center field for a single. Turkey Stearnes steps into the batter's box. Shocker falls behind 2-0 and throws his fast ball. Stearnes hits it to deep right, and it is out of here for a walk-off 2-run home run. Two games in a row, walk-off wins for the BB Stars have evened the series 3-3.

!0 Innings	R	H	E	LOB
Browns/Orioles	5	13	0	8
BB Stars	7	13	0	7

Winning Pitcher – H. Smith   Losing Pitcher – Shocker

The series is tied, 3-3.

Game Seven, Friday May 14, Milwaukee County Stadium, 1 pm (Palmer vs. Newcombe)

It is a warm, cloudy day, no wind. Stone leads off the first with a double to center. Wallace hits a chopper to Wells (SS), and he is thrown out as Stone moves to third. Singleton goes down swinging on a low fast ball (two outs). Robinson walks. Powell hits a line drive that short-hops Wells (SS). He cannot make the play (E6), and the run scores (unearned). **Browns/Orioles 1, BB Stars 0.**

It remains 1-0 until the bottom of the fourth. Irvin leads off with a home run to left. Mackey lines a base hit to center. Dandridge goes down swinging (high heat, one out). Allen singles (hit-and-run); Mackey goes to third. They are looking for the bunt. Newcombe lays down a beauty that only the catcher, McGuire, can handle. His only play is at first (DeCinces covering) as Mackey scores, and Allen goes to second (two outs). The BB Stars are now leading 2-1. Charleston clobbers Palmer's first pitch with a long home run to right field (4-1). **BB Stars 4, Browns/Orioles 1.**

Palmer is lifted for a pinch hitter in the fifth. Palmer's line is 4 IP, 8 H, 4 R, 2 HR, 2 K, 0 BB. Haddix replaces Palmer and pitches three shut-out innings. It is now the top of the eighth. Newcombe is still on the mound for the BB Stars. He has given up 4 hits and one unearned run (first inning). Porter pinch hits for Haddix and doubles off the wall in center field. Moore is ready in the bullpen. Newcombe walks Stone. Moore replaces Newcombe. Jennings pinch hits for Wallace. He singles (on hit-and-run) to score Williams and send Stone to third (4-2); still none out. Singleton hits a high fly to Charleston in fairly deep left field; Stone easily scores on the sac fly (4-3). Moore gets the next two batters. Newcombe's line is 7+ IP, 5 H, 3 R, 2 ER, 0 HR, 2 K, 2 BB. **BB Stars 4, Browns/Orioles 3.**

Ned Garver (1950 St. Louis Browns) is pitching in the bottom of the eighth. He retires the side with only a one-out single (Mackey). Moore is now pitching his second inning of relief. McGuire singles to left field. Clift forces McGuire at second (Wells to Allen). Doug DeCinces steps to the plate. He is 0 for 3 (2 Ks). Moore's 2-1 pitch (fast ball) is crushed; 2-run home run to deep left. Browns/Orioles take the lead (5-4) for the first time since the first inning. For the second game in a row, the BB Stars bullpen has given up the lead on 2-run HRs in the ninth (Singleton off Rogan and Decinces off Moore). **Browns/Orioles 5, BB Stars 4.**

Can the BB Stars make another dramatic comeback (two walk-off wins in a row)? Williams stays in the game, replacing Stone in center field. Dave Smith replaces Garver and will bat in lead-off spot. Dave Smith will try to close the door and put the Browns/Orioles back in the series lead, 4-3. He will be tested right off the bat. Josh Gibson is pinch hitting for Donnie Moore. Smith gets Gibson to top a changeup down to Clift at third base, and he is thrown out (one out). Charleston walks. Wells is caught looking at a fast ball at the knees, strike three (two outs). Bell (pinch hit for Torriente in seventh) hits Smith's first pitch to Decinces (2B). He flips to Jennings for the force, and the game is over. **Browns/Orioles 5, BB Stars 4.**

	R	H	E	LOB
Browns/Orioles	5	9	0	6
BB Stars	4	10	1	8

Winning Pitcher – Garver   Save – D. Smith   Losing Pitcher – Moore
The Browns/Orioles lead the series, 4-3.

Game Eight, Saturday May 15, Sportsman's Park (St. Louis), 1 pm (Foster vs. Hendrix)

It is a warm, clear day, no wind. In the bottom of the second, the Browns/Orioles strike first. Ken Williams doubles off the right field wall. Clift flies out to Bell in center. Stone singles to right; with Williams holding at third. McGuire lines a single to left field, scoring Williams; Stone stops at second. Pratt lines into an unassisted double play (Allen 2B). **Browns/Orioles 1, BB Stars 0.**

In the bottom of the third, Sisler homers over the wall in right. **Browns/Orioles 2, Bb Stars 0.**

After seven innings, the score remains 2-0. Remember in Game Four, Hendrix pitched a complete game and won 3-2; both runs were unearned. He has now pitched 16 innings against the BB Stars without giving up an earned run. Foster left the game after 4 innings (4 IP, 5 H, 2 R, 1 HR, 1 K, 0 BB). Day pitched 3 scoreless innings.

Allen leads off the top of the eighth with a double into the right field corner. Mackey pinch hits for Day and singles to right, Allen races around and scores from second (2-1). Haddix (lefty) and Smith (righty) are ready in the bullpen. Hendrix walks Bell on four pitches. Haddix is coming in to pitch to Lloyd and Charleston (none out). Hendrix receives a warm ovation from the crowd. Wells pinch hits for Lloyd and tops one past Haddix, but Pratt bare hands the ball and throws Wells out (one out). Runners move into scoring position. They decide to pitch to Charleston with first and third basemen on the edge of the infield grass. Charleston bloops one over Pratt (2B) into shallow right field, scoring both runners. The BB Stars now lead 3-2. The final line for Hendrix is 7+ IP, 8 H, 3 R, 2 K, 1 BB. Smith relieves Haddix and gets Gibson (ground out) and Stearnes (swinging strikeout). **BB Stars 3, Browns/Orioles 2.**

J. R. Richard relieves Day and retires the side in order in the eighth, finishing with a fast ball that Ken Williams cannot catch up with. Smith pitches a scoreless top of the ninth. It is now up to J. R. to save it. The inning does not start out well. Clift lines a base hit into center field. Stone singles to left center, and Charleston does a great job holding Stone to a single as Clift races to third (none out). No one is warming up for the BB Stars; it is up to J. R. He gets McGuire looking at a fast ball on the inside corner for strike three (one out). John Tudor (P) is pinch hitting for Pratt (Tudor is an excellent bunter). They are in at the corners. Tudor pushes it up the third base line as Clift heads for the plate. Johnson bare hands the ball and fires a strike to Gibson, who puts the tag on Clift in a bang-bang play at the plate (two outs). Stone goes to second, Tudor is on first. Singleton is pinch hitting for Smith. He lines one to the left of Allen (2B). He leaps and makes a great catch for out number three. The game is over.

	R	H	E	LOB
BB Stars	3	11	0	7
Browns/Orioles	2	10	0	7

Winning Pitcher – Day   Save – J. R. Richard   - Losing Pitcher – Hendrix
The BB Stars have tied the series, 4-4.

Game Nine, Sunday May 16, Sportsman's Park (St. Louis), 1 pm (Paige vs. Radbourn)

It is warm and partly cloudy in St. Louis. Paige vs. Radbourn with the series tied is a perfect ending to a great series. In the bottom of the first, with one out, George Sisler triples to deep center. He has been the offensive star for the Browns/Orioles in this series. Frank Robinson grounds out to deep short as Sisler scores the first run of the game. Williams flies out to center. **Browns/Orioles 1, BB Stars 0.**

In the top of the third, the BB Stars come back against Radbourn. Bell bounces one up the middle into center field for a base hit. Bell gets a good jump and steals second. Lloyd goes down swinging (one out). Charleston singles into right, and Bell races home with the tying run. With Stearnes at the plate, Radbourn uncorks a wild pitch as Charleston moves into scoring position. Stearnes singles to right, and Charleston scores the go-ahead run. **BB Stars 2, Browns/Orioles 1.**

In the bottom of the fourth inning, Paige walks the lead-off hitter, Williams. He retires Clift and Stone on fly balls. Porter singles to center field with Williams hustling to beat the throw to third. Paige steps up on to the rubber and drops the ball. "Balk!" shouts the home plate umpire. Williams scores, and Porter goes to second. DeCinces lines out Dandridge (3B) **Browns/Orioles 2, BB Stars 2.**

In the top of the fifth, with one out, Charleston (single, run scored, RBI in the third) hits a long home run to right field (3-2). **BB Stars 3, Browns/Orioles 2.**

In the seventh, Griffith is in his second inning of relief (one-two-three sixth). With one out, Charleston doubles off the wall in right center. Griffith intentionally walks Stearnes. He gets Suttles to swing and miss at a pitch in the dirt for strike three (two outs). Mackey singles through the box into center field as Charleston comes in to score (4-2). Charleston has figured in all the BB Star's scoring. Dandridge lofts a high fly ball down the left field line; Stone runs back and leaps, catching the ball as he crashes into the wall. He holds on for the third out. **BB Stars 4, Browns/Orioles 2.**

The BB Stars threaten in the top of the eighth. They do not score, as Tudor replaces Griffith with runners on first and second (one out), but he gets Lloyd and Charleston. In the bottom of the eighth, Paige, who had retired the last ten batters, walks Singleton (pinch hitting for Tudor). Pratt pinch runs for Singleton. Jennings flies out to center (Bell). Sisler gets his third hit, base hit to right center, with Pratt moving to third. Paige gets Robinson to fly out to Bell in shallow center, and Pratt stays on third (two out). Williams lines out to Johnson for the third out. **BB Stars 4, Browns/Orioles 2.**

Neither team scores in the ninth (Paige retires side in order). The BB Stars come back from down four games to three for the second straight series. Paige's final line is 9 IP, 5 H, 2 R, 0 HR, 3 K, 2 BB.

	R	H	E	LOB
BB Stars	4	12	0	12
Browns/Orioles	2	5	0	5

Winning Pitcher – Paige   Losing Pitcher – Radbourn

The BB Stars win the series, 5-4.

Recap of Best Season Series 2 (BB Stars vs. Browns/Orioles)

If all 15 Best Season Series are as good as the first two series, we are in for some great baseball played by the best players of all time (1880s-1980s). Chart 6-2 on page 59 has BB Stars individual/team statistics for this series. Chart 6-3 on page 60 has Browns/Orioles individual/team statistics for this series.

The turning point of the series occurred when the BB Stars were down three games to one, trailing in Game Five 4-0 after five innings vs. Old Hoss Radbourn, yet they won Games Five and Six with walk-off hits to tie the series, 3-3. When the BB Stars blew a 4-1 lead in Game Seven with Singleton winning it with a 2-run HR off Rogan in the ninth, it could have been a turning point. The Browns/Orioles 4-3 series lead created another potential turning point in Game Eight. The BB Stars rallied for three runs off Hendrix (in the previous 16 innings, he held the BB Stars to two unearned runs) It was a very entertaining, well-played series.

MVP of Series – George Sisler (31 AB, 7 R, 15 H, 6 RBI, 2 T, 2 HR, 25 TB, .484 B.Avg, .500 OBP, .806 Slg.Pct., 1.306 OPS) had an outstanding series.

BB Stars Results vs. Browns/Orioles 5-4, .556

Pos.	E	R	TH	PB	Hitters	G	AB	R	H	RBI	2B	3B	HR	TB	W	HB	SO	SF	SH	SB	B.AVG.	OBP	S.PCT.	OPS
LF	5	A	-1		Charleston	9	39	5	11	7	3	0	2	20	1	0	3	0	0	0	0.282	0.300	0.513	0.813
CF	8	AA	-1		CP Bell	9	32	3	10	2	1	2	0	15	4	1	2	0	0	2	0.313	0.405	0.469	0.874
OF	5	A	-1		Stearnes	9	30	2	5	4	0	1	2	13	0	0	8	0	0	0	0.167	0.167	0.433	0.600
OF	6	B	-2		M Irvin	2	7	2	2	3	0	0	2	8	0	0	0	0	0	0	0.286	0.286	1.143	1.429
OF	6	A	-1		Torriente	6	11	2	2	2	0	0	0	2	0	0	1	0	0	0	0.182	0.182	0.182	0.364
SS	7	A			P Lloyd	9	30	1	6	2	1	0	0	7	0	0	4	0	0	0	0.200	0.200	0.233	0.433
SS	7	AA			W Wells	4	10	1	2	0	0	0	0	2	1	0	1	0	0	0	0.200	0.273	0.200	0.473
3B	6	A			J Johnson	6	21	2	2	1	1	0	0	3	0	0	5	0	0	0	0.095	0.095	0.143	0.238
3B	5	B			Dandridge	5	14	0	0	0	0	0	0	0	0	0	5	0	0	0	0.000	0.000	0.000	0.000
2B	8	A			N Allen	8	22	6	11	4	3	0	1	17	2	0	1	0	1	0	0.500	0.542	0.773	1.314
2B	3	A			F Warfield	3	5	0	1	0	0	0	0	1	3	0	0	0	0	0	0.200	0.500	0.200	0.700
1B	7	A			Suttles	7	23	6	8	3	2	2	1	17	0	0	3	0	0	0	0.348	0.348	0.739	1.087
1B	6	B			B Leonard	6	13	0	4	1	1	0	0	5	0	0	1	0	0	0	0.308	0.308	0.385	0.692
C	7	A	-2	Fr	J Gibson	8	26	3	9	2	3	1	0	14	1	0	3	0	0	0	0.346	0.370	0.538	0.909
C	6	B	-2	Av	B Mackey	7	15	1	9	3	2	0	0	11	1	0	2	0	0	0	0.600	0.625	0.733	1.358
					pitchers	9	16	2	5	1	0	0	0	5	0	0	5	0	1	1	0.313	0.313	0.313	0.625
					TOTAL	9	314	36	87	35	17	6	8	140	13	1	44	0	2	3	0.277	0.308	0.446	0.754

Fat.	H	WP	E	R	Pitchers	G	GS	QS	CG	S	W	L	IP	H	SO	BB	HB	HR	R	ER	ERA
10/L	Vg	N	9	B	BJ Rogan	2	2	1	0	0	0	1	6.3	11	2	2	1	3	9	9	12.80
9/L	Ex	R	7	B	B Foster	3	1	1	0	0	0	1	12.3	14	8	1	0	1	4	4	2.92
10/L	Vg	NL	8	B	L Day	2	1	1	0	0	0	1	10	8	4	3	0	0	3	2	1.80
10/L	Av	NL	7	B	M Dihigo	1	0	0	0	1	0	0	1	3	1	0	0	0	1	1	9.00
8/L	Md	R	8	C	S Paige	3	3	1	1	0	1	0	22	14	13	3	0	2	9	7	2.86
L/9	Vg	R	8	A	H Smith	4	0	0	0	1	1	0	7	7	3	0	0	0	2	2	2.57
9/L	Av	R	9	A	Newcombe	2	1	0	0	0	2	0	8.3	8	8	3	0	0	7	6	6.48
10/L	Ex	NL	8	D	L Tiant	1	1	1	1	0	0	1	7	8	2	0	1	1	3	3	3.86
9	Av	N	5	C	J R Richard	3	0	0	0	0	1	0	5	6	4	0	0	0	1	1	1.80
Long	Md	NL	4	B	D Moore	1	0	0	0	0	0	0	2	4	3	1	0	1	2	2	9.00
9	Md	NL			**TOTAL**	22	9	5	2	2	5	4	81	83	48	13	2	8	41	37	4.11

Chart 6-2 – BB Stars Statistics for this series

Browns/Orioles Best Season Series vs. BB All-Stars 4-5, .444

Team	Year	WS	Hitters	G	AB	R	H	RBI	2B	3B	HR	TB	W	HB	SO	SF	SH	SB	B.AVG.	OBP	S.PCT.	OPS
Baltimore	1966	41	F Robinson	9	36	5	5	2	2	0	0	7	3	0	6	0	0	0	0.139	0.205	0.194	0.400
St. Louis (A)	1923	29	K Williams	9	26	6	8	5	2	0	1	13	4	0	5	0	0	0	0.308	0.400	0.500	0.900
St. Louis (A)	1905	27	G Stone	7	26	8	12	4	3	1	0	20	0	0	0	0	1	0	0.462	0.462	0.769	1.231
St. Louis (A)	1928	35	H Manush	6	15	3	5	0	1	0	0	6	0	0	1	0	0	0	0.333	0.333	0.400	0.733
Baltimore	1979	32	K. Singleton	6	7	1	2	3	0	0	1	5	1	0	1	1	0	0	0.286	0.375	0.714	1.089
Baltimore	1896	36	H Jennings	8	31	2	5	1	0	0	0	5	0	0	5	0	0	0	0.161	0.161	0.161	0.323
St. Louis (N)	1901	26	B Wallace	2	7	0	0	0	1	0	0	0	0	0	0	0	0	0	0.000	0.000	0.000	0.000
St. Louis (A)	1937	23	H Clift	8	30	5	9	4	3	0	1	15	0	0	4	0	0	0	0.300	0.300	0.500	0.800
Baltimore	1967	24	B Robinson	2	7	0	0	0	0	0	0	0	0	0	1	0	0	0	0.000	0.000	0.000	0.000
Baltimore	1978	27	D DeCinces	5	11	3	3	2	0	0	1	6	1	0	3	1	0	0	0.273	0.273	0.545	0.818
St. Louis (A)	1916	24	D Pratt	8	19	1	3	3	3	2	0	3	1	0	2	0	0	0	0.158	0.200	0.158	0.358
St. Louis (A)	1920	33	G Sisler	9	31	7	15	6	6	0	2	25	1	0	0	0	0	1	0.484	0.500	0.806	1.306
Baltimore	1969	27	B Powell	4	8	0	1	0	0	0	0	1	0	0	4	0	0	0	0.125	0.125	0.125	0.250
Kansas City	1979	31	D Porter	7	26	4	8	6	3	1	1	16	0	0	2	0	0	0	0.308	0.308	0.615	0.923
Washington	1895	17	D McGuire	3	12	0	4	1	0	0	0	4	0	0	0	0	0	0	0.333	0.333	0.333	0.667
			pitchers	9	24	2	2	0	0	0	0	2	0	0	12	1	1	1	0.083	0.083	0.083	0.167
			TOTAL	9	316	41	82	38	14	4	8	128	10	0	48	1	1	1	0.259	0.282	0.405	0.687

Team	Year	WS	Pitchers	G	GS	QS	CG	S	W	L	IP	H	SO	BB	HB	HR	R	ER	ERA
Providence	1884	89	ORadbourn	3	3	2	1	1	1	0	21.3	23	15	4	1	2	10	10	4.22
Baltimore	1975	31	J Palmer	2	2	1	1	0	0	1	13	15	7	0	0	2	6	6	4.15
Chicago (F)	1914	37	C Hendrix	2	2	1	2	0	1	1	16	13	6	3	3	0	5	3	1.69
Chicago (N)	1898	32	C Griffith	2	1	0	0	1	0	0	8.7	12	5	1	0	1	5	5	5.19
St. Louis	1985	27	J Tudor	2	1	0	0	0	0	1	6	7	3	1	1	2	6	6	9.00
St. Louis (A)	1922	29	U Shocker	3	0	0	0	0	0	1	3	6	6	2	0	1	3	3	9.00
St. Louis (A)	1950	25	N Garver	2	0	0	0	0	0	0	3	1	1	1	0	0	0	0	0.00
St. Louis (N)	1953	27	H Haddix	4	0	0	0	0	0	0	4.3	3	3	1	3	0	0	0	0.00
Indianapolis	1914	34	H Falkenberg	2	0	0	0	0	1	0	0.7	4	4	2	2	0	2	2	27.00
Houston	1987	15	D Smith	3	0	0	0	1	0	0	4.3	4	3	0	1	0	0	0	0.00
			TOTAL	25	9	4	3	1	4	4	80.3	88	44	15	8	8	37	35	3.92

Chart 6-3 – Browns/Orioles statistics for this series

Chapter 7

Best Season Nine Game Series 3 - BB Stars vs.White Sox

White Sox Roster Review

SIXTY-FOUR PERCENT OF THE ROSTER are made up of Chicago White Sox. Thirty-six percent of the roster are free agents. . See the White Sox Roster (Chart 7-1 on page 62).

Offensive Leaders (White Sox) Ranked by OPS

Player	OBP	SPct	OPS	R +	RBI -	HR =	NR
W. McCovey	.458	.656	1.114	101	126	45	182
B. Hamilton	.518	.528	1.046	192	87	4	275
W. Keeler	.460	.539	.999	145	74	0	219
L. Appling	.473	.508	.981	111	128	6	233
O. Cepeda	.354	.609	.963	105	142	46	201
F. Clarke	.415	.532	.947	88	70	5	153
M. Minoso	.402	.535	.937	119	116	35	200
E. Collins	.460	.436	.896	118	77	4	191
B. Horner	.344	.552	.896	66	98	33	131
B. Bell	.379	.498	.877	76	83	17	137

The following players would be base-stealing threats – Hamilton 98, Keeler 64, Aparicio 51, Collins 46 (numbers listed SB for their best season).

White Sox Roster Best Season Series vs. BB All-Stars

Team	Year	WS Hitters	G	AB	R	H	RBI	2B	3B	HR	TB	W	HB	SO	SF	SH	SB	B.AVG.	OBP	S.PCT.	OPS
Philadelphia	1894	29 B Hamilton	129	544	192	220	87	25	15	4	287	126	3	17	-	-	98	0.404	0.519	0.528	1.046
Baltimore	1897	32 WW Keeler	129	564	145	239	74	27	19	0	304	35	3	6	-	-	64	0.424	0.460	0.539	0.999
Chicago (A)	1954	32 M Minoso	153	568	119	182	116	29	18	19	304	77	0	46	-	-	18	0.320	0.402	0.535	0.937
Pittsburgh	1903	25 F Clarke	104	427	88	150	70	32	15	5	227	41	6	27	-	-	21	0.351	0.416	0.532	0.947
Chicago (A)	1960	20 L Aparicio	153	600	86	166	61	20	7	6	206	43	1	39	-	-	51	0.277	0.326	0.343	0.669
Chicago (A)	1936	29 L Appling	138	526	111	204	128	31	7	6	267	85	0	25	-	-	10	0.388	0.473	0.508	0.981
Chicago (A)	1971	23 B Melton	150	543	72	146	86	18	2	33	267	61	1	87	-	-	3	0.269	0.344	0.492	0.836
Texas	1980	21 B Bell	129	490	76	161	83	24	4	17	244	40	0	39	-	-	3	0.329	0.379	0.498	0.877
Chicago (A)	1915	40 E Collins	155	521	118	173	77	22	10	4	227	119	5	27	-	-	46	0.332	0.460	0.436	0.896
Chicago (A)	1957	32 N Fox	155	619	110	196	61	27	8	6	257	75	16	13	-	-	5	0.317	0.404	0.415	0.819
SF Giants	1969	39 W McCovey	149	491	101	157	126	26	2	45	322	121	4	66	-	-	0	0.320	0.458	0.656	1.114
SF Giants	1961	29 O Cepeda	152	585	105	182	142	28	4	46	356	39	0	91	-	-	12	0.311	0.354	0.609	0.963
Atlanta	1979	19 B Horner	121	487	66	153	98	15	1	33	269	22	0	74	-	-	12	0.314	0.344	0.552	0.896
Chicago (A)	1922	22 R Schalk	142	442	57	124	60	22	3	4	164	67	3	36	-	-	12	0.281	0.379	0.371	0.750
Detroit (N)	1881	15 C Bennett	76	299	44	90	64	18	7	7	143	18	2	37	-	-	6	0.301	0.345	0.478	0.823

Team	Year	WS Pitchers	G	GS	QS	CG	S	W	L	IP	H	SO	BB	HB	HR	R	ER	ERA
Chicago (A)	1908	47 E Walsh	66	49	-	42	6	40	15	464	343	269	56	2	-	-		1.42
Chicago (A)	1955	23 B Pierce	33	26	-	16	1	15	10	206	162	157	64	16	-	-		1.97
Chicago (A)	1919	32 E Cicotte	40	35	-	30	1	29	7	307	256	110	49	5	-	-		1.82
Chicago (A)	1906	25 D White	28	24	-	20	0	18	6	219	160	95	38	2	-	-		1.52
Chicago (A)	1941	32 T Lee	35	34	-	30	1	22	11	300	258	130	92	18	-	-		2.37
Chicago (A)	1963	25 G Peters	41	30	-	13	1	19	8	243	192	189	68	9	-	-		2.33
Chicago (A)	1971	33 W Wood	44	42	-	22	1	22	13	334	272	210	62	21	-	-		1.91
Chicago (A)	1927	30 T Lyons	39	34	-	30	2	22	14	308	291	71	67	7	-	-		2.84
Chicago (A)	1921	37 R Faber	43	39	-	32	1	25	15	331	293	124	87	10	-	-		2.48
Chicago (N)	1885	62 J Clarkson	70	70	-	68	0	53	16	623	497	308	97	21	-	-		1.85

Chart 7-1 – White Sox Best Season Roster

62

Fielding Leaders	Pos	Range	Error	Throwing
B. Hamilton	CF	A	6	0
M. Minoso	LF	A	6	-1

For outfielders, range (AA is best) and throwing (-4 is exceptional, -3 is excellent) are most important. Error rating (10 is best, 1 is poor) is not as critical as for infielders, because outfielders normally do not make as many errors.

L. Aparicio	SS	AA+	10	-
L. Appling	SS	AA+	4	-
B. Bell	3B	AA	10	-
B. Melton	3B	AA	9	-
N. Fox	2B	AA+	9	-
E. Collins	2B	A	7	-

For infielders, range (AA is best), + increase in DPs because of excellent pivot, error rating is as important as range (10 is excellent, 1 is poor).

Catcher Throwing - Schalk is -3 (excellent); Bennett is -2 (very good).

Pitcher Hold Rating - Clarkson, Cicotte, White, and Peters are excellent (less successful steal attempts); Lee and Lyons are average.

Pitching - Ed Walsh (40-15, 1.42 in 1908), Doc White (18-6, 1.51 in 1906), Wilbur Wood (22-13, 1.91 in 1971), and Eddie Cicotte (29-7, 1.82 in 1919) lead a very good staff (including one free agent from Chicago-N 1885, John Clarkson).

Game One, Tuesday May 18, Astrodome (Houston), 7 pm (Walsh vs. Rogan)

The home park for the BB Stars for this series is the Houston Astrodome (Games One, Two, Six, and Seven). Ed Walsh (in my opinion, the best White Sox pitcher of all time) and Bullet Joe Rogan have no problems in the first three innings. The White Sox put two men on with two outs in the second off Rogan (walk to Collins, single to right by Appling, Collins to third), but Schalk bounces into a force play (64) to end the mini-threat. The only base runner off of Ed Walsh is Rogan when he doubles off a "hanging speaker" in the third. **White Sox 0, BB Stars 0.**

In the fourth, Rogan retires the side in order. Walsh, who does not walk many, walks Lloyd to lead-off the bottom of the fourth. He gets Charleston and Leonard on infield grounders, with Lloyd moving over to third. Walsh hangs a curve ball to Cristobal Torriente, and it is gone, a long home run to right field. Mackey flies out to Hamilton (CF). **BB Stars 2, White Sox 0.**

Neither team scores in the fifth. Walsh escapes a two-on, two-out situation in the fifth when Lloyd lines out to Eddie Collins (2B). In the top of the sixth, the White Sox finally get to Rogan. Billy Hamilton (free agent, Philadelphia, 1894) triples off the wall in center field. Keeler lays down a perfect bunt, and Mackey's throw to Allen (covering first) is too late (infield hit), scoring Hamilton. Keeler steals second. Minoso bounces out to second, moving Keeler to third (one out). McCovey is walked intentionally. Melton singles to left, scoring Keeler; McCovey stops at second (2-2). Collins and Appling hit into force-outs to end the inning. **White Sox 2, BB Stars 2.**

Two players are ejected from the game. Both incidents involve the first base umpire. In the fourth inning, Collins makes a great play on a smash by Leonard, knocking it down, then recovering to throw him out at first. He looked safe. Leonard did not like the call, argues too vehemently and is ejected (replaced by Suttles). In the sixth inning, on Keeler's bunt single, Allen (2B covering first) argues the safe call and is ejected (replaced by Warfield).

There is a scary moment in the top of the seventh, when Rogan tries to brush back Hamilton (single, walk, triple, run scored) and hits him in the head. Hamilton goes down in a heap. He is helped off the field as Fred Clarke (free agent, 1903 Pirates) goes in to pinch run. Defensively, Clarke will play left field. Minoso moves to center field.

The score remains tied going into the ninth inning. Rogan retires the first two batters. Ed Walsh is due up. The White Sox decide to bring up Orlando Cepeda. Red Faber (1921 White Sox) will replace Walsh. The final line for Walsh is 8 IP, 5 H, 2 R, 1 HR, 1 K, 1 BB. Cepeda flies to left, ending the inning.

In the bottom of the ninth, Suttles singles to left off Faber. Torriente hits a smash up the middle into center; Suttles stops at second (none out). Mackey (batting left-handed against righty Faber) slaps one into left field. Clarke charges the ball, gloves it, and fires a strike to home plate as Suttles makes the turn at third and holds. The bases are loaded (none out). Josh Gibson pinch hits for Judy Johnson. The infield and outfield move in. Faber makes a good pitch, and Gibson hits a one-hopper to Collins (2B), who fires to the plate. Suttles slides hard into Schalk, so there is no chance to get Gibson for the double play (one out). Warfield hits a fly ball to medium right center. Minoso waives off Keeler (Minoso has a much better arm than Keeler) and makes the catch as Torriente tags at third. Torriente slides in, beating the throw, giving the BB Stars a walk-off sac fly win in Game One, 3-2. The final line for Rogan is 9 IP, 5 H, 2 R, 0 HR, 2 K, 5 BB, 1 HB.

	R	H	E	LOB
White Sox	2	5	0	7
BB Stars	3	8	0	6

Winning Pitcher – Rogan   Losing Pitcher – Faber
The BB Stars lead the series, 1-0.

Game Two, Wednesday May 19, Astrodome (Houston), 1 pm (Pierce vs. Foster)

The White Sox receive some disturbing news before the game. Ray Schalk, their starting catcher, is back at the hotel, apparently sick from food poisoning. He probably will miss two games. Charlie Bennett, an excellent defensive catcher from the 1881 Detroit club, will be starting the next two games. In an emergency, Bill Melton (3B) would come in to catch.

In the top of the first with one out, "Wee Willie, hit them where they ain't" Keeler slaps one into left field for a base hit. Minoso grounds out to Warfield (hit-and-run), and Keeler stops at second (two outs). Cepeda smashes one to deep center. Bell crashes into the wall trying to make the catch, but the ball rolls away from him. Keeler scores. Cepeda, watching Bell go down and the ball rolling away, races toward third and then heads home. Bell finally relays the ball to Pop Lloyd in shallow left center. Lloyd turns and fires a strike to Gibson, and he applies the tag to an exhausted Cepeda to end the inning. **White Sox 1, BB Stars 0.**

The BB Stars even things up in the bottom of the first. Bell singles to right. Wells flies out to Minoso in left (one out). Gibson doubles down the left field line. Bell holds at third, as Minoso cuts it off and quickly throws it into the infield. Stearnes hits a high fly down the right field line. Keeler makes the catch as Bell trots in with the tying run. Gibson remains at second; credit Turkey Stearnes with the sac fly. Buddy Bell (3B) makes a great play on a smash in the hole and throws out Mule Suttles to end the inning. **BB Stars 1, White Sox 1.**

The left-handed Bill Foster gets himself in trouble in the second. Buddy Bell and Luke Appling lead-off with singles into left field. Runners are on first and second when Foster hits Nellie Fox in the arm, and the bases are loaded (none out). Foster gets Bennett looking at a called third strike (at the knees, on the corner, one out). Billy Pierce comes to the plate. Dandridge (3B) and Suttles (1B) are looking for the bunt. Pierce drops a beauty between the pitcher's mound and first base. Suttles fields the ball; his only play is to first base with Warfield (2B) covering the bag.

Pierce executes the squeeze bunt perfectly, scoring Bell and sending Appling to third and Fox to second (two outs). Hamilton works Foster for a base on balls, loading the bases again. Hilton Smith is warming up for the BB Stars. The dangerous Willie Keeler comes to the plate. He is not a home run threat, but he could still clear the bases with a double or triple. This could be Foster's last batter. Foster jams Keeler, who hits a lazy fly ball to shallow center field. Cool Papa Bell catches it for the third out. **White Sox 2, BB Stars 1.**

The White Sox add to their lead in the third. With two outs, Bell doubles into the left field corner. Appling lines a single to right, and Bell comes around to score. Fox strikes out. **White Sox 3, BB Stars 1.**

With one out in the bottom of the third, the lefty Pierce, with some help from his shortstop Appling, gives it back in threes. Wells singles to center. Gibson hits a tailor-made double play ball to Appling, who lets the ball play him (E6), and runners are on first and second (one out). Stearnes flies out to Hamilton (CF) for the second out (should have been third out). Suttles hits Pierce's first pitch to deep left, gone, a home run. Irvin strikes out looking. **BB Stars 4, White Sox 3 (three unearned runs)**

Clarkson relieves Pierce in the bottom of the sixth (Pierce- 5 IP, 7 H, 4 R, 1 ER, 1 HR, 3 K, 0 BB). Clarkson retires the side in order. **BB Stars 4, White Sox 3.**

In the top of the seventh, the BB Stars make defensive changes. Johnson replaces Dandridge at 3B (range upgrade from B to A). Charleston, who pinch hit for Irvin, replaces him in left (upgrade on range B to A; downgrade on throwing arm from -2 to -1). Foster makes a mistake (fast ball on inner part of plate, just above the knees). Hamilton golfs it into the first row in deep right field for a home run to tie the game, 4-4. Keeler lines a single to left. Hilton Smith replaces Foster (6 IP+, 9 H, 4 R, 1 HR, 5 K, 1 BB, 1 HB). Keeler breaks for second; Gibson guns him down with a strike to Warfield (one out). Smith gets Minoso to pop-up into shallow right field; Stearnes waves off Warfield to make the catch (two outs). Cepeda reaches on an error by Suttles (1B). Buddy Bell flies out to Stearnes (RF). **White Sox 4, BB Stars 4.**

Clarkson retires Allen (batting for Warfield) on a ground out to Fox (2B). Mackey pinch hits for Smith and singles to right. C. P. Bell lines out to Fox (two outs). Wells hits a one-hopper to Appling (SS), who throws him out. **White Sox 4, BB Stars 4.**

J. R. Richard (1979 Astros) gets a good hand from his home crowd as he replaces Smith to start the eighth inning. J. R. walks Appling. Luis Aparicio pinch runs for Appling and promptly steals second. Fox hits a fly ball toward the right field foul line (not too deep). Stearnes runs over and makes the catch as Aparicio tags and beats the throw to third with a head-first slide. The infield is in on the edge of the grass (Astroturf). Bennett bunts it right back to Richard on a one-hop. Aparicio is a dead duck at the plate (two outs).

McCovey bats for Clarkson. He walks. Bennett moves to second. Donnie Moore is warming up for the BB Stars. J. R. Richard fires a fast ball on the inside corner that freezes the dangerous Hamilton, strike three, inning over. **White Sox 4, BB Stars 4.**

Lyons replaces Clarkson and retires the side in order to end the eighth inning. J. R. Richard has an easy ninth inning. The final out is a great stop by Judy Johnson on Cepeda. **White Sox 4, BB Stars 4.**

Charleston leads off the bottom of the ninth with a one-hop double off the wall in right center. Johnson is walked intentionally (first and second, none out). Allen hits a high chopper off the turf; Cepeda (1B) grabs it and steps on first (one out) as the runners move up. Lloyd pinch hits for Richard, and Lyons intentionally walks him to load the bases. Bell hits a fly ball to center. Hamilton comes in two steps, makes the catch, and throws a low one-hop throw to Bennett. His sweeping tag gets Charleston's hand just before it touches the plate for an inning-ending double play. **White Sox 4, BB Stars 4.**

Donnie Moore is on to pitch in the top of the tenth. He easily retires the side (ground out, pop out and a fly out). Lyons is beginning his third inning. He escapes a serious jam in the ninth thanks to Hamilton (great throw) and Bennett (acrobatic tag). He walks Wells to start the inning. Josh Gibson ends the inning and the game with a mammouth walk-off home run to left.

10 Innings	R	H	E	LOB
White Sox	4	9	1	9
BB Stars	6	10	2	6
Winning Pitcher – Moore		Losing Pitcher – Lyons		

Three unearned runs cost the White Sox the chance to even the series. The BB Stars lead the series, 2-0.

Game Three, Thursday May 20, Comiskey Park (Chicago), 1 pm, (Day vs. Cicotte)

The BB Stars run themselves out of a potentially big, first inning. Bell singles to right. Lloyd pops out to Collins (2B). Charleston singles to center, and Bell races to third. Leonard doubles over Hamilton's head; Bell scores. Hamilton plays it off the wall with a quick throw to Aparicio. He fires a strike to Bennett, who tags out Charleston (two outs, 1-0). Torriente grounds out to Collins (2B). **BB Stars 1, White Sox 0.**

In the fourth inning, with two outs, the BB Stars score again, but poor base running ends the threat. Dandridge singles to center. Mackey bloops one into center for a base hit, with Dandridge stopping at second. Allen grounds one into left field for a single. Dandridge comes in to score. Clarke fires to Melton (3B) to nail Mackey, a split second after Dandridge crosses home plate. **BB Stars 2, White Sox 0.**

In the bottom of the sixth inning, Nellie Fox (1957 White Sox) pinch hits for Eddie Cicotte (6 IP, 8 H, 2 R, 0 HR, 3 K, 1 BB). Fox singles sharply to right field. Hamilton flies out to deep right; Torriente catches it on the warning track. Fox holds at first. On the hit-and-run, Keeler lines a single to right, and Fox scampers to third base. On the first pitch to Clarke, Keeler steals second (runners on second and third, one out). Clarke singles into left center, and Fox and Keeler score to tie the game (2-2). McCovey and Melton ground out. **White Sox 2, BB Stars 2.**

The knuckleballer Wilbur Wood (1971 White Sox) is in to pitch in the top of the seventh. Newt Allen hits one into the gap in right center; Hamilton makes a nice sliding catch to take away a potential double or triple (one out). Leon Day singles up the middle into center field. Cool Papa Bell lines a single to center, with Day stopping at second. Wood recovers and strikes out Lloyd, swinging on a nasty fluttering knuckleball (two outs). Charleston falls behind 0-2 on two nasty knuckleballs, and Wood strikes him out (looking) on a fast ball on the inside corner. **White Sox 2, BB Stars 2.**

Day retires the White Sox in order in the home half of the seventh. In the top of the eighth, Suttles (righty) pinch hits for Leonard (lefty) against the southpaw Wood. Suttles is retired on a fly to Clarke in shallow left (one out). Monte Irvin is announced to pinch hit for Torriente, and the White Sox bring in John Clarkson (1885 Chicago-N). Wood does his job (1.3 IP, 0 R). The strategy backfires as Irvin hits the ball into the lower deck in left field (3-2). Clarkson retires Dandridge (K), and Mackey (Clarkson makes a great play on a sharp grounder). **BB Stars 3, White Sox 2.**

In the bottom of the eighth, the BB Stars make a pitching change as well as defensive changes (double switch). Leon Day (7 IP, 6 H, 2 R, 0 HR, 3 K, 1 BB) is replaced by Hilton Smith (batting in the seventh spot). Josh Gibson replaces Mackey and will bat ninth (second man up in ninth inning). Suttles is now playing first base. Irvin is in right field. Judy Johnson has replaced Dandridge at third base. Hilton Smith retires the White Sox one-two-three. **BB Stars 3, White Sox 2.**

In the top of the ninth, with one out, Josh Gibson smashes one into the second deck in left field (Clarkson's second gopher ball) to make it 4-2. Bell doubles to left center. Gary Peters (1963 White Sox) replaces Clarkson and retires Lloyd (fly out) and Charleston (ground out). **BB Stars 4, White Sox 2.**

Clarke leads off with a base hit to center. Donnie Moore is warming up for the BB Stars. Smith pitches too carefully to McCovey and walks him on four pitches. Moore replaces Smith to face Bob Melton (1971 White Sox).

Melton represents the winning run. Could the White Sox reverse things and get their own walk-off win?

Melton hits it hard on the ground but right to Pop Lloyd, who starts the 6-4-3 double play with Clarke moving to third (two outs). Eddie Collins flies out to Charleston in left field to end the game. The White Sox had chances to win all three games, and they find themselves in a deep hole down three games to none.

	R	H	E	LOB
BB Stars	4	13	0	8
White Sox	2	7	0	4

Winning Pitcher – Day   Save – Moore   Losing Pitcher – Clarkson
The BB Stars lead the series 3-0.

Game Four, Friday May 21, Comiskey Park (Chicago), 7 pm (Paige vs. White)

It is a cool, cloudy Friday evening with the wind blowing in from center field. Left-hander Doc White (1906 World Champion White Sox) is blessed by the wind when the switch-hitting Bell (batting right-handed) hits a deep fly ball to left that Clarke catches in front of the fence (a home run with no wind). Charleston bounces out to Fox at second (two outs). Josh Gibson doubles into the left field corner. Mule Suttles lines White's first pitch just inside the foul pole into the lower deck in left field (2-0). Wells hits a screamer right at Appling (SS) and he boots it (E6). Irvin bounces into a force play. **BB Stars 2, White Sox 0.**

In the top of the third, the BB Stars add to their lead. Charleston leads off with a single to right. Gibson bloops one into center field, but Hamilton makes a great running catch. Charleston has to hustle back to first (one out). White hits Suttles on the left arm (runners on first and second, one out). Wells booms one to deep center, just beyond the reach of Hamilton. Both runners score, and Wells slides into third with a triple (4-0). Gary Peters is warming up. Irvin hits a fly ball to center field; Hamilton makes the catch as Wells races home (sac fly for Irvin). Dandridge takes a called third strike. **BB Stars 5, White Sox 0.**

With two outs in the bottom of the third (Paige has retired first eight hitters), Collins bats for White (3 IP, 4 H, 5 R, 1 HR, 1 K, 0 BB, 1 HB) and grounds out to Warfield (2B). **BB Stars 5, White Sox 0.**

Gary Peters escapes a bases-loaded jam in the top of the fifth when he entices Dandridge to hit into a 4-6-3 double play. Judy Johnson replaces Dandridge defensively in the bottom of the fifth inning. Paige retires the side in order. He has retired all 15 batters through five innings. **BB Stars 5, White Sox 0.**

In the top of the sixth, Warfield leads off with a triple. With two outs, Charleston singles to center to score Warfield. Red Faber (1921 White Sox) replaces Peters. Aparicio replaces Appling at short (double switch). Gibson flies out. **BB Stars 6, White Sox 0.**

Paige retires Fox on a fly to center (16 retired in a row) before Ray Shalk (1922 White Sox) singles to right, breaking up Paige's no-hitter with one out in the sixth. Aparicio (batting ninth) takes a called third strike (two outs). Hamilton is also caught looking on Paige's famous hesitation pitch. **BB Stars 6, White Sox 0.**

In the bottom of the seventh, the White Sox get on the board. Keeler singles to right. Clarke doubles to right-center, scoring Keeler (6-1). Paige retires the next three hitters (last out, Melton pinch hitter for Faber). **BB Stars 6, White Sox 1.**

In the top of the eighth, Wilbur Wood replaces Faber. Johnson leads off with a single. Warfield bangs out a second triple (7-1). Paige strikes out (one out). Bell singles, scoring Warfield (8-1). This ends the scoring. Paige retires the side in order in the bottom of the ninth (9 IP, 5 H, 1 R, 0 HR, 8 K, 1 BB).

	R	H	E	LOB
BB Stars	8	11	0	7
White Sox	1	5	3	5

Winning Pitcher – Paige   Losing Pitcher – White
The BB Stars lead the series, 4-0.

Game Five, Saturday May 22, Comiskey Park (Chicago), 1 pm (Tiant vs. Walsh)

It is a hot, cloudy, no-wind day in Chicago. In the first three innings, there is only one scoring threat. In the top of the second with two out, Mackey singles through the middle into center field off Big Ed Walsh. Judy Johnson doubles into the left field corner, but Minoso cuts it off and makes a strong one-bounce throw to the plate to throw out Mackey on a bang-bang play at home. Schalk makes a great sweeping tag as Mackey tries to tag the plate with his hand. **BB Stars 0, White Sox 0.**

Tiant has retired the first nine White Sox (3 Ks). In the top of the fourth, with one out, Turkey Stearnes doubles off the wall in right center. Leonard fouls out to McCovey (two outs). Mackey singles to right, and Stearnes comes home to score (1-0). **BB Stars 1, White Sox 0.**

Tiant retires the side in order in the fourth (12 in a row). The White Sox bats have been anemic. In the bottom of the fifth, the White Sox execution nearly stops them from scoring. McCovey singles to center. Melton hits one to third (potential DP), and it bounces off Johnson's glove (E5), leaving runners on first and second. Fox swings and misses; Mackey throws out McCovey at third (McCovey thought hit-and-run was on, one out). Finally the hit-and-run is on. Fox singles to right, and Melton races to third. Johnson (3B) and Leonard (1B) move in on the grass, expecting Aparicio to bunt. Aparicio bunts, but Tiant is off the mound quickly and throws to Mackey. Melton is out (two outs). Tiant goes to a 3-2 count on Schalk. On the next pitch, Fox (from second) and Aparicio (from first) take off. Schalk lines it off the left field wall on one-bounce as both runs score, 2-1. Walsh grounds out to end the inning. Both runs were unearned. **White Sox 2, BB Stars 1.**

In the top of the sixth, Walsh gives up two singles, but Johnson flies out to end the inning with runners on first and third. In the bottom of the sixth, Hamilton triples off the wall in center field. Keeler brings him home with a sac fly to Stearnes in right. Tiant strikes out Minoso and McCovey (both swinging). **White Sox 3, BB Stars 1.**

In the seventh, Newt Allen leads off with a single. Josh Gibson (representing the tying run) bats for Tiant (6 IP, 4 H, 3 R, 1 ER, 0 HR, 5 K, 0 BB). Gibson hits a hard smash, but Aparicio snares it on the short hop and flips to Fox (2B), who relays to McCovey for the double play. Bell grounds out to Aparicio, ending the inning.

The only other scoring threat is in the bottom of the eighth for the White Sox. With one out, Hamilton hits a J. R. Richard fast ball over Bell's head in right center and goes into third, standing, his second triple. Hamilton tries to steal home, but J. R. Richard throws him out. Keeler strikes out. Walsh gives up a one-out single in the ninth (BB Stars tenth hit) but retires Suttles (pinch hitting for Johnson) on a fly to Keeler (RF) and Allen, hitting into a game-ending force play.

	R	H	E	LOB
BB Stars	1	10	1	7
White Sox	3	5	0	2

The BB Stars lead the series, 4-1. The White Sox have only generated 12 runs (2.4/g) and 31 hits (6.2/g). Walsh (9 IP, 10 H, 1 R, 4 K, 0 BB) has given them two excellent starts (17 IP, 3 R, 1.59 ERA).

Game Six, Sunday May 23, Astrodome (Houston), 1 pm (Lee vs. Dihigo)

In the bottom of the second, with one out, Suttles triples to deep center. Johnson doubles off the wall in left field, scoring Suttles (1-0). After Warfield flies out to right, Dihigo singles to center, scoring Johnson (2-0). Torriente singles to center; Dihigo stops at second. Lloyd flies out to Hamilton (CF). **BB Stars 2, White Sox 0.**

In the bottom of the fourth, Johnson hits his second double into the left field corner. Lee fans Warfield and Dihigo, but Torriente singles to right, scoring Johnson (2-0). Billy Pierce is warming up. Lloyd singles, with Torriente moving to third. Charleston flies out to Keeler. **BB Stars 3, White Sox 0.**

In the bottom of the fifth, Stearnes homers into the right field seats. **BB Stars 4, White Sox 0.**

Dihigo retires the White Sox one-two-three in the top of the sixth. In the bottom of the sixth, the White Sox do a double switch. Pierce replaces Lee (5 IP, 9 H, 4 R, 1 HR, 5 K, 2 BB) and bats fourth. McCovey replaces Cepeda and bats ninth. Pierce gives up a one-out single to Lloyd, but he retires Charleston and Gibson on fly balls (Gibson to warning track). **BB Stars 4, White Sox 0.**

With one out in the top of the seventh, Collins walks. Appling slaps a hit-and-run single to right center; Collins moves to third. Schalk doubles to left center, scoring Collins; Appling holds at third. Foster and Rogan begin warming up. McCovey bounces out to Warfield as Collins crosses the plate with the second run. Hamilton flies out to Bell. **BB Stars 4, White Sox 2.**

In the bottom of the seventh, with two outs, Johnson slams his third double off the wall in right center. Warfield singles to center, and Johnson comes around to score the BB Stars' fifth run. Dihigo pops out to Collins (2B). **BB Stars 5, White Sox 2.**

In the eighth, Keeler singles up the middle. Bill Foster replaces Dihigo (7+ IP, 7 H, 2 R, 0 HR, 2 K, 1 BB). Minoso hits a slow chopper to Lloyd, who throws him out (one out). Fox pinch hits for Pierce (clean-up spot) and strikes out swinging (two outs). Rogan replaces Foster. Buddy Bell pops out to Warfield. There is no more scoring.

	R	H	E	LOB
White Sox	2	7	0	6
BB Stars	5	14	1	11

Winning Pitcher – Dihigo   Losing Pitcher – Lee

The BB Stars lead the series, 5-1.

Game Seven, Monday May 24, Astrodome (Houston), 7 pm (Cicotte vs. Richard)

Richard strikes out Collins swinging. Keeler singles to left. Richard walks Hamilton, and Keeler goes over to second. Cepeda doubles off the wall in left field, scoring Keeler and Hamilton. McCovey pops out to first. Melton flies out to Bell in center. **White Sox 2, BB Stars 0.**

Cicotte retires the first two batters in the bottom of the first. Charleston singles to right. Suttles lines a single to right center; Charleston hustles to third. Stearnes hits a long home run to right center. Mackey grounds out. **BB Stars 3, White Sox 2.**

In the top of the third, Collins reaches on an error by Lloyd (SS). On the hit-and-run, Keeler lines a single to right; Collins goes around to third. Hamilton hits one toward the hole on the right side. Suttles (1B) stabs it and throws to Richard, covering the bag as Collins crosses the plate with the tying run (3-3). With Keeler on second, Cepeda flies out to Charleston (LF) for the second out. McCovey takes a called third strike (Richard now has three strike outs). **White Sox 3, BB Stars 3.**

With two outs in the bottom of the third, Cicotte throws one up-and-in that bounces off Charleston's shoulder. Charleston leaps up and yells at Cicotte, then scrambles for the mound. Before any fisticuffs can take place, the umpires and teammates separate the combatants, and both are ejected.

Torriente runs for Charleston, and Doc White replaces Cicotte. Suttles singles to right, and Torriente heads for third and beats the throw with a head-first slide. Stearnes singles to right, scoring Torriente, and Suttles moves to third (BB Stars taking advantage of Keeler's bad arm, +1). Mackey singles to right, scoring Suttles, and Stearnes is into third with no throw. Dandridge strikes out swinging to end the inning. **BB Stars 5, White Sox 3.**

The rest of the game is the J. R. Richard show in front of a packed Astrodome, his home park. He strikes out the side in the fourth. Appling is ejected after arguing a strike call. Richard retires 21 out of 23 batters (15 Ks). His final line is 9 IP, 5 H, 3 R, 2 ER, 0 HR, 17 K, 1 BB. The BB Stars do not score after the third inning.

	R	H	E	LOB
White Sox	3	5	0	4
BB Stars	5	9	2	4

Winning Pitcher – Richard   Losing Pitcher - Cicotte

The BB Stars lead the series, 6-1.

Game Eight, Tuesday May 25, Comiskey Park (Chicago), 7 pm (Day vs. Peters)

It is a cool, cloudy day, and the wind is favorable for the hitters (blowing out). In the bottom of the first, Hamilton lashes one down the right field line into the corner; it bounces past Irvin. As Irvin chases it down, Hamilton heads for third. Irvin's throw is wide going into the dugout, and Hamilton trots home with the first run. Keeler singles to right. Day recovers and retires the side. **White Sox 1, BB Stars 0.**

Peters has been tough in the clutch. He gives up four hits in the first three innings, but the BB Stars strand all four runners. In the bottom of the third, Peters helps himself with a base hit to left field. Hamilton singles to center. Keeler singles to center, Peters scores, and Hamilton moves to third. Where would these White Sox be without these two free agents from the 1890s? Day picks Keeler off first base (one out). Minoso hits a fly ball to Suttles in left, and Hamilton scores (sac fly for Minoso). McCovey flies out to Bell (CF). **White Sox 3, BB Stars 0.**

Irvin taps a slow roller toward short. Appling charges, bare hands the ball, and throws it into right field. Credit Irvin with an infield single; he takes second on Appling's throwing error. Peters bares down and gets the next two hitters (Wells and Johnson) to hit routine fly ball outs. Warfield singles to center, scoring Irvin (unearned run). Day grounds out. **White Sox 3, BB Stars 1.**

In the top of the fifth inning, Aparicio, the better defensive shortstop, replaces Appling, who has struggled defensively in this series. Peters has been in trouble every inning, and he walks Bell to start the fifth. Lloyd flies out to Hamilton (CF). Suttles hits the ball to Buddy Bell, who throws to Collins (2B) for the force on Bell (two outs). Gibson singles to right, and Suttles moves over to third. Irvin also hits into a Bell to Collins force-out to end the inning. **White Sox 3, BB Stars 1.**

The BB Stars have left seven runners stranded in five innings. Day escapes a two-out, two-on jam in the fifth getting Minoso to foul out to Gibson behind the plate. With one out in the top of the sixth, Aparicio makes a nice play in the hole. But his foot slips and his throw is high, bouncing into the stands for a two-base error (so much for a defensive upgrade). Warfield lines a single to center. Hamilton fields it on a one-hop and throws a strike to the plate as Johnson turns third and stops. Day, a good hitter, is not up there to bunt, and he lines out to Aparicio (two outs, should be three). Cool Papa Bell hits it to deep center field, off the wall and scoring both runners. Bell is standing on third with a triple (3-3; all the BB Stars runs are unearned). Lloyd grounds out. **BB Stars 3, White Sox 3.**

In the top of the seventh inning, Red Faber has replaced hard luck starter Gary Peters (6 IP. 9 H, 3 R, 0 ER, 0 HR, 2 K, 1 BB). Faber gets Suttles looking at a curve ball on the outside corner (one out). Then Josh Gibson crushes one to deep left near the foul pole, fair ball, upper deck, home run. Faber gives up two more singles but no more runs in the seventh. **BB Stars 4, White Sox 3.**

In the top of the eighth (Clarkson pitching), two more White Sox errors (Fox and Aparicio again) around Lloyd's triple lead to two more unearned runs. This ends the scoring. In the bottom of the eighth, Hilton Smith replaces Day. His final line is 7 IP, 7 H, 3 R, 0 HR, 3 K, 1 BB.

	R	H	E	LOB
BB Stars	6	16	1	14
White Sox	3	9	4	6

The BB Stars lead the series, 7-1. The White Sox hit a little better, but their defense fell apart; pitching was ok. If the BB Stars got more clutch hits, they could have scored 2-3 more runs.

Game Nine, Wednesday May 26, Comiskey Park (Chicago), 1 pm (Paige vs. Walsh)

It is a beautiful day for baseball, warm and clear. The White Sox would like to finish with a win before their home crowd. Ed Walsh knows he needs to shut down the BB Stars because these White Sox Hitless Wonders will probably not do much against Satchel Paige, based on the previous eight games.

Walsh does his job in the first with three ground ball outs. Hamilton and Keeler (the White Sox offense in this series) start things off well in the bottom of the first inning. Hamilton singles to center. He steals second on first pitch to Keeler. Then Keeler lines one into right center for a single, with Hamilton coming around to score (1-0). Keeler breaks for second as Cepeda swings and misses on a 2-1 pitch, another stolen base. Satchel is only mediocre at holding runners. This does not bode well for Paige if Hamilton and Keeler continue to get on base. Paige retires the next three batters in order. **White Sox 1, BB Stars 0.**

Walsh escapes a jam in the top of the third. With one out, Paige hits a slow-roller past Walsh; Collins bare hands the ball but throws it into the dugout. Paige is on second base. Bell hits a Texas League single into center. Paige has to hold up halfway to third to see if Hamilton might catch it. As it drops in, Paige continues to third but has no chance to score. Walsh bears down. He jams Lloyd with a fast ball, and he pops out to Collins (two outs). Charleston bounces one toward the hole between first and second, but McCovey grabs it and throws to Walsh, covering. Charleston is out by a step. **White Sox 1, BB Stars 0.**

In the bottom of the third, Paige has to escape a none-out runner on third situation. Hamilton leads off with a single to left. He steals second, and Mackey's throw is low and rolls into shallow center. Hamilton goes to third. No problem for Satchel. Keeler pops out to Allen (2B). Cepeda takes a called third strike, and McCovey grounds out to Allen. **White Sox 1, BB Stars 0.**

With two outs in the fourth, Mackey hits one to deep center, and it's gone, home run. Dandridge singles to center, but Allen forces him at second to end the inning. **BB Stars 1, White Sox 1.**

In the top of the sixth, with one out, Buck Leonard hits a deep drive to center. Hamilton races back to the wall and makes the catch (two outs). Stearnes singles sharply to left. Mackey singles to center, and Stearnes races around to third. Walsh freezes Dandridge with a fast ball on the inside corner, strike three. **BB Stars 1, White Sox 1.**

With two outs in the bottom of the sixth, Allen knocks down McCovey's hard smash, but it rolls away from him. McCovey has an infield hit. Fred Clarke pinch runs for him (he will stay in the game and play left field, with Cepeda moving to first). Melton grounds one to Lloyd (SS), who flips to Allen, ending the inning. **BB Stars 1, White Sox 1.**

Walsh gives up a two-out single to Bell in the top of the seventh, but Lloyd grounds out to Aparicio (SS), ending the inning. Walsh has 13 ground ball outs through seven innings. As expected, we have a low-scoring (1-1) game between Walsh and Paige.

In the bottom of the seventh, Paige walks the first batter of the game, Eddie Collins (Walsh has none). Dandridge (3B) and Leonard (1B) are in on the grass, expecting the bunt. Aparicio is an excellent bunter. He drops down a beauty that Leonard picks up, but his only play is to Allen, covering first. Collins, the go-ahead run, is on second. Wilbur Wood is warming up for the White Sox. Paige gets Schalk to hit a one-hopper to Lloyd (SS); he looks Collins back to second and throws Schalk out at first (two outs). Nellie Fox is going to bat for Walsh (7 IP, 7 H, 1 R, 1 HR, 3 K, 0 BB). Fox hits it hard, but Allen grabs it on the second hop and throws out Fox. **BB Stars 1, White Sox 1.**

In the top of the eighth, Wilbur Wood is now pitching. Charleston tries to start something with a smash between first and second, but Collins dives, knocks it down, and throws Charleston out from his knees, great play. Leonard hits one to deep right; Keeler goes to the edge of the warning track and hauls it in (two outs). Stearnes takes a called third strike. **BB Stars 1, White Sox 1.**

In the bottom of the eighth, Paige faces the top of the order (Hamilton, Keeler, and Cepeda). Paige gets Hamilton to ground out to Allen (one out). Keeler singles sharply to right. Paige makes a couple of throws over to first to try to hold Keeler close. However, with the count on Cepeda 1-1, Paige rushes his delivery and throws it low in the dirt as Keeler breaks for second. Mackey's throw is not in time, stolen base. Keeler takes a good lead-off on second. On the next pitch, Keeler steals third without a throw. Keeler has three stolen bases, and Hamilton has two (off Paige), today. On the next pitch (2-2), Cepeda lines a single into center field, and Keeler scores the go-ahead run (2-1). Clarke goes

THE BEST SEASON-THE FIRST NINETY GAMES:

down swinging (two outs). Melton flies out to Bell (CF). **White Sox 2, BB Stars 1.**

Josh Gibson comes out to bat for Mackey to try to tie up the game on one pitch. Wood strikes out Gibson with a nasty knuckleball (Gibson waves at it). Dandridge lofts a fly ball right to Hamilton (CF). Allen hits the ball on one-hop to Aparicio, who throws him out to end the game. The White Sox win their second game to end the series. Wood retires all six batters (2 Ks) for the win.

	R	H	E	LOB
BB Stars	1	7	1	7
White Sox	2	7	1	6

Winning Pitcher – Wood   Losing Pitcher – Paige

The BB Stars win the series, 7-2.

Recap of Best Season Series 3 (BB Stars vs. White Sox)

This series could have been closer, but the BB Stars clearly dominated offensively, defensively, and on the mound. Chart 7-2 on page 78 has BB Stars individual/team statistics for this series. Chart 7-3 on page 79 has White Sox individual/team statistics for this series.

The turning point of the series - Is it possible to have a turning point in a series that was dominated by the BB Stars? Yes. After the White Sox lost the first two games to a walk-off sac fly and a home run, Game Three (at home) became pivotal. Clarke's 2-run single in the sixth ties the game. Wood does a good job with 1.3 innings of shut out relief. When Irvin (righty) is announced to bat for Torriente (lefty), Clarkson relieves Wood. Irvin hits a home run. In the ninth, Gibson hits a home run off Clarkson. Obviously, Clarkson did not do his job. For the rest of the series, Clarkson gives up only two unearned runs in 6.7 more innings of relief. In the bottom of the ninth, the White Sox get their first two runners on base off Smith. Moore comes in to pitch to Melton (representing the winning run at the plate). Melton raps into a double play. Melton had a terrible series (20 AB, 0 R, 2 H, 1 RBI, 6 K, .200 OPS). Collins flied out to end the game (1 for 18, .056 for series). The White Sox team did not come through in the clutch.

MVP of Series – BB Stars Pitching Staff - 8 QS, 4 CG, 2 S, 2.14 ERA. The highlight was J. R. Richard's 17 K complete game. The staff dominated the White Sox.

BB Stars Results vs. White Sox 7-2, .778

Pos.	E	R	TH	PB	Hitters	G	AB	R	H	RBI	2B	3B	HR	TB	W	HB	SO	SF	SH	SB	B.AVG.	OBP	S.PCT.	OPS
LF	5	A	-1		Charleston	8	29	3	6	3	1	1	0	9	1	1	4	0	0	0	0.217	0.258	0.310	0.568
CF	8	AA	-1		CP Bell	8	35	2	14	1	1	0	2	17	2	0	3	1	0	0	0.400	0.432	0.486	0.918
OF	5	A	-1		Steames	5	19	2	7	6	1	0	2	14	2	0	1	1	0	0	0.368	0.368	0.737	1.105
OF	6	B	-2		M Irvin	4	10	2	3	2	0	0	1	6	2	0	2	0	0	0	0.300	0.417	0.600	1.017
OF	6	A	-1		Torriente	4	13	4	5	3	0	0	1	8	1	0	5	0	0	0	0.385	0.429	0.615	1.044
SS	7	A			P Lloyd	8	31	2	7	1	1	1	0	9	2	0	1	0	0	0	0.226	0.273	0.290	0.563
SS	7	AA			W Wells	4	14	3	4	2	0	1	0	6	1	0	0	0	0	0	0.286	0.333	0.429	0.762
3B	7	A			J Johnson	7	16	5	6	1	4	0	0	10	1	0	6	0	0	0	0.375	0.412	0.625	1.037
3B	6	B			Dandridge	5	17	1	5	0	0	0	0	5	0	0	2	0	0	0	0.294	0.294	0.294	0.588
2B	7	A			N Allen	6	19	0	2	1	0	0	0	2	0	0	3	0	0	0	0.105	0.105	0.105	0.211
2B	7	A			F Warfield	5	16	3	7	4	2	0	0	11	0	0	3	1	0	0	0.438	0.438	0.688	1.125
1B	7	A			Suttles	8	22	6	7	6	1	0	2	14	1	2	5	0	0	0	0.318	0.400	0.636	1.036
1B	8	B			B Leonard	6	15	0	1	1	0	0	0	2	0	0	2	0	0	0	0.067	0.067	0.133	0.200
C	7	A	-2	Fr	J Gibson	9	24	5	8	4	1	0	3	19	0	0	4	0	0	1	0.333	0.333	0.792	1.125
C	6	B	-2	Av	B Mackey	6	20	1	11	3	1	0	0	14	0	0	0	0	1	0	0.550	0.550	0.700	1.250
					pitchers	9	27	0	5	1	1	0	0	6	0	1	6	1	1	0	0.185	0.185	0.222	0.407
					TOTAL	9	327	39	98	39	11	7	10	153	13	4	44	3	1	1	0.300	0.328	0.468	0.796

Fat.	H	WP	E	R	Pitchers	G	GS	QS	CG	S	W	L	IP	H	SO	BB	HB	HR	R	ER	ERA
10/L	Vg	N	9	B	BJ Rogan	2	2	1	1	0	1	0	10.3	5	5	4	0	1	2	2	1.74
9/L	Ex	R	7	B	B Foster	2	1	1	0	0	0	2	6.7	9	6	1	0	1	4	4	5.37
10/L	Vg	NL	8	B	L Day	2	2	0	0	0	2	1	14	13	6	2	0	0	5	5	3.21
10/L	Av	NL	7	B	M Dihigo	1	1	0	0	0	0	1	7	6	7	1	0	1	2	2	2.57
8/L	Md	R	8	C	S Paige	2	2	2	2	0	1	1	17	12	16	2	1	0	3	3	1.59
L/9	Vg	R	8	A	H Smith	3	0	0	0	1	0	0	4	3	3	1	0	0	0	0	0.00
9/L	Av	R	9	A	Newcombe	0	0	0	0	0	0	0	0	0	0	0	0	0	0	0	
10/L	Ex	NL	8	D	L Tiant	1	1	1	0	0	0	1	13	6	4	0	0	0	3	2	1.50
9	Av	N	5	C	J R Richard	3	1	1	1	0	1	1	2	2	6	4	0	0	3	2	1.39
Long	Md	NL	4	B	D Moore	2	0	0	0	1	1	0	6	3	7	1	1	0	0	0	0.00
					TOTAL	18	9		4	2	7	7	80	59	60	16	2	1	22	19	2.14

Chart 7-2 – BB Stars Statistics for this series

White Sox Best Season Series vs. BB All-Stars 2-7, .222

Team	Year	WS Hitters	G	AB	R	H	RBI	2B	3B	HR	TB	W	HB	SO	SF	SH	SB	B.AVG	OBP	S.PCT	OPS
Philadelphia	1894	29 B Hamilton	9	32	7	10	2	0	5	1	23	4	1	6	0	0	2	0.313	0.405	0.719	1.124
Baltimore	1897	32 WW Keeler	9	36	6	15	3	0	0	0	15	0	0	4	1	0	5	0.417	0.417	0.417	0.833
Chicago (A)	1954	32 M Minoso	6	17	0	1	1	0	0	0	1	0	0	5	1	0	0	0.059	0.059	0.059	0.118
Pittsburgh	1903	25 F Clarke	5	11	0	3	3	1	0	0	4	1	0	2	0	0	0	0.273	0.333	0.364	0.697
Chicago (A)	1960	20 L Aparicio	7	15	1	2	0	0	0	0	2	0	0	3	0	0	1	0.133	0.133	0.133	0.267
Chicago (A)	1936	29 L Appling	7	17	1	4	1	0	0	0	4	2	0	2	0	0	0	0.235	0.316	0.235	0.551
Chicago (A)	1971	23 B Melton	7	20	0	2	0	0	0	0	2	0	0	6	0	0	0	0.100	0.100	0.100	0.200
Texas	1980	21 B Bell	3	13	2	3	0	1	0	0	4	0	0	0	0	1	0	0.231	0.231	0.308	0.538
Chicago (A)	1915	40 E Collins	3	18	2	1	1	0	0	0	1	3	0	6	0	0	0	0.056	0.190	0.056	0.246
Chicago (A)	1957	32 N Fox	7	15	2	4	0	0	0	0	4	1	1	4	0	0	0	0.267	0.353	0.267	0.620
SF Giants	1969	39 W McCovey	9	25	0	3	1	0	0	0	3	3	0	3	0	0	0	0.120	0.120	0.214	0.334
SF Giants	1961	29 O Cepeda	6	21	0	3	4	1	1	0	6	0	0	3	0	0	0	0.143	0.143	0.286	0.429
Atlanta	1979	19 B Horner	4	7	0	1	0	0	0	0	1	1	0	1	0	0	0	0.143	0.143	0.143	0.286
Chicago (A)	1922	22 R Schalk	6	19	0	5	3	2	0	0	7	2	0	1	0	0	0	0.263	0.333	0.368	0.702
Detroit (N)	1881	15 C Bennett	3	10	0	0	0	0	0	0	0	0	0	3	0	0	0	0.000	0.000	0.000	0.000
		pitchers	9	12	1	2	1	0	0	0	2	0	0	3	0	2	0	0.167	0.167	0.167	0.333
		TOTAL	9	288	22	59	20	5	6	1	80	16	2	55	2	3	8	0.205	0.252	0.278	0.529

Team	Year	WS Pitchers	G	GS	CG	S	W	L	IP	H	SO	BB	HB	HR	R	ER	ERA
Chicago (A)	1908	47 E Walsh	3	3	3	1	1	0	24	24	8	1	1	2	4	4	1.50
Chicago (A)	1955	23 B Pierce	2	2	1	0	0	1	7	7	5	0	0	1	5	2	2.57
Chicago (A)	1919	32 E Cicotte	2	2	1	0	0	1	8.7	11	4	1	1	1	6	6	6.21
Chicago (A)	1906	25 D White	2	1	0	0	0	1	4.3	8	3	1	0	1	6	6	12.47
Chicago (A)	1941	32 T Lee	1	1	0	0	0	1	5	9	5	0	0	1	4	4	7.20
Chicago (A)	1963	25 G Peters	3	3	1	0	1	0	9.3	13	3	3	0	0	4	1	0.96
Chicago (A)	1971	33 W Wood	5	5	0	0	0	1	6.7	7	8	0	0	0	2	2	2.69
Chicago (A)	1927	30 T Lyons	2	2	0	0	0	1	2.3	3	1	1	0	1	2	2	7.73
Chicago (A)	1921	37 R Faber	2	2	0	0	0	0	3	6	3	1	1	1	2	2	6.00
Chicago (N)	1885	62 J Clarkson	5	5	5	1	0	1	8.3	9	6	3	0	2	4	2	2.16
		TOTAL	28	9			2	7	78.7	98	46	11	3	10	39	31	3.55

Chart 7-3 – White Sox statistics for this series

Clutch Performers - Josh Gibson's three key home runs gives him an edge over Turkey Stearnes, who also had a great series. Gibson seems to hit HRs when they mean something (Turkey does, too). In Game Two, Gibson's walk-off HR in the tenth gives the BB Stars a 2-0 edge in the series. In Game Three, Gibson enters the game in an eighth inning double switch and hits a HR in his only at bat. This gives the BB Stars an insurance run in a 4-2 win and a 3-0 lead in the series. In Game Four, with two outs and none on, he doubles before Suttles' 2-run HR in the 8-1 fourth straight win. In Game Eight, he breaks the 3-3 tie in the seventh with third HR of the series. The BB Stars go on to a 6-3 win (Gibson is 3 for 5).

Highlight of White Sox problems - Let us first give credit to what the White Sox did right. Hamilton and Keeler were the offense. Hamilton hit the only HR the White Sox had in the series. Hamilton and Keeler created 17 of the 22 runs the White Sox scored. The Keeler/Hamilton OPS was .970. The pitching staff, led by Ed Walsh (24 innings, 1.50 ERA), had a 3.55 ERA. There were four other good performances to go with Walsh – Pierce 7 IP, 2.57 ERA; Peters 9.3 IP, 0.96 ERA; Clarkson 8.3 IP, 2.16 ERA; Wood 6.7 IP, 2.69 ERA. The rest of the staff was terrible (23.7 IP, 7.60 ERA, 0 W, 6 L).

Defensively, they gave up eight unearned runs (Appling and Aparicio at SS were responsible for seven unearned runs). Keeler, who was the co-star of the offense with Hamilton, was a liability in right field because of his poor arm (+1). The BB Stars were always taking the extra base. Offensively (excluding Hamilton/Keeler), the White Sox key offensive stats were 9 R, 15 RBI, 0 HR, 44 K, .159 Avg., .205 OBP, .192 S. Pct., .397 OPS. Ugly!

Chapter 8

Review and Analysis of Series 1 to 3

Playoff rank (to date) by W-L .Pct

	Team	W-L	Pct.	Run Differential
1.	BB Stars	17-10	.630	+18
2.	Browns/Orioles	4-5	.444	+5
3.	Braves/Pirates	4-5	.444	-6
4.	White Sox	2-7	.286	-17

Keys to success for the BB Star opponents (based on first three series)

1. When offense/defensive trade-offs are relatively equal, put your best defensive team on the field (range, throwing arms, error rating).
2. When OPS stats (OBP/S.Pct.) are relatively equal, use left-handed or switch hitters unless Foster (L) is pitching.
3. When you get a lead in the late innings, be sure to upgrade your defense, even if your offense loses some punch.

Review of key stats/facts from first three series

1. **Braves/Pirates** – the key factors were outfield defense (range/arm) and bullpen.

2. **Browns/Orioles** – the key factor was lefty/righty splits (see chart below).

3. **White Sox** – lack of an attack other than Hamilton/Keeler and poor defense (infield errors, primarily SS, and below average throwing arm in right field, Keeler).

Summary of the First Three Series (27 Games)

As I stated earlier, the Best Season Series would be more competitive than the 1880-1970 Decade Series. The reason is the level of competition. Remember, the 30 games (10 three-game series) in the Decades competition were against the average season of these great players' careers. I predicted the BB Stars would win 20 games (.667 winning percentage), and they won 21 games (.700). They outscored their opponents on average 7.2 runs vs. 3.6 runs per game.

In the first 27 games of the Best Season Series, the first 3 nine-game series, the BB Stars are 17-10 (.630). More importantly, the BB Stars have outscored their opponents on average 4.4 runs to 3.8 runs per game.

I expect that going forward, the BB Stars winning percentage will continue to come down. Why, you may ask? I have tried to have the stronger competition toward the end. Some may question that assumption, since the BB Stars' final opponent will be my favorite team (Red Sox) with my favorite player (Ted Williams) in his best season (1941, .406).

Remember Appendix One for Baseball Definitions when looking at any of the charts in the book. In the charts below, there is a column L/R (lefty/righty). T means the total team statistics. L means left-handed batter statistics and the R means right handed batter statistics. The White Sox series isolates Hamilton and Keeler vs. all other (AO) batters.

Lefty/Righty Splits - BB Stars Opponents (non-pitchers)

Team	L/R	NR	B.Avg	OBP	S.Pct	OPS
B/P*	T	68	.224	.281	.360	.641
B/P	L	28	.216	.295	.381	.676
B/P	R	40	.230	.269	.344	.613

* Braves/Pirates

Team	L/R	NR	B.Avg	OBP	S.pct	OPS
B/O*	T	71	.274	.308	.453	.761
B/O	L	45	.382	.438	.649	1.087
B/O	R	26	.186	.273	.255	.528

* Browns/Orioles

Team	L/R	NR	B.Avg	OBP	S.pct	OPS
WS*	T	37	.210	.256	.283	.539
WS	H/K**	15	.367	.411	.559	.970
WS	AO***	22	.159	.205	.192	.397

* White Sox;
** Hamilton and Keeler
*** All other White Sox non-pitcher hitters

Chapter 9

Best Season Nine-Game Series 4 - BB Stars vs.Reds

Reds Roster Review

SEVENTY-SIX PERCENT OF THE ROSTER are made up of Cincinnati Reds. Twenty-four percent of the roster are free agents. . See the Reds Roster (Chart 9-1 on page 86).

Offensive Leaders (Reds) Ranked by OPS

Player	OBP	SPct	OPS	R +	RBI -	HR =	NR
S. Thompson	.428	.654	1.082	131	165	18	278
T. Kluszewski	.410	.642	1.052	104	141	49	196
J. Morgan	.453	.576	1.029	113	111	27	197
G. Foster	.382	.631	1.013	124	149	52	221
T. Perez	.404	.589	.993	107	129	40	196
C. Seymour	.431	.559	.990	96	121	8	209
P. Rose	.432	.512	.944	120	82	16	186
J. Bench	.350	.587	.937	97	148	45	200
C. Cedeno	.384	.537	.921	103	82	22	163
E. Lombardi	.391	.524	.915	60	95	19	136

The following players would be base-stealing threats – Morgan 60, Cedeno 55 (numbers listed SB for their best season).

Fielding Leaders	Pos	Range	Error	Throwing
S. Thompson	RF	AA	5	-2
C. Seymour	CF	A	4	-2
E. Roush	CF	A	5	-1
G. Foster	LF	A	8	-2
C. Cedeno	LF	A	6	-1

For outfielders - range (AA is best) and throwing (-4 is exceptional, -3 is excellent, -2 is very good) are most important. Error rating (10 is best, 1 is poor) is not as critical as infielders because outfielders normally do not make as many errors.

H. Groh	3B	AA	10	-
M. Huggins	2B	AA	4	-
D. Concepcion	SS	A+	6	-
J. Beckley	1B	A	4	-
T. Kluszewski	1B	C	10	-
J. Morgan	2B	C	7	-

For infielders, range (AA is best), + increase in DPs because of excellent pivot, error rating is as important as range (10 is excellent, 1 is poor).

Catcher Throwing - Bench is very good (-2); Lombardi is above average (-1).

Pitcher Hold Rating - Rusie is excellent (less successful steal attempts). Hahn, Hecker, King Lucas, Luque, and Rixey are very good.

RedsRoster Best Season Series vs. BB All-Stars

Team	Year	WS	Hitters	G	AB	R	H	RBI	2B	3B	HR	TB	W	HB	SO	SF	SH	SB	B.AVG.	OBP	S.PCT.	OPS
Philadelphia	1895	28	SThompson	119	538	131	211	165	45	21	18	352	31	2	11	-	-	-	27	0.392	0.427	0.654	1.082
Houston	1972	33	C Cedeno	139	559	103	179	82	39	8	22	300	56	2	62	-	-	-	55	0.320	0.384	0.537	0.921
Cincinnati	1905	42	C Seymour	149	581	96	219	121	40	21	8	325	51	4	35	-	-	-	21	0.377	0.431	0.559	0.990
Cincinnati	1917	30	E Roush	136	522	82	178	67	19	14	4	237	27	5	24	-	-	-	21	0.341	0.379	0.454	0.833
Cincinnati	1969	37	P Rose	156	627	120	218	82	33	11	16	321	88	5	65	-	-	-	7	0.348	0.432	0.512	0.944
Cincinnati	1977	32	G Foster	158	615	124	197	149	31	2	52	388	61	0	107	-	-	-	6	0.320	0.382	0.631	1.013
Cincinnati	1979	24	Concepcion	149	590	91	166	84	25	3	16	245	64	5	73	-	-	-	19	0.281	0.357	0.415	0.772
Cincinnati	1917	37	H Groh	156	599	91	182	53	39	11	1	246	71	2	30	-	-	-	15	0.304	0.385	0.411	0.796
Cincinnati	1970	33	T Perez	158	587	107	186	129	28	6	40	346	83	2	134	-	-	-	8	0.317	0.403	0.589	0.993
Cincinnati	1976	37	J Morgan	141	472	113	151	111	30	5	27	272	114	1	41	-	-	-	60	0.320	0.453	0.576	1.029
Cincinnati	1905	27	M Huggins	149	564	117	154	38	11	8	1	184	103	1	50	-	-	-	27	0.273	0.386	0.326	0.712
Cincinnati	1954	33	Kluszewski	149	573	104	187	141	28	3	49	368	78	3	35	-	-	-	0	0.326	0.410	0.642	1.052
Cincinnati	1900	21	J Beckley	141	558	98	190	94	26	10	2	242	40	1	46	-	-	-	23	0.341	0.386	0.434	0.819
Cincinnati	1970	34	J Bench	158	605	97	177	148	35	4	45	355	54	0	102	-	-	-	0	0.293	0.351	0.587	0.937
Cincinnati	1938	24	E Lombardi	129	489	60	167	95	30	1	19	256	40	0	14	-	-	-	0	0.342	0.391	0.524	0.915

Team	Year	WS	Pitchers	G	GS	OS	CG	S	W	L	IP	H	SO	BB	HB	HR	R	ER	ERA
Cincinnati	1902	29	N Hahn	36	36	-	35	0	23	12	321	282	142	58	-	2	-	-	1.77
Louisville	1884	74	G Hecker	75	73	-	72	0	52	20	671	526	385	56	-	4	-	-	1.80
Cincinnati	1923	39	D Luque	41	37	-	28	2	27	8	322	279	151	88	-	2	-	-	1.93
Cincinnati	1925	26	E Rixey	39	36	-	22	1	21	11	287	302	69	47	-	8	-	-	2.88
Cincinnati	1947	28	E Blackwell	33	33	-	23	0	22	8	273	227	193	95	-	10	-	-	2.47
Montreal	1982	24	S Rogers	35	35	-	14	0	19	8	277	245	179	65	-	12	-	-	2.40
Cincinnati	1939	38	B Walters	39	36	-	31	0	27	11	319	250	137	109	-	15	-	-	2.29
NY (N)	1894	56	A Rusie	54	50	-	45	1	36	13	444	426	195	200	-	10	-	-	2.78
St. Louis	1898	71	S King	66	65	-	64	0	45	19	585	437	258	76	-	6	-	-	1.64
Cincinnati	1929	26	R Lucas	32	32	-	28	0	19	12	270	267	72	58	-	14	-	-	3.60

Chart 9-1 – Reds Best Season Roster

Pitching - Luque (1923, 27-8, 1.93), King (free agent 1888, 45-21, 1.64), Hecker (free agent 1884, 52-20, 1.80), and Hahn (1902, 23-12, 1.77) lead the staff. In *The New Bill James Historical Baseball Abstract* [1] the highest ranking of a Cincinnati Reds pitcher in his Top 100 pitchers is Bucky Walters, ranked sixty-ninth.

Game One, Friday May 28, Crosley Field (Cincinnati), 7 pm (Newcombe vs. Hahn)

Thunderstorms delay the start of the game for over an hour. It is warm and muggy, and the outfield is wet. After a scoreless first, the BB Stars score in the second. With one out, Wells triples to center. Dandridge singles to center, scoring Wells (1-0). Dandridge moves to second when Warfield hits a high-hopper to Concepcion (SS), who throws Warfield out at first. New-combe (a good-hitting pitcher) lines a single into right center, with Dandridge scoring (2-0). Torriente flies out to Seymour (CF). **BB Stars 2, Reds 0.**

In the bottom of the fourth, with two out and Kluszewski on first (single), Tony Perez (3B), hits a long HR to left off Newcombe to tie the game. **Reds 2, BB Stars 2.**

With one out in the bottom of the fifth, Noodles Hahn hits a home run just inside the right field foul pole (3-2). This appears to rattle Newcombe. Seymour doubles into the right field corner. Morgan singles to right, and Sey-mour stops at third. He does not want to challenge Irvin's arm (-2) with the heart (middle, best hitters) of the order coming up. Foster doubles into the gap in left center as both runners score (Morgan is extremely fast on the bases). On the throw to the plate, Foster goes to third. It is now 5-2, and Bullet Joe Rogan is warming up for the BB Stars. Newcombe intentionally walks Kluszewski, setting up a double play possibility with Bench coming to the plate. Bench lines a ball between short and third. Wells dives, knocks it down, and throws out Bench (great play). Morgan scores, and Kluzewski moves to second (two out; 6-2). Perez flies out to Torriente in left field. Newcombe ambles off the field, wiping sweat off his face. **Reds 6, BB Stars 2.**

In the top of the sixth, the BB Stars waste no time in responding to the challenge. Suttles lines a single to left. Gibson also hits a line drive, but it's right to Perez (one out). Irvin doubles off the wall in center, and Suttles takes the turn at third but holds. Willie Wells, who made the great play in the bottom of the fifth, jacks a Hahn fast ball over the left field fence to make it a 1-run game (6-5). Hahn continues to struggle as Bucky Walters warms up. Dandridge singles to right, and Warfield walks. Turkey Stearnes will bat for Newcombe (5 IP, 7 H, 6 R, 2 HR, 2 K, 1 BB). The decision is made to let Hahn (lefty) pitch to the lefty, Stearnes. This is a mistake, Stearnes lashes the ball into right center. Seymour tries to cut it off, but it goes by him to the wall. Two runs score, and Stearnes is standing on third with a big smile on his face. The BB Stars now lead, 7-6. Hahn is on his way to the showers (5.3 IP, 10 H, 7 R (so far), 1 HR, 2 K, 1BB). Walters gets Torriente to fly out to shallow center field; Stearne stays at third (two outs). Bell hits a soft line drive to Joe Morgan (2B) for the third out. **BB Stars 7, Reds 6.**

The Reds fail to score off Rogan in the bottom of the sixth. Walters, however, cannot stop the BB Stars' bats. With one out, Josh Gibson lines a ball over the left field fence (8-6), Irvin doubles into the left field corner, and Wells hits his second HR (5 RBIs) in as many at bats. Amos Rusie replaces Walters and retires Dandridge and Warfield (fly out, ground out). **BB Stars 10, Reds 6.**

The fans are stunned - a 6-2 lead within two innings has become a 10-6 deficit. In the bottom of the eighth, after walking Perez to lead-off the inning, Rogan retires the next two batters. Rose pops out to Wells (SS) in short left field, and Wells makes another great defensive play, charging Concepcion's slow grounder and throwing him out at first (two outs), with Perez moving to second. Lombardi pinch hits for Rusie (1.1 IP, 0 R) and singles to center; Perez stops at third. Beckley pinch runs for Lombardi. Hilton Smith is ready in the BB Stars' pen. After Rogan walks Seymour on four pitches, Smith is brought in to face Joe Morgan (2 for 4) with the bases loaded. The crowd is back into the game. Smith falls behind Morgan 2-1, and his next pitch (fast ball) is right down the middle. Joe hits a high drive to deep right center field; it is going, going, gone. Morgan has hit a grand slam home run to tie the game, 10-10. Foster flies out to Torriente in left field to end the inning. **Reds 10, BB Stars 10.**

Silver King (free agent from the 1880s) is on to pitch in the top of the ninth for the Reds. With two outs, he gives up a double to left center to Wells, who is having an outstanding game (offensively and defensively). King walks Dandridge. Allen pinch hits for Warfield and bounces out to Kluszewski (1B). **Reds 10, BB Stars 10.**

In the bottom of the ninth, Smith gives up a two-out single to Perez, but Pete Rose flies out to Bell (CF). We are headed to extra innings. **Reds 10, BB Stars 10.**

The Reds do a double switch. Rogers (1982 Expos) replaces King on the mound and will bat seventh. Sam Thompson (free agent 1890s) will bat ninth and play right field in place of Rose. Oscar Charleston will pinch hit for Hilton Smith. Charleston hits Rogers' first pitch over the right field fence, home run (11-10). With one out, Cool Papa Bell triples to deep center. The infield is pulled in for Mule Suttles to try to keep a second run from scoring. The Reds are gambling. Suttles could be walked intentionally to set up the double play with Josh Gibson on deck. The strategy fails, as Suttles is able to drive the ball to medium left center field. Foster makes the catch, but Bell scores easily (sac fly for Suttles, 12-10). Gibson bounces out to short, ending the inning. **BB Stars 12, Reds 10.**

Donnie Moore (1985 Angels, free agent) retires the Reds in order without the ball leaving the infield.

10 Innings	R	H	E	LOB
BB Stars	12	17	1	7
Reds	10	13	0	6

Winning Pitcher – Smith   Save – Moore   Losing Pitcher – Rogers

An exciting opener, but a tough opening game loss for the Reds.
The BB Stars lead the series, 1-0.

Game Two, Saturday May 29, Crosley Field (Cincinnati), 1 pm (Smith vs. Hecker)

In the bottom of the first, the Reds get on the board. Sam Thompson singles to center. On a hit-and-run play, Seymour bounces out to Allen (2B), with the speedy Thompson moving into scoring position. Joe Morgan lines a ball into the right field corner (just fair) for a double, and Thompson scores. It is Morgan's fourth hit and fifth RBI of the series, and this is only the first inning of the second game. Smith throws a wild pitch, and Morgan moves to third. Foster hits a high fly to left; Charleston makes the catch as Morgan races home with the second run (his third in the series). It is a sac fly for Foster. Kluszewski singles. Lombardi grounds into a force-out (at second) to end the inning. **Reds 2, BB Stars 0.**

Hecker has had three easy innings (two singles) when his team goes to work on Smith in the third. With one out, Seymour doubles to right center. Morgan slashes another ball into the right field corner, and it bounces away from Stearnes. Morgan rounds second as Stearnes fires a strike to Dandridge. Morgan and the ball arrive at about the same time. Morgan slides into Dandridge, who makes the tag. Morgan is safe with a triple. Both players are hurt. Morgan limps off as Muller Huggins goes in to pinch run. Dandridge has to be helped off the field. Morgan will miss Game Three, and Dandridge will miss Games Three and Four. Johnson replaces Dandridge at third base. Smith has faced Morgan three times (grand slam HR, double, and triple) in the series. Smith strikes out Foster (two outs). Kluszewski hits one up the middle; Allen dives and knocks it down but cannot make a play (infield hit), and Huggins scores. Lombardi bounces one to Lloyd (SS) who flips to Allen, forcing Klu to end the inning. **Reds 4, BB Stars 0.**

In the fifth inning, the BB Stars finally get to Hecker. Mackey singles to center. Judy Johnson strikes out swinging (one out). Allen tops one down the third base line, but Groh throws the ball into right field for a two-base error. Mackey stops at third. Irvin bats for Smith (4 IP, 9 H, 4 R, 0 HR, 0 K, 0 BB). Irvin hits it off the wall in left for a 2-run double (4-2). Hecker retires the next two batters on ground balls. **Reds 4, BB Stars 2.**

Bullet Joe Rogan replaces Smith. With one out, Rogan walks Foster. Kluszewski flies out to Charleston in left (two outs). Lombardi lines one just fair into the left field corner. Charleston picks it up throws it to the cut-off man (Lloyd), who throws wide of the mark at home, blocked nicely by Mackey as Foster scores.. Lombardi, a very slow runner, ends up on third (double advanced to third on throw home). The Reds lead 5-2. Groh grounds out to Lloyd at short. **Reds 5, BB Stars 2.**

Yesterday, the BB Stars scored five in the sixth to take the lead, 7-6. Today the BB Stars score six in the sixth. Hecker faces five batters they all get hits, and they all score (5+ IP, 9 H, 7 R, 6 ER, 0 HR, 1 K, 0 BB). Silver King gives up an RBI double to Allen (runners on first and second), scoring Mackey (fourth run off Hecker in the inning), and tying the score, 6-6. Johnson goes to third. Torriente pinch hits for Rogan (infield is in) and flies out to Seymour in shallow center for the first out. Bell bounces one to Huggins (2B), who looks Johnson back to third before throwing Bell out at first (two outs). The infield moves back to normal depth. Lloyd lines it over Concepcion's glove into left field as both runners score (8-5). Charleston singles to right (eighth hit of the inning), and Lloyd races around to third. Leonard (eleventh batter of the inning) goes down swinging. **BB Stars 8, Reds 5.**

The Reds score a run off J. R. Richard in the eighth inning to complete the scoring.

	R	H	E	LOB
BB Stars	8	13	1	6
Reds	6	12	2	8

Winning Pitcher – Rogan   Save – Richard   Losing Pitcher – Hecker
The BB Stars lead the series, 2-0.

Game Three, Sunday May 30, Crosley Field (Cincinnati), 1 pm (Day vs. Luque)

It is a warm, partly cloudy day in Cincinnati. Neither team scores in the first. Stearnes and Suttles open the second inning with back-to-back singles, runners on first and second. Johnson flies out to Rose (LF), and Warfield hits a routine ground ball to Perez. He has trouble getting the ball out of his glove but is still able to force Suttles at second. There is no chance for the double play (two outs). Day bloops one into shallow right field that falls in for a hit (Stearnes scores and Warfield scampers to third). Bell singles up the middle, scoring Warfield. Day stops at second (2-0). Lloyd doubles off the right field wall as both runners score (4-0). Charleston singles to right, and Bell scores the fifth run of the inning. Gibson (ninth batter) grounds into a force play at second. **BB Stars 5, Reds 0.**

In the bottom of the second, Day gives it all back. He walks the first two batters (Beckley and Huggins). Concepcion doubles into the gap in left center. Beckley scores; Huggins stops at third. Seymour pinch hits for Luque (2 IP, 7 H, 5 R, 0 HR, 0 K, 0 BB). Seymour lines one over Bell's head in center. It rolls to the fence. Seymour is into third standing with a 2-run triple (5-3). Day bounces the next pitch. It goes over Gibson's head for a wild pitch, scoring Seymour (5-4). Dihigo is warming up for the BB Stars. Hecker (yesterday's starter) is warming up for the Reds. Rose flies out to left (one out). Roush singles to right. Thompson singles to left; Roush stops at second. Bench flies out to Charleston (LF) for the second out. Perez lines one between first and second into right field as Roush comes around to score, tying the game, 5-5. Beckley forces Perez at second to end the long, high-scoring, second inning. **Reds 5, BB Stars 5.**

No starting pitcher in the first three games has come close to a quality start (23.3 innings, 33 earned runs, 12.73 ERA). In the top of the fourth (Hecker's second inning), Charleston hits a 3-run home run. **BB Stars 8, Reds 5.**

The BB Stars get an unearned run in the fifth (9-5), and Stearnes singles in their final run in the eighth (10-5). In the meantime, Martin Dihigo, who replaced Leon Day in the third (Huggins lead-off double), gives up a seventh inning single and an eighth inning walk with seven shutout innings for the win (7 IP, 1 H, 0 R, 3 K, 1 BB).

	R	H	E	LOB
BB Stars	10	16	0	8
Reds	5	9	0	7

Winning Pitcher – Dihigo   Losing Pitcher – Luque

The BB Stars lead the series, 3-0.

Game Four, Tuesday June 1, Royals Stadium (Kansas City), 7 pm (Rixey vs. Foster)

It is warm and partly cloudy with a slight breeze at game time. In the bottom of the first, Bell singles to left. Torriente singles to center, with Bell racing around to third. Seymour lets the ball get by him; Bell scores, and Torriente slides safely into second. Suttles lines a single to left; Torriente stops at third. Gibson hits a fly ball to Foster in left center. Torriente tags and scores (credit Gibson with a sac fly). Irvin grounds into a 5-4-3 double play. **BB Stars 2, Reds 0** (one run is unearned).

In the bottom of the third, Bell singles to right. Torriente goes down swinging (one out). Suttles smashes one to deep center; Seymour goes back to the wall and jumps, but it is off his glove. Suttles slides into third with a triple (Bell scores). Gibson lines a single to center scoring Suttles (4-0). Rixey strikes out Irvin and Johnson around a single to Wells. **BB Stars 4, Reds 0.**

Foster retires the side in order in the fourth; he has allowed one base runner (Cedeno reached on Johnson's error in the second). In the top of the fifth, Perez hits a home run for Reds first hit, Beckley also singles. **BB Stars 4, Reds 1.**

In the bottom of the fifth, Rixey gives up his tenth and eleventh hits around a fly out. Luque comes in to replace him. Luque gets Wells to foul out to Bench behind home plate (two outs). Johnson and Warfield each produce run-scoring singles before Foster takes a called third strike (Rixey 4.3 IP, 11 H, 6 R, 5 ER, 0 HR, 6 K, 0 BB). **BB Stars 6, Reds 1.**

Seymour's run scoring double after Morgan's lead-off walk makes it 6-2. Foster retires the next three batters. **BB Stars 6, Reds 2.**

In the top of the seventh, with help from the BB Stars defense, the Reds close the gap. Cedeno doubles off the left field wall. Beckley hits the ball to the right of Warfield, who backhands the ball but throws it over Suttles' head into the dugout. Cedeno is waved home from third, and Beckley is given second base (6-3). Concepcion flies out to Bell (one out). Lombardi, pinch hitting for Luque, singles to right, and Beckley scores. Foster bears down to strike out Morgan (swinging) and get Seymour to pop-up to the shortstop, Wells. **BB Stars 6, Reds 4.**

The Reds do a double switch. Rusie replaces Luque and will bat second. Roush replaces Seymour and will bat ninth. Rusie makes a leaping stab of Irvin's one-hopper and throws him out. Rusie then walks Wells and Johnson. Warfield triples over Roush's head, scoring Wells and Johnson (Warfield has 3 RBIs). Charleston pinch hits for Foster and flies out to Roush (CF). Foster's final line is 7 IP, 5 H, 4 R, 3 ER, 1 HR, 5 K, 1 BB. Bell flies out to Cedeno (RF) to end the inning. **BB Stars 8, Reds 4.**

Donnie Moore, in relief of Bill Foster, gives up a lead-off HR to George Foster in the eighth. That ends the scoring.

	R	H	E	LOB
Reds	5	6	2	4
BB Stars	8	14	2	9

Winning Pitcher – Foster   Losing Pitcher – Rixey

The BB Stars lead the series, 4-0.

Game Five, Wednesday June 2, Royals Stadium (Kansas City), 1 pm (Blackwell vs. Paige)

The game is delayed about 45 minutes due to storms in the area. The field is wet. It is a warm, muggy afternoon. Charleston's 2-run home run in the bottom of the first off Blackwell sets the tone. In the bottom of the third, the BB Stars score four more runs on four hits, an intentional walk, and Seymour's error in center field. The key blows were an RBI double by Stearnes and a two-out bases-loaded single by Dandridge (2 RBIs) that cleared the bases when Seymour misplayed the ball in center field. **BB Stars 6, Reds 0.**

The Reds score an unearned run in the top of the fourth. Lloyd's HR in the bottom of the fourth offsets it. **BB Stars 7, Reds 1.**

Roush pinch hits for Blackwell in the fifth. The final line for Blackwell is 4 IP, 8 H, 7 R, 6 ER, 2 HR, 5 K, 1 BB. Paige retires the side in order. In the sixth, Bench hits a 2-run home run off Paige (7-3), and Morgan hits a 2-run home run off of him in the seventh (7-5). Paige pitches eight innings (8 IP, 9 H, 5 R, 4 ER, 2 HR, 7 K, 0 BB). J. R. Richard gives up a lead-off single in the ninth and than strikes out the side for the save.

	R	H	E	LOB
Reds	5	10	0	7
BB Stars	7	10	2	5

Winning Pitcher – Paige   Save – Richard   Losing Pitcher – Blackwell

The BB Stars lead the series 5-0, which means that they cannot lose the overall series.

Game Six, Thursday June 3, Royals Stadium (Kansas City), 7 pm (Hahn vs. Tiant)

This is the third of four games in a row at Royals Stadium before returning to Cincinnati to play the final two games at Riverfront Stadium. It is a warm and partly cloudy evening that starts out promising for the Reds. Thompson booms a triple off the wall in center. Morgan hits a fly ball toward the line in right. Thompson is tagging at third. Torriente makes the catch and fires the ball to Gibson, who applies the tag, double play. George Foster goes

93

down swinging. The Reds fail to score with a lead-off triple.

In the bottom of the first, Bell takes a called third strike. Torriente walks. Then Suttles smashes one off the wall in left center; the ball rebounds past Roush. Torriente scores, and Suttles has a triple (1-0). Gibson bounces out to deep short; he is thrown out by Concepcion as Suttles crosses the plate with the second run. Irvin walks. Wells grounds out to third. **BB Stars 2, Reds 0.**

Hahn does not help himself in the second inning when he walks Dandridge and Warfield to open the inning. Tiant is trying to bunt the runners over, but he tops it in front of the plate. Lombardi pounces on it and fires to Concepcion, covering third for the force (one out). Bell doubles into the corner in left, scoring Warfield with the third run, and Tiant stops at third. With the third baseman and first baseman looking for the bunt, Torriente tries to slap it by Groh. He stabs it, looks at Tiant (standing on third base), and throws out Torriente (two outs). After fouling off four two-strike pitches, however, Suttles lines a 2-run single to center (5-0). Gibson flies out to Foster (LF). **BB Stars 5, Reds 0.**

In the fourth, George Foster hits a bases-empty home run (5-1), but in the bottom of the fourth, Bell hits a 2-run HR off Hecker (in his second inning of relief) to add to the BB lead. **BB Stars 7, Reds 1.**

In the fifth inning, the teams trade runs (8-2). Tiant leaves in the eighth inning (7.7 IP, 7 H, 2 R, 1 HR, 7 K, 1 BB). Roush hits a 2-run HR off Moore in the ninth to close out the scoring.

	R	H	E	LOB
Reds	4	9	0	6
BB Stars	8	9	0	4

Winning Pitcher – Tiant   Losing Pitcher – Hahn

The BB Stars lead the series, 6-0.

Game Seven, Friday June 4, Royals Stadium (Kansas City), 7 pm (King vs. Dihigo)

It is a warm, partly cloudy evening in Kansas City. The Reds are down six games to none, despite averaging nearly six runs/game. What is the problem? The Reds' pitching has been non-existent (nearly nine runs/game). In the bottom of the first, the BB Stars continue the offensive attack. Torriente singles to center. Cool Papa Bell doubles to left center; Torriente stops at third. Silver King gets Charleston looking at a called third strike (one out). Stearnes hits a slow roller to second for out number two. Torriente scores, and Bell moves to third (1-0). Mackey drops a Texas League bloop into center field that falls in front of Seymour. Bell scores the second run. Lloyd grounds out to Morgan. **BB Stars 2, Reds 0.**

In the top of the second, Kluszewski smashes one down the first base line that Charleston (1B) knocks down, but it rolls into foul territory for an infield hit. If Charleston had made the play, Dihigo would probably have escaped the inning without a run. Bench is called out on strikes (one out). Seymour singles to right on the hit-and-run, with Kluszewski hustling to third. Concepcion singles up the middle, scoring Kluszewski. Seymour holds up at second base. Johnson (3B) and Charleston (1B) are in on the grass looking for King to bunt.

On Dihigo's first pitch (King squares to bunt), Mackey is ready to pounce on the bunt. The pitch bounces off Mackey's glove and rolls away as the runners move up to second and third (passed ball). On a 2-2 pitch, King bounces one up the middle, Lloyd grabs it on a one-hop and throws out King as Seymour scores the tying run and Concepcion stays at second (two outs). Rose lines a single to center, scoring Concepcion (3-2).

Morgan hits a high drive to deep right, and it is gone, home run (5-2). Newcombe is warming up for the BB Stars. Sam Thompson singles to right. Perez lines a single to left with the speedy Thompson racing to third. Newcombe is coming in; Dihigo is headed to the showers. Kluszewski hits Newcombe's first pitch over Warfield's head into right center for a base hit (his second of the inning). Thompson scores (6-2), and Perez stops at second. Bench hits Newcombe's first pitch 420 feet over the left-field fence for a 3-run homer (9-2). The final line for Dihigo is 2.7 IP, 8 H, 7 R, 1 HR, 2 K, 0 BB. The twelfth man up in the inning, Seymour, strikes out. **Reds 9, BB Stars 2.**

In the bottom of the third, Mackey's 2-run triple closes the gap. **Reds 9, BB Stars 4.**

In the fourth, Newcombe gives up his second home run (Kluszewski 2-run HR). **Reds 11, BB Stars 4.**

With two outs and none on in the top of the fifth, Rose singles to center. Morgan then lines the ball over Bell's head in center for a triple. Thompson (3 for 3) flies out to Bell on the warning track. **Reds 12, BB Stars 4.**

In the meantime, King retires the side in order in the fifth. He has now settled down and retired seven in a row. In the top of the sixth, the BB Stars do a double switch. Paige replaces Newcombe but will bat third. Leonard replaces Charleston (1B) and will bat ninth. In the bottom of the sixth, a two-out double by Allen puts runners on second and third. Josh Gibson comes out to pinch hit for Warfield. Gibson goes down swinging. **Reds 12, BB Stars 4.**

Gibson stays in the game. Johnson replaces Allen at 3B (bats in Mackey's fifth spot). Allen moves to second base. Paige retires the side in order. In the bottom of the seventh, Leonard leads off with a single to right. Blackwell begins to throw in the Reds bullpen. Torriente doubles off the wall in right.

Leonard stops at third. Bell lines a single to center. Leonard scores; Torriente stops at third (12-5). Blackwell replaces King. Suttles pinch hits for Paige. Blackwell jams him and Suttles pops out to Concepcion in shallow left field (one out). Stearnes flies out to Rose in left center; Torriente scores (sac fly, 12-6, two outs). Johnson flies out to Thompson (RF). **Reds 12, BB Stars 6.**

Moore replaces Paige. With one out in the eighth, Morgan slams his second triple over a leaping Bell. Morgan is having an awesome series (even if the Reds have not one a game, yet). Thompson hits a high chopper to first as Morgan races home (two outs). Perez grounds out to second. **Reds 13, BB Stars 6.**

Reds do a double switch; Luque replaces Blackwell (bats fourth). Groh replaces Perez and will bat ninth. Other defensive changes for Reds are Cedeno replacing Rose (LF), Huggins replaces Morgan (2B) and Beckley replaces Kluszewski (1B). Lloyd leads off with a single into right field. Allen takes a called third strike (one out). Gibson hits one to deep left; it is out of here, 2-run home run (13-8). Leonard strikes out swinging (two outs). Irvin pinch hits for Torriente and singles to left. Bell triples to center as Seymour's attempt for a diving catch fails (13-9). Bucky Walters replaces Luque and walks Wells (batting for Moore). It is hard to believe, but the BB Stars have the potential tying run in the on deck circle. Stearnes flies to left, ending the inning. **Reds 13, BB Stars 9.**

Hilton Smith relieves Moore and keeps the Reds scoreless. In the bottom of the ninth, Walters tries to save the game for Silver King (6+ IP, 10 H, 6 R, 0 HR, 5 K, 1 BB). Johnson grounds out to Concepcion. Lloyd hits one to deep center, but Seymour has room and makes the catch on the edge of the warning track (two outs). Newt Allen tops one in front of the plate. Bench pounces on the ball, but his throw glances off Allen's arm and rolls out into shallow right field (error Bench). Allen, hustling all the way, ends up on second.

Walters now has to face the dangerous Josh Gibson. He falls behind 3-1 and throws a fast ball down the middle. Gibson hits it high and deep, gone, home run to left center. Walters gets Leonard to hit a high fly ball to shallow right, and Thompson comes in to make the catch, game over. Reds win, 13-11.

	R	H	E	LOB
Reds	13	17	1	4
BB Stars	11	15	0	7

Winning Pitcher – King   Save – Walters   Losing Pitcher – Dihigo
The BB Stars lead the series, 6-1.

Game Eight, Saturday June 5, Riverfront Stadium (Cincinnati), 1 pm (Rogan vs. Rusie)

The game has been delayed about an hour due to a thunderstorm. It is hot and muggy. The field is wet. Rusie retires the side in order. Rogan retires the first two batters. George Foster lines one past Johnson (3B) that Lloyd knocks down, but Foster is safe at first with an infield single. Kluszewski hits Rogan's first pitch (fast ball, inner part of the plate) over the fence in right, home run. Lombardi flies out to deep left. **Reds 2, BB Stars 0.**

The BB Stars come right back in the second. With one out, Stearnes and Suttles get back-to-back singles (first and third). Johnson triples off the center field wall (2-2). Allen walks. Rogan hits into a 6-4-3 double play. **BB Stars 2, Reds 2.**

Kluszweski leads off the bottom of the fourth (2-run homer in second). Rogan falls behind 3-1. There's the pitch, there it goes, headed to deep center field, and it's gone, home run (3-2). Rogan gives up a two-out single to Groh before Concepcion grounds out to Johnson (3B). **Reds 3, BB Stars 2.**

In the top of the sixth, Rusie gets in a slight jam. With one out, Charleston singles to center. Rusie walks Gibson. Rusie strikes out Stearnes, swinging at a pitch out of the strike zone. Leonard flies to left. **Reds 3, BB Stars 2.**

Big Klu (two HRs, 3 RBIs) leads off the bottom of the sixth. Rogan throws a fast ball, high and tight, as Kluszewski spins away, ball one. Rogan throws a knee-high fast ball. Kluszewski smashes a line drive down the right field line, and it is gone.. Kluszewski has just hit his third home run in three at bats; Reds lead 4-2. Rogan retires the next three batters. **Reds 4, BB Stars 2.**

It is the top of the eighth. The Reds make defensive changes – Huggins replaces Morgan at second base (bats in lead-off spot). Thompson replaces Rose in RF and bats second (lead-off bottom of the eighth). Rusie has been solid (5 hits, 3 walks, two runs). Lloyd grounds out to Kluszewski (one out). The Reds have a lefty (Rixey) and a righty (Walters) ready as Rusie faces Charleston. He walks Charleston on a 3-2 pitch (a little low). Rusie wanted that pitch to be strike three. Gibson flares one into center field; it drops in front of Seymour. Charleston stops at second. Rixey will be brought in to pitch to Stearnes.

Rusie receives a standing ovation from the sellout crowd at Riverfront Stadium. Irvin (righty) will bat for Stearnes against the southpaw, Rixey. Irvin pops it up behind the pitchers mound. Concepcion calls for it and takes it (Irvin was out anyway because of the infield fly rule). Suttles will pinch hit for Leonard. Walters will be brought in to pitch to Suttles. Walters jams Suttles, who bounces it to Groh (3B), who throws to second, forcing Gibson to end the inning (Rusie 7.1 IP, 6 H, 2 R, 0 HR, 2 K, 4 BB). **Reds 4, BB Stars 2.**

With two out in the bottom of the eighth, Rogan will pitch to Kluszewski again. Rogan has not had trouble with any other hitter. However, Big Klu (3 HRs, 4 RBIs) is a different story. Kluszewski lines one into the gap in left center; it rolls to the wall. Bell picks it up and throws to Lloyd (cut-off man). Kluszewski is standing on second with a double. Beckley runs out to second to pinch run and goes in defensively at first base. The final line for Kluszewski is 4 AB, 3 R, 4 H, 4 RB1, 1 2B, 3 HR, 14 TB. He leaves to a standing ovation. Lombardi strikes out swinging to end the inning. The final line for Rogan is 8 IP, 8 H, 4 R, 3 HR, 3 K, 1 BB. **Reds 4, BB Stars 2.**

The Reds make one more defensive change in the ninth inning; Bench replaces Lombardi behind the plate. Walters retires the side in order, retiring pinch hitter, Biz Mackey (batting for Rogan) on an infield pop-up to Concepcion.

	R	H	E	LOB
BB Stars	2	6	1	7
Reds	4	8	0	4

Winning Pitcher – Rusie   Save – Walters   Losing Pitcher – Rogan
The BB Stars lead the series, 6-2.

Game Nine, Sunday June 6, Riverfront Stadium (Cincinnati), 1 pm (Day vs. Rogers)

The Reds open the scoring in the bottom of the second inning. Kluszewski singles up the middle (he is on fire). Perez walks; runners are on first and second. Bench tops one up the third base line. Dandridge bare hands the ball and fires to Suttles (1B) to retire Bench; runners advance to second and third (one out). Roush hits a high fly to fairly deep right center. Bell makes the catch as both runners advance on the sac fly (1-0). Concepcion singles to left, scoring Perez (2-0). Concepcion steals second. Rogers grounds out to Lloyd, ending the inning. **Reds 2, BB Stars 0.**

Rogers has blanked the BB Stars through four innings (five hits, five LOB). In the bottom of the fourth, Kluszewski smashes one through Suttles' legs into the right field corner (two-base error). Perez strikes out swinging. Bench doubles into the left field corner; Klu scores (3-0). Roush singles to right; Bench stops at third. Concepcion hits a slow roller to Warfield (2B), who throws him out (2 outs). Bench scores; Roush moves to second. Rogers takes a called third strike to end the inning. **Reds 4, BB Stars 0.**

The BB Stars cut the lead in half on Charleston's 2-run home run in the top of the fifth. **Reds 4, BB Stars 2.**

In the bottom of the sixth, the Reds chase Day. Red hot Kluszewski singles up the middle. Beckley goes in to run for Klu. Groh singles to left, and Beckley stops at second. J. R. Richard replaces Day, and Allen replaces Warfield (double switch). Bench drives Charleston back to the warning track for the first out; both runners advance. Roush lines a single to center, scoring Beckley and Perez. Leon Day's final line is 5+ IP, 6 H, 6 R, 4 ER, 0 HR, 2 K, 1 BB. Concepcion flies out to Charleston, and Rogers strikes out. **Reds 6, BB Stars 2.**

Groh has replaced Perez defensively at third base. Allen leads off the seventh and flies out to Roush (CF). Rogers walks Bell; Blackwell begins to warm up. Lloyd slaps a single to left; Allen stops at second. Charleston singles to left center. Allen scores, and Lloyd stops at second (6-3). Gibson singles to left, Lloyd scores, and Charleston holds at second (6-4). Blackwell replaces Rogers. Blackwell walks Suttles on four pitches to load the bases. Torriente lines one to left that Foster decides to play on one-hop; Charleston scores, and the bases remain loaded (6-5). Six men in a row have reached base. Stearnes bats for Dandridge. Rixey replaces Blackwell. Stearnes pops out to Morgan (infield fly rule, 2 outs). Johnson bats for Richard and hits into a force play, ending the inning. Rogers' final line is 6.3 IP, 12 H, 5 R, 1 HR, 5 K, 1 BB. **Reds 6, BB Stars 5.**

In the bottom of the seventh, the BB Stars do another double switch; Johnson replaces Dandridge at third base. Paige is in to pitch and retires the side in order. Rixey gets out of the eighth when Lloyd lines into a double play (Concepcion to Beckley). In the bottom of the eighth, Beckley singles to right off Paige. Beckley steals second (Paige is mediocre at holding runners). Groh bounces out to Johnson (3B) as Beckley stays at second base (one out). Paige tries to jam Bench, but he does not get it inside enough, and it is a long home run to left field (8-5). Roush flies out to Bell (two outs). Concepcion doubles into the left field corner. Rixey, who has pitched well in relief and has a 3-run lead, will bat. He singles to left, and Concepcion scores easily (9-5). Thompson raps into a force play at second. **Reds 9, BB Stars 5.**

Rixey enters the ninth with a 4-run lead. Hecker and Hahn are ready in the Reds bullpen. Charleston leads off with his second home run and his fourth RBI (9-6). Hecker replaces Rixey. Gibson beats out an infield single to deep short. Suttles singles to center, with Gibson holding at second base. Hahn has replaced Hecker, still none out. Hahn gets Torriente to hit a one-hopper to Huggins (replaced Morgan at second in eighth), who starts a 4-6-3 double play. Gibson moves to third. Wells bats for Paige, and he bloops one into left field that drops in, scoring Gibson (9-7). Walters (righty) is ready in the pen, but Hahn (lefty) will pitch to Johnson. Big mistake. Johnson hits a line drive down the left field line; if it stays fair, it is a home run. The third base umpire gives the home run signal as Johnson leaps into the air as he heads for second. The game is tied, 9-9. Allen bounces out to end the top half of the ninth. **BB Stars 9, Reds, 9.**

In the bottom of the ninth, Donnie Moore is in to pitch for the the BB Stars. He fans Huggins (replaced Morgan in eighth) and Foster. Beckley gets a double, his second hit since replacing Big Klu (pinch runner in sixth). Groh flies out to left, and we are going into extra innings in Game Nine. **BB Stars 9, Reds 9.**

In the top of the tenth, Hahn strikes out Bell (looking). Lloyd walks. Charleston takes a called third strike (two outs). Walters replaces the lefty, Hahn, to face Josh Gibson. Walters gets Gibson to hit into a force at second to end the inning. **BB Stars 9, Reds 9.**

Bench leads off with a smash into the left center field gap, and Charleston makes a great catch (one out). Roush bloops a hit into left field. Concepcion hits one to Lloyd, who knocks it down and flips to Allen for the force at second (two outs). Pete Rose bats for Walters. He pops out to Lloyd in shallow left field. **BB Stars 9, Reds 9.**

Dolf Luque is the seventh pitcher for the Reds. He starts the 11th inning. He will face Suttles, Torriente, and Moore (or pinch hitter) in the eleventh inning. Luque retires Suttles on a pop-out to Concepcion (one out). Torriente goes down swinging (two outs). Leonard will bat for Moore. Leonard lifts a fly to Roush (CF) to end the inning. **BB Stars 9, Reds 9.**

The Reds have fought hard in this high-scoring series and would like to finish with three straight victories. Bullet Joe Rogan is the fifth BB Stars pitcher in the game. He will face the free agent Sam Thompson in the bottom of the eleventh. Thompson is hitless in five at bats. Rogan's first two pitches are outside. Rogan throws a 2-0 fast ball, knee-high, and Thompson jumps on it. There it goes over the right field wall, home run. The Reds win in eleven innings, 10-9.

11 Innings	R	H	E	LOB
BB Stars	9	19	1	10
Reds	10	14	0	6
Winning Pitcher – Luque	Losing Pitcher – Rogan			

The BB Stars win the series, 6-3.

Recap of Best Season Series 4 (BB Stars vs. Reds)

The Reds score 62 runs. However, they give up 75 runs. Chart 9-2 on page 101 has BB Stars individual/team statistics for this series. Chart 9-3 on page 102 has Reds individual/team statistics for this series.

BB Stars Results vs. Reds 6-3, .667

Pos.	E	R	TH	PB	Hitters	G	AB	R	H	RBI	2B	3B	HR	TB	W	HB	SO	SF	SH	SB	B.AVG.	OBP	S.PCT.	OPS
LF	5	A	-1		Charleston	7	27	8	11	11	1	0	1	27	2	0	2	0	0	0	0.407	0.448	1.000	1.448
CF	8	AA	-1		CP Bell	8	38	8	15	6	3	2	0	25	1	0	6	0	0	1	0.395	0.410	0.658	1.068
OF	5	A	-1		Stearnes	7	23	5	8	7	2	1	0	12	0	0	2	1	0	0	0.348	0.348	0.522	0.870
OF	6	B	-2		M Irvin	6	15	5	6	2	4	0	0	10	1	0	2	0	0	0	0.400	0.438	0.667	1.104
OF	6	A	-1		Torriente	6	25	5	7	1	1	0	0	8	1	0	4	0	0	0	0.280	0.308	0.320	0.628
SS	7	A			P Lloyd	8	26	9	8	5	1	0	1	12	3	0	0	0	0	0	0.308	0.379	0.462	0.841
SS	7	AA			W Wells	7	14	5	6	6	1	1	1	15	2	0	0	0	0	0	0.429	0.500	1.071	1.571
3B	7	A			J Johnson	6	20	3	7	6	1	1	0	13	1	0	3	0	0	0	0.350	0.381	0.650	1.031
3B	6	B			Dandridge	6	14	2	5	2	0	0	0	5	3	0	3	0	0	0	0.357	0.471	0.357	0.828
2B	7	A			N Allen	7	24	4	6	1	3	0	0	9	1	0	2	0	0	0	0.250	0.280	0.375	0.655
2B	6	A			F Warfield	6	17	4	4	4	0	3	0	10	2	0	2	0	0	0	0.235	0.316	0.588	0.904
1B	7	A			Suttles	7	26	5	9	5	1	2	0	14	1	0	0	1	0	0	0.346	0.370	0.538	0.909
1B	8	B			B Leonard	6	15	4	4	1	1	0	0	5	1	0	3	0	0	0	0.267	0.313	0.333	0.646
C	7	A		-2 Fr	J Gibson	8	32	4	8	9	0	0	3	17	1	0	6	0	0	0	0.250	0.273	0.531	0.804
C	6	B		-2 Av	B Mackey	5	12	2	7	3	0	0	0	9	0	0	1	0	0	0	0.583	0.583	0.750	1.333
					pitchers	9	23	2	8	3	0	1	0	8	0	0	5	0	1	1	0.348	0.375	0.348	0.723
					TOTAL	9	351	75	119	72	19	11	10	153	21	0	43	3	1	1	0.339	0.376	0.436	0.812

Fat.	H	WP	E	R	Pitchers	G	GS	OS	CG	S	W	L	IP	H	SO	BB	HB	SO	HR	R	ER	ERA
10/L	Vg	N	9	B	BJ Rogan	3	1	1	1	0	1	0	11.7	13	5	4	0	3	0	8	8	6.17
9/L	Ex	R	7	B	B Foster	2	1	1	0	0	1	0	9	5	6	3	0	0	1	4	3	3.00
10/L	Vg	NL	8	B	L Day	2	2	0	0	0	0	1	7	14	3	3	0	0	0	11	9	11.57
10/L	Av	NL	7	B	M Dihigo	2	1	0	0	0	0	1	8.7	9	5	1	0	1	1	7	7	7.27
8/L	Md	R	8	C	S Paige	3	1	1	0	0	1	0	12	13	10	0	0	0	0	8	7	5.25
L/9	Vg	R	8	A	H Smith	3	1	1	0	0	1	0	6.3	12	6	0	0	0	0	5	5	7.11
9/L	Av	R	9	A	Newcombe	2	1	0	0	0	0	1	8.3	14	7	1	0	0	4	11	11	11.88
10/L	Ex	NL	8	D	L Tiant	1	1	0	0	0	1	0	7.7	7	7	1	0	0	1	2	2	2.35
9	Av	N	5	C	J R Richard	3	0	0	0	2	1	0	4	4	4	1	0	0	0	2	1	2.25
Long	Md	NL	4	B	D Moore	5	0	0	0	1	0	0	7.3	7	0	1	0	0	3	5	5	6.14
					TOTAL	26	9	4	1	3	6	3	82	98	53	15	0	3	17	62	58	6.37

Chart 9-2 – BB Stars Statistics for this series

Reds Best Season Series vs. BB All-Stars 3-6, .333

Team	Year	WS Hitters	G	AB	R	H	RBI	2B	3B	HR	TB	W	HB	SO	SF	SH	SB	B.AVG.	OBP	S.PCT.	OPS
Philadelphia	1895	28 S Thompson	8	32	5	13	3	2	1	1	20	1	0	3	0	0	0	0.406	0.424	0.625	1.049
Houston	1972	33 C Cedeno	4	5	1	1	1	0	0	0	2	1	0	0	0	0	0	0.200	0.200	0.400	0.600
Cincinnati	1905	42 C Seymour	8	28	5	8	4	4	1	0	14	1	0	1	0	0	0	0.286	0.310	0.500	0.810
Cincinnati	1917	30 E Roush	5	15	3	6	5	0	0	1	9	0	0	0	1	0	0	0.400	0.400	0.600	1.000
Cincinnati	1969	37 P Rose	8	27	3	7	1	0	0	0	7	0	0	4	0	0	0	0.259	0.259	0.259	0.519
Cincinnati	1977	32 G Foster	6	24	5	5	5	1	0	2	12	2	0	6	1	0	0	0.208	0.269	0.500	0.769
Cincinnati	1979	24 Concepcion	9	38	4	6	5	2	0	0	8	0	0	4	0	0	1	0.158	0.158	0.211	0.368
Cincinnati	1917	37 H Groh	5	12	0	3	0	0	0	0	3	1	0	0	0	0	0	0.250	0.308	0.250	0.558
Cincinnati	1970	33 T Perez	6	23	6	6	4	2	0	2	12	2	0	9	0	0	0	0.261	0.320	0.522	0.842
Cincinnati	1976	37 J Morgan	8	31	7	9	11	1	3	3	25	1	0	3	0	0	0	0.290	0.313	0.806	1.119
Cincinnati	1905	27 M Huggins	7	6	2	2	0	1	0	0	3	4	0	1	0	0	0	0.333	0.600	0.500	1.100
Cincinnati	1954	33 Kluszewski	8	29	10	14	8	1	0	4	27	1	0	2	0	0	1	0.483	0.500	0.931	1.431
Cincinnati	1900	21 J Beckley	9	13	4	3	0	1	0	0	4	2	0	2	0	0	0	0.231	0.333	0.308	0.641
Cincinnati	1970	34 J Bench	7	26	4	7	8	1	0	3	17	0	0	5	0	0	0	0.269	0.269	0.654	0.923
Cincinnati	1938	24 E Lombardi	5	14	0	5	2	1	0	1	6	0	0	2	0	0	0	0.357	0.357	0.429	0.786
		pitchers	9	20	1	3	3	0	0	1	6	0	0	7	0	0	0	0.150	0.150	0.300	0.450
		TOTAL	9	343	60	98	59	16	5	17	175	15	0	50	2	0	2	0.286	0.316	0.510	0.826

Team	Year	WS Pitchers	G	GS	QS	CG	S	W	L	IP	H	SO	BB	HB	HR	R	ER	ERA
Cincinnati	1902	29 N Hahn	3	2	0	0	0	0	0	9	15	5	6	2	2	14	14	14.00
Louisville	1884	74 G Hecker	5	1	0	0	0	0	0	13	21	6	2	1	2	12	12	8.31
Cincinnati	1923	39 D Luque	5	1	0	0	0	0	2	6.3	13	4	2	0	1	8	8	11.37
Cincinnati	1925	26 E Rixey	3	1	0	0	0	0	1	6.3	13	6	1	0	1	7	6	8.53
Cincinnati	1947	28 E Blackwell	3	1	0	0	0	0	1	5	9	5	1	1	2	7	6	10.80
Montreal	1982	24 S Rogers	4	0	0	0	0	0	1	9.3	14	5	1	1	2	7	6	6.75
Cincinnati	1939	38 B Walters	5	0	0	0	0	2	0	6	5	5	1	1	3	5	3	4.50
NY (N)	1894	56 A Rusie	3	1	0	0	0	0	1	11	8	8	4	0	0	2	2	1.64
St. Louis	1896	71 S King	3	1	0	0	0	0	1	8	14	4	2	0	0	7	7	7.88
Cincinnati	1929	26 R Lucas	3	0	0	0	0	0	0	7	7	7	1	0	0	2	2	2.57
		TOTAL	37	9	1	0	0	2	3	81	119	46	21	3	13	73	67	7.78

Chart 9-3 – Reds statistics for this series

The turning point of the series - The Reds' pitching failure was the dominant factor. Offensively, the Reds scored 62 runs with 17 HRs. They had a .286 team batting average with a .510 slugging percentage. Defensively, there were no critical errors that cost any games. While the Reds' pitching was outstanding during Game Eight with Rusie, Rixey, and Walters in a 4-2 win, it was overshadowed by Kluszewski's 3 home runs, double and 4 RBIs. In addition to saving Game Eight, Walters also saved Game Seven.

MVP of Series – Oscar Charleston - OPS-1.448; Slg. Pct.-1.000; OBP-.448; B.Avg.-.407; 5 HRs, 11 RBIs, 8 RS and solid defense. He won Game One with a pinch-hit HR in the tenth. His 3-run HR in the fourth inning was a game-winning hit in Game Three. In Game Five, his 2-run HR in the first inning led to a 7-5 win. He was 3 for 6 in Game Nine, with 2 HRs and 4 RBIs, but the BB Stars lost in eleven innings.

Hitting Stars for the Reds - Joe Morgan and Ted Kluszewski led the Reds in a losing cause.

	RS	RBI	HR	.Avg	OBP	SPct	OPS
Morgan	7	11	3	.290	.313	.806	1.119
Kluszewski	10	8	4	.483	.500	.931	1.431

Chapter 10

Best Season Nine Game Series 5 - BB Stars vs. Senators/Twins

Senators/Twins Roster Review

TWENTY-EIGHT PERCENT OF THE roster are made up of Washington Senators. Twenty-four percent of the roster are Minnesota Twins. Forty-eight percent are free agents. See the Senators/Twins Roster (Chart 10-1 on page 106).

Offensive Leaders (Senator/Twins) Ranked by OPS

Player	OBP	SPct	OPS	R +	RBI -	HR =	NR
G. Goslin	.443	.614	1.057	80	102	17	165
R. Carew	.452	.570	1.022	128	100	14	214
K. Kelly	.486	.534	1.020	155	79	4	230
H. Killebrew	.430	.584	1.014	106	140	49	197
F. Howard	.403	.574	.977	111	111	48	174
R. Staub	.419	.526	.945	89	79	29	139
J. Cronin	.422	.513	.935	127	126	13	240
C. Travis	.410	.520	.930	106	101	7	200
T. Oliva	.361	.557	.918	109	94	32	171
D. Johnson	.363	.546	.909	84	99	43	140

The following players would be base-stealing threats – Sam Rice 63, Stirnweiss 55, and King Kelly 53 (numbers listed SB for their best season).

Fielding Leaders	Pos	Range	Error	Throwing
S. Rice	R/CF	AA	4	-2
R. Staub	RF	A	3	-1
G. Goslin	L/CF	A	4	0
T. Oliva	RF	A	6	+1
K. Kelly	RF	A	5	-2

For outfielders - range (AA is best) and throwing (-4 is exceptional, -3 is excellent, -2 is very good) are most important. Error rating (10 is best, 1 is poor) is not as critical as infielders because outfielders normally do not make as many errors.

J. Cronin	SS	AA+	7	-
R. Smalley	SS	AA+	7	-
C. Travis	SS	A	7	-
S. Stirnweiss	2B	AA+	8	-
R. Carew	1B	B	8	-
C. Travis	3B	B	6	

For infielders, range (AA is best) + increase in DPs because of excellent pivot. Error rating is as important as range (10 is excellent, 1 is poor).

Catcher Throwing - Battey and K. Kelly are above average (-1).

Pitcher Hold Rating - Kaat and Galvin are excellent (less successful steal attempts). Johnson, McCormick, Chance, and Pennock are very good. Leonard and Stottlemyre are average. Perry and Kern are mediocre (more successful steal attempts).

Pitching - Walter Johnson is the ace of the staff (1913 – 36-7 with a 1.14 ERA). He will start three games.

Senators/Twins Roster Best Season Series vs. BB All-Stars

Team	Year	WS	Hitters	G	AB	R	H	RBI	2B	3B	HR	TB	W	HB	SO	SF	SH	SB	B.AVG.	OBP	S.PCT.	OPS
Montreal	1969	27	R Staub	158	549	89	166	79	26	5	29	289	110	0	61	-	-	3	0.302	0.419	0.526	0.945
Minnesota	1964	27	T Oliva	161	672	109	217	94	43	9	32	374	34	6	68	-	-	12	0.323	0.361	0.557	0.918
Washington	1920	23	S Rice	153	624	83	211	80	29	9	3	267	39	2	23	-	-	63	0.338	0.379	0.428	0.807
Buffalo	1884	25	O'Rourke	108	467	119	162	63	33	7	5	224	35	1	17	-	-	15	0.347	0.394	0.480	0.873
Washington	1928	28	G Goslin	135	456	80	173	102	36	10	17	280	48	4	19	-	-	16	0.379	0.443	0.614	1.057
Washington	1969	34	F Howard	161	592	111	175	111	17	2	48	340	102	5	96	-	-	1	0.296	0.403	0.574	0.978
Washington	1930	33	J Cronin	154	587	127	203	126	41	9	13	301	72	5	36	-	-	17	0.346	0.422	0.513	0.934
Minnesota	1979	24	R Smalley	162	621	94	168	95	28	3	24	274	80	1	80	-	-	2	0.271	0.355	0.441	0.796
Minnesota	1969	34	H Killebrew	162	555	106	153	140	20	2	49	324	145	5	84	-	-	8	0.276	0.430	0.584	1.014
Washington	1941	34	C Travis	152	608	106	218	101	39	19	7	316	52	1	25	-	-	2	0.359	0.410	0.520	0.930
New York A	1944	35	Stirnweiss	154	643	125	205	43	35	16	8	296	73	2	87	-	-	55	0.319	0.390	0.460	0.850
Atlanta	1973	21	D Johnson	157	559	84	151	99	25	0	43	305	81	1	93	-	-	5	0.270	0.363	0.546	0.909
Minnesota	1977	37	R Carew	155	616	128	239	100	38	16	14	351	69	3	55	-	-	23	0.388	0.452	0.570	1.022
Minnesota	1963	20	E Battey	147	508	64	145	84	17	1	26	242	61	5	75	-	-	0	0.285	0.368	0.476	0.844
Chicago N	1886	35	K Kelly	118	451	155	175	79	32	11	4	241	83	3	33	-	-	53	0.388	0.486	0.534	1.020

Team	Year	WS	Pitchers	G	GS	QS	CG	S	W	L	IP	H	SO	BB	HB	HR	R	ER	ERA
Washington	1913	54	W Johnson	48	36	-	29	2	36	7	346	232	243	38	-	9	-	-	1.14
Cleveland	1883	40	McCormick	43	43	-	36	1	28	12	342	316	145	65	-	1	-	-	1.84
Minnesota	1966	26	J Kaat	41	41	-	19	0	25	13	305	271	205	55	-	29	-	-	2.75
LA (A)	1964	32	D Chance	46	35	-	15	4	20	9	278	194	207	86	-	7	-	-	1.65
Buffalo	1884	57	P Galvin	72	72	-	71	0	46	22	636	566	369	63	-	23	-	-	1.99
Cleveland	1972	39	G Perry	41	40	-	29	1	24	16	342	253	234	82	-	17	-	-	1.92
New York A	1965	23	Stottlemyre	37	37	-	16	0	20	9	291	250	155	88	-	18	-	-	2.63
New York A	1924	23	H Pennock	40	34	-	25	3	21	9	286	302	101	64	-	13	-	-	2.83
Washington	1939	21	D Leonard	34	34	-	21	0	20	8	269	273	88	59	-	16	-	-	3.54
Texas	1979	25	J Kern	71	0		0	29	13	5	143	99	136	62		5			1.57

Chart 10-1 – Senators/Twins Best Season Roster

Game One, Tuesday June 8, Griffith Stadium (Washington DC), 7 pm (Paige vs. Johnson)

It is a warm and partly cloudy evening at the ball park. There is a buzz about this series. According to Bill James, Walter Johnson is the #1 pitcher of all time, and Satchel Paige is #2. They are scheduled to face each other three times in this series. The BB Stars have won the first four Best Season nine-game series, winning 23 games while losing only 13. However, they are on a three-game losing streak. The Reds won the last three games in their series after losing the first six. The Reds' pitchers were overmatched (7.88 ERA). Walter Johnson gives up a one-out single to Lloyd before retiring the dangerous duo of Oscar Charleston and Josh Gibson.

In the bottom of the first inning, Paige struggles. Goslin singles sharply to right. On the hit-and-run, Cecil Travis hits a soft liner over Allen's head (2B), and Goslin scoots to third. Carew smashes a single up the middle, scoring Goslin (1-0), and Travis stops at second. Killebrew bounces one past Paige, but Lloyd makes the play on Killebrew with the runners advancing to second and third (one out). Oliva is walked intentionally, setting up the possible double play with Earl Battey coming to the plate. However, Battey foils that plan, lashing a single into left center, scoring two runs. Oliva makes the turn at second and holds (3-0). Paige escapes further damage (Stirnweiss FC forceout at second; Rice lines out to Bell in center.) **Sen-Twins 3, BB Stars 0.**

In the top of the fourth inning, the BB Stars finally get to Johnson. Gibson leads off with a one-hop double off the wall in left center. Leonard hits a slow-hopper charged by Travis (SS), who throws him out as Gibson moves to third. Torriente walks. Dandridge pops out to Stirnweiss (2B) for the second out. Allen singles to center to score Gibson (3-1); Torriente stops at second. Paige hits a fly to Rice in shallow center, but Rice drops the ball. Torriente scores, but Allen slips rounding second, and Rice throws to Travis, who tags Allen out. **SenTwins 3, BB Stars 2.**

In the bottom of the fifth, a one-out triple by Travis looks promising. Carew lofts a fly to medium left center; Cool Papa Bell makes the catch and throws a strike to Gibson, who tags Travis for an inning-ending double play.

In the bottom of the sixth, Paige is in trouble again. Killebrew singles to center. Oliva follows with another base hit up the middle. Killebrew stops at second. Paige walks Battey on a 3-2 pitch that is just outside, bases loaded, none out. Luis Tiant (free agent, 68 Indians) is warming up for the BB Stars. Paige gets both Stirnweiss and Rice to fly out to shallow center, and Killebrew is not about to challenge Bell's arm (two outs). Walter Johnson is not a bad-hitting pitcher, and he has a chance to help himself. Johnson jumps on the first pitch and lines it into center field to score two runs (5-2). Goslin bounces out (Leonard to Paige). **Sen Twins 5, BB Stars 2.**

In the seventh, Johnson retires the side in order (final out occurs when Mackey flies out to deep center while batting for Paige). Johnson has retired eight in a row. The final line on Satchel Paige is 6 IP, 8 H, 5 R, 0 HR, 3 K, 2 BB. Tiant replaces Paige and gives up a lead-off single (Travis), but he retires the next three batters. Neither team gets a base runner on in the eighth (Johnson has retired eleven in a row).

In the top of the ninth, Walter Johnson quickly retires the first two batters (Gibson and Leonard) for 13 in a row. Torriente hits a drive over Rice's head in center and races to third with a two-out triple. Dandridge singles to left, scoring Torriente (5-3). Allen steps to the plate. He represents the tying run. Kern begins to warm up. Johnson walks him. Turkey Stearnes will bat for Tiant. Stearnes singles to right center, Dandridge scores, and Allen hustles to third (5-4). The tying run is 90 feet away. Four BB Stars hitters in a row have reached base. Will the manager pull Johnson and bring in Kern? No, he is going with the Big Train all the way. The count goes to 1-2 with Bell. The runners take their lead, Johnson fires, strike three called, and the game is over.

	R	H	E	LOB
BB Stars	4	9	1	6
Sen Twins	5	9	1	6

Winning Pitcher – Johnson   Losing Pitcher – Paige
The Sen Twins lead the series, 1-0.

Game Two, Wednesday June 9, Griffith Stadium (Washington DC), 1 pm (Foster vs. McCormick)

It is a hot, partly cloudy day at Griffith Stadium. Oscar Charleston will lead-off for the BB Stars as Cool Papa Bell gets a well-deserved day off. McCormick tries to get a quick first strike with a fast ball on the inside corner, but Charleston jumps on it, home run to deep right (1-0). Lloyd doubles into the right field corner. McCormick has his work cut out for him. He gets Suttles looking at a called third strike (one out). Stearnes goes down swinging (two outs). McCormick walks Irvin. McCormick strikes out Mackey (swinging). **BB Stars 1, Sen Twins 0.**

Bill Foster, the tough left-hander, gives up a lead-off single (right field) to nineteenth century free agent King Kelly. Joe Cronin flies out to Charleston (CF), one out. Big Frank Howard lines a single to center, with Kelly racing to third. Harmon Killebrew steps to the plate. Foster falls behind 2-0 and needs to get a fast ball over the plate, and Killebrew knows it. There it goes to deep left, going, going and gone, 3-run HR for Harmon Killebrew. SenTwins lead 3-1. Foster strikes out Staub (free agent, 1969 Expos). Carew bounces out to Warfield (2B). **SenTwins 3, BB Stars 1.**

McCormick gives up two hits in second and two hits in the third but allows no runs (BB Stars have stranded six runners in the first three innings). In the bottom of the third, the SenTwins add to their lead. With one out, Cronin doubles off the left field wall. Foster is not going to give Howard anything on the inside part of the plate. His first pitch is way outside, ball one. His second pitch is a fast ball on the outside corner, and Howard, going with the pitch, slashes a single into right field. Cronin races home with the fourth run. Foster retires Killebrew and Staub to end the inning. **SenTwins 4, BB Stars 1.**

In the fourth, the BB Stars make a move. Warfield leads off with a single to left. Howard misplays the ball, and Warfield ends up on third (single and two base error). Leonard bats for Foster. McCormick ends up walking Leonard. McCormick misses outside on a 3-2 pitch to Charleston, bases loaded (none out). Gaylord Perry begins to warm up for the SenTwins. Lloyd hits a high fly to shallow center; Kelly makes the catch. Warfield bluffs, heading for home. Kelly throws a strike to Battey (one out). Suttles hits a fly ball down the left field line; Howard races over to make the catch as Warfield tags and scores (Suttles sac fly, 4-2). Stearnes forces Charleston at second to end the inning. **SenTwins 4, BB Stars 2.**

Martin Dihigo comes in to pitch for the BB Stars. He gives up a two-out single to Sam Rice. Mackey has to leave the game when he is hit on the hand with a foul tip; Gibson replaces Mackey. McCormick fans to end the inning. Through the first four innings, the BB Stars have left eight men on base. McCormick comes out to pitch the fifth inning (could be his last). Perry is ready in the SenTwins bullpen. McCormick retires the first two batters. Judy Johnson lines one over the left-field fence (4-3). Warfield doubles into the gap in right center. Dihigo, a very good hitter, bats for himself and slaps one into right field, scoring Warfield and tying the score, 4-4. Charleston bounces one to Cronin (SS), who flips to Johnson (2B) to force Dihigo. This ends the top of the fifth. **BB Stars 4, SenTwins 4.**

King Kelly leads off the bottom of the fifth with a double into the left field corner. Cronin taps one to the left of the mound. Dihigo fields it; his only play is at first base as Kelly moves to third (one out). Frank Howard hits a high fly ball to fairly deep left. Stearnes makes the catch as Kelly tags and scores the go-ahead run (5-4, sac fly Howard, two outs). Killebrew flies out to Stearnes. **SenTwins 5, BB Stars 4.**

Lloyd leads off with a double into the gap in right center. McCormick is done. Perry is in to pitch. The SenTwins make some defensive changes. Travis replaces Killebrew at third and will bat ninth. Perry will bat fourth. Suttles grounds one to Johnson (2B), who throws out Suttles as Lloyd moves to third. Stearnes hits one to Johnson's right. He backhands the ball and throws Stearnes out as Suttles scores the tying run (5-5). The final line on McCormick is 5 IP, 11 H, 5 R, 2 HR, 4 K, 3 BB. Perry is now the pitcher of record for the SenTwins. Dihigo is the same for the BB Stars. Irvin and Mackey get back-to-back singles (Irvin to second). Judy Johnson flies out to Kelly (CF). The BB Stars have left eleven men on base in six innings. **BB Stars 5, SenTwins 5.**

In the bottom of the sixth, Rusty Staub hits Dihigo's 2-2 fast ball over the right field wall as the SenTwins retake the lead (6-5). With one out, Davey Johnson doubles. Rice hits a line drive into center field. Charleston makes a great sliding catch (two outs) as Johnson holds at second. Travis (batting ninth) bounces out to Suttles to end the inning. **SenTwins 6, BB Stars 5.**

In the top of the seventh, the SenTwins make two more defensive changes; Goslin replaces Howard in left. Howard did his job (2 AB, 1 R, 2 H, 2 RBI, sac fly). Stirnweiss replaces Davey Johnson at second base. Allen pinch hits for Warfield. He beats out an infield hit, as Perry cannot pick up his roller to the right of the pitcher's mound. Perry retires the next three batters, including Cool Papa Bell, batting for Dihigo.

In the bottom of the seventh, J. R. Richard is in to pitch (batting in first position). Bell stays in the game, replacing Charleston. Richard retires the side in order (Kelly, Cronin, Goslin).

Perry begins his third inning of relief in the top of the eighth. Suttles hits his first pitch over the wall in left to tie the game 6-6. With two outs, Gibson and Judy Johnson get back-to-back singles (six hits off Perry, seventeen hits for the BB Stars). Kern is ready in the SenTwins pen. Perry gets Allen to hit a one-hopper back to him, and he throws him out. The BB Stars have now stranded fourteen base runners in eight innings. **BB Stars 6, SenTwins 6.**

In the bottom of the eighth, Richard strikes out Oliva (pinch hitting for Perry). Perry's final pitching line is 3 IP, 6 H, 1 R, 1 HR, I K, 0 BB. Staub grounds out, and Carew flies out. J. R. Richard has retired all six batters he has faced.

Kern is on to pitch the ninth. Cool Papa Bell hits a long fly ball to center, and Rice tracks it down on the edge of the warning track, just a long out. Torriente pinch hits for Richard and singles to right. Lloyd hits a one-hopper to Stirnweiss, who starts a 4-6-3 double play. **BB Stars 6, SenTwins 6.**

Hilton Smith replaces J. R. Richard and quickly retires the first two batters in the bottom of the ninth. Travis singles to center. On the hit-and-run, Kelly singles to left, and Travis slides safely into third, beating Stearnes' throw. Cronin hits a smash; Judy Johnson (3B) dives, but he cannot get it, and Lloyd (SS) dives. It is a game-winning single to left. The SenTwins have a "walk off" win to go up 2-0 in the series!

	R	H	E	LOB
BB Stars	6	18	0	14
SenTwins	7	12	1	5

Winning Pitcher – Kern   Losing Pitcher – Smith
The SenTwins lead the series, 2-0.

Game Three, Thursday June 10, Griffith Stadium (Washington DC), 1 pm (Rogan vs. Kaat)

It is a warm, clear day in the nation's capital. Jim Kaat fans Bell (one out). Wells singles up the middle. Kaat walks Charleston on four pitches as Wells goes to second. Josh Gibson lines the first pitch into right center; Wells comes around to score, with Charleston holding at second base (1-0). Kaat is out of the inning when he gets Suttles looking at a third strike and Irvin forcing Gibson (Killebrew – Stirnweiss). **BB Stars 1, SenTwins 0.**

Rogan limits the SenTwins to a Carew single and a Goslin steal of second after hitting into a force play. The BB Stars add single runs in second and third (both runs scoring on infield DPs). Rogan blanks the SenTwins over the first three innings. **BB Stars 3, SenTwins 0.**

In the top of the fourth, the BB Stars score three unearned runs (6-0). With one out, Killebrew misplays Dandridge's grounder to third. Back-to-back singles (Allen and Rogan) score the first run (Dandridge). Bell strikes out for the third time in four innings (should have been third out). Wells triples to deep center, scoring two runs. Charleston flies out to Goslin (LF). **BB Stars 6, SenTwins 0.**

In the bottom of the fourth, an error by Wells (SS) contributes to a Sen-Twins rally. Goslin leads off with a double off the right field wall. Rogan hits Killebrew with a pitch. Oliva bounces one to short, but Wells bobbles the ball to load the bases (none out). Travis flies out to center (sac fly, one out); Goslin scores (6-1). Stirnweiss bounces one back to Rogan who makes a play at second, erasing Oliva (two outs, should have been three outs). Killebrew moves to third base. Rice singles to left, scoring Killebrew; Stirnweiss races around to third (6-2). Rusty Staub (1969 Expos) will pinch hit for Kaat (4 IP, 9 H, 6 R, 3 ER, 0 HR, 4 K, 1 BB). Staub smashes one down the first base line; Suttles dives and knocks the ball into foul territory as Stirnweiss scores. Rice takes a turn but holds at second. King Kelly flies to right. **BB Stars 6, SenTwins 3.**

Stottlemyre (1965 Yankees) is now pitching for the SenTwins. Gibson grounds out to Killebrew (one out). Suttles triples over Sam Rice's head in center. Irvin grounds out to deep short, scoring Suttles (7-3). Dandridge flies out to Rice, ending the inning. **BB Stars 7, SenTwins 3.**

The score remains 7-3 until the bottom of the seventh. King Kelly leads off with a single to left that Charleston misplays, and Kelly hustles to second. Carew grounds out (slow chopper to Wells), and Kelly moves to third. Goslin flies out to Bell in deep center (sac fly) as Kelly scores. Killebrew walks. Tiant is warming up for the BB Stars. Allen robs Oliva of a base hit and throws him out to end the inning. **BB Stars 7, SenTwins 4.**

With one out in the bottom of the ninth, Carew walks, and Goslin gets his third hit (single to left-center). Carew moves to third. Tiant is brought in. Rogan's line is 8.3 IP, 11 H, 4 R, 1 ER, 0 HR, 3 K, 2 BB, 1 HB, and he is responsible for two runners on base. Tiant retires both Killebrew and Oliva on fly balls to save the win for Rogan.

	R	H	E	LOB
BB Stars	7	16	2	9
SenTwins	4	11	1	10

Winning Pitcher – Rogan;   Save – Tiant   Losing Pitcher – Kaat
The SenTwins lead the series, 2-1.

Game Four, Friday June 11, Atlanta County Stadium (Atlanta), 7 pm (Chance vs. Day)

Day walks Goslin to start the game. A hit-and-run single by Carew puts runners on the corners (none out). Day jams Frank Howard, forcing him to hit into a 5-4-3 double play as Goslin scores (1-0). Killebrew flies to right. **SenTwins 1, BB Stars 0.**

Cool Papa Bell singles to right. Bell steals second base. Lloyd grounds out to Johnson (second base); Bell moves to third. Charleston grounds out to Johnson as Bell scores the tying run. Gibson singles to left. Stearnes takes a called third strike. **BB Stars 1, SenTwins 1.**

Day escapes a one-out, two-on situation (first and second) by striking out Smalley and getting Chance to hit into an inning-ending force out.

Dean Chance is roughed up in the bottom of the second. Leonard triples off the wall in center. Dandridge hits one up the middle, but Smalley grabs it and throws him out as Leonard scores (one out). The next five batters (Allen, Day, Bell, Lloyd and Charleston) single for three more runs in the inning before Chance retires Gibson and Stearnes. **BB Stars 5, SenTwins 1.**

Chance is gone after four innings (4 IP, 8 H, 5 R, 0 HR, 3 K, 0 BB). Day strikes out Carew to end the top of the fifth, with two runners left on. Paul Galvin (46-game winner, Buffalo 1884) is now pitching in the bottom of the fifth. With one out, Gibson singles to center. Stearnes doubles off the wall in right as Gibson scores all the way from first (6-1). Galvin retires Leonard and Dandridge. **BB Stars 6, SenTwins 1.**

Frank Howard leads off the sixth with a home run. With one out, Oliva singles to center; Day hits Battey with a pitch (runners on first and second). Hilton Smith starts warming up for the BB Stars. Dave Johnson flies to right. Cecil Travis (1941) pinch hits for Smalley. Day uncorks a wild pitch, moving runners to second and third before retiring Travis on a ground ball to second (Allen). This was the SenTwins' last opportunity (only one batter reaches base in last three innings, Howard walked in eighth). Leon Day goes the distance (9 IP, 5 H, 2 R, 1 HR, 4 K, 4 BB, 1 HB).

	R	H	E	LOB
SenTwins	2	5	0	7
BB Stars	6	14	0	9

Winning Pitcher – Day   Losing Pitcher – Chance

The series is now tied, 2-2.

Game Five, Saturday June 12, Atlanta County Stadium (Atlanta), 1 pm (Johnson vs. Paige)

This is a rematch of Game One pitching greats Walter Johnson #1 vs. Satchel Paige #2 (ranking of Bill James). Johnson outpitched Paige in Game One, with a complete game win.

It is a warm, partly cloudy day. For the first five and one-half innings, Johnson and Paige are in a 0-0 tie. Johnson has had to escape more jams (BB Stars 6 men LOB). With one out in the sixth, Wells triples into the gap in left center. Mackey goes down swinging on a letter-high fast ball from the Big Train (Johnson) for the second out. Judy Johnson hits one off the wall in center for a double scoring Wells (1-0). Warfield slices one down the right field line, but King Kelly makes an outstanding sliding catch to end the inning. **BB Stars 1, SenTwins 0.**

Walter Johnson is lifted for a pinch hitter in the top of the ninth, trailing 1-0. Johnson's final line is 8 IP, 9 H, 1 R, 0 HR, 8 K, 1 BB. Paige fans Oliva (pinch hitter, one out), Paige's eighth K. King Kelly booms one to deep center, but Bell cannot reach it as it bounces off the wall. Kelly slides into third with a one-out triple. Travis hits a fly ball to Torriente (RF), and Kelly races home with the tying run (Travis sac fly). Goslin goes down swinging. **Sen-Twins 1, BB Stars 1.**

Jim Kern (1979 Rangers closer) relieves Walter Johnson in the bottom of the ninth and retires the side in order (Judy Johnson strikes out. Irvin pinch hits for Warfield and flies out to Goslin. Josh Gibson, pinch hitting for Paige, flies to right).

In the tenth, J. R. Richard replaces Paige (9 IP, 5 H. 1 R, 0 HR, 9 K, 1 BB). The SenTwins generate only a two-out walk.

In the bottom of the tenth, with one out, Torriente triples off the center field wall. The infield and outfield are pulled in. Kern walks Suttles (first and third). Turkey Stearnes goes down swinging (two outs). Lloyd bats for Wells, and he flies to right to end the inning.

Richard shuts down the SenTwins in the top of the eleventh. McCormick is pitching for the SenTwins in the bottom of the eleventh. The BB Stars do not score.

In the top of the twelfth, Hilton Smith is in to pitch for the BB Stars. Travis singles to center. Goslin flies to right (one out). Killebrew hits a slow bouncer to Judy Johnson (3B), who guns him down as Travis moves to second (two outs). Cronin grounds a base hit between Johnson and Lloyd. Travis races around third; Stearnes picks up the ball and fires to the plate. Travis slides in before Mackey can apply the tag, 2-1. Rice fans. **SenTwins 2, BB Stars 1.**

In the bottom of the twelfth, Charleston flies out to Kelly in deep right, Torriente grounds out to Stirnweiss (2B), and Suttles flies out to Goslin. The SenTwins win.

12 Innings	R	H	E	LOB
SenTwins	2	8	0	4
BB Stars	1	10	0	11

Winning Pitcher – McCormick   Losing Pitcher – Smith
The SenTwins lead the series, 3-2.

Game Six, Sunday June 12, Atlanta County Stadium (Atlanta), 1 pm (Perry vs. Foster)

This is the first game of a Sunday double header. It is delayed an hour by a passing thunderstorm. The game will be played on a wet field. King Kelly leads off with a triple that tips off Bell's glove in center. Kelly scores as Carew grounds out to Lloyd (SS). Foster retires Howard and Killebrew without the ball leaving the infield. **SenTwins 1, BB Stars 0.**

The game remains 1-0 until the BB Stars come to bat in the bottom of the sixth. Torriente bats for Bill Foster (6 IP, 3 H, 1 R, 0 HR, 1 K, 0 BB), who was brilliant. Torriente bounces back to Perry, who throws him out. Bell singles to center, then steals second. Lloyd doubles into the right field corner for a run-scoring double (1-1). Charleston walks. Stearnes hits a slow chopper, charged by Stirnweiss (2B), who throws him out as the runners advance to second and third. Leonard doubles into the gap in right center, scoring both runners (3-1). Leonard is 3 for 3. Mackey bounces out to Stirn-weiss. **BB Stars 3, Sen Twins 1.**

Luis Tiant replaces Foster in the top of the seventh. If Tiant holds the lead, Foster gets the win. Tiant retires the first two batters (Killebrew and Cronin). Rice singles to right. Tiant walks Stirnweiss. Oliva bats for Battey and flies out to Stearnes in right field. Oliva stays in the game and will play right field. King Kelly will switch from right field to catcher. Perry blanks the BB Stars in the seventh (one base runner reached on Killebrew error). Perry is done for the day (7 IP, 6 H, 3 R, 0 HR, 2 K, 1 BB). He did a fine job. In the bottom of the eighth, with one out, Galvin gives up three hits in a row (Charleston HR, Stearnes triple, Leonard's fourth hit, RBI single). He is replaced by Dutch Leonard, who gives up the fourth successive hit (Mackey single) before he retires Judy Johnson (K) and Allen (fly to center). **BB Stars 5, Sen Twins 1.**

In the ninth, Tiant gives up a lead-off double to Travis and retires the next three batters for a three-inning save.

	R	H	E	LOB
Sen Twins	1	5	1	5
BB Stars	5	10	0	6

Winning Pitcher – Foster   Save – Tiant   Losing Pitcher – Perry
The series is tied again, 3-3.

Game Seven, Sunday June 12, Atlanta County Stadium (Atlanta), 4 pm (Kaat vs. Rogan)

The second game of the doubleheader begins a little after four. In the bot-tom of the first with two outs, Wells is on second. Suttles is on first (both sin-gles) when Irvin lines a shot into the gap in left center that bounces off the fence as both runners score. Irvin is on third with a triple. Torriente lines out to Carew (1B). **BB Stars 2, Sen Twins 0.**

With one out in the top of the third, the Sen Twins get to Rogan. Kaat sin-gles to right. Kelly tops one that rolls past Rogan, and no one can make the play. Kelly is on with an infield single. Kaat is at second. Travis slams one over Bell's head that rolls to the fence scoring two, with Travis sliding safely into third with a triple (2-2). Carew tops one about six feet in front of the plate. Travis breaks for the plate; Gibson has only one play and throws Carew out at first (3-2). Goslin grounds out (Suttles to Rogan, covering first). **Sen Twins 3, BB Stars 2.**

In the bottom of the fourth inning, the BB Stars regain the lead off of Kaat. With one out, Kaat loads the bases (singles by Torriente and Dandridge and a walk to Warfield). Rogan, a good-hitting pitcher, lines a single to center, scoring two, Warfield stops at second (4-3). Bell flies out to deep center, and Wells forces Rogan at second. **BB Stars 4, SenTwins 3.**

Cronin pinch hits for Kaat in the fifth, but Rogan retires the side in order. Chance replaces Kaat in the bottom of the fifth and quickly retires the first two batters before Charleston, pinch hitting for Irvin, goes "yard" to make it 5-3. Torriente follows with a single. Dandridge doubles, but Rice guns Torriente out at home with a perfect throw to King Kelly at the plate for the out. **BB Stars 5, SenTwins 3.**

In the top of the seventh, Rice singles to left, and Dave Johnson smacks a 2-run home run to left, tying the game, 5-5. Rogan retires the next three batters, including pinch hitter Staub, batting for Chance. **BB Stars 5, SenTwins 5.**

McCormick comes in to pitch for the SenTwins in the bottom of the seventh and retires the side in order. Killebrew leads off the eighth with a walk. Killebrew entered the game in the fifth after Travis was ejected on a close play at first base. Moore replaces Rogan. Carew hits Moore's first pitch over the wall in right, and the SenTwins lead 7-5. Rogan's final line is 7+ IP, 7 H, 6 R, 1 HR, 1 K, 3 BB. Goslin doubles down the right-field line. Oliva is walked intentionally. J. R. Richard replaces Moore. On the hit-and-run, Goslin steals third, and Oliva is thrown out at second (one out). Rice fans (two outs). Richard walks Dave Johnson. Stirnweiss runs for Johnson. Smalley slaps a single to right, scoring Goslin. Stirnweiss stops at second. Frank Howard bats for McCormick and strikes out. **SenTwins 8, BB Stars 5.**

Walter Johnson is coming out of the bullpen to try to hold off the BB Stars. Charleston greets him with a double off the wall in right. Torriente grounds out to Stirnweiss (2B, one out). Charleston advances to third. Johnson strikes out Dandridge, swinging (two outs). Allen bats for Warfield, and Johnson strikes Allen out, looking to end the inning.

The SenTwins do not score in the top of the ninth; it is up to Walter Johnson to hold off the BB Stars. He strikes out Stearnes (third strikeout in a row, one out). Johnson hits Bell. Wells doubles into right center as Bell comes around to score (8-6). Suttles represents the tying run at the plate. He bounces one to third; Killebrew charges in, picks it up, and throws out Suttles. Wells moves to third. Josh Gibson steps to the plate. The count goes to 2-2. Gibson hits a one-hopper to Killebrew, who throws him out. Game over. Walter Johnson gets the save.

	R	H	E	LOB
SenTwins	8	11	0	5
BB Stars	6	12	0	6

Winning Pitcher – McCormick   Save – W. Johnson   Losing Pitcher – Rogan
The SenTwins lead the series, 4-3.

Game Eight, Tuesday June 15, Metrodome (Minneapolis), 7 pm (Day vs. Pennock)

The SenTwins lead the series, 4-3. The BB Stars are going with Leon Day, who pitched a complete game 6-2 win (Game Three). The SenTwins will go with free agent Herb Pennock (1924 Yankees). He has not seen any action in this series. The last two games of this nine-game series will be played indoors on Astroturf.

Pennock quickly runs into trouble. Bell doubles to right center. Wells bloops one into left center for a single as Bell races home with the first run. Pennock escapes with only a two-out single by Suttles but no more scoring. **BB Stars 1, SenTwins 0.**

Day continues where he left off in Game Three, giving up one hit in the first two innings but no threats. With two out in the top of the third, Charleston homers to right (2-0). Gibson grounds out to short. **BB Stars 2, SenTwins 0.**

In the top of the fifth, with one out, Day helps himself out with a double into the right center field gap. Bell singles Day home (3-0). Bell steals second. Killebrew makes a good play on a slow grounder by Wells and throws him out. Bell moves to third. Charleston goes down swinging to end the inning. **BB Stars 3, SenTwins 0.**

In the bottom of the fifth, Sam Rice singles (second hit off Day). Stirnweiss flies out to Bell (CF, one out). Earl Battey hits a hard one-hopper to Wells (SS), who turns it into a 6-4-3 double play.

The SenTwins make defensive changes to start the sixth inning. Battey is lifted as catcher. Kelly moves in from right field to catch. Free agent Mel Stottlemyre (1965 Yankees) replaces Pennock and will bat eighth. Oliva goes to right field and will bat ninth. Pennock did not pitch that badly (5 IP, 6 H, 3 R, 1 HR, 5 K, 0 BB). In the top of the seventh with two out, none on, Bell singles to right (his third hit). Wells doubles off the wall in center; Bell comes around to score (4-0). Charleston grounds out. **BB Stars 4, SenTwins 0.**

Goslin doubles to lead-off the seventh for the SenTwins. Day retires the next three batters on ground balls; Goslin gets as far as third base but does not score.

Day retires the side in order in the eighth. As Leon Day takes the mound in the ninth, he leads 4-0. He has given up 3 hits and hit a batter, facing three men over the minimum. Hilton Smith is ready in the bullpen. King Kelly leads off the bottom of the ninth with a single to left field. Travis pops out to Allen, who had pinched hit for Warfield in the seventh (one out). Day walks Carew; runners are on first and second (the first time the SenTwins have had two base runners on in an inning).

Day looks in for the sign; both runners take a good lead. Day fires as both runners break on a hit-and-run. Goslin lines the ball to right center, and Irvin dives. Did he catch it? No, it rolls a few feet away. Irvin picks up the ball and fires to third base. Goslin has turned second, headed for third, and he slides into the bag; Kelly and Carew are also on the bag. Judy Johnson looks at the umpire and tags Kelly (umpire gives the safe sign). He tags Carew (out) and Goslin (out). The game is over. Three SenTwins end up on third. It is the first time in the game the SenTwins had three base runners in an inning. What happened? It appears after Kelly turned third, he slipped on the turf and did not think he could make it home and retreated to third. Carew was sliding into third, thinking Kelly had gone home. Goslin, confident that both runners would score, believed he could get to third safely, and he did. However, you can only have one man on a base. Leon Day, who was backing up third, could not believe his good fortune.

	R	H	E	LOB
BB Stars	4	12	0	9
SenTwins	0	5	0	4

Winning Pitcher – Day   Losing Pitcher – Pennock
The series is tied, 4-4.

Game Nine, Wednesday June 16, Metrodome (Minneapolis), 7 pm (Paige vs. Johnson)

The key to this series, so far, is that Walter Johnson has had the edge over Satchel Paige, and Walter Johnson saved another game. Whoever has the edge in this game between these two great pitchers probably determines the series.

The BB Stars draw first blood in the first inning. With two outs and Bell on first (walk), Stearnes drives the ball over Rice's head that rolls to the wall in center, scoring Bell. Stearnes ends up on third with a triple. Leonard bounces one to third that glances off Killebrew's glove into short left field (error) as Stearnes scores the second run. Mackey fans to end the inning. **BB Stars 2, SenTwins 0.**

Paige singles in a third run in the second inning. The SenTwins get one back in the bottom of the second with two singles (Goslin and Killebrew) and Rice reaching on a fielder's choice (Killebrew force out at second base) as Goslin scores from third. Stirnweiss raps into a 6-4-3 double play. **BB Stars 3, SenTwins 1.**

In the bottom of the fifth inning, the SenTwins tie it up. Killebrew singles, and Rice walks to start the rally. Stirnweiss lines a double (just fair) down the left field line to score Killebrew and send Rice to third (3-2). Oliva flies out to shallow center, and the runners hold (one out). Walter Johnson is not bunting. He grounds one to the right side, and Allen throws him out as Rice scores, and Stirnweiss goes to third. Kelly goes down swinging. **SenTwins 3, BB Stars 3.**

In the top of the sixth, Stearnes crushes a Johnson fast ball for a home run over the right field fence (bag), 4-3. Johnson strikes out three of the next four batters (Leonard, Dandridge, and Allen around a Mackey single). **BB Stars 4, SenTwins 3.**

The score remains the same when Satchel Paige comes out to pitch the bottom of the eighth. Rusty Staub will bat for Johnson (8 IP, 5 H, 4 R, 3 ER, 1 HR, 7 K, 1 BB). Can Paige hold on to finally beat Walter Johnson? Staub flies to right (one out). Paige strikes out King Kelly swinging (two outs). Travis lines one off the wall in right center and goes in to second with a stand-up double. The BB Stars make a pitching change; lefty Bill Foster comes in with two tough left-handed batters due up (Carew and Goslin). Suttles comes in to play first base and bat ninth. Foster will bat in Leonard's spot, fifth in the order. Carew hits one up the middle past Foster into center field as Travis comes around to score the tying run (4-4). The final line on Paige is 7.7 IP, 6 H, 4 R, 0 HR, 3 K, 1 BB. Goslin forces Carew at second to end the inning. **SenTwins 4, BB Stars 4.**

The BB Stars are trying to win their fifth consecutive nine-game series. In the first two series against the Braves/Pirates and Browns/Orioles, the BB Stars trailed four games to three before coming back to win both series. They also trailed the SenTwins four games to three, when Game Eight had the bizarre ending with three SenTwins all ending up on third base to end the game. Can they make it five in a row?

Jim Kern, the hard-throwing free agent (1979 Rangers), is in to pitch the ninth. It does not start well, as Mackey doubles off the baggy in right field. Dandridge lines one into the gap in left center, but Sam Rice makes a diving catch, and Mackey scampers back to second (one out). Allen hits a two-hopper to Killebrew at third. Killebrew looks Mackey back to second and guns out Allen at first (two outs). Kern blows a fast ball past the hard swing of Mule Suttles, ending the inning.

J. R. Richard is coming in to pitch for the BB Stars. He retires the Sen-Twins in order with two Ks (Rice and Stirnweiss). **SenTwins 4, BB Stars 4.**

In the top of the tenth, Bell bounces out to Stirnweiss. Lloyd pops one up into shallow right field; Oliva is racing in, but Stirnweiss (2B) dives and makes an outstanding catch to rob Lloyd of a possible double. Kern pitches too care-fully to Oscar Charleston, and he walks him. The dangerous Turkey Stearnes comes to the plate. He triples, driving in a run in the first inning. He flies out to Oliva in deep right (third inning). He homers in the sixth and bounces out to Carew at first in the eighth inning. Kern's 2-2 pitch is strike three called.

In the bottom of the tenth, Richard retires his fourth batter in a row as Oliva hits a one-hopper to Suttles, who makes the putout unassisted (one out). Frank Howard will bat for Kern (two shutout innings of relief). Richard walks him on four pitches. Cronin will run for Howard. Richard goes to 3-2 on King Kelly, and the pitch is way high, ball four. Runners are now on first and second (one out). Hilton Smith is warming up. The first pitch to Travis is lined to deep right center, hitting off the base of the wall. It is a walk-off, series-winning double for Travis. The SenTwins are the first team to down the BB Stars in the Best Season tournament!

Ten Innings	R	H	E	LOB
BB Stars	4	6	0	6
SenTwins	5	8	2	5

Winning Pitcher – Kern Losing Pitcher – Richard
Senators/Twins win the series 5-4.

Recap of Best Season Series 5 (BB Stars vs. SenTwins)

The SenTwins scored 28 fewer runs than the Reds (34-62) in Series 4 and 41 fewer runs than the BB Stars in Series 4. They also scored nine fewer runs than the BB Stars (34-43) in this Series 5, but they were the first opponent to defeat the BB Stars, winning the series 5-4. Chart 10-2 on page 121 has BB Stars individual/team statistics for this series. Chart 10-3 on page 122 has Senators/Twins individual/team statistics for this series.

The turning point of the series - The SenTwins were 5-0 in 1-run and 2-run games. They were 0-4 in 3- and 4-run games.

MVP of Series – Walter Johnson appeared in four games (three starts, one close). The SenTwins won all four games (80% of their wins). He out-pitched Satchel Paige with one win and one save to Paige's one loss; three quality starts to one; 2.67 ERA vs. 3.97; 27 IP to 22.7 IP; K:BB/HB ratio Johnson 5.75:1 vs.Paige 3.75:1.

BB Stars Results vs. Senators/Twins 4-5, .444

Pos.	E	R	TH	PB	Hitters	G	AB	R	H	RBI	2B	3B	HR	TB	W	HB	SO	SF	SH	SB	B.AVG.	OBP	S.PCT.	OPS
LF	5	A	-1		Charleston	9	37	5	9	7	1	0	4	22	4	0	5	0	0	0	0.243	0.317	0.595	0.912
CF	8	AA	-1		CP Bell	8	33	6	10	2	2	0	1	11	2	0	7	0	0	3	0.303	0.343	0.333	0.676
OF	5	A	-1		Stearnes	7	25	3	7	5	2	2	1	16	0	0	5	0	0	0	0.280	0.280	0.640	0.920
OF	6	B	-2		M Irvin	5	15	0	4	3	0	1	0	6	2	0	2	0	0	0	0.267	0.353	0.400	0.753
OF	6	A	-1		Torriente	5	15	3	7	0	0	2	0	11	1	0	2	0	0	0	0.467	0.500	0.733	1.233
SS	7	A			P Lloyd	7	27	2	8	2	4	0	0	12	0	0	0	0	0	0	0.296	0.296	0.444	0.741
SS	7	AA			W Wells	4	15	4	8	4	1	0	2	13	2	0	2	0	0	0	0.533	0.588	0.867	1.455
3B	7	A			J Johnson	4	18	1	5	2	1	0	1	9	0	0	4	0	0	0	0.278	0.278	0.500	0.778
3B	6	B			Dandridge	5	21	4	6	2	1	0	0	7	0	0	1	0	0	0	0.286	0.286	0.333	0.619
2B	7	A			N Allen	9	23	3	7	1	0	0	0	7	3	0	4	0	0	1	0.304	0.385	0.304	0.689
2B	7	A			F Warfield	3	10	2	3	0	1	0	0	4	1	0	0	0	0	0	0.300	0.364	0.400	0.764
1B	7	A			Suttles	6	24	3	8	2	0	1	1	13	1	0	6	1	0	0	0.333	0.36	0.542	0.902
1B	8	B			B Leonard	6	17	1	5	3	1	0	0	8	1	0	1	0	0	0	0.294	0.333	0.471	0.804
C	7	A	-2	Fr	J Gibson	7	27	2	8	1	1	1	0	11	0	0	4	0	0	0	0.296	0.296	0.407	0.704
C	6	B	-2	Aw	B Mackey	4	14	0	4	0	0	0	0	4	0	0	4	0	0	0	0.286	0.286	0.286	0.571
					pitchers	9	27	3	7	5	1	0	0	8	0	0	7	1	0	0	0.259	0.259	0.296	0.556
					TOTAL	9	348	42	106	36	15	10	7	158	17	0	54	1	0	4	0.305	0.337	0.454	0.791

Fat.	H	WP	E	R	Pitchers	G	GS	QS	CG	S	W	L	IP	H	SO	BB	HB	HR	R	ER	ERA
10/L	Vg	N	9	B	BJ Rogan	2	2	1	0	0	0	1	15.3	18	4	5	1	1	7	10	3.50
9/L	Ex	R	7	B	B Foster	3	2	1	0	0	1	0	9.3	9	7	5	0	1	5	5	4.82
10/L	Vg	NL	8	B	L Day	2	2	2	0	2	0	2	18	10	2	5	2	0	2	2	1.00
10/L	Aw	NL	7	B	M Dihigo	1	0	0	0	0	0	0	3	4	2	0	1	2	2	2	6.00
8/L	Md	R	8	C	S Paige	3	3	1	0	0	0	0	22.7	19	15	4	0	0	10	10	3.97
L/9	Vg	R	8	A	H Smith	2	0	0	0	0	0	0	1.7	5	2	0	0	0	2	2	10.79
9/L	Av	R	9	A	Newcombe	0	0	0	0	0	2	0	0	0	0	0	0	0	0	0	0.00
10/L	Ex	NL	8	D	L Tiant	3	0	0	0	0	0	0	5.7	3	4	1	0	0	0	0	0.00
9	Av	N	5	C	JR Richard	4	0	0	0	0	0	0	7.3	4	7	4	0	0	1	2	1.23
Long	Md	NL	4	B	D Moore	1	0	0	0	0	0	0	0	2	1	0	0	1	2	2	0.00
			9		TOTAL	21	9	5	0	2	2	4	83	74	43	20	3	5	34	31	3.36

Chart 10-2 – BB Stars Statistics for this series

Senator/TwinsRoster Best Season vs. BB All-Stars 5.4, .556

Team	Year	WS	Hitters	G	AB	R	H	RBI	2B	3B	HR	TB	W	HB	SO	SF	SH	SB	B.AVG.	OBP	S.PCT.	OPS
Montreal	1969	27	R Staub	5	8	1	2	2	0	0	1	5	0	0	1	1	0	0	0.250	0.250	0.625	0.875
Minnesota	1964	27	T Oliva	9	24	3	3	0	0	0	0	3	1	0	3	0	0	0	0.125	0.16	0.125	0.285
Washington	1920	23	S Rice	9	30	2	7	2	2	0	0	7	3	0	3	0	0	0	0.233	0.303	0.233	0.536
Buffalo	1884	25	O'Rourke	3	3	0	0	0	0	0	0	0	0	0	0	0	0	0	0.000	0.000	0.000	0.000
Washington	1928	28	G Goslin	9	30	5	10	1	2	0	1	14	2	0	5	0	1	2	0.333	0.375	0.467	0.842
Washington	1969	34	F Howard	6	11	2	4	3	0	0	1	7	2	0	1	1	0	0	0.364	0.462	0.636	1.098
Washington	1930	33	J Cronin	4	14	2	3	2	1	0	0	4	0	0	3	0	0	0	0.214	0.214	0.286	0.500
Minnesota	1979	24	R Smalley	3	6	0	2	1	0	1	0	3	0	0	1	0	0	0	0.333	0.333	0.500	0.833
Minnesota	1969	34	H Killebrew	9	31	5	5	5	0	0	1	8	2	1	7	0	0	0	0.161	0.235	0.258	0.493
New York A	1941	34	C Travis	9	27	5	11	4	3	2	0	18	2	0	1	2	0	0	0.407	0.448	0.667	1.115
Atlanta	1944	35	Stirmweiss	8	22	1	3	1	1	0	0	4	1	0	6	0	0	0	0.136	0.174	0.182	0.356
Minnesota	1973	21	D Johnson	8	9	3	3	2	0	0	1	6	2	0	2	0	0	0	0.333	0.455	0.667	1.121
Minnesota	1977	37	R Carew	8	32	2	6	6	1	0	0	10	1	1	2	0	0	0	0.188	0.235	0.313	0.548
Minnesota	1963	20	E Battey	4	10	0	2	2	0	0	0	2	1	1	5	0	0	0	0.200	0.333	0.200	0.533
Chicago N	1886	35	K Kelly	7	30	6	11	0	1	2	2	16	2	0	4	0	1	2	0.367	0.424	0.533	0.958
			pitchers	9	13	0	1	3	0	0	0	1	0	0	4	0	1	0	0.077	0.077	0.077	0.154
			TOTAL		300	33	73	34	10	4	5	108	20	3	45	3	1	4	0.243	0.297	0.360	0.657

Team	Year	WS	Pitchers	G	GS	QS	CG	S	W	L	IP	H	SO	BB	HB	HR	R	ER	ERA
Washington	1913	54	W Johnson	4	3	3	1	0	1	1	27	25	23	4	1	1	10	8	2.67
Cleveland	1883	40	McCormick	3	1	0	0	0	0	2	8	11	4	4	0	2	5	5	5.63
Minnesota	1966	26	J Kaat	3	1	0	0	0	0	0	8.3	16	7	2	0	1	10	7	7.56
LA (A)	1964	32	D Chance	3	1	0	0	0	0	0	6.3	11	5	1	0	1	6	6	8.53
Buffalo	1884	57	P Galvin	2	0	0	0	0	0	0	2.3	7	1	0	0	0	3	3	11.59
Cleveland	1972	39	G Perry	3	1	1	1	0	0	0	11	13	3	2	0	1	4	4	3.27
New York A	1965	23	Stottlemyre	3	0	0	0	0	0	0	7	9	4	1	0	0	2	2	2.57
New York A	1924	23	H Pennock	1	0	0	0	1	0	0	5	6	5	0	0	1	3	3	5.40
Washington	1939	21	D Leonard	3	0	0	0	0	0	1	3	5	4	0	0	0	0	0	0.00
Texas	1979	25	J Kern	3	0	0	0	1	0	0	5	3	4	0	0	0	0	0	0.00
			TOTAL	28	9	4	1	1	1	5	83	106	61	16	1	7	43	38	4.12

Chart 10-3 – Senators/Twins statistics for this series

Hitting Star for the SenTwins - Cecil Travis (1941 Senators)

	RS	RBI	HR	.Avg	OBP	SPct	OPS
C. Travis	5	5	0	.407	.448	.667	1.115

Hitting Star for the BB Stars - Oscar Charleston

	RS	RBI	HR	.AVG	OBP	SPct	OPS
O. Charleston	5	7	4	.243	.317	.595	.912

Best Pitcher for the BB Stars – Leon Day

	G	GS	QS	CG	W-L	IP	H	HR	R/ER	ERA
L. Day	2	2	2	2	2-0	18	10	1	2	1.00

Chapter 11

Best Season Nine Game Series 6 - BB Stars vs.Phillies

Phillies Roster Review

SIXTY PERCENT OF THE ROSTER ARE MADE up of Philadelphia Phillies. Forty percent of the roster are free agents. See the Phillies Roster (Chart 11-1 on page 126).

Offensive Leaders (Phillies) Ranked by OPS

Player	OBP	SPct	OPS	R +	RBI -	HR =	NR
C. Klein	.436	.687	1.123	158	170	40	288
D. Allen	.398	.632	1.030	112	110	40	182
M. Schmidt	.388	.624	1.012	104	121	48	177
E. Flick	.437	.545	,982	106	110	11	205
C. Anson	.436	.544	.980	117	147	10	258
G. Cravath	.403	.568	.971	78	128	19	187
J. Fournier	.421	.536	.957	93	116	27	182
A. Seminick	. .393	.524	.917	55	68	24	99
C. Childs	.466	.446	.912	106	106	1	211
B. Grich	.366	.537	.903	78	101	30	149

The following players would be base-stealing threats – M. Ward 111, Glasscock 57, Flick 35, Ashburn 30, Anson 29, and Childs 25 (numbers listed SB for their best season).

Fielding Leaders	Pos	Range	Error	Throwing
R. Ashburn	CF	AA	7	-1
C. Klein	RF	AA	4	-3
E. Flick	L/RF	A	4	0
S. Magee	LF	A	4	0
G. Cravath	RF	B	4	-4

For outfielders - range (AA is best) and throwing (-4 is exceptional, -3 is excellent, -2 is very good) are most important. Error rating (10 is best, 1 is poor) is not as critical as infielders because outfielders normally do not make as many errors.

M. Ward	SS	AA+	6	-
J. Glasscock	SS	AA	5	-
M. Schmidt	3B	AA	6	-
C. Childs	2B	AA	5	-
B. Grich	2B	A+	8	-
J. Fournier	1B	A	5	
C. Anson	1B	A	5	

For infielders, range (AA is best), + increase in DPs because of excellent pivot, error rating is as important as range (10 is excellent, 1 is poor).

Catcher Throwing - Boone and Seminick are average (0).

Pitcher Hold Rating - Carlton, McGraw, and Quisenberry are excellent (less successful steal attempts). Alexander, Caldwell, Foutz, and Davis are very good. Bunning and Roberts are average. M. Scott is mediocre (more successful steal attempts).

PhilliesRoster Best Season Series vs. BB All-Stars

Team	Year	WS Hitters	G	AB	R	H	RBI	2B	3B	HR	TB	W	HB	SO	SF	SH	SB	B.AVG.	OBP	S.PCT.	OPS
Philadelphia	1930	28 C Klein	156	648	158	250	170	59	8	40	445	54	4	50	-	-	4	0.386	0.436	0.687	1.123
Philadelphia	1913	29 G Cravath	147	525	78	179	128	34	14	19	298	55	0	63	-	-	10	0.341	0.403	0.568	0.971
Philadelphia	1900	32 E Flick	138	545	106	200	110	32	16	11	297	56	12	30	-	-	35	0.367	0.437	0.545	0.982
Philadelphia	1958	28 R Ashburn	152	615	98	215	33	24	13	2	271	97	4	48	-	-	30	0.350	0.441	0.441	0.882
Philadelphia	1914	29 S Magee	146	544	96	171	103	39	11	15	277	55	3	42	-	-	25	0.314	0.380	0.509	0.890
Indianapolis	1889	27 JGlasscock	134	582	128	205	85	40	3	7	272	31	6	10	-	-	57	0.352	0.391	0.467	0.858
New York N	1887	25 M Ward	129	537	114	184	53	16	5	1	213	29	-	12	-	-	111	0.343	0.377	0.397	0.774
Philadelphia	1980	37 M Schmidt	150	548	104	157	121	25	8	48	342	89	2	119	-	-	12	0.286	0.388	0.624	1.012
Philadelphia	1966	35 D Allen	141	524	112	166	110	25	10	40	331	68	3	136	-	-	10	0.317	0.398	0.632	1.030
Cleveland N	1896	27 C Childs	132	498	106	177	106	24	9	1	222	100	3	18	-	-	25	0.355	0.466	0.446	0.912
California	1979	28 B Grich	153	534	78	157	101	30	5	30	287	59	2	84	-	-	1	0.294	0.366	0.537	0.904
Chicago (N)	1886	30 C Anson	125	504	117	187	147	35	11	10	274	55	3	19	-	-	29	0.371	0.436	0.544	0.980
Brooklyn	1924	34 J Fournier	154	563	93	188	116	25	4	27	302	83	2	46	-	-	7	0.334	0.421	0.536	0.958
Philadelphia	1978	17 B Boone	132	435	48	123	62	18	4	12	185	46	1	37	-	-	2	0.283	0.353	0.425	0.778
Philadelphia	1950	22 A Seminick	130	393	55	113	68	15	3	24	206	68	0	50	-	-	0	0.288	0.393	0.524	0.917

Team	Year	WS Pitchers	G	GS	QS	CG	S	W	L	IP	H	SO	BB	HB	HR	R	ER	ERA
Philadelphia	1915	43 GAlexander	49	42	-	36	3	31	10	376	253	241	64	-	3	-	-	1.22
Philadelphia	1972	40 S Carlton	41	41	-	30	0	27	10	346	257	310	87	-	17	-	-	1.97
Philadelphia	1952	32 R Roberts	39	37	-	30	2	28	7	330	292	148	45	-	22	-	-	2.59
St. Louis AA	1886	62 D Foutz	59	57	-	55	1	41	16	504	418	283	144	-	5	-	-	2.11
Houston	1986	27 M Scott	37	37	-	7	0	18	10	275	182	306	72	-	17	-	-	2.22
Philadelphia	1967	25 J Bunning	40	40	-	16	0	17	15	302	241	253	73	-	18	-	-	2.29
Milwaukee A	1978	28 M Caldwell	37	34	-	23	1	22	9	293	258	131	54	-	14	-	-	2.36
Philadelphia	1934	24 C Davis	51	31	-	18	5	19	17	274	283	60	99	-	14	-	-	2.95
Philadelphia	1980	18 T McGraw	57	0	0	-	20	5	4	92	62	75	23	-	3	-	-	1.46
Kansas City	1983	28 Quisenberry	69	0	0	-	45	5	3	139	118	48	11	-	6	-	-	1.94

Chart 11-1 – Phillies Best Season Roster

Pitching - Four excellent starters in Alexander, Carlton, Roberts, and Scott and two great closers in Quisenberry and McGraw lead a solid pitching staff.

Game One, Friday June 18, Shibe Park (Philadelphia), 7 pm (Tiant vs. Alexander)

It is a warm, cloudy evening at Shibe Park. Pete Alexander (1915 Phillies) will face Cool Papa Bell, Pop Lloyd, and Oscar Charleston in the first inning of Game One of this nine-game series. Alexander and Tiant (free agent, 1968 Indians) will probably face each other three times. Alexander does not start well. Bell homers over the right field fence to start the game. Lloyd doubles into the gap in left center. Charleston flies out to Klein in short right field (one out). Leonard lines a single to right. Klein fields the ball on a one-hop and fires toward the plate. Lloyd takes the turn at third and holds. He has tremendous respect for Klein's throwing arm (-3). Alexander goes to 2-2 count with Cristobal Torriente. He wants to keep this to a 1-run inning. Alexander winds and throws; strike three called (a slow curve catches the outside corner for the second out). Torriente glares back at the umpire as he heads back to the dugout. Biz Mackey hits a hard shot between first and second; Cupid Childs (free agent, 1896 Cleveland N) dives and catches the ball on the short hop and throws Mackey out while still on his knees. It is a great run-saving play. **BB Stars 1, Phillies 0.**

In the bottom of the second, the Phillies tie the score. Tiant strikes out Schmidt, walks Fournier (free agent, 1924 Dodgers), then strikes out Seminick (1950 Phillies) for the second out. Ward hits a shot off the base of the fence in right center for a double as Fournier zooms around to score the tying run. Alexander pops one up into shallow left field, and Lloyd, with his back to the plate, makes a great catch to end the inning. **Phillies 1, BB Stars 1.**

In the third, Lloyd leads off with a single to center off Alexander. Charleston bounces one to Monte Ward (SS), who tries to play it on the short hop. But the ball runs up his arm for an error (runners on first and second, none out). Leonard bounces a ball over Alexander's head, but Ward grabs it and throws out Leonard as the runners advance (one out). Torriente hits a fly to right center. Klein makes the catch as Lloyd tags up and scores (unearned run). Mackey flies out to Flick (LF). **BB Stars 2, Phillies 1.**

With two outs in the bottom of the fourth, Andy Seminick homers to left (2-2). Lloyd makes a great play on a smash up the middle to rob Ward of a hit. **Phillies 2, BB Stars 2.**

In the top of the fifth, Lloyd doubles down the right field line. Charleston strikes out swinging (one out). Leonard grounds out to Childs (2B) as Lloyd moves over to third (two outs). Torriente lines a single into right center, scoring Lloyd. Mackey flies out to Flick. **BB Stars 3, Phillies 2.**

The score remains 3-2 until the top of the seventh, two out, no one on base. Alexander knows this is his last inning, trailing 3-2 and due up in the bottom of the seventh. The count goes to 3-2 on Charleston (Alexander has not walked a batter). Charleston is looking fast ball all the way. He gets one on the inside corner and hits a tremendous home run (just fair) over the fence in right field. Ashburn ends the inning by robbing Buck Leonard of an extra base hit with a diving catch. The final line for Alexander is 7 IP, 9 H, 4 R, 3 ER, 2 HR, 6 K, 0 BB. **BB Stars 4, Phillies 2.**

Suttles has gone in as a defensive replacement for Leonard (Suttles A Range, Leonard B Range). Tiant retires the side in order (Anson pinch hitting for Alexander flies out). In the top of the eighth, the left-hander Caldwell (free agent, 1978 Brewers AL) is now pitching. Torriente singles up the middle. Mackey (batting right-handed) flies out to Flick (LF), one out. Right-hander Curt Davis (1934 Phillies) is coming in to pitch to Judy Johnson; he flies out to Klein (RF), two outs. Newt Allen (switch hitter) will bat left-handed against Davis. They could walk him to pitch to Tiant. The decision is to pitch to Allen, and he launches a double off the wall in right. Torriente comes around to score (5-2). Tiant goes down swinging. **BB Stars 5, Phillies 2.**

That ends the scoring. Tiant gives up a lead-off double to Childs in the bottom of the eighth and retires the final six men in a row (4 Ks). The final line for Tiant is 9 IP, 6 H, 2 R, 1 HR, 7 K, 2 BB).

	R	H	E	LOB
BB Stars	5	12	1	9
Phillies	2	6	1	6

Winning Pitcher – Tiant   Losing Pitcher – Alexander
The BB Stars lead the series, 1-0.

Game Two, Saturday June 19, Shibe Park (Philadelphia), 1 pm (Foster vs. Carlton)

It is a hot, clear day in Philadelphia. Steve Carlton (1972 Phillies, 27-10 for a terrible Phillies team, 59-103) retires the first two batters, then Gibson triples off the wall in center field. Stearnes singles to right; Gibson scores (1-0). Suttles hits a high fly ball to left field; Sherry Magee (1914 Phillies) tracks it down on the edge of the warning track. **BB Stars 1, Phillies 0.**

In the top of the fourth, Carlton fans Stearnes (swinging). Suttles doubles off the wall in left center. Irvin pops out to Dick Allen (3B). Johnson bloops one into left field that drops in front of Magee for a single, as Suttles races home (2-0). Carlton walks Warfield. Foster goes down swinging for the second time. **BB Stars 2, Phillies 0.**

With one out, Gabby Cravath (1913 Phillies) triples over Bell's head in center field. Klein bounces out to Newt Allen (2B) on the edge of the outfield grass, and Cravath scores (2-1). Dick Allen (1966 Phillies) flies out to Cool Papa Bell (CF). **BB Stars 2, Phillies 1.**

In the bottom of the fifth, Bobby Grich (1979 Angels) singles to left field. Magee chops one to Wells (SS), who underhands to Allen (2B) for the force on Grich. It appears that Grich has been hurt on the play. He is helped off the field. He is definitely favoring his right leg. He may have jammed his leg trying to beat the throw.

Foster falls behind Bob Boone (1978 Phillies), 3-0 and throws a fast ball right down the middle. Boone hits one to deep left; it is going, going, and gone for a 2-run home run. Phillies take the lead, 3-2. Boone was given the green light, and he crushed that ball. Carlton hits a high fly to right; Stearnes loses the ball in the sun, and it lands behind him. Carlton hustles to second with a sun-assisted double. There is still only one out, and the top of the order is coming up for the Phillies. Hilton Smith is beginning to throw in the BB Stars bullpen. Glasscock hits a smash that Warfield dives and knocks down. He still manages to throw out Glasscock as Carlton moves to third (two outs). Anson hits a one-hopper to Judy Johnson (3B), who throws him out. **Phillies 3, BB Stars 2.**

Childs has replaced Grich at second base. The preliminary report on Grich is he jammed his foot and ankle and could possibly miss a couple of games. Mule Suttles hits Carlton's first pitch over the left field fence (3-3). Carlton walks off the mound and plants his hands on his hips. He is obviously upset with his pitch location. Carlton bears down and retires the next three batters – Irvin and Johnson strike out. Warfield grounds out. **BB Stars 3, Phillies 3.**

In the bottom of the sixth, Cravath gets his second hit of the game (single to right). Klein flies out to Stearnes (RF). Dick Allen takes a called third strike (two outs). Childs walks, and Hilton Smith is coming in to relieve Foster with runners on first and second. Newt Allen also comes in to replace Warfield (double switch). Mike Schmidt is coming out to bat for Magee. Schmidt lofts a lazy fly ball to Bell (CF) for out number three.

In the top of the seventh, the Phillies are making some defensive changes. Schmidt stays in the game and replaces Dick Allen at 3B. Flick will replace Magee in LF and bat in Allen's slot, fifth. Ashburn replaces Cravath and will play CF, while Klein moves from CF to RF. Carlton retires Newt Allen (batting ninth) and Charleston on ground balls to Glasscock (SS). Wells doubles into the left field corner. The decision is to walk Gibson intentionally. Carlton jams Stearnes, who flies out to Klein in short right field.

In the bottom of the seventh, Boone leads off with his second home run in as many at bats (4-3). Smith gets out of the inning with no further scoring. Ashburn flies out to Stearnes on the warning track in right to end the inning (Anson was on first base with a two out walk). **Phillies 4, BB Stars 3.**

In the top of the eighth, Suttles reaches on first baseman Anson's error. With three right-handed batters to follow, Quisenberry replaces Carlton. Quisenberry retires the next three batters, including Leonard batting for Smith. The final line for Steve Carlton is 7+ IP, 8 H, 3 R, 1 HR, 8 K, 2 BB. **Phillies 4, BB Stars 3.**

J. R. Richard is in to pitch for the BB Stars. He does not help himself; he misplays Klein's ground ball for an error. Flick bounces out to Allen (2B) as Klein moves to second base. Childs singles to left, scoring Klein with an unearned insurance run. Richard retires Schmidt and Boone to end the inning. **Phillies 5, BB Stars 3.**

Newt Allen leads off the ninth with a single to center. Charleston puts a scare into the home crowd when he launches a shot to deep center. On the warning track, Ashburn makes the catch (one out). Pop Lloyd pinch hits for Wells and raps into a game-ending double play (4-6-3).

	R	H	E	LOB
BB Stars	3	9	1	7
Phillies	5	7	1	6

Winning Pitcher – Carlton   Save – Quisenberry   Losing Pitcher – Smith
The series is tied, 1-1.

Game Three, Sunday June 20, Skydome (Toronto), Noon (Roberts vs. Paige)

This is the first game of a double header. It is cloudy in Toronto, and the roof is closed. With one out in the top of the first, the Phillies get to Paige. Ashburn doubles to the wall in left center. Klein launches a long home run to right before Paige retires Schmidt and Fournier. **Phillies 2, BB Stars 0.**

The BB Stars quickly get one back. Bell singles. Lloyd doubles off the wall in left, and Bell scores from first (2-1). Roberts fans Stearnes and Gibson. Leonard grounds out to Childs (2B). **Phillies 2, BB Stars 1.**

Roberts and Paige throw blanks through the next four innings. In the top of the sixth, Klein hits another home run (3-1). **Phillies 3, BB Stars 1.**

In the top of the eighth, with one out, the Phillies threaten to add to their lead. Klein gets his third hit with a single to center. Schmidt hits one through the middle, with Klein stopping at second. Dihigo and Day are warming up for the BB Stars. Paige bears down and strikes out Fournier (swinging) and

Flick (looking). This completes the line on Paige (8 IP, 8 H, 3 R, 2 HR, 11 K, 1 BB).

In the bottom of the eighth, Mackey is pinch hitting for Paige, and he singles to center. McGraw and Foutz are ready in the Phillies bullpen. Roberts hits Bell, putting runners on first and second. McGraw replaces Roberts. He gets Lloyd and Stearnes before Gibson singles to center. Mackey is held at third, loading the bases. Suttles comes out to pinch hit for Leonard. Foutz replaces McGraw and fans Suttles (swinging). The final line on Roberts is 7+ IP, 5 H, 1 R, 0 HR, 7 K, 1 BB, 1 HB.

In the bottom of the ninth, Torriente leads of with a double to left and takes third when Flick lets the ball slip by him. Dandridge flies out to Ashburn in shallow center (one out), Torriente holds at third. Newt Allen hits one to Ward's left. Ward dives, knocks it down, and throws Allen out on a close play, as Torriente scores (3-2). Charleston bats for Day and flies out to Flick. Phillies go up one in the series.

	R	H	E	LOB
Phillies	3	8	1	6
BB Stars	2	7	0	7

Winning Pitcher – Roberts   Save – Foutz   Losing Pitcher – Paige
The Phillies lead the series, 2-1.

Game Four, Sunday June 20, Skydome (Toronto), 4 pm (Scott vs. Rogan)

This is the second game of a doubleheader. The game is scoreless until the top of the third. There are two outs with the pitcher Mike Scott on first base when lead-off hitter Cupid Childs lines one to deep center over Bell's head. Scott scores, and Childs has a stand-up triple. Ashburn flies out to end the inning. **Phillies 1, BB Stars 0.**

In the bottom of the third, Newt Allen leads off with a home run, just fair, inside the right field foul pole. Scott fans Rogan, Bell, and Lloyd. **BB Stars 1, Phillies 1.**

In the bottom of the fifth, with one out, Newt Allen hits his second HR of the game. Allen's two home runs are the only hits off Scott. Rogan strikes out (Scott's 10th K). Bell singles to deep short. Glasscock makes a great stop but has no chance to throw out Bell. Lloyd flies out to Ashburn. **BB Stars 2, Phillies 1.**

In the top of the sixth, Childs leads off and sends one to deep right, but Stearnes tracks it down on the warning track. Ashburn hits one through on the right side for a single. Rogan walks Cap Anson; Ashburn moves into scoring position at second base. Klein lines one into the gap in left center; Bell cuts it off, but Ashburn scores the tying run, with Anson scampering to third. Klein beats the throw to second for a double. Dick Allen lines one on one-hop to Lloyd, who holds Anson at third with a stare and then guns down Allen (two outs). Glasscock pops out to Newt Allen (2B). **Phillies 2, BB Stars 2.**

In the bottom of the sixth, Mike Scott retires the first two batters (Charleston and Stearnes). Mule Suttles gets a fast ball on the inside part of the plate and launches one over the left field wall. Mackey pops out to Glasscock (SS). **BB Stars 3, Phillies 2.**

In the top of the seventh, Rogan gets into trouble quickly. Sherry Magee leads off with a triple off the center field wall. Rogan walks Seminick on four pitches. Donnie Moore and Don Newcombe have been warming up. Jack Fournier will bat for Scott (6 IP, 4 H, 3 R, 3 HR, 10 K, 0 BB). Fournier smashes one past Rogan into center field, tying the game. Magee scores, and Seminick stops at second. Newcombe is coming in, and Rogan heads to the showers. Newcombe walks Childs to load the bases; then he walks Ashburn, forcing in the go-ahead run (4-3). Newk settles down and gets Anson and Klein to pop out (infield fly rule). If Newcombe can get the dangerous Dick Allen, the damage will be minimal. However, Dick hits a "seeing eye" single between Dandridge and Lloyd into left field, scoring two runs. Donnie Moore is coming in to replace Newcombe. The Phillies now lead 6-3. Glasscock is the ninth batter of the inning. Glasscock lines a base hit to right, scoring Ashburn with the fifth run of the inning (7-3). Mike Schmidt will pinch hit for Magee, who led off the inning with a triple. Mike bounces one to Dandridge, who throws to second, forcing Glasscock. The final line on Rogan is 6+ IP, 7 H, 5 R, 0 HR, 3 K, 3 BB). **Phillies 7, BB Stars 3.**

The Phillies are making a number of changes in the bottom of the seventh. Bunning is in to pitch and will bat in Dick Allen's fifth spot. Fournier will stay in the game and play first base. Flick will replace Magee in left, batting in Anson's third spot. Schmidt stays in the game and plays third. Bunning pitches the final three innings, giving up one single.

The Phillies add two runs in the eighth off Moore. **Phillies 9, BB Stars 3.**

	R	H	E	LOB
Phillies	9	12	2	7
BB Stars	3	5	0	4

Winning Pitcher – Scott   Save – Bunning   Losing Pitcher – Rogan
The Phillies lead the series, 3-1.

Game Five, Tuesday June 22, Cleveland Municipal Stadium, 7 pm (Alexander vs. Tiant)

This game was scheduled for the Skydome. However, a violent storm tore the roof, and the games scheduled for the Skydome (Games Five, Eight, and Nine) have to be moved to another venue, Cleveland Municipal Stadium.

The game is scoreless through four innings. Alexander has worked harder. In the first inning, he has to strike out Mackey with the bases loaded to end the inning. Also, in the first, Cool Papa Bell is injured when he steals second base. Stearnes replaces him. The BB Stars leave six men on base through the first four innings.

Tiant does not give up a hit until one out in the fourth, when Ashburn doubles. He strikes out the next two batters (Klein and Schmidt). He starts the fifth by striking out Fournier but Flick, Ward, and Boone follow with singles, and the Phillies lead 1-0. Tiant then retires Alexander and Childs. **Phillies 1, BB Stars 0.**

In the top of the sixth, the Phillies score again. Ashburn singles, and Klein triples him in (2-0). Schmidt is intentionally walked. Fournier takes a called third strike (one out). Flick hits a fly to Turkey Stearnes (CF). Klein tags and heads home, but Stearnes throws a perfect strike to Mackey, who tags Klein out (inning-ending double play). **Phillies 2, BB Stars 0.**

Alexander retires the BB Stars in order with two Ks (Torriente and Mackey). In the top of the seventh, the Phillies chase Tiant. Monte Ward (1887 New York N) leads off with a single to left. Tiant walks Boone; runners are on first and second, with none out. Alexander bunts; Tiant makes a play at third, but Ward beats the throw. The bases are now loaded (none out). Hilton Smith is warming up for the BB Stars. Childs drops a bunt down the first base line, fielded by Suttles whose only play is at first with Warfield covering.

Ward scores as the other runners move up to second and third (successful squeeze by Childs, 3-0). Ashburn drives a fair ball down into the right-field corner for a double, scoring Boone and Alexander. It is 5-0 Philadelphia, and Tiant is headed for the showers. Smith strikes out the dangerous Chuck Klein (two outs). Mike Schmidt lines a single to center as Ashburn races home with the sixth run. The final line on Tiant is 6.1 IP, 8 H, 6 R, 0 HR, 4 K, 2 BB. Fournier fouls out to Suttles. **Phillies 6, BB Stars 0.**

The Phillies are in a great position to go up 4-1 in the series. Alexander has settled down and retired five in a row. Newt Allen leads off the bottom of the seventh, pinch hitting for Frank Warfield (2B) and triples into right center. Josh Gibson pinch hits for Smith. Gibson drives the ball to deep center. Ashburn races to the fence, leaps, and robs Gibson of a home run. The sac fly scores Allen (6-1). Stearnes grounds out to Childs (2B) for the second out.

Lloyd singles to center. Alexander faces Oscar Charleston, who lines one to right center. Ashburn dives but cannot get it. Klein picks the ball up on the warning track and throws it in; Charleston is standing on third with a triple as Lloyd scores the second run. Suttles hits one to deep left. It is going, going, gone, and so is Pete Alexander.

The BB Stars have closed the gap, 6-4. The final line for Alexander is 6.7 IP, 9 H, 4 R, 1 HR, 5 K, 2 BB, 1 HB. The left-hander Caldwell is brought in to pitch to Cristobal Torriente. Curt Davis (1934 Phillies) and Dan Quisenberry (1983 Royals) are warming up. Caldwell walks Torriente. Mackey singles to center as Torriente scoots to third. Davis replaces Caldwell and walks Johnson to load the bases.

Quisenberry replaces Davis. Allen, who led off the inning with a pinch triple, gets his second hit of the inning, a 2-run single to right. This ties the score as Johnson races to third. Josh Gibson singles to center, scoring Johnson with the seventh run of the inning (Allen to third). Stearnes makes his second out of the inning to end the inning. **BB Stars 7, Phillies 6.**

In the eighth, Leon Day is in to pitch to the stunned Phillies. Flick flies out to Torriente (RF). Ward gets his third hit in a row (single to center). Boone forces Ward at second (6-4). Magee pinch runs for Boone. Dick Allen will bat for Quisenberry. Day walks him. Childs hits one to Newt Allen (2B), who flips to Lloyd. This forces Dick Allen, ending the inning.

McGraw (lefty) is now pitching for the Phillies in the bottom of the eighth. Lloyd flies out to Ashburn (CF); McGraw walks Charleston. Suttles bloops a single to center, and Charleston stops at second. Torriente smashes one off the fence in right center for a double as Charleston and Suttles race home (9-6). Mackey bounces one to Fournier (1B), who flips to McGraw, covering first (two outs). Torriente moves to third. Johnson singles up the middle, scoring Torriente with the BB Stars' tenth run to take a 10-6 lead after trailing 6-0. Newt Allen walks; Johnson goes to second. Foutz (1886 St. Louis AA) replaces McGraw to face Leon Day. He lines a base hit to left, loading the bases. Ward makes a great play on a hot smash from Stearnes and throws him out, ending the inning. **BB Stars 10, Phillies 6.**

In the ninth inning, Day retires the Phillies in order to end the Phillies nightmare.

	R	H	E	LOB
Phillies	6	10	0	7
BB Stars	10	16	0	12

Winning Pitcher – H. Smith   Save – Day   Losing Pitcher – Davis
The Phillies lead the series, 3-2.

Game Six, Wednesday June 23, Veteran Stadium (Philadelphia), 8 pm (Foster vs. Carlton)

The game is delayed an hour by showers. It is a cool night with a wet turf. The Phillies score first in the second. Glasscock singles and steals second. Grich hits one to Lloyd at short, but his throw to first is wild, heading into the dugout and scoring Glasscock, with Grich going to second. Foster retires the next three batters. **Phillies 1, BB Stars 0.**

The Phillie fans seem anxious entering the fourth inning; they know that no lead is safe. They get downright nasty after Gibson triples. Suttles singles him in, and Wells beats out a hit to deep short. Dandridge walks (loading the bases), and Warfield singles to left, scoring Suttles. Foster lays down a perfect squeeze bunt (3-1) scoring Wells with Dandridge and Warfield moving to third and second, respectively... Schmidt throws Foster out at first (Grich covering). Charleston tops one to second; Grich throws him out as Dandridge score the fourth run of the inning. Lloyd flies to left. **BB Stars 4, Phillies 1.**

In the bottom of the fourth, the Phillies close the gap. Glasscock doubles to left. Grich singles to center. Glasscock stops at third. Seminick hits a slow roller to third, but Dandridge bare hands it and throws him out as Glasscock scores, and Grich moves to second. Dick Allen bats for Carlton and lines a single to left center, scoring Grich. Foster settles down and retires Ashburn on a ground ball (2B) and Anson lofts a lazy fly to Suttles (LF). The final line on Carlton is 4 IP, 5 H, 4 R, 0 HR, 3 K, 3 BB. **BB Stars 4, Phillies 3.**

Suttles hits a 2-run HR off Bunning in the fifth. **BB Stars 6, Phillies 3.**

In the bottom of the eighth, Gabby Cravath homers to left, 6-4. J. R. Richard is warming up. Foster strikes out Klein, and Richard replaces Foster. The final line for Foster is 7.3 IP, 7 H, 4 R, 3 ER, 1 HR, 4 K, 2 BB. J. R. Richard closes out the Phillies in the eighth and ninth to even the series 3-3.

	R	H	E	LOB
BB Stars	6	8	2	7
Phillies	4	8	0	7

Winning Pitcher – Foster   Save – Richard   Losing Pitcher – Carlton
The series is tied 3-3.

Game Seven, Thursday June 24, Veteran Stadium (Philadelphia), 1 pm (Paige vs. Roberts)

It is warm and partly cloudy. The Phillies need to regain their momentum. In the bottom of the second, Flick reaches on an error by Dandridge, who could not pick up the short-hop. Ward hits a bloop into shallow right, toward the line. Stearnes races over and makes a nice sliding catch (one out).

Boone flies out to Stearnes (two outs but should be three). Robin Roberts doubles to right center as Flick scores all the way from first. Childs walks (second time). Ashburn singles to center, and Roberts beats the throw with a nice slide (Childs to third). Klein lines one to Leonard (1B). Two unearned runs give the Phillies the lead. **Phillies 2, BB Stars 0.**

With one out in the top of the fourth, Torriente doubles off the right field wall. Stearnes grounds a single through the left side; Torriente races home with their first run. Mackey singles to left, and Stearnes stops at second. Leonard chops one toward second, Childs charges, bare hands the ball and, while falling, throws the ball past Fournier into right field. Stearnes scores (unearned run) with the other runners, ending up on second and third. Roberts recovers by striking out Dandridge and enticing Newt Allen to pop out on a slow curve. **BB Stars 2, Phillies 2.**

In the top of the fifth, with one out, Charleston walks and steals second. Roberts walks Lloyd. The crowd begins to stir. Torriente drives one to left center. It looks like trouble, but Ashburn makes a spectacular catch, and both runners have to hustle back to their respective bases. What a catch. Turkey Stearnes loops one to shallow right toward the line, and Klein makes a great sliding catch near the foul line to end the inning. Roberts waits for both of his outfielders (Klein and Ashburn) to pat them on the back.

In the bottom of the fifth, Newt Allen makes a second crucial throwing error (into the dugout), sending Childs to second base. Ashburn steps to the plate. He gets a standing ovation. He is 2 for 2, with an RBI and the great catch that prevented two runs. He hits Paige's first pitch over Charleston's outstretched glove for a triple, scoring Childs and restoring the Phillies lead, 3-2. Klein gets a big hand, and he responds with a double into the right field corner. It is now 4-2 as Ashburn scores. Paige retires the next three batters. He has given up four runs, but only one is earned. **Phillies 4, BB Stars 2.**

The sixth inning is scoreless. Paige strikes out the side for his last inning (6 IP, 5 H, 4 R, 1 ER, 0 HR, 5 K, 2 BB).

Newt Allen leads off the seventh with a sinking liner to left. Flick makes a shoestring catch (one out). The Phillies outfield has made four great catches today. Klein has made two;; Ashburn and Flick, one each.. Wells singles to left, pinch hitting for Paige. Roberts retires both Charleston and Lloyd on fly balls.

Wells will remain in the game and play shortstop. Hilton Smith will pitch and bat second. With one out in the bottom of the seventh, Ashburn slams another triple (4 for 4), and Klein hits a sac fly scoring Ashburn. Klein and Ashburn each have 2 RBIs. Schmidt singles to left, and Fournier grounds out to Leonard who flips the ball to Smith covering first. **Phillies 5, BB Stars 2.**

With one out in the top of the eighth, Stearnes doubles off the center-field wall. Mackey singles to right, scoring Stearnes (5-3). Quisenberry is warming up. Leonard hits a hard one-hopper to Fournier, who starts a 3-6-3 double play. **Phillies 5, BB Stars 3.**

The Phillies try to increase their lead. Flick singles to right, then steals second base (his second stolen base of the game). Ward moves him to third with a sacrifice bunt. Smith then strikes out Boone and Magee (batting for Roberts). The final line for Roberts is 8 IP, 7 H, 3 R, 2 ER, 0 HR, 3 K, 3 BB, 1 HB. Roberts has pitched 15 innings so far in the series, giving up three earned runs, 1.80 ERA in the series.

Quisenberry gives up a single to Newt Allen with one out in the top of the ninth, but strikes out Wells and gets Charleston to hit into a game-ending force out.

	R	H	E	LOB
BB Stars	3	8	2	6
Phillies	5	8	1	7

Winning Pitcher – Roberts   Save – Quisenberry   Losing Pitcher – Paige
The Phillies lead the series, 4-3.

Game Eight, Friday June 25, Cleveland Municipal Stadium, 7 pm (Scott vs. Rogan)

It is a cool, partly cloudy evening with the wind blowing in off Lake Erie. Games Eight and Nine were also scheduled to be played in the Skydome, but the roof is still under repair. The Phillies open fast in the first inning. Childs walks. Ashburn moves Childs to third on a hit-and-run single to center. Anson one-hops a double off the wall in left center, scoring Childs and Ashburn. Klein flies to Bell (CF), and Dick Allen goes down swinging (two outs). Three singles in a row (Flick, Ward, and Seminick) plate the third and fourth runs of the inning. Scott strikes out. Day and Dihigo are throwing hard in the BB Stars bullpen. **Phillies 4, BB Stars 0.**

In the second inning, the Phillies threaten again. Childs singles and steals second base. Anson lines a one-out single, but Childs holds third. Klein goes down swinging. Dick Allen hits a ball to deep left, but the wind holds it up and Charleston catches it at the fence.

In the fourth, the Phillies add to their lead. With two out, Ashburn walks and moves to second on a Rogan wild pitch. Anson bloops a single into shallow center, scoring Ashburn. Klein strikes out swinging. **Phillies 5, BB Stars 0.**

In the bottom of the fourth, the BB Stars begin to stir. Gibson singles to center. Stearnes lines one to center, but Ashburn gets a great jump and makes the catch. Suttles gets a base hit to left, with Gibson stopping at second.

Johnson lines a single to left, but Gibson has to hold at third (bases loaded). Allen chops one to Childs at second; he flips to Ward to force Johnson (two outs) as Gibson scores the BB Stars' first run. Torriente is pinch hitting for Rogan. He bounces to Childs for an inning-ending force play at second. **Phillies 5, BB Stars 1.**

Leon Day relieves Rogan (4 IP, 8 H, 5 R, 0 HR, 4 K, 2 BB, 1 WP). Dick Allen greets Day with a monster HR to left field (6-1). Flick singles up the middle. Day uncorks a wild pitch, Flick moves into scoring position. Ward pops out to Newt Allen (2B). Seminick singles into left center as Flick comes around to score (7-1). Scott sacrifices Seminick to second. Childs grounds out to Allen (2B). **Phillies 7, Bb Stars 1.**

In the bottom of the fifth, Schmidt is a defensive change for Dick Allen. Bell triples to deep center. Lloyd singles to left, scoring Bell (7-2). Scott throws a pitch in the dirt that scoots past Seminick for a wild pitch, and Lloyd moves to second base. Scott bears down, striking out Charleston and Gibson. Klein robs Stearnes of a hit (Ashburn robbed him, last inning.). **Phillies 7, BB Stars 2.**

The score remains 7-2 going into the bottom of the seventh. With one out, Bell singles to right. Lloyd doubles into the left center field gap, with Bell stopping at third. The Phillies are making a change; Jim Bunning is now pitching. On Bunning's first pitch, the ball bounces off of Seminick's glove (passed ball), scoring Bell. Lloyd moves to third (7-3). Charleston lines a single to right, scoring Lloyd (7-4). The final line for Scott is 6.3 IP, 10 H, 4 R, 0 HR, 7 K 0 BB. Gibson fouls out to Anson (two outs). Stearnes triples over Ashburn's head, scoring Charleston (7-5). Bunning throws one outside, going all the way to the back stop (wild pitch). It is now 7-6. Suttles pops out to Anson. **Phillies 7, BB Stars 6.**

Dihigo replaces Day in the top of the eighth and, despite throwing a wild pitch after walking Ashburn (5 wild pitches and passed ball in the game), he escapes when Anson lines to Lloyd, who doubles Ashburn off second (unassisted double play).

Foutz has replaced Bunning and will bat in Anson's third spot. Fournier will replace Anson and bat eighth. Boone replaces Seminick and will bat ninth. Foutz retires the first batter, Judy Johnson, on a ground ball to Schmidt (3B). Newt Allen drives one just out of the reach of Ashburn; it rolls to the wall. Allen slides into third with a triple. Irvin bats for Dihigo and lofts a high fly to Ashburn in fairly deep center. Allen trots home with the tying run (7-7). The Phillies have blown a 6-run lead for the second time in this series. Bell hits one high and deep to center, but Ashburn catches it on the edge of the warning track. **BB Stars 7, Phillies 7.**

J. R. Richard is in to pitch the top of the ninth. Klein flies out to Bell. Mike Schmidt fouls off a couple of tough 2-2 pitches and then smashes one deep to left. It is out of here, home run. The Phillies regain the lead, 8-7. Richard walks Flick, and Ward follows with a single to center as Flick hustles to third. With Fournier coming to the plate, Johnson (3B) and Suttles (1B) are in on the edge of the grass. Lloyd (SS) and Allen (2B) are midway, hoping to turn double play. Fournier hits a ground ball to Allen's left; he grabs it, turns, and fires to Lloyd for the force on Ward. But Fournier beats the throw to first as Flick scores the insurance run (9-7). Boone pops one up into shallow left toward the line; Lloyd dives and makes a great catch. **Phillies 9, BB Stars 7.**

Tug McGraw is now pitching for Philadelphia. Lloyd hits a fly to fairly deep right center, but Ashburn has room and runs it down (one out). Charleston takes a called third strike (two outs). The Phillies are one out from winning the series. Gibson hits one up the middle, but Childs dives, snares it on a one-hop, and, from his knees, throws Gibson out. The Phillies win the series.

	R	H	E	LOB
Phillies	9	15	0	9
BB Stars	7	13	0	6

Winning Pitcher – Foutz   Save – McGraw   Losing Pitcher – Richard
The Phillies win the series 5-3 and will try to be the first team to win six games against the BB Stars.

Game Nine, Friday June 26, Cleveland Municipal Stadium, 1 pm (Alexander vs. Tiant)

It is a warm and partly cloudy day with a light wind (not a factor). The Phillies open the scoring in the top of the first. Childs singles up the middle. It looks like Tiant has a chance to at least knock it down, but it deflects off the top of his glove. Tiant walks Ashburn. With the count 2-2 on Cap Anson, the runners take off. Anson swings and misses, strike three. Gibson fires to third, and Johnson tags out the sliding Childs for the double play. Tiant bears down on Chuck Klein, but he drops one into short center field, and Ashburn scores from second. Schmidt fouls out to Josh Gibson near the backstop. **Phillies 1, BB Stars 0.**

In the bottom of the second, Josh Gibson hits one deep, down the line in left field. If it stays fair, it is gone. Home run, it is fair by about two feet. Alexander retires the next three batters (Stearnes, Suttles, and Johnson). **BB Stars 1, Phillies 1.**

In the bottom of the third, Alexander retires Newt Allen and Luis Tiant on ground outs to Childs (2B). Alexander's first pitch to Bell is in tight and hits him on the shoulder. Bell goes to first base. Bell gets a good jump on the first pitch to Lloyd and breaks for second. Seminick throws the ball into center field, and Bell moves to third. Lloyd smashes one between Anson and Childs into right as Bell scores. Alexander is rattled. He flings the resin bag to the ground.

He falls behind Charleston 2-0, and Charleston drills a ground-rule double that one-hops the fence near the right field foul pole. Lloyd must go back to third. Alexander has a chance to hold the BB Stars to just one run this inning. However, he must get Josh Gibson out first. Gibson jumps on the first pitch and hits a towering drive to left field. Fournier is going back, but he will not get this one. It is a 3-run home run for Gibson. Alexander slouches on the mound, head down, hands on hips, kicking the dirt. He realizes he created this mess when he hit Bell after retiring the first two batters. The Phillies now trail 5-1. Stearnes grounds out to Childs (2B). **BB Stars 5, Phillies 1.**

In the top of the fourth, the Phillies take advantage of a lead-off walk to Klein and Johnson's error (potential double play ball off Schmidt's bat). Fournier bounces out to Allen (2B) as the runners move up. Glasscock lines one just fair over third and into the left field corner for a 2-run double (5-3). Seminick takes a called third strike (two outs). The Phillies manager decides to let Alexander bat, and he lines out to Lloyd (SS). **BB Stars 5, Phillies 3.**

In hindsight, the Phillies should have pinched hit for Alexander. Tiant retires 15 of the next 16 batters. Glasscock, who did reach base on a single in the seventh, was thrown out trying to steal. Alexander and three relievers shut down the BB Stars the rest of the way. The final line for Alexander is 6 IP, 5 H, 5 R, 2 HR, 5 K, 2 BB, 1 HB.

With two outs in the ninth, the Phillies have one last chance. Fournier reaches when Lloyd misplays a ground ball hit right at him. Glasscock singles to center, and Fournier moves around to third. The Phillies have the tying runs on base with Andy Seminick, their powerful hitting catcher coming to the plate. Hilton Smith is relieving Luis Tiant, who pitched a great game. The count goes to 1-2, and Smith blows a fast ball over the inside corner that freezes Seminick, strike three. The BB Stars salvage Game Nine of the series, their fourth win. The final line for Tiant is 8.7 IP, 6 H, 3 R, 2 ER, 0 HR, 7 K, 2 BB.

	R	H	E	LOB
Phillies	3	6	2	5
BB Stars	5	7	2	4

Winning Pitcher – Tiant   Save – Smith   Losing Pitcher – Alexander

The Phillies win the series, 5-4.

Recap of Best Season Series 6 (BB Stars vs. Phillies)

This was a very evenly matched series. The Phillies scored 46 runs. The BB Stars scored 44 runs. The BB Stars batted .272, which was low for them, and the Phillies batted .254. The ERA for the BB Stars pitching was 4.56. The ERA for the Phillies staff was 4.67. Chart 11-2 on page 142 has BB Stars individual/team statistics for this series. Chart 11-3 on page 143 has Phillies individual/team statistics for this series.

The turning point of the series - After the BB Stars won Game Five (trailed 6-0 and won 10-6) and Game Six to even the series, the Phillies won Games Seven and Eight to win the series. In Game Seven, Robin Roberts beat Satchel Paige for the second time in the series. Paige pitched well in both games (ERA – 2.77). Defense let him down in Game Seven (three unearned runs in a 5-3 loss). In Game Eight, like Game Five, the Phillies blow a 6-run lead (7-1). However, they recovered to win 9-7. Schmidt's home run in the ninth is the winning blow.

MVP of Series – I have co-winners, Richie Ashburn and Robin Roberts, though Chuck Klein, despite hitting .216, drove in 9 runs. He was the offense in Robin Roberts' Game Three win (3-2) with 2 HRs and all 3 RBIs. The Phillies outfield made many great defensive plays, led by Ashburn and Klein. Below are the reasons for Ashburn and Roberts sharing the Series MVP.

Hitting Star for the Phillies - Richie Ashburn (1958 Phillies)

	RS	RBI	HR	.Avg	OBP	SPct	OPS
R. Ashburn	10	6	0	.452	.541	.710	1.251

Best Pitcher for Phillies – Robin Roberts (1952 Phillies)

	G	GS	QS	CG	W-L	IP	H	HR	R/ER	ERA
R. Roberts	2	2	2	0	2-0	15	12	0	4-3	1.80

Hitting Star for the BB Stars - Newt Allen

	RS	RBI	HR	.Avg	OBP	SPct	OPS
N. Allen	6	7	2	.440	.481	.880	1.361

Best Pitcher for the BB Stars – Satchel Paige*

	G	GS	QS	CG	W-L	IP	H	HR	R/ER	ERA
S. Paige	2	2	2	0	0-2	14	12	2	7-4	2.57

* Even though Satchel did not win either game (both vs. Robin Roberts), he did everything needed to win. He also struck out 16 and walked only 3 batters.

BB Stars Results vs. Phillies 4-5, .556

Pos.	E	R	TH	PB	Hitters	G	AB	R	H	RBI	2B	3B	HR	TB	W	HB	SO	SF	SH	SB	B.AVG.	OBP	S.PCT.	OPS
LF	5	A	-1		Charleston	9	35	4	7	4	1	2	1	15	4	0	9	0	0	0	0.200	0.282	0.429	0.711
CF	8	AA	-1		CP Bell	7	22	5	7	1	0	0	1	10	0	2	7	0	0	3	0.318	0.375	0.455	0.830
OF	5	A	-1		Stearnes	8	30	3	5	3	1	1	0	8	0	0	6	0	0	0	0.167	0.167	0.267	0.433
OF	6	B	-2		M Irvin	3	5	0	0	1	0	0	0	0	1	0	2	1	0	0	0.000	0.167	0.000	0.167
OF	6	A	-1		Torriente	8	18	5	6	4	3	0	0	9	2	1	2	1	0	0	0.333	0.429	0.500	0.929
SS	7	A			P Lloyd	9	33	5	14	4	3	0	0	18	4	0	2	0	0	0	0.424	0.486	0.545	1.032
SS	7	AA			W Wells	3	8	1	4	0	2	0	0	6	1	0	3	0	0	0	0.500	0.556	0.750	1.306
3B	7	A			J Johnson	5	21	1	5	2	0	0	0	5	1	0	4	0	0	0	0.238	0.273	0.238	0.511
3B	6	B			Dandridge	4	14	1	0	0	0	0	0	0	1	0	6	0	0	0	0.000	0.067	0.000	0.067
2B	7	A			N Allen	8	25	6	11	7	1	2	2	22	1	0	2	0	0	0	0.440	0.481	0.880	1.361
2B	7	A			F Warfield	3	7	0	3	1	0	0	0	3	2	0	0	0	0	0	0.429	0.556	0.429	0.984
1B	8	B			Suttles	8	26	7	8	7	1	0	4	21	1	0	4	0	0	0	0.308	0.333	0.808	1.141
1B	8	B			B Leonard	4	12	0	1	0	0	0	0	1	0	0	0	0	0	0	0.083	0.083	0.083	0.167
C	7	A	-2	Fr	J Gibson	7	22	5	7	6	0	2	2	17	1	0	5	1	0	0	0.318	0.348	0.773	1.121
C	6	B	-2	Aw	B Mackey	7	17	1	6	1	1	0	0	7	0	1	3	0	0	0	0.353	0.389	0.412	0.801
					pitchers	9	17	0	0	0	0	0	0	0	0	0	10	0	6	1	0.000	0.000	0.000	0.000
					TOTAL	9	312	44	85	41	14	7	10	143	20	4	65	3	6	4	0.272	0.324	0.458	0.783

Fat.	H	WP	E	R	Pitchers	G	GS	QS	CG	S	W	L	IP	H	SO	BB	HB	HR	R	ER	ERA
10/L	Vg	N	9	B	BJ Rogan	2	2	2	0	0	0	0	10	15	7	5	0	0	10	10	9.00
9/L	Ex	R	7	B	B Foster	2	2	1	0	0	0	1	13	12	7	4	2	1	7	6	4.16
10/L	Vg	NL	8	B	L Day	3	0	0	0	0	1	0	6	6	6	2	1	0	2	2	3.00
10/L	Aw	NL	7	B	M Dihigo	2	0	0	0	0	0	0	1	1	1	1	1	0	0	0	0.00
8/L	Md	R	8	C	S Paige	2	2	2	0	0	0	0	14	12	16	3	0	2	7	4	2.57
L/9	Vg	R	8	A	H Smith	4	0	0	0	0	1	1	4.3	5	4	1	0	0	2	2	4.16
9/L	Aw	R	9	A	Newcombe	1	0	0	0	0	0	0	0.7	1	0	2	0	0	2	2	27.00
10/L	Ex	NL	8	D	L Tiant	3	3	2	0	2	1	0	24	20	18	6	0	1	11	10	3.75
9 Aw		N	5	C	JR Richard	4	0	0	0	0	0	0	5.3	4	3	1	0	1	3	2	3.38
Long	Md	NL	4	B	D Moore	1	0	0	0	0	0	1	0.7	4	1	1	0	0	2	2	27.00
					TOTAL	24	9				3	4	79	79	59	25			46	40	4.56

Chart 11-2 – BB Stars Statistics for this series

Phillies Best Season Series vs. BB All-Stars 5-4, .556

Team	Year	WS	Hitters	G	AB	R	H	RBI	2B	3B	HR	TB	W	HB	SO	SF	SH	SB	B.AVG	OBP	S.PCT	OPS
Philadelphia	1930	28	C Klein	9	37	4	8	9	2	2	1	18	1	0	7	1	0	0	0.216	0.237	0.486	0.723
Philadelphia	1913	29	G Cravath	2	7	2	4	1	1	1	1	10	0	0	0	0	0	0	0.571	0.571	1.429	2.000
Philadelphia	1900	32	E Flick	7	22	5	7	1	0	0	0	7	1	0	2	2	0	3	0.318	0.348	0.318	0.666
Philadelphia	1958	28	R Ashburn	9	31	10	14	6	4	2	0	22	6	0	1	0	0	0	0.452	0.541	0.710	1.250
Philadelphia	1914	29	S Magee	5	4	2	1	0	0	1	0	3	2	0	1	0	0	0	0.250	0.500	0.750	1.250
Indianapolis	1889	27	JGlasscock	4	17	1	8	1	3	0	0	11	0	0	0	0	0	1	0.471	0.471	0.647	1.118
New York N	1887	25	M Ward	5	20	1	8	1	0	0	0	8	0	0	3	0	1	0	0.400	0.400	0.400	0.800
Philadelphia	1980	37	M Schmidt	9	29	2	4	2	2	0	1	7	2	0	6	0	0	0	0.138	0.194	0.241	0.435
Philadelphia	1966	35	D Allen	5	12	1	3	4	0	0	1	6	1	0	3	0	0	0	0.250	0.308	0.500	0.808
Cleveland N	1896	27	C Childs	8	26	4	5	3	0	1	0	8	6	0	5	0	1	1	0.192	0.344	0.308	0.651
California	1979	28	B Grich	2	6	1	2	0	0	0	0	2	0	0	2	0	0	0	0.333	0.333	0.333	0.667
Chicago (N)	1886	30	C Anson	5	19	1	4	3	1	1	0	5	3	0	3	0	0	0	0.211	0.318	0.263	0.581
Brooklyn	1924	34	J Fournier	6	23	3	3	2	0	0	0	3	1	0	7	0	0	0	0.130	0.167	0.130	0.297
Philadelphia	1978	17	B Boone	5	16	2	3	4	2	0	0	6	1	0	3	0	0	0	0.188	0.235	0.563	0.798
Philadelphia	1950	22	A Seminick	6	19	3	3	1	1	0	1	6	1	0	6	0	1	0	0.158	0.200	0.316	0.516
			pitchers	9	23	3	2	2	0	0	0	4	0	0	11	1	0	1	0.087	0.087	0.174	0.261
			Total	9	311	46	79	42	15	6	8	130	25	0	61	3		4	0.254	0.310	0.418	0.728

Team	Year	WS	Pitchers	G	GS	QS	CG	S	W	L	IP	H	SO	BB	HB	HR	R	ER	ERA
Philadelphia	1915	43	GAlexander	3	3	1	0	0	0	0	19.7	23	16	4	2	5	13	12	5.48
Philadelphia	1972	40	S Carlton	2	2	1	0	0	0	1	11	13	11	5	0	1	7	7	5.73
Philadelphia	1952	32	R Roberts	2	2	2	0	0	0	2	15	12	10	4	2	0	4	3	1.80
St. Louis AA	1886	62	D Foutz	4	0	0	0	0	1	1	4.7	5	5	1	0	0	2	1	1.93
Houston	1986	27	M Scott	2	2	1	0	0	0	1	13.3	14	17	0	0	0	7	7	4.72
Philadelphia	1967	25	J Bunning	4	0	0	0	0	1	0	7	4	4	2	0	3	4	4	5.14
Milwaukee A	1978	28	M Caldwell	3	0	0	0	0	0	0	1.7	2	2	0	1	1	3	3	20.31
Philadelphia	1934	24	C Davis	3	0	0	0	0	0	0	1.7	4	1	1	1	0	1	1	5.39
Philadelphia	1980	18	T McGraw	3	0	0	0	0	1	0	2.3	4	4	2	2	0	3	3	11.59
Kansas City	1983	28	Quisenberry	4	0	0	0	0	0	0	4	4	3	0	0	0	0	0	0.00
			TOTAL	9	9	5	0	0	5	5	79	85	65	20		10	44	41	4.67

Chart 11-3 – Phillies statistics for this series

Chapter 12

Best Season Nine Game Series 7 - BB Stars vs.Indians

Indians Roster Review

EIGHTY PERCENT OF THE ROSTER are made up of Cleveland Indians. Twenty percent of the roster are free agents. See the Indians Roster (Chart 12-1 on page 145).

Offensive Leaders (Indians) Ranked by OPS

Player	OBP	SPct	OPS	R +	RBI -	HR =	NR
E. Averill	.438	.627	1.065	136	126	28	234
S. J. Jackson	.468	.590	1.058	126	83	7	202
A. Rosen	.422	.613	1.035	115	145	43	217
R. Colavito	.408	.620	1.028	80	113	41	152
L. Boudreau	.453	.534	.987	116	106	18	208
L. Doby	.442	.545	.987	110	102	25	187
E. Howard	.390	.549	.939	64	77	21	120
J. Sewell	.456	.479	.935	98	109	3	204
R. Connor	.436	.495	.931	102	65	1	166
A. Otis	.387	.525	.912	74	96	22	148

The following players would be base-stealing threats – T. McCarthy 83, B. Ewing 53, SJ Jackson 41, and A. Otis 32 (numbers listed SB for their best season).

IndiansRoster Best Season Series vs. BB All-Stars

Team	Year	WS Hitters	G	AB	R	H	RBI	2B	3B	HR	TB	W	HB	SO	SF	SH	SB	B.AVG.	OBP	S.PCT.	OPS
Cleveland	1958	32 R Colavito	143	489	80	148	113	26	3	41	303	84	3	89	-	-	0	0.303	0.408	0.620	1.028
St. Louis (N)	1890	24 T McCarthy	133	548	137	192	74	28	9	6	256	66	0	17	-	-	83	0.350	0.420	0.467	0.887
Cleveland	1950	30 L Doby	142	503	110	164	102	25	5	25	274	98	6	71	-	-	8	0.326	0.442	0.545	0.986
Cleveland	1936	27 E Averill	152	614	136	232	126	39	15	28	385	65	1	35	-	-	3	0.378	0.438	0.627	1.065
Cleveland	1911	39 SJ Jackson	147	571	126	233	83	45	19	7	337	56	8	15	-	-	41	0.408	0.468	0.590	1.058
Kansas City	1978	29 A Otis	141	486	74	145	96	30	7	22	255	66	4	54	-	-	32	0.298	0.387	0.525	0.911
Cleveland	1948	34 L Boudreau	152	560	116	199	106	34	6	18	299	98	2	9	-	-	3	0.355	0.453	0.534	0.987
Cleveland	1923	29 J Sewell	153	553	98	195	109	41	10	3	265	98	7	12	-	-	9	0.353	0.456	0.479	0.935
Cleveland	1953	42 A Rosen	155	599	115	201	145	27	5	43	367	85	0	48	-	-	8	0.336	0.422	0.613	1.034
Cleveland	1941	23 K Keltner	149	581	83	156	84	31	13	23	282	51	1	56	-	-	2	0.269	0.328	0.485	0.813
Cleveland	1954	34 B Avila	143	555	112	189	67	27	2	15	266	59	1	31	-	-	9	0.341	0.405	0.479	0.884
Cleveland	1980	25 M Hargrove	160	589	86	179	85	22	2	11	238	111	0	36	-	-	4	0.304	0.414	0.404	0.818
New York N	1885	36 R Connor	110	455	102	169	65	23	15	1	225	51	1	8	-	-	23	0.371	0.436	0.495	0.930
New York A	1961	29 E Howard	129	446	64	155	77	17	5	21	245	28	3	65	-	-	0	0.348	0.390	0.549	0.939
New York N	1888	27 B Ewing	103	415	83	127	58	18	15	6	193	24	0	28	-	-	53	0.306	0.344	0.465	0.809

Team	Year	WS Pitchers	G	GS	OS	CG	S	W	L	IP	H	SO	BB	HB	HR	R	ER	ERA
Cleveland	1946	32 B Feller	48	42	-	36	4	26	15	371	277	348	153	-	11	-	-	2.18
Cleveland	1908	35 A Joss	42	35	-	29	2	24	11	325	232	130	30	-	2	-	-	1.16
Cleveland	1956	25 H Score	35	33	-	16	0	20	9	249	162	263	129	-	18	-	-	2.52
Cleveland	1920	32 S Coveleski	41	38	-	26	2	24	14	315	284	133	65	-	6	-	-	2.49
Cleveland	1948	26 B Lemon	43	37	-	20	2	20	14	294	231	147	129	-	12	-	-	2.82
Cleveland	1956	28 E Wynn	38	35	-	18	2	20	9	278	233	158	91	-	19	-	-	2.72
Cleveland	1965	25 S McDowell	42	35	-	14	4	17	11	273	178	325	132	-	9	-	-	2.18
Cleveland	1954	24 M Garcia	45	34	-	13	5	19	8	259	220	129	71	-	6	-	-	2.64
Cleveland	1948	22 G Bearden	37	29	-	15	1	20	7	230	187	80	106	-	9	-	-	2.43
Cleveland	1934	27 M Harder	44	29	-	17	4	20	12	255	246	91	81	-	6	-	-	2.60

Chart 12-1 – Indians Best Season Roster

Fielding Leaders	Pos	Range	Error	Throwing
A. Otis	CF	AA	9	-1
T. McCarthy	RF	A	5	-1
S. J. Jackson	L/RF	A	4	-2
L. Doby	L/CF	B	8	0
R. Colavito	RF	B	7	-1
E. Averill	CF	B	5	0

For outfielders - range (AA is best) and throwing (-4 is exceptional, -3 is excellent, -2 is very good) are most important. Error rating (10 is best, 1 is poor) is not as critical as infielders because outfielders normally do not make as many errors.

K. Keltner	3B	AA	10	-
L. Boudreau	SS	A+	9	-
B. Avila	2B	A+	6	-
R. Connor	1B	A	5	-
J. Sewell	SS	A	3	-
A. Rosen	3B	B	9	
M. Hargrove	1B	B	7	

For infielders, range (AA is best), + increase in DPs because of excellent pivot, error rating is as important as range for an infielder (10 is excellent, 1 is poor).

Catcher Throwing - Ewing has a very good throwing arm (-2), and Howard is above average (-1).

Pitcher Hold Rating - There are no Indians pitchers with a hold rating above average. McDowell is mediocre, and Feller is poor. Expect opponents to take advantage on the bases. Ewing and Howard behind the plate offsets the pitchers' weakness in holding runners.

Pitching - This a strong, adaptable, pitching staff with two overpowering left-handers (Score and McDowell).

Game One, Sunday June 27, Cleveland Municipal Stadium, 1 pm (Paige vs. Joss)

It is a warm, partly cloudy day for the opener of Series Seven. The BB Stars have lost the last two series (Phillies and SenTwins), as well as the final three games vs. the Reds, for a record of 8 wins and 13 losses (.381).

In the bottom of the first, the Indians get on the board vs. Satchel Paige. Shoeless Joe Jackson (1911 Indians) doubles into the right field corner. Roger Connor (1885 New York N) goes down swinging (one out). Al Rosen (1953 Indians) hits a towering pop-up near the pitcher's mound; Pop Lloyd makes the catch (two outs). Earl Averill (1936 Indians) lines one over Newt Allen's outstretched glove into right center, and Jackson races around with the first run of the game. Rocky Colavito (1958 Indians) forces Averill at second to end the inning. **Indians 1, BB Stars 0.**

In the bottom of the second, the Indians add to their lead. Boudreau (1948 Indians) leads off with a single to right. Avila (1954 Indians) chops a ground ball to Allen (2B) and is thrown out as Boudreau moves to second base. Ewing (1888 New York N) slams a ground rule double (one-hop over fence in left center), scoring Boudreau with the Indians' second run. Joss (1908 Indians) strikes out (two outs). Jackson gets his second hit with a base hit into right field, and Ewing comes around to score. Connor strikes out (second time). **Indians 3, BB Stars 0.**

In the top of the third, Newt Allen singles to center, and on the first pitch to Paige, Allen steals second base. Paige lines a one-hop single to Jackson in left. Allen stops at third, respecting Shoeless Joe's throwing arm (-2). Paige is on first (none out). Joss strikes out Bell (swinging). Lloyd lifts a fly ball to Averill as Allen tags and scores (sac fly, Lloyd). Charleston doubles into the gap in left center. Averill cuts it off and fires to Boudreau (cut-off man), and Paige is held at third base. Josh Gibson bounces out to Rosen (3B) to end the threat. **Indians 3, BB Stars 1.**

Paige is not up to par today. Al Rosen leads off with a home run to left field (4-1). Averill lines one to deep center; Bell leaps, and it tips off his glove as he falls to the ground. Before he can retrieve the ball, Averill is on his way to third with a stand-up triple. Newcombe is warming up for the BB Stars. Colavito takes a called third strike (one out). Boudreau smashes one to Dandridge's left. Dandridge knocks the ball down, but it is an infield single, scoring Averill (5-1). Avila hits one hard and deep to center, but Bell catches up with it on the edge of the warning track. Boudreau, who has already turned past second, has to retrace his steps and slide back into first before Bell's throw reaches Leonard (1B). Ewing flies out to Bell in shallow center. **Indians 5, BB Stars 1.**

In the top of the fourth, with two outs and Leonard on second (his second double of the game), Newt Allen triples over Averill's head (center field); Leonard scores (5-2). Cristobal Torriente bats for Paige and takes a called third strike. **Indians 5, BB Stars 2.**

Newcombe is now pitching for the BB Stars. The final line on Paige is 3 IP, 8 H, 5 R, 1 HR, 4 K, 0 BB. Newcombe keeps the Indians scoreless in the fourth.

Joss has been struggling the last two innings, and it continues. Bell singles to center and goes to third on a hit-and-run single by Lloyd. Bearden (left-hander, 1948 Indians) is beginning to warm up. Charleston chops one up the middle; Boudreau (SS) gloves it and throws him out. Bell scores, and Lloyd moves to second (5-3). Josh retires Gibson (K) and Stearnes (ground out) to end the inning. **Indians 5, BB Stars 3.**

Newcombe does a great job in the bottom of the fifth. Averill and Rosen both go down swinging, and Boudreau flies out to Bell.

In the sixth, Addie Joss retires the first two hitters. Allen singles to center. Monte Irvin is coming out to bat for Newcombe (two shutout innings in relief). Irvin hits the first pitch from Joss to deep left field near the foul pole. If it is fair, it is out of here. The third base umpire signals fair ball. Monte Irvin has just tied the game with a 2-run pinch hit home run (5-5). The Indians had led 5-1. Paige is now off the hook. This would be a tough loss for the Indians after chasing Paige so early in the game. Bell hits a deep fly to center, but Averill chases it down near the warning track. **BB Stars 5, Indians 5.**

Hilton Smith is now pitching for the BB Stars. Avila hits one to deep left, and Charleston catches it in front of the fence. Avila thought he had a home run (one out). Ewing lines one into the gap in right center, and Bell cuts it off. Ewing, who has great speed, is trying to stretch it into a double. Bell's throw is on target, but Ewing's head-first slide to the inside part of the base beats the throw. Larry Doby (1950 Indians) is pinch hitting for Joss. The final line on Joss is 6 IP, 10 H, 5 R, 1 HR, 4 K, 1 BB.

They decide to pitch to Doby, and he smashes the ball past the diving Leonard (1B) into right field. There is no chance to throw out Ewing. The Indians quickly regain the lead (6-5). Bullet Joe Rogan begins to warm up. McCarthy is pinch running for Doby. Jackson hits a ground ball to Leonard (1B), who makes a good play to force the speedy McCarthy at second base (two outs). Connor singles to right, and Jackson easily makes it to third. Rosen lines one into left center. Bell races over and dives, but he cannot get it. The ball rolls to the wall, two runs score, and Al Rosen slides into third with a 2-run triple. Indians lead 8-5. Averill bloops one that drops in shallow center for an RBI single as Rosen scores the ninth run (fourth of the inning). Rogan replaces the usually dependable Smith. Colavito flies out to Charleston. **Indians 9, BB Stars 5.**

Bearden is in to pitch. Joss, despite a poor performance, is in line to win the game if the Indians can hold the lead. McCarthy stays in the game and is playing right field. Bearden is batting in Colavito's spot, fifth. Bearden strikes out Lloyd on a pitch that looks outside. Lloyd slams his bat on home plate and screams at the plate umpire. He is tossed from the game. Wells will replace him in the field in the bottom of the seventh. Bearden retires Charleston and Gibson. Boudreau dives to grab Josh Gibson's rocket for out number three.

Rogan retires the Indians in order (bottom of the seventh). **Indians 9, BB Stars 5.**

Bearden gives up a lead-off triple to Stearnes (Averill almost made a great catch). Mule Suttles is going to bat for Leonard. Mel Harder (1934 Indians) is now pitching for Cleveland. Suttles hits a high fly to shallow right field;

McCarthy makes the catch, and Stearnes stays at third base. Dandridge goes with Harder's curve on the outside corner and slaps it into right field for a single, scoring Stearnes (9-6).

There is no further scoring. Despite blowing a 5-1 lead, the Indians hang on to win the first game of the series.

	R	H	E	LOB
BB Stars	6	13	0	7
Indians	9	15	0	6

Winning Pitcher – Joss   Save – Harder   Losing Pitcher – Paige
The Indians lead the series, 1-0.

Game Two, Monday June 28, Cleveland Municipal Stadium, 7 pm (Foster vs. Feller)

It is cool and cloudy. There were showers an hour before game time. The outfield is wet. The BB Stars score early off Bob Feller (1946 Indians). He walks Bell on four pitches. Wells lines Feller's first pitch over the left field fence for a 2-run home run. Feller escapes further trouble. After striking out Charleston, Suttles and Stearnes get back-to-back singles (runners on first and second). Mackey hits a one-hopper to Rosen, who turns it into an around the horn double play (5-4-3). **BB Stars 2, Indians 0.**

The left-handed Foster no-hits the Indians through the first four innings. Feller also has settled down. It is 2-0 going into the bottom of the fifth. Howard (1961 Yankees) leads off with a home run over the fence in left center (2-1). Foster walks Feller on a 3-2 pitch. Jackson singles to right on a hit-and-run, with Feller going to third. Boudreau hits a fly ball to shallow right; Stearnes waves off Warfield (2B) and makes the catch. Feller never leaves third base. Jackson stays at first (one out).

McCarthy is fooled by Foster's changeup and pops it up in the infield, Wells (SS) makes the catch (two outs). Foster is trying to get out of the inning with the lead. Amos Otis (1978 Royals) hits a "seeing eye" ground ball between the diving Johnson and the diving Wells into left field. Feller scores as Jackson slides into third, beating the throw from Charleston (2-2). Keltner hits a one-hopper to Wells, who flips to Warfield for the force on Otis, ending the inning. **Indians 2, BB Stars 2.**

In the bottom of the seventh, Al Rosen pinch hits for Feller. After the quick two runs in the first, Feller shuts down the BB Stars. The final line for Bob Feller is 7 IP, 6 H, 2 R, 1 HR, 4 K, 2 BB. Rosen takes a called third strike. Jackson and Boudreau ground out.

Sam McDowell (1965 Indians) is now pitching to start the top of the eighth. He faces a challenge right away. Josh Gibson is coming off the bench to bat for Foster. The final line on Foster is also very good (7 IP, 3 H, 2 R, 1 HR, 2 K, 5 BB). On a 2-2 pitch, McDowell freezes Gibson with a fast ball on the outside corner, strike three. McDowell retires the side in order.

Martin Dihigo is now pitching for the BB Stars in the bottom of the eighth. Gibson is now catching. McCarthy singles and steals second on the first pitch to Otis. Dihigo walks Otis intentionally to set up for the potential double play. Keltner pops out to Wells (infield fly rule). On the 2-2 pitch, both runners take off. Hargrove strikes out, and Gibson throws a strike to Wells (SS), who tags out Otis, double play.

In the top of the ninth, Charleston reaches on an error by Hargrove. McDowell does not let the error rattle him. He retires the next three batters. **BB Stars 2, Indians 2.**

In the bottom of the ninth, Avila reaches on a two-base throwing error by Judy Johnson (3B). Ewing bats for Howard. Johnson (3B) and Suttles (1B) are in on the grass. Ewing is an excellent bunter. He drops a bunt down the first base line. Suttles' only play is on Ewing, and he throws to Allen, covering first base (Allen pinched hit for Warfield in seventh, hitting in to DP). Avila is now on third; credit Ewing with a sacrifice hit. Joe Sewell is batting for McDowell. The BB Stars have the outfield and infield pulled in. Sewell also is an excellent bunter. He squares to bunt and rolls it about four feet in front of the plate. There is no play. Avila slides in safely as Sewell crosses first base with a walk-off bunt single. The winning run is unearned.

	R	H	E	LOB
BB Stars	2	6	1	4
Indians	3	5	1	8

Winning Pitcher – McDowell   Losing Pitcher – Dihigo

The Indians lead the series, 2-0.

Game Three, Tuesday June 29, Shea Stadium (New York), 7 pm (Score vs. Richard)

The BB Stars continue to struggle and hope to break out of it, being the home team for the next three games at Shea Stadium. J. R. Richard (1979 Astros), who usually comes out of the pen, gets the start for the BB Stars. With two outs and Sewell on first base (walk), Doby lines one over the right field fence for a 2-run home run. Colavito grounds out. **Indians 2, BB Stars 0.**

In the top of the third, the BB Stars get another bad break. Josh Gibson is injured trying to catch a foul pop-up and falls down the stairs of the Indian dugout. He will probably miss at least three games.

In the bottom of the third, Score retires the first two batters. He has retired the first eight men he has faced in the game. J. R. Richard singles to left. Bell bounces one to Sewell, but he drops the ball and cannot pick it up. Everybody is safe. Wells splits the gap in right center; the ball rolls to the wall. Doby picks it up and throws it in to Avila (cut-off man). Wells slides safely into third with a 2-run triple, tying the game with two unearned runs. Mackey strikes out to end the inning. **BB Stars 2, Indians 2.**

In the bottom of the fifth, the BB Stars take the lead. Judy Johnson walks to lead-off the inning. Warfield goes down swinging. J. R. Richard bunts; Score slips as he tries to pick up the ball. Both runners are safe; credit Richard with a single. Score strikes out Bell (looking) for the second out of the inning. Wells doubles into the left field corner, scoring Johnson, with Richard stopping at third. Wells has driven in all three runs. Score fools Mackey (replaced Gibson, third inning) with a curve on the outside corner, strike three. **BB Stars 3, Indians 2.**

Richard retires the first two batters in the sixth. He walks Colavito. Connor crushes the first pitch from Richard to straight away center; Bell cannot get it. Connor has tripled to tie the score. Avila hits one deep in the hole (left side); Wells grabs it on a one-hop, but he cannot make a play (infield single). Connor scores the go-ahead run (4-3). Ewing flies out to Charleston (LF). **Indians 4, BB Stars 3.**

In the bottom of the sixth, Suttles ties the game with a home run off Score over the center field fence. **BB Stars 4, Indians 4.**

Averill pinch hits for Score. The final line for Score is 6 IP, 6 H, 4 R, 2 ER, 1 HR, 8 K, 1 BB. Averill lines a single to right. Tiant is warming up in the bullpen for the BB Stars. Richard walks Jackson on four pitches. Tiant replaces Richard in a double switch. Allen replaces Warfield at second base and will bat ninth (lead-off in the bottom of the seventh). Tiant bats eighth (Warfield's spot). Johnson and Suttles move in, looking for the bunt. Sewell bunts in front of the plate. Mackey pounces on it and fires to Wells, covering third for the force on Averill (one out). Rosen chops one to Wells, who charges the ball and throws to Suttles (1B), but Suttles drops the ball. The bases are loaded with only one out. Doby lofts a fly ball into left center; Charleston (LF) makes the catch as Shoeless Joe Jackson races home with the go-ahead run (5-4). Credit Doby with a sac fly. This completes the final line on J. R. Richard (6+ IP, 7 H, 5 R, 4 ER, 1 HR, 3 K, 3 BB). Tiant walks Colavito to reload the bases. Tom McCarthy pinch runs for Colavito and will play right field. Tiant goes to 3 and 2 on Connor. The runners take off as Tiant throws the ball in the dirt blocked by Mackey. It is ball four, forcing in the sixth run, which is unearned. Avila ends the inning, forcing Connor at second base. **Indians 6, BB Stars 4.**

Bob Lemon is now pitching and will bat fourth, replacing Doby (CF) in the lineup. Averill stays in the game and is playing center field. Allen singles to center, and Averill bobbles the ball. Allen hustles to second (single and error). Bell bounces one back to Lemon. He looks Allen back to second and throws out Bell (one out). Wells steps to the plate. He is 2 for 3 (triple, double, 3 RBIs). Wells drives one into the gap in left center. Jackson picks it up on the warning track as Allen scores. Wells has a stand-up double and his fourth RBI (6-5). Lemon strikes out Mackey and Charleston (both hitters have struck out three times today). **Indians 6, BB Stars 5.**

Ewing leads off the eighth with a home run just inside the right field foul pole to give the Indians a 2-run cushion again (7-5). Averill singles to right before Tiant retires the side (striking out Sewell and Rosen to end the inning). **Indians 7, BB Stars 5.**

With one out in the bottom of the eighth, Stearnes will bat for Irvin. Stearnes lines one that Lemon is able to knock down with his glove before it hits him in the face. He is unable to make a play. Stearnes is on first with a hard, infield single. Judy Johnson slaps a base hit into left field, and Stearnes stops at second base. Early Wynn is warming up for the Indians. Buck Leonard will bat for Tiant. Leonard is fooled by a changeup and tops it to Avila at second base, who throws Leonard out while the runners move to second and third. Lemon walks Allen. Early Wynn is being brought in to pitch to the switch-hitting Cool Papa Bell with the bases loaded. Bell hits a high fly ball to McCarthy (RF) to end the inning. The BB Stars miss a big opportunity.

Hilton Smith comes in to pitch the ninth. He gives up a two-out single to Connor; however, Connor is thrown out attempting to steal (Mackey-Allen).

In the eighth inning, Wynn escaped a bases-loaded situation. In the ninth inning, Wynn creates a bases-loaded situation. He walks the first three batters he faces (Wells, Mackey, and Charleston). Harder is now pitching for the Indians. Suttles tops one in front of the plate. Buck Ewing grabs it and fires to second to force Charleston (one out). There is no chance to double-up Suttles at first. Wells scores (7-6), and Mackey goes to third. Can Harder retire Turkey Stearnes without Mackey scoring the tying run? Harder strikes out Stearnes (looking). Johnson hits a high fly down the right field line; McCarthy hustles over and makes the catch. Mel Harder saves the win for Herb Score. The Indians have won the first three games of the series.

	R	H	E	LOB
Indians	7	10	2	8
BB Stars	6	8	1	10

Winning Pitcher – Score   Save – Harder   Losing Pitcher – Richard
The Indians lead the series 3-0.

Game Four, Wednesday June 30, Shea Stadium (New York), 7 pm (Coveleski vs. Day)

The BB Stars have called on Leon Day to get them back on track. Stan Coveleski would like to lead the Indians to their fourth straight win. It is a warm, clear evening with just a very light wind at Shea Stadium. It is a beautiful night for baseball. Each team gets a couple of base runners and a run in the first. Both runs score on force plays at second base in first and third situations. **Indians 1, BB Stars 1.**

In the bottom of the third, the BB Stars score two unearned runs off Coveleski to take a 3-1 lead. Coveleski gives up a single (to center) to Bell, leading off, but Coveleski gets Bell leaning the wrong way and picks him off first base (one out). Lloyd bounces out to Avila (2B) for the second out. Charleston walks, and Leonard moves him to third with a single up the middle. Torriente hits a soft line drive into shallow right; Colavito gets a good jump but drops the routine fly ball. Charleston scores, Leonard ends up on third, and Torriente is on first. Colavito seems to have taken his eye off the ball; instead of three outs and no runs, there is one unearned run and runners on first and third. I wonder what Coveleski is thinking? Mackey lines a single to center, scoring Leonard with the second unearned run in the inning. Torriente is at second, Mackey is at first, and Coveleski pitches to Dandridge. He lines one to Sewell's right; Sewell knocks it down, but it is an infield hit, loading the bases. Coveleski avoids further damage by striking out Warfield. **BB Stars 3, Indians 1.**

In the top of the fourth, with two outs and no one on base, the Indians come to life. Connor singles to right. Avila singles to center, with Connor moving to third. Ewing lines a ball deep down the right-field line. It hits the foul pole about six feet above the fence for a 3-run home run. Coveleski strikes out swinging to end the inning. **Indians 4, BB Stars 3.**

Day singles to center, leading off the bottom of the fourth. Bell hits a potential double play ball to Avila (2B), and he bobbles the ball; everybody is safe (first and second, none out). Lloyd bounces one between Connor and Avila into right field. Day scores from second, and Bell moves to third (4-4). Mike Garcia begins to warm up for the Indians. Charleston hits a ground ball that Connor (1B) fields and throws to Sewell (SS) for the force on Lloyd at second base. Bell scores the go-ahead run (5-4). Leonard chops the ball over Coveleski's head. Sewell makes a good play but a horribly wide throw into the dugout; runners are on second and third. The Indians have made four errors.

153

There is one out but should be three outs. One of the two runs this inning is unearned; any additional runs will be unearned. Both runs in the third were unearned. Coveleski is definitely a victim of poor support. Torriente singles to left, scoring Charleston (6-4); Leonard stops at third. Mackey hits one on two hops to Connor, who throws to Sewell, forcing Torriente. The return throw is too late to double up Mackey, as Leonard scores the seventh run for the BB Stars. Dandridge fouls out to Connor to end the disastrous inning. **BB Stars 7, Indians 4.**

Day walks Jackson and Sewell to open the fifth. Day looks like he might escape without any runs. Averill grounds out to second with both runners advancing. Rosen hits a high fly to shallow left; Charleston makes the catch. Shoeless Joe Jackson fakes a dash to the plate to force Charleston to make a throw. It is a strike to Mackey, as Jackson retreats to third. Colavito singles to left, and the ball bounces past Charleston as both runners score. Colavito takes second on the error. Connor flies out to Torriente, ending the inning. **BB Stars 7, Indians 6.**

In the bottom of the fifth, the BB Stars make some changes. Newt Allen pinch hits for Warfield and grounds out to Connor (unassisted). Stearnes pinch hits for Leon Day (5 IP, 7 H, 6 R, 1 HR, 1 K, 4 BB). Stearnes hits one up the middle. Avila dives, knocks it down, and throws out Stearnes from his knees (great play). Coveleski walks Bell. Lloyd chases Averill to the warning track for the third out.

Martin Dihigo is now pitching for the BB Stars in the sixth. The Indians pinch hit for Coveleski in the sixth but do not score. The final line on Coveleski is 5 IP, 8 H, 7 R, 2 ER, 0 HR, 1 K, 3 BB.

Mike Garcia is now pitching in the bottom of the sixth. The BB Stars get a two-out single (Torriente) but fail to score.

Martin Dihigo strikes out Sewell (swinging) for the first out in the seventh. Averill gets all of a Dihigo fast ball for a home run to right field, tying the score 7-7.

The pitching stiffens. Garcia is replaced in the eighth by Bob Lemon. Dihigo is replaced in the tenth by Bullet Joe Rogan. It is a double switch, and Johnson replaces Dandridge at third.

The Indians can put the BB Stars in a deep hole if they can overcome the four errors that led to five unearned runs. The BB Stars do not want to fall behind four games to none.

In the bottom of the twelfth, Bob Lemon is beginning his fifth inning. Allen leads off with a single to center. Judy Johnson (batting ninth) will probably be bunting. Connor (1B) and Rosen (3B) are in on the grass looking for the bunt. Johnson drops an excellent bunt up the first base line. Connor fields it and throws to Avila, covering first (one out), and Allen advances to second (credit sacrifice hit to Johnson). Lemon pitches around Bell, who walks. Lemon wants a ground ball and a double play. Lemon's first pitch is a knee-high fast ball that Lloyd drives into the gap in right center, scoring Allen with the winning run (a walk-off run scoring double)..

12 Innings	R	H	E	LOB
Indians	7	10	4	9
BB Stars	8	16	1	12

Winning Pitcher – Rogan   Losing Pitcher – Lemon

The Indians lead the series, 3-1.

Game Five, Thursday July 1, Shea Stadium (New York), 2 pm (McDowell vs. Paige)

The game is delayed for an hour by a passing thunderstorm. It is hot and very muggy. The field is wet. With two out in the bottom of the first, Bell is on first (lead-off single). Mule Suttles hits the ball off the base of the center field wall for a run scoring double. Irvin taps the ball back to McDowell, who throws him out. **BB Stars 1, Indians 0.**

Through the first six innings, Satchel Paige is coasting. Four of the first six batters in the game reach base off Paige. However, Averill raps into a double play to end the first. In the second, Rosen singles, and Hargrove walks to lead-off the inning. Paige retires the next 15 batters (through six innings).

Suttles leads off in the bottom of the sixth against McDowell. The BB Stars have not had a hit since the second. In the fourth, McDowell loaded the bases with three walks, but Sewell made a great catch of Satchel Paige's pop-up near the foul line to end that inning.

Suttles has an RBI double and a walk. McDowell falls behind 3-0. Suttles is sitting on a fast ball that he drives high and deep to center field. Averill runs to the fence and looks up; it is gone, home run (2-0). McDowell escapes from a hit batter and an error when Averill throws out Irvin, trying to score after a fly out (double play). **BB Stars 2, Indians 0.**

Paige retires the side in order (top of the seventh, 18 retired in a row).

Addie Joss is warming up for the Indians. In the bottom of the seventh, McDowell fans Paige, his seventh strike out (one out). Bell singles to left. Bell steals second. McDowell walks Wells. Charleston will probably be the last batter McDowell will face. McDowell blows Charleston away with three fast balls (two outs). Joss is coming in to pitch to Suttles (run-scoring double, walk, and bases empty HR). It is a double switch; Connor replaces Hargrove at first base. Joss fares no better; Suttles lines a sharp single to left center, scoring Bell with Wells stopping at second. Stearnes bats for Irvin. On the first pitch, Stearnes foul tips the ball, and it hits Elston Howard's thumb on his bare hand. He falls to his knees in pain. Ewing replaces Howard. It looks doubtful that Howard will be available for the rest of the series.

Joss falls behind 3-1; Stearnes crushes a fast ball for a 3-run home run. The BB Stars lead 6-0. The final line on McDowell is 6.7 IP, 5 H, 4 R, 1 HR, 8 K, 4 BB, 1 HB. Mackey strikes out to end the inning. **BB Stars 6, Indians 0.**

In the eighth, Paige retires the side in order (three ground balls by Avila, Ewing, and Hargrove). He has now retired 21 in a row.

In the bottom of the eighth, the BB Stars score one more run (7-0).

Paige walks the lead-off man in the ninth (Jackson). Sewell raps into a double play. McCarthy hits it hard and fairly deep to right center, but Cool Papa Bell makes a nice running catch to end the game. The final line on Paige is a complete game shutout, 9 IP, 3 H, 0 R, 5 K, 2 BB.

	R	H	E	LOB
Indians	0	3	1	3
BB Stars	7	8	0	7

Winning Pitcher - Paige   Losing Pitcher - McDowell

The Indians lead the series, 3-2.

Game Six, Saturday July 3, Cleveland Municipal Stadium, 1 pm (Foster vs. Feller)

It is a perfect day for baseball (warm, clear, no wind). The BB Stars are trying to even the series 3-3 after being down 3-0. They strike first. In the top of the second, Turkey Stearnes takes Bob Feller deep, home run to right field. **BB Stars 1, Indians 0.**

In the bottom of the second, Larry Doby leads off with a double into the right field corner. Colavito is robbed by Stearnes' shoestring catch (CF), Doby has to slide back to second to avoid being doubled off the bag. Connor grounds out to Allen (2B); Doby goes to third (two outs). Avila slaps a single to right field, scoring Doby with the tying run. Ewing flies out to Torriente (RF). **Indians 1, BB Stars 1.**

In the top of the third, Allen singles to right. He steals second. Foster strikes out trying to bunt. Feller strikes out Torriente (looking) for the second out. Feller gives up a double to Lloyd (one run), a single to Charleston (scores Lloyd), and a triple to Stearnes (scores Charleston) before Mackey grounds out to Avila (2B). Three runs score after two outs. How many times do the BB Stars do that? **BB Stars 4, Indians 1.**

In the top of the fifth (with two outs) and Lloyd on first (single), Stearnes gets his third hit (HR and two triples), a triple that scores Lloyd. Mackey grounds out to Avila. **BB Stars 5, Indians 1.**

Otis pinch hits for Feller in the bottom of the fifth and makes the third out with a long fly ball to left field. Charleston catches it near the foul pole. The final line on Feller is 5 IP, 8 H, 5 R, 1 HR, 6 K, 1 BB.

Bearden relieves Feller in the top of the sixth. The BB Stars close out the scoring with a solo home run by Ray Dandridge. Foster gives the BB Stars a second complete game in a row (9 IP, 6 H, 1 R, 0 HR, 3 K, 2 BB).

	R	H	E	LOB
BB Stars	6	11	1	3
Indians	1	6	0	8

Winning Pitcher – Foster   Losing Pitcher – Feller

The BB Stars even the series, 3-3.

Game Seven, Sunday July 4, Cleveland Municipal Stadium, 1 pm (Newcombe vs. Score)

It is a scorcher, a very hot, partly cloudy day at the ball park with the wind blowing out toward left field. It is scoreless going into the top of the fourth inning. Score escapes a bases loaded situation in the third (a single, a walk, and an error by Ewing).

Stearnes walks to lead-off the fourth. Suttles singles to left, with Stearnes stopping at second base. Irvin forces Suttles at second, while Stearnes goes to third (one out). Score walks Johnson, loading the bases for the second inning in a row. Warfield lines a double into the left field corner, scoring two and moving Johnson to third. Newcombe lays down a perfect bunt, scoring a run and moving Warfield to third (Newcombe out, Score to Avila covering first). Score walks his third batter of the inning (Bell). Wells singles in the fourth run of the inning with Bell stopping at second. Gibson hits a deep fly to left that Jackson takes on the warning track. **BB Stars 4, Indians 0.**

In the fifth, Mule Suttles takes Score deep to left. With the wind blowing out, it is gone, home run. It is now 5-0.

Newcombe is pitching well as he goes into the bottom of the sixth. Sewell flies out to center, pinch hitting for Feller (6 IP 5 H, 5 R, 1 HR, 4 K, 4 BB). Jackson strikes out (two outs). Boudreau bloops a single to center field. Averill doubles to the gap in left center; Bell cuts it off, which holds Boudreau at third. Rosen flies out to Stearnes (LF). Newcombe escapes a threatening situation. **BB Stars 5, Indians 0.**

As part of a double switch (Sewell replaces Boudreau), Mel Harder relieves Feller and pitches a scoreless seventh.

With one out, Newcombe walks Connor in the bottom of the seventh. Avila (on the hit-and-run) singles to right, sending Connor to third. On the first pitch to Ewing, the ball bounces off of Gibson's glove (passed ball); Connor scores, and Avila goes to second. Bell robs Ewing of a potential double (two outs). Sewell bounces out to Allen. The Indians are on the board. **BB Stars 5, Indians 1.**

Each team adds two runs in the eighth (Rosen 2-run home run for Indians). **BB Stars 7, Indians 3.**

The BB Stars do not score in the ninth off the third Indian pitcher (Garcia).

Hilton Smith is ready in the BB Stars bullpen. Connor leads off the bottom of the ninth, with a single to center. The BB Stars will make a pitching change. Hilton Smith relieves Don Newcombe, who pitched eight plus innings very effectively. Smith retires all three batters he faces. The final line for Newcombe is 8 IP, 9 H, 3 R, 1 HR, 2 K, 1 BB. The BB Stars have now won four straight.

	R	H	E	LOB
BB Stars	7	9	0	7
Indians	3	9	2	6

Winning Pitcher – Newcombe   Losing Pitcher – Score
The BB Stars lead the series, 4-3.

Game Eight, Monday July 5, Shea Stadium (New York), 7 pm (Joss vs. Rogan)

It is warm and clear for Game Eight at Shea Stadium. With one out in the top of the second, Boudreau doubles over Charleston's head in left field. Hargrove punches a soft line drive over shortstop Lloyd's head for an RBI single. On the hit-and-run, Ewing singles to right, with Hargrove scampering to third. Keltner chops one to the right side fielded by Allen, who throws Keltner out at first (Hargrove scores and Ewing moves to second, 2-0). Rogan strikes out Addie Joss (swinging). **Indians 2, BB Stars 0,**

In the bottom of the second, Gibson and Leonard lead-off with singles (runners on first and second), but Joss retires the next three batters with no runs scoring.

With one out in the bottom of the third, the BB Stars finally score off Joss. Bell singles to center. Lloyd singles to right with Bell easily making it to third. Charleston brings in a run with a sac fly to Doby (LF). Josh hits a one-hop smash down the third base line. Keltner dives, fields the ball, and guns Gibson out at first to end the inning. Note that Keltner's AA range vs. Rosen's B range is the difference between a double and an out. **Indians 2, BB Stars 1.**

Rogan gets two quick outs in the fourth; Boudreau and Hargrove both fly out to Bell (CF). Rogan does not retire another batter. Ewing gets his second hit (single to right). Ewing steals second on the first pitch to Keltner. Rogan walks Keltner. Joss singles to center; Ewing scores and Keltner stops at second (3-1). Leon Day is warming up for the BB Stars. Jackson singles to right, scoring Keltner with the fourth run, Joss stops at second. Rogan walks Sewell to load the bases. Rogan walks Doby, forcing in the fifth run. Leon Day replaces Rogan.

Day falls behind Averill, 3-1. Averill gets what he wants, a fast ball over the heart of the plate. He swings and hits a drive to deep right center. Bell is racing to the fence; he leaps and makes a great catch, taking a grand slam home run from Averill and keeping the game relatively close (5-1 vs. 9-1). The final line on Rogan is 3.7 IP, 7 H, 5 R, 0 HR, 2 K, 3 BB. **Indians 5, BB Stars 1.**

In the bottom of the fifth, one out back-to-back doubles by Bell and Lloyd make it 5-2 (Joss also walks Gibson). The BB Stars have had men on base every inning (8 hits and 6 left on base through five innings). **Indians 5, BB Stars 2.**

In the top of the seventh, Donnie Moore replaces Day, who retired all seven batters he faced. Cool Papa Bell did help him a lot on the first batter in the fourth (Averill). Moore gives up a two-out single to Averill but no runs.

The Indians make two defensive changes in the bottom of the seventh. McCarthy replaces Doby but will play right field, as Shoeless Joe Jackson moves from right to left. Amos Otis replaces Averill in center field. In the sixth Avila (2B) replaced Boudreau (SS), as Sewell moved from second base to short stop. Connor had replaced Hargrove at first base in the bottom of the sixth, also.

Lloyd singles to center (his fourth hit of the game). Joss has never retired the side in order. Charleston chops one to the right of mound. Connor (1B) makes a good play and flips to Joss, who tags Charleston just before he steps on first base (one out). Lloyd is now in scoring position at second base. Gibson lines a sharp single to left. Lloyd stops at third as Jackson fires a strike to Ewing at home plate. Leonard booms one off the fence in right center. It takes a funny bounce past Otis as two runs score. Leonard slides into third with a triple, making it a 1-run game (5-4). Coveleski and McDowell are both ready in the Cleveland bullpen. Connor and Keltner are in on the grass, playing for the bunt with Cristobal Torriente at the plate. Torriente is swinging away and hits one toward the hole on the right side. Connor dives getting the ball on the first hop. Leonard takes two steps toward home and decides to go back to third as Connor flips to Joss at first base (two outs). Joss strikes out Dandridge (looking). **Indians 5, BB Stars 4.**

In the top of the eighth, Moore retires the Indians in order.

In the bottom of the eighth, Addie Joss is still on the mound. With one out, Mackey bats for Moore and singles to right. Coveleski is coming in to pitch. Coveleski retires both batters he faces to end the inning. The final line on Addie Joss is 7.3 IP, 14 H, 4 R, 0 HR, 0 K, 1 BB. **Indians 5, BB Stars 4.**

In the ninth, J. R. Richard is the fourth pitcher for the BB Stars, and he retires the side in order (including pinch hitter Rosen, K batting for Coveleski).

Sudden Sam McDowell is in to protect the 1-run lead. He jams Charleston, who pops out to Avila (2B). However, Josh Gibson slams a McDowell fast ball into the left field seats to tie the game. Leonard hits his second triple off the fence in center field. The Indians move the infield and outfield in as Torriente comes to bat. McDowell gets Torriente to hit a high fly to shallow center. Otis makes the catch and fires the ball to Ewing but there is no runner coming to the plate. Leonard holds at third base. Dandridge takes a called third strike to end the inning. **BB Stars 5, Indians 5.**

We are headed to extra innings in Game Eight with the BB Stars holding a 4-3 lead in the series. The Indians have been shut down by the BB Stars bullpen. In the tenth, they do get a one out base runner (Otis walks). Otis steals second but is stranded at second.

In the bottom of the tenth, Allen leads off with a single. Wells is announced as the pinch hitter for Richard, and the Indians bring the right-hander, Mike Garcia, in to pitch. Wells lines out to Keltner. Carcia retires Bell and Lloyd on fly balls to Otis (CF).

The BB Stars do a double switch to start the eleventh. Wells stays in the game and will play shortstop; Luis Tiant is pitching and batting second in Lloyd's spot. Dandridge robs Ewing of a base hit with a great play, moving to his left and throwing the speedy Ewing out at first. Keltner flies out to Charleston (two outs). Rocky Colavito bats for Garcia. Rocky hits a high drive to deep left, but Charleston has room and makes the catch.

In the bottom of the eleventh, Early Wynn is now pitching for the Indians (their fifth pitcher of the game). Charleston leads off with a double to the wall in right center. Gibson is intentionally walked. Leonard hits a tailor-made double play ball to Sewell (SS). Sewell bobbles it, and the bases are loaded, none out.

Wynn is a veteran pitcher. He does not panic. The infield and outfield are moved in. Torriente is 0 for 5 and has had chances with men on base three times previously. He has left Leonard on third, twice. Torriente bunts down the third-base line. Keltner charges bare hands the ball and fires to Ewing as Charleston slides, out at home (force play, one out). Dandridge pops it up (infield fly rule, batter is out); Avila makes the catch behind the pitcher's mound (two outs). The infield and outfield go back to normal positions. Allen flies out to McCarthy (RF). What a great job by Wynn. Keltner again makes a great play in the clutch.

In the top of the twelfth, Tiant faces the top of the Indians order. Bell makes a sliding catch to rob Jackson of a double or triple (one out). Sewell walks and McCarthy singles to right, with Sewell hustling to third. Otis hits a line drive over Bell's head in center; this may score two runs. McCarthy beats the throw, 7-5 Indians. Otis is standing on second base with a double. Avila grounds out to Wells (SS) and Otis remains at second base (two outs). Connor lines a single to right, Otis is being waved home and Torriente's throw is cut off, 8-5 Indians. Hilton Smith is ready in the bullpen. Ewing singles to center and Connor races to third. Smith replaces Tiant. Keltner hits a ground ball past Wells into left field, scoring Connor and sending the speedy Ewing over to third. It is 9-5 Indians. Wynn, the ninth batter of the inning strikes out. **Indians 9, BB Stars 5.**

In the bottom of the twelfth, Otis runs a long way and catches Wells' drive on the warning track (one out). Bell walks. The BB Stars have had base runners in every inning of this game. Monte Irvin will bat for Hilton Smith. Irvin hits a routine fly ball to Jackson for the second out. Wynn strikes out Charleston (swinging).

12 Innings	R	H	E	LOB
Indians	9	13	1	9
BB Stars	5	18	0	16

Winning Pitcher – Wynn   Losing Pitcher – Tiant
The series is tied, 4-4.

Game Nine, Tuesday July 6, Shea Stadium (New York), 7 pm (Lemon vs. Paige)

It is warm and partly cloudy for Game Nine. Lemon and Paige breeze through the first three innings. In the top of the fourth, Jackson doubles down the right field line. Paige then retires the next three batters. Over the last twelve innings Paige has pitched in this series, he has faced 37 batters, one over the minimum.

In the bottom of the fourth, Lemon strikes out Lloyd. Charleston beats out an infield hit just beyond Lemon's reach. With the count 1-1 on Gibson, Lemon throws a wild pitch in the dirt that skips by Ewing; Charleston advances to second. Gibson bounces out to Connor (1B); Charleston moves to third. Turkey Stearnes hits a high fly deep down the right-field line, if it stays fair it could be trouble. Colavito runs to the fence; it is gone, a home run, just fair (2-0). Leonard flies to Colavito ending the inning. **BB Stars 2, Indians 0.**

In the fifth, Colavito leads off with a home run to cut the lead in half. **BB Stars 2, Indians 1.**

In the top of the seventh, Paige retires the first two batters.. Avila doubles over Charleston's head in left. Ewing bloops one that drops between Lloyd

(SS) and Charleston (LF) for an RBI single tying the game (Ewing is 2 for 3). On the first pitch to Lemon, Ewing steals second. Lenon flies out to Stearnes (RF). **Indians 2, BB Stars 2.**

In the bottom of the seventh, Leonard leads off with a double down the right field line, Torriente pinch runs for Leonard (Suttles will play first base). After Judy Johnson flies to center, Allen walks. Mackey pinch hits for Paige and goes down swinging. The final line for Paige is 7 IP, 6 H, 2 R, 1 HR, 6 K, 0 BB. Lemon fans Bell to end the threat.

Hilton Smith is now pitching. He retires the Indians in order (top of the eighth).

In the bottom of the eighth with one out, Charleston lines a home run over the right field-fence. The BB Stars take the lead again, 3-2. Lemon retires the next two batters to end the eighth. **BB Stars 3, Indians 2.**

This is the last chance for the Indians. They won the first three games, lost four straight and then won the exciting eighth game in 12 innings. Smith is starting his second inning of relief. He will be facing Rosen, Colavito and Connor. Smith gets Rosen to ground out to Lloyd (SS). Rosen is 0 for 4. Colavito walks on a 3-2 pitch in the dirt. Tommy McCarthy will run for Colavito. Smith walks Connor on four pitches. Left-hander Bill Foster is warming up for the BB Stars. Coveleski is warming up for the Indians. Avila hits a ground ball up the middle and through into center field. McCarthy scores easily and Connor legs it around to third. This game is tied, again (3-3).

Johnson (3B) and Suttles (1B) are playing in for the bunt. Buck Ewing is a great bunter, and he has been having a great series. (Howard, the other catcher, has been unavailable since his finger injury in Game Five). Ewing squares to bunt. He drops down a beauty. Johnson can only make the play on Ewing at first as Connor scores the go-ahead run (4-3). Avila goes to second. Doby has been announced to bat for Bob Lemon (8 IP, 5 H, 3 R, 2 HR, 7 K, 2 BB). Foster will be brought in to pitch (lefty vs. lefty). Amos Otis will now bat for Larry Doby. Otis lines a single into left field. Avila is being waved home. Charleston's throw is on the money; Gibson blocks the plate and tags out Avila to end the inning. **Indians 4, BB Stars 3.**

The Indians will make a number of defensive changes. McCarthy will now play right field. Otis stays in the game and will play center. Keltner replaces Rosen but will bat in Averill's third spot. Coveleski, the new pitcher will bat fourth (Rosen's spot). Suttles leads off the bottom of the ninth and grounds out (Avila-Connor). Johnson hits a one-hopper to Keltner's left, he spears it and throws out Johnson. Allen will try to keep things alive; Monte Irvin is on deck hoping to bat for Foster. The count goes to 3-2 on Allen. Coveleski jams him with a fast ball. It is popped up to shallow right field;

McCarthy is coming on and makes the catch. The Indians have rallied to take the series five games to four!

	R	H	E	LOB
Indians	4	8	1	5
BB Stars	3	5	0	5

Winning Pitcher – Lemon   Save – Coveleski   Losing Pitcher – Smith
The Indians win the series, 5-4.

Recap of Best Season Series 7 (BB Stars vs. Indians)

The BB Stars have now lost three series in a row after having won their first four series. Chart 12-2 on page 165 has BB Stars individual/team statistics for this series. Chart 12-3 on page 166 has Indians individual/team statistics for this series.

This was an exciting Series played in three acts.
- Act One – Indians win Games One, Two, and Three.
- Act 2 - The BB Stars win Games Four through Seven.
- Act 3 - The Indians win Games Eight and Nine to win the series. There were many other twists and turns throughout this exciting series.

Hitting Star for the Indians - Buck Ewing (1888 New York-N)

	RS	RBI	HR	.Avg	OBP	SPct	OPS
B. Ewing	5	7	2	.300	.323	.600	.923

Note: He had two successful bunts that led to key victories, also. His speed on bases was critical, including two stolen bases.

Best Pitcher for Indians – Bob Lemon (1948 Indians)

	G	GS	QS	CG	W-L	IP	H	HR	R/ER	ERA
B. Lemon	3	1	1	0	1-1	14	14	2	5	3.21

Note: His first relief appearance was not effective (Game 3, Indians 7-6 win); he did a great job in the tough twelve-inning loss (Game Five – 4.3 IP, 5 H, 1 ER); Lemon was very solid as the winning pitcher in Game Nine (8 IP, 5 H, 3 R, 2 HR, 7 K, 2 BB).

Hitting Star for the BB Stars - Mule Suttles

	RS	RBI	HR	.Avg	OBP	SPct	OPS
M. Suttles	4	6	3	.350	.381	.850	1.231

Best Pitcher for the BB Stars – B. Foster

	G	GS	QS	CG	W-L	IP	H	HR	R/ER	ERA
B. Foster	3	2	1	1	1-0	16.3	10	1	3	1.60

Foster had two solid starts. In his first start, he pitched 7 innings (3 hits, 2 runs, no decision in a 3-2 loss). His second start was a complete game six-hitter (6-1 win). He finished Game Nine giving up a hit (runner thrown out at the plate).

Game by Game Recap

This was an excellent nine-game series. Let us review the highlights by game.

Game One - Indians blow 5-1 lead but win the game with a 4-run sixth inning. Paige goes only three innings (eight hits, five runs). Indians win 9-6.

Game Two - Solid starting pitching by Foster and Feller; neither one involved in decision. Indians win in the ninth with a Judy Johnson two-base error; Ewing sac bunt and Sewell's walk-off bunt single, 3-2.

BB Stars Results vs. Indians 4-5, .444

Pos.	E	R	TH	PB	Hitters	G	AB	R	H	RBI	2B	3B	HR	TB	W	HB	SO	SF	SH	SB	B.AVG.	OBP	S.PCT.	OPS
LF	5	A	-1		Charleston	8	35	5	10	5	2	0	1	15	3	0	9	1	0	0	0.286	0.342	0.429	0.771
CF	8	AA	-1		CP Bell	8	35	8	8	2	2	1	0	12	7	0	6	0	0	1	0.229	0.357	0.343	0.700
OF	5	A	-1		Stearnes	8	25	5	8	8	0	3	3	23	1	0	3	0	0	0	0.320	0.346	0.920	1.266
OF	6	B			M Irvin	4	6	2	1	2	0	1	1	4	1	1	3	0	0	0	0.167	0.375	0.667	1.042
OF	6	A	-2		Torriente	5	17	4	3	2	0	0	0	3	0	0	2	1	0	0	0.176	0.176	0.176	0.353
SS	7	A			P Lloyd	5	21	4	11	5	3	0	1	14	2	0	4	1	0	0	0.524	0.565	0.667	1.232
SS	7	AA			W Wells	6	19	3	6	7	2	1	0	13	2	0	2	0	0	0	0.316	0.381	0.684	1.065
3B	7	A			J Johnson	6	18	4	4	0	1	0	0	5	3	0	3	0	1	0	0.222	0.333	0.278	0.611
3B	6	B			Dandridge	4	19	1	6	3	0	0	1	9	0	0	2	0	0	0	0.316	0.316	0.474	0.789
2B	7	A			N Allen	7	22	5	8	1	0	1	0	10	3	0	1	0	0	2	0.364	0.440	0.455	0.895
2B	7	A			F Warfield	5	13	2	2	3	1	0	0	3	2	0	3	0	0	0	0.154	0.267	0.231	0.497
1B	8	B			Suttles	6	20	4	7	6	1	0	3	17	1	0	1	0	0	0	0.350	0.381	0.850	1.231
1B	8	B			B Leonard	6	21	3	8	3	3	2	0	15	2	0	2	0	0	0	0.381	0.381	0.714	1.095
C	7	A	-2	Fr	J Gibson	6	20	2	4	1	0	0	1	7	2	0	4	0	0	0	0.200	0.273	0.350	0.623
C	6	B	-2	Aw	B Mackey	8	23	0	3	1	0	0	0	3	1	0	0	0	2	0	0.130	0.167	0.130	0.297
					pitchers	9	30	2	7	1	0	0	0	7	0	0	5	0	3	0	0.233	0.233	0.233	0.467
					TOTAL	9	344	50	96	50	15	8	11	160	28	1	56	3	0	3	0.279	0.335	0.465	0.800

Fat.	H	WP	E	R	Pitchers	G	GS	QS	CG	S	W	L	IP	H	SO	BB	HB	HR	R	ER	ERA
10/L	Vg	N	9	B	BJ Rogan	3	1	0	0	0	0	1	8	8	5	4	0	0	5	5	5.63
9/L	Ex	R	7	B	B Foster	2	2	1	0	0	0	1	16.3	10	5	7	0	1	3	3	1.65
10/L	Vg	NL	8	B	L Day	2	1	0	0	0	0	0	7.3	7	5	4	0	0	6	6	7.37
10/L	Aw	NL	7	B	M Dihigo	2	0	0	0	0	0	0	5.3	4	3	4	0	1	2	2	1.69
8/L	Md	R	8	C	S Paige	3	3	2	1	0	1	1	19	17	15	3	0	2	7	7	3.32
L/9	Vg	R	8	A	H Smith	5	0	0	0	2	0	0	4.7	8	6	2	0	0	6	6	11.56
9/L	Aw	R	9	A	Newcombe	2	1	1	0	0	1	1	10	10	6	1	0	1	3	3	2.70
10/L	Ex	NL	8	D	L Tiant	2	0	0	0	0	0	0	3.7	6	2	3	0	0	6	5	12.26
9	Aw	N	5	C	J R Richard	2	1	0	0	0	0	0	8	7	5	4	0	0	5	4	4.50
Long	Md	NL	4	B	D Moore	2	0	0	0	0	0	0	3	2	2	0	0	0	0	0	0.00
					TOTAL	26	9	5	2	2	4	4	85.3	79	43	32	0	8	43	40	4.22

Chart 12-2 – BB Stars Statistics for this series

Indians Best Season Series vs. BB All-Stars 5-4, .556

Team	Year	WS	Hitters	G	AB	R	H	RBI	2B	3B	HR	TB	W	HB	SO	SF	SH	SB	B.AVG.	OBP	S.PCT.	OPS
Cleveland	1958	32	R Colavito	7	23	2	3	4	0	0	1	7	4	0	3	0	0	3	0.130	0.259	0.304	0.564
St. Louis (N)	1890	24	T McCarthy	6	11	2	4	0	0	0	1	4	1	0	1	0	0	3	0.364	0.417	0.364	0.780
Cleveland	1950	30	L Doby	6	13	2	4	5	2	0	1	9	1	0	2	1	0	0	0.308	0.357	0.692	1.049
Cleveland	1936	27	E Averill	7	21	3	8	4	1	1	1	14	1	0	2	0	0	0	0.381	0.409	0.667	1.076
Cleveland	1911	39	SJ Jackson	9	39	5	11	2	4	0	0	15	3	0	6	0	0	1	0.282	0.333	0.385	0.718
Kansas City	1978	29	A Otis	5	5	1	3	3	1	0	0	4	2	0	0	0	0	0	0.600	0.714	0.800	1.514
Cleveland	1948	34	L Boudreau	6	21	2	4	1	1	0	0	5	1	0	2	0	0	0	0.190	0.227	0.238	0.465
Cleveland	1923	29	J Sewell	7	21	4	4	1	1	1	0	5	5	0	0	0	0	0	0.190	0.346	0.238	0.584
Cleveland	1953	42	A Rosen	9	31	3	5	5	0	1	2	13	1	0	4	0	0	0	0.161	0.188	0.419	0.607
Cleveland	1941	23	K Keltner	6	11	1	1	2	0	0	0	1	1	0	6	0	0	0	0.091	0.167	0.091	0.258
Cleveland	1954	34	B Avila	9	34	3	9	3	1	0	0	10	2	0	2	0	0	0	0.265	0.306	0.294	0.600
Cleveland	1980	25	M Hargrove	4	9	1	1	1	0	0	0	1	2	0	1	0	0	0	0.111	0.273	0.111	0.384
New York N	1885	36	R Connor	9	28	6	10	3	1	1	0	13	4	0	3	0	0	0	0.357	0.438	0.464	0.902
New York A	1961	29	E Howard	9	5	1	1	1	0	0	1	4	0	0	0	0	0	0	0.200	0.200	0.800	1.000
New York N	1888	27	B Ewing	9	30	5	9	7	3	0	2	18	1	0	2	0	2	2	0.300	0.323	0.600	0.923
			Pitchers	9	24	2	2	1	0	0	0	2	2	0	10	0	0	0	0.083	0.154	0.083	0.237
			Total	9	326	43	79	43	15	3	8	124	31	0	44	1	2	6	0.242	0.308	0.380	0.688

Team	Year	WS	Pitchers	G	GS	QS	CG	S	W	L	IP	H	SO	BB	HB	HR	R	ER	ERA
Cleveland	1946	32	B Feller	2	2	1	0	0	1	1	12	14	10	3	0	2	7	7	5.25
Cleveland	1908	35	A Joss	3	2	0	0	0	0	1	14	27	5	3	0	2	12	12	7.71
Cleveland	1956	25	H Score	2	2	1	0	0	1	1	12	11	12	5	0	2	9	7	5.25
Cleveland	1920	32	S Coveleski	3	3	0	1	0	1	0	6.7	8	1	3	0	0	7	2	2.70
Cleveland	1948	26	B Lemon	3	1	0	1	0	0	1	14	14	12	4	0	2	5	5	3.21
Cleveland	1956	28	E Wynn	4	0	0	0	0	0	1	5	2	1	5	0	0	1	1	1.80
Cleveland	1965	25	S McDowell	3	1	0	0	0	0	1	9.7	8	11	4	1	2	5	5	4.65
Cleveland	1954	24	M Garcia	3	0	0	0	0	0	0	4	3	2	1	0	0	0	0	0.00
Cleveland	1948	22	G Bearden	3	0	0	0	0	0	0	3	3	1	1	0	1	2	2	6.00
Cleveland	1934	27	M Harder	3	0	0	0	2	0	0	5	6	1	0	0	0	2	2	3.60
			TOTAL	29	9	3	3	0	3	5	4	85.3	96	56	28	1	11	50	43	4.53

Chart 12-3 – Indians statistics for this series

Game Three - Indians win a wild one, 7-6. Gibson injured (misses next three games but the BB Stars win all three). Ewing home run in the eighth is decisive. Mel Harder saves the game in the ninth after Wynn walks the bases loaded with none out.

Game Four - Indians make four errors that cost them the game (five unearned runs). They lose in twelve innings, 8-7.

Games Five, Six, and Seven - BB Stars pitching dominates 5) Paige 7-0 win; 6) Foster 6-1 win: 7) Newcombe 7-3 win. 26 innings by three starting pitchers, outscore Indians 20-4.

Game Eight - Cool Papa Bell robs Averill of grand slam in fourth but the Indians prevail in 12 innings, 9-5. The BB Stars leave 16 men on base.

Game Nine - Lemon and Paige both pitch very well. Indians rally in ninth; a couple of walks; Avila ties game with single and Ewing wins it with a perfect squeeze bunt, 4-3. Coveleski retires the BB Stars in order for the save. Coveleski, who had been the victim of the Indians' shoddy defense in Game Four, saved the deciding game. It was a great series.

Chapter 13

Best Season Nine Game Series 8 - BB Stars vs.Cardinals

Cardinals Roster Review

NINETY-TWO PERCENT OF THE ROSTER are made up of St. Louis Cardinals. Eight percent of the roster are free agents. See the Cardinals Roster (Chart 13-1 on page 170).

Offensive Leaders (Cardinals) Ranked by OPS

Player	OBP	SPct	OPS	R +	RBI -	HR =	NR
R. Hornsby	.507	.698	1.205	121	94	25	190
S. Musial	.450	.702	1.152	135	131	39	227
J. Medwick	.414	.641	1.056	111	154	31	234
J. Milligan	.401	.623	1.024	53	76	12	117
C. Hafey	.391	.632	1.023	101	125	29	197
B. Dahlen	.448	.566	1.014	149	107	15	241
J. Bottomley	.413	.578	.992	92	128	21	199
J. Torre	.421	.555	.976	97	137	24	210
K. Boyer	.373	.562	.935	95	97	32	160
K. Hernandez	.421	.513	.934	116	105	11	210

The following players would be base-stealing threats – L. Brock 118, F. Frisch 48, B. Dahlen 42 (numbers listed SB for their best season).

Fielding Leaders	Pos	Range	Error	Throwing
E. Slaughter	RF	A	8	-2
J. Medwick	LF	A	9	-2
S. Musial	L/RF	B	7	-1
C. Hafey	CF	C	5	-1
L. Brock	LF	B	3	0

For outfielders - range (AA is best) and throwing (-4 is exceptional, -3 is excellent, -2 is very good) are most important. Error rating (10 is best, 1 is poor) is not as critical as infielders because outfielders normally do not make as many errors.

R. Schoendienst	2B	AA+	8	-
F. Frisch	2B	AA+	8	-
K. Boyer	3B	AA	8	-
K. Hernandez	1B	AA	8	-
B. Dahlen	SS/3B	AA	5	-
R. Hornsby	2B	B+	3	-
J. Bottomley	1B	B	6	-

For infielders, range (AA is best), + increase in DPs because of excellent pivot, error rating is as important as range for an infielder (10 is excellent, 1 is poor).

Catcher Throwing - Milligan has an above-average throwing arm (-1) and Simmons is average (0).

Cardinals Roster Best Season Series vs. BB All-Stars

Team	Year	WS	Hitters	G	AB	R	H	RBI	2B	3B	HR	TB	W	HB	SO	SF	SH	SB	B.AVG.	OBP	S.PCT.	OPS
St. Louis (N)	1942	37	E. Slaughter	152	591	100	188	98	31	17	13	292	88	6	30	-	-	9	0.318	0.412	0.494	0.906
St. Louis (N)	1948	46	S. Musial	155	611	135	230	131	46	18	39	429	79	3	34	-	-	7	0.376	0.450	0.702	1.152
St. Louis (N)	1937	40	J. Medwick	156	633	111	237	154	56	10	31	406	41	2	50	-	-	4	0.374	0.414	0.641	1.056
St. Louis (N)	1929	22	C. Hafey	134	517	101	175	125	47	9	29	327	45	0	42	-	-	7	0.338	0.391	0.632	1.024
St. Louis (N)	1974	22	L. Brock	153	635	105	194	48	25	7	3	242	61	2	88	-	-	118	0.306	0.368	0.381	0.749
Chicago (N)	1894	21	B. Dahlen	121	502	149	179	107	32	14	15	284	76	7	33	-	-	42	0.357	0.448	0.566	1.014
St. Louis (N)	1927	34	F. Frisch	153	617	112	208	78	31	11	10	291	43	7	10	-	-	48	0.337	0.387	0.472	0.858
St. Louis (N)	1960	31	K. Boyer	151	552	95	168	97	26	10	32	310	56	4	77	-	-	8	0.304	0.373	0.562	0.934
St. Louis (N)	1971	41	J. Torre	161	634	97	230	137	34	8	24	352	63	1	70	-	-	4	0.363	0.421	0.555	0.976
St. Louis (N)	1924	38	R. Hornsby	143	536	121	227	94	43	14	25	374	89	2	32	-	-	5	0.424	0.507	0.698	1.205
St. Louis (N)	1953	27	Schoendi'st	146	564	107	193	79	35	5	15	283	60	0	23	-	-	3	0.342	0.405	0.502	0.907
St. Louis (N)	1979	29	Hernandez	161	610	116	210	105	48	11	11	313	80	1	78	-	-	11	0.344	0.421	0.513	0.934
St. Louis (N)	1925	27	Bottomley	153	619	92	227	128	44	12	21	358	47	2	36	-	-	3	0.367	0.413	0.578	0.992
St. Louis (N)	1978	30	T. Simmons	152	516	71	148	80	40	5	22	264	77	1	39	-	-	1	0.287	0.380	0.512	0.892
St. Louis	1889	17	J. Milligan	72	273	53	100	76	30	2	12	170	16	0	19	-	-	2	0.366	0.401	0.623	1.024

Team	Year	WS	Pitchers	G	GS	QS	CG	S	W	L	IP	H	SO	BB	HB	HR	R	ER	ERA
St. Louis (N)	1968	36	B. Gibson	34	34	-	28	0	22	9	305	198	268	62	11	-	-	-	1.12
St. Louis (N)	1934	37	D. Dean	50	33	-	24	7	30	7	312	288	195	75	14	-	-	-	2.66
St. Louis (N)	1946	27	H. Pollet	40	32	-	22	5	21	10	266	228	107	86	12	-	-	-	2.10
St. Louis (N)	1942	29	M. Cooper	37	35	-	22	0	22	7	279	207	152	68	9	-	-	-	1.78
St. Louis (N)	1943	23	M. Lanier	32	25	-	14	3	15	7	213	195	123	75	3	-	-	-	1.89
St. Louis (N)	1927	28	J. Haines	38	36	-	25	1	24	10	301	273	89	77	11	-	-	-	2.72
St. Louis (N)	1960	25	L. McDaniel	65	2	-	1	26	12	4	116	85	105	24	8	-	-	-	2.09
St. Louis (N)	1948	27	H. Brecheen	33	30	-	21	1	20	7	233	193	149	49	6	-	-	-	2.23
St. Louis	1975	19	A. Hrabosky	65	0	-	0	22	13	3	97	72	82	33	3	-	-	-	1.66
St. Louis	1984	23	B. Sutter	58	0	-	0	45	5	7	123	109	77	23	9	-	-	-	1.54

Chart 13-1 – Cardinals Best Season Roster

Pitcher Hold Rating - Gibson, Brecheen, and Cooper have excellent hold ratings; Haines is very good; the rest of the staff is average except Hrabosky, who is poor at holding runners.

Pitching - This is a solid pitching staff with an excellent bullpen (Sutter, McDaniel, Hrabosky and Brecheen).

Game One, Thursday July 8, Sportsman's Park (St. Louis), 3 pm (Day vs. Gibson)

The game is delayed two hours as a thunderstorm comes through about an hour before game time. When the storm moves out, it is hot and muggy, and the field is wet. Bob Gibson (1968 Cardinals, 22-9, 1.12 ERA) struggles in the first inning. Bell singles; Lloyd forces him at second. Charleston doubles off the wall in right; Lloyd stops at third. They decide to walk the dangerous right-hander, Josh Gibson, loading the bases to face the left-hander, Cristobal Torriente. The strategy works as Torriente hits a hard one-hopper to Hornsby (2B) who starts the 4-6-3 double play.

In the second inning, Buck Leonard leads off with a home run to right field. **BB Stars 1, Cardinals 0.**

Leon Day escapes a two-out jam in the fourth. Boyer triples over Bell's head in center. Hernandez walks but Day strikes out Frisch with a great curve ball on the outside corner.

With the BB Stars still leading 1-0 in the top of the sixth, they score again. Torriente singles to right field. Leonard flies out to Slaughter (RF). Dandridge singles to center and Torriente goes to third. Boyer (3B) and Hernandez (1B) move in looking for the bunt. Newt Allen slaps one to the right side; Hernandez lunges, grabs the ball on one-hop, and throws to Frisch, covering second for the force on Dandridge. There is no chance to double up Allen as the second run scores. Bob Gibson hits Day with a fast ball that grazes Day's arm. Bell forces Day at second. **BB Stars 2, Cardinals 0.**

In the bottom of the sixth with two outs and Hornsby on second (single), Boyer singles into left center, scoring Hornsby with the Cardinals' first run. Hernandez singles (two hits and a walk); Boyer moves to second. Rogan begins to throw in the BB Stars bullpen. Simmons flies out to Bell. **BB Stars 2, Cardinals 1.**

In the bottom of the seventh with one out, Bottomley bats for Bob Gibson (7 IP, 6 H, 2 R, 1 HR, 4 K, 2 BB, 1 HB). Bottomley lines a double into the right-field corner. Brock pinch runs for Bottomley. Day strikes out Medwick (swinging). Slaughter flies out to Bell.

Lanier (left-hander) is now pitching for the Cardinals in the top of the eighth. He retires Torriente on a fly to Musial in center field. Suttles is going to pinch hit for Leonard. McDaniel is now pitching for the Cardinals. McDaniel retires Suttles on a ground ball to Hernandez, and he strikes out Dandridge.

Hornsby leads off the bottom of the eighth with a single to center (his second hit). Rogan is ready in the BB bullpen. Dahlen will pinch run for Hornsby. Musial hits a slow ground ball to Allen (2B), who throws Musial out as Dahlen goes to second (one out). Boyer flies out to Charleston (LF) for the second out. Keith Hernandez is coming to the plate. Hernandez has been on base three times (two singles and a walk). The count goes to 3-2, and Dahlen breaks for third. Hernandez lines the pitch into center for a base hit as Dahlen scores easily (tying the game, 2-2). Frisch bounces into a force-out at second base. **Cardinals 2, BB Stars 2.**

In the top of the ninth for the Cardinals, Frisch moves from shortstop to second base. Dahlen stays in the game and will play shortstop. The defense up the middle has been upgraded at both positions. Allen leads off with a pop fly into shallow right field, Slaughter gets a great jump and makes a tumbling shoe-string catch for the first out. Day is a good hitting pitcher and he will bat. He hits it right at Dahlen on two hops and Dahlen throws him out (two outs). McDaniel walks Cool Papa Bell, the BB Stars' best base runner. Lloyd hits one up the middle into center field, and Bell races to third. With Oscar Charleston coming to the plate, the Cardinals will bring in the lefty, Harry The Cat Brecheen. The count goes to 3-1; Charleston will be waiting on the fast ball. Brecheen fires and Charleston lines it and Hernandez (1B) leaps and makes a great catch to rob Charleston of a double into the right-field corner. More than likely, two runs would have scored. **Cardinals 2, BB Stars 2.**

In the bottom of the ninth, Simmons flies out to Charleston (one out). Hafey bats for Brecheen and he flies out to Bell (CF). Medwick is called out on strikes. We are headed to extra innings.

Bruce Sutter is the fifth Cardinal pitcher (Leon Day has pitched the first nine innings for the BB Stars). Josh Gibson lines a base hit to center. Frankie Warfield will run for Gibson. Warfield gets a great jump and steals second. Torriente is intentionally walked (first and second, none out). Hrabosky is warming up for the Cardinals, and J. R. Richard is warming up for the BB Stars. Mule Suttles is coming up for the second time (pinched hit for Leonard in eighth). Suttles hits a one-hopper back to Sutter, who wheels and throws a strike to Dahlen covering second. Dahlen fires the relay to Hernandez, double play, Warfield moves to third (two outs). Dandridge grounds out Dahlen to Hernandez ending the threat.

The BB Stars make several changes in the bottom of the tenth. J. R. Richard is pitching, and he will bat seventh. Judy Johnson is playing third and will bat fourth. Mackey is catching and will bat ninth. The final line on Day is 9 IP, 9 H, 2 R, 0 HR, 5 K, 1 BB.

Richard gives up a one out single, but the Cardinals do not score. **Cardinals 2, BB Stars 2.**

In the top of the eleventh, Sutter retires the BB Stars one, two, three.

J. R. Richard retires Hernandez on a ground ball to Suttles (one out in the bottom of the eleventh). Hernandez had been on base four times (three singles, walk, RBI). Frisch hits the ball over Bell's head in center field. Frisch ends up on third with a triple. The infield and outfield are moved in. J. R. Richard walks Simmons on four pitches (first and third, one out). Schoendienst is batting for Sutter. Schoendienst hits a soft line-drive down the right field line; Torriente gets a great break and makes a sliding catch. The speedy Frisch tags at third as Torriente quickly stands up and fires the ball toward the plate. The ball lands in Mackey's glove (on the fly). Mackey, blocking the plate with his left leg, spins and dives on to Frisch (head-first slide) as Frisch reaches back for home plate in vain, double play. **Cardinals 2, BB Stars 2.**

Al Hrabosky, great Cardinal relief pitcher (1975, 13-3, 22 saves, 1.66 ERA) is now pitching in the top of the twelfth inning. Hrabosky has one weakness. He is poor at holding runners and Ted Simmons (C) has an average throwing arm. Lloyd singles to right. Everyone in the ball park knows that Lloyd will probably be attempting to steal second. On the first pitch, the Cardinals call a pitch out and Lloyd is only a couple of steps off the bag (ball one). On the second pitch, Lloyd takes off and steals second easily. On the next pitch, Hrabosky retires Charleston on a fly to Slaughter in short right field. Lloyd stays at second. Judy Johnson flies out to Musial (CF) for the second out. Up comes Torriente. He gets a good hand from the crowd for his great defensive play in the bottom of the eleventh that saves the game for the BB Stars. Torriente lines a base hit into left center field as Lloyd races around third base with the go-ahead run, 3-2. Suttles flies out to Medwick to end the inning. **BB Stars 3, Cardinals 2.**

In the bottom of the twelfth, the Cardinals have the top of the order to face J. R. Richard, working his third inning in relief. Richard is throwing aspirins and strikes out Medwick and Slaughter (two outs). Dahlen hits one on the ground (right side); Allen scoops it up and throws him out. A great win for the BB Stars and a tough loss for the Cardinals. I believe the odds of Torriente and Mackey to make that play on the speedy Frisch (bottom of the eleventh) was at least 5:1 against. Will the results of Game One determine the winner of this series?

12 Innings	R	H	E	LOB
BB Stars	3	10	0	12
Cardinals	2	11	2	10

Winning Pitcher – Richard   Losing Pitcher – Hrabosky

The BB Stars lead the series, 1-0.

Game Two, Friday July 9, Sportsman's Park (St. Louis), 7 pm (Foster vs. Dean)

It is a cool, partly cloudy day at Sportsman's Park. In the top of the second inning, the BB Stars score first. With one out, Leonard singles to center. Mackey reaches on an error (Hornsby, 2B), and Leonard stops at second. Johnson lines a single to center; Leonard is heading for the plate. Musial throws to third and gets Mackey as he slides into the bag. Warfield takes a called third strike. **BB Stars 1, Cardinals 0.**

Foster coasts through the first three innings. Dean struggles in the fourth. Stearnes singles, and Leonard hits a long home run to right field (3-0). Mackey singles to right. Johnson doubles into the left field corner, and Mackey stops at third. Dean strikes out Warfield (one out). Haines is throwing in the Cardinals bullpen. Bottomley and Boyer are playing in for the bunt. Foster drops a great bunt down third base line. Boyer throws over to Hornsby (covering first) as Mackey scores the fourth run. Bell strikes out swinging. **BB Stars 4, Cardinals 0.**

Charleston homers off Dean in the fifth. **BB Stars 5, Cardinals 0.**

The Cardinals get single runs off Foster in the seventh and eighth. **BB Stars 5, Cardinals 2.**

The Cardinals bullpen (Haines 2.0, Lanier 1.7 and McDaniel 0.3 innings) shuts down the BB Stars over the last four innings. Hilton Smith pitches a shut-out ninth to save the game for Foster.

	R	H	E	LOB
BB Stars	5	8	2	5
Cardinals	2	8	1	9

Winning Pitcher – Foster   Save – Smith   Losing Pitcher – Dean
The BB Stars lead the series, 2-0.

Game Three, Saturday July 10, Texas Arlington Stadium, 1 pm (Pollet vs. Paige)

It is a hot, partly cloudy day with the wind blowing from right field to left field. Howie Pollet (1946 Cardinals) and Satchel Paige both put up zeros in the run column until the BB Stars come to bat in the bottom of the fourth.

Left-hander Pollet walks Willie Wells to start the inning. Suttles singles up the middle into center field; Wells stops at second. Josh Gibson doubles to the fence in right center, scoring Wells with Suttles stopping at third. Pollet throws a fast ball on the outside part of the plate to the left-handed hitting Charleston. He goes with the pitch and hits it high and deep to left field and the prevailing right to left wind takes it over the fence, three run home run (4-0). Jesse Haines is warming up. Pollet escapes any more damage (walks Irvin and throws a wild pitch), but no more runs score. **BB Stars 4, Cardinals 0.**

In the top of the fifth, the Cardinals get a couple of singles around a warning track fly ball to Irvin (RF) by Hernandez (1979 Cardinals) but do not score.

In the bottom of the fifth, Pollet retires the first two batters. Suttles triples and Gibson scores him with a single to center (5-0). It was Gibson's second RBI in as many innings. Charleston strikes out to end the inning. **BB Stars 5, Cardinals 0.**

In the top of the sixth, Frankie Frisch bats for Pollet (5 IP, 6 H, 5 R, 1 HR, 2 K, 2 BB). On Satchel Paige's first pitch, uncharacteristically high for ball one, Paige grabs his fore arm and grimaces in pain. Martin Dihigo is being brought in to replace Paige (5+ IP, 4 H, 0 R, 0 HR, 1 K, 0 BB). Note: Paige will be lost to the BB Stars for the next 10 days. Dihigo retires the side in order.

Jesse Haines is now pitching for the Cardinals. Haines retires the first two batters then Warfield, Dihigo and Bell single producing another run (6-0). Wells flies out to Brock in left field to end the inning. **BB Stars 6, Cardinals 0.**

The Cardinals come to life in the seventh. Slaughter (1942 Cardinals) singles to right. Dihigo walks Musial. Bullet Joe Rogan is warming up. Torre lines a single to right, scoring Slaughter; Musial stops at second (6-1). Hernandez doubles into the right field corner scoring Musial with Torre stopping at third (6-2). Rogan replaces Dihigo. Rogan retires the next two batters on infield ground balls (includes Bottomley batting for Brock); however, two more runs have now crossed the plate (6-4). Chick Hafey bats for Haines and doubles to left. Dahlen singles to right plating the fifth run of the inning (6-5). Schoendienst hits into a force play at second to finally end the inning. **BB Stars 6, Cardinals 5.**

Lindy McDaniel (1960 Cardinals) is now pitching for the Cardinals. Defensively, Medwick has replaced Brock in left field. Like Haines did in the sixth, McDaniel retires the first two batters in the bottom of the seventh. Charleston doubles and Turkey Stearnes, batting for Monte Irvin, singles to left, Charleston beats Medwick's throw to the plate and Stearnes advances to second (7-5). Dandridge flies out to Musial. **BB Stars 7, Cardinals 5.**

This ends the scoring as the BB Stars go up three games to none.

	R	H	E	LOB
Cardinals	5	9	0	3
BB Stars	7	12	0	6

Winning Pitcher – Paige   Save – Rogan   Losing Pitcher – Pollet
The BB Stars lead the series, 3-0.

Game Four, Sunday July 11, Texas Arlington Stadium, 1 pm (M. Cooper vs. Tiant)

It is a hot, sunny day with the wind blowing from right field to left as it did on Saturday. In the top of the second the Cardinals get to Tiant. Stan "The Man" Musial (1948 Cardinals) leads off with a double to right field. Medwick bounces one back to Tiant, who looks Musial back to second and throws out Medwick. Bottomley singles to right with Musial holding at third base. Boyer bounces one to the right side; Allen fields it and throws out Boyer as Musial scores and Bottomley moves to second. Simmons singles to right, bringing Bottomley around to score (2-0). Cooper strikes out. **Cardinals 2, BB Stars 0.**

Tiant settles down and blanks the Cardinals from the third through the eighth inning. Mort Cooper blanks the BB Stars through seven innings on three hits.

With one out in the bottom of the eighth, Mackey pinch hits for Tiant and doubles into the gap in left center. Bell grounds out to the right side (Frisch-Hernandez) as Mackey moves to third. Lloyd singles to center, scoring Mackey (2-1). Gibson bounces out to Cooper. **Cardinals 2, BB Stars 1.**

Donnie Moore comes in to pitch in the top of the ninth. The final line on Tiant is 8 IP, 7 H, 2 R, 0 HR, 7 K, 2 BB, 1 HB. Moore retires the first two batters then Cooper singles and Moore hits Frisch (runners on first and second). Frisch has been hit by a pitch twice in the game. Slaughter forces Frisch at second base to end the threat.

Turkey Stearnes leads off the bottom of the ninth with a long home run to right field to tie the game (2-2). Cooper retires the next three batters. **BB Stars 2, Cardinals 2.**

Moore retires the Cardinals one-two-three in the top of the tenth.

Hrabosky is warming up for the Cardinals as Cooper begins his tenth inning. Allen leads off and hits a drive to deep center, but Musial makes the catch at the edge of the warning track (one out). Charleston strikes out (pinch hitting for Moore). Bell doubles into the corner in left field. Hrabosky is coming in to pitch. What a performance by Mort Cooper. Lloyd bounces out, Hernandez to Hrabosky covering first. The final line on Cooper is 9.7 IP, 7 H, 2 R, 1 HR, 5 K, 1 BB. **BB Stars 2, Cardinals 2.**

In the eleventh inning, J. R. Richard pitches for the BB Stars. Hernandez reaches on an error by Suttles (1B). Boyer strikes out (one out). Ted Simmons is three for four (single, double, triple) with an RBI as he steps to the plate. Richard fires, and Simmons hits a high drive deep to left. Stearnes is back to the fence and it is gone, home run about three feet fair. Simmons has hit for the cycle, Cardinals lead 6-4. Hrabosky strikes out. Frisch grounds out to Allen (2B). **Cardinals 6, BB Stars 4.**

In the bottom of the eleventh, Hrabosky retires Josh Gibson on a fly ball to Medwick (LF). Hrabosky strikes out Stearnes (swinging). Monte Irvin bats for Torriente. Bruce Sutter comes in to pitch to Irvin. Sutter strikes out Irvin. Cardinals win a big one.

11 Innings	R	H	E	LOB
Cardinals	4	9	0	9
BB Stars	2	7	1	6

Winning Pitcher – Hrabosky   Save – Sutter   Losing Pitcher – Richard
The BB Stars lead the series, 3-1.

Game Five, Monday July 12, Texas Arlington Stadium, 7 pm (Gibson vs. Newcombe)

In the bottom of the third inning, Cool Papa Bell hits a home run to right-field off Bob Gibson to open the scoring. **BB Stars 1, Cardinals 0.**

Hornsby opens the Cardinal fourth with a base hit to right field. Musial takes Newcombe deep over the right-field fence. **Cardinals 2, BB Stars 1.**

In the Cardinals sixth, Newcombe walks Hornsby to lead-off the inning. Musial forces Hornsby at second (one out). Medwick flares one that drops in front of Bell for a single; Musial stops at second. Rogan begins to loosen in the BB Stars' bullpen. Hernandez flies out to Charleston (LF). Ken Boyer slams a two-out base hit to left center; Musial races around to score and Medwick stops at second. (3-1). Milligan flies out to Bell. **Cardinals 3, BB Stars 1.**

The sixth inning is the first inning Bob Gibson retires the side in order. Charleston makes sure that will not happen again with a triple off the center-field fence to start the home half of the seventh inning. Haines begins to throw for the Cardinals. Dandridge lines a single to center, scoring Charleston (3-2). Warfield tops one down the third base line. Boyer bare hands the ball and fires to Hernandez, retiring Warfield by half a step (Dandridge to second). With one out Stearnes will bat for Newcombe (7 IP, 8 H, 3 R, 1 HR, 2 K, 1 BB). Stearnes hits a ground ball through the right side. Slaughter (RF) charges the ball, picks it up and fires to Simmons (replaced Milligan in sixth due to injury) as Dandridge barrels into Simmons and jars the ball loose (3-3). On his knees, Simmons fires to first, and Stearnes has to dive back to the bag. Bob Gibson retires Bell and Lloyd on ground balls. **BB Stars 3, Cardinals 3.**

Rogan is now pitching in the top of the eighth inning. He retires the Cardinals in order.

Bob Gibson gives up a lead-off triple to Charleston in the bottom of the eighth. The infield is in close all the way around. Gibson calls time and asks for a new baseball. He is ready to pitch and looks very determined. His first pitch knocks Suttles back off the plate (purpose pitch?). He strikes out Suttles on a letter high fast ball (one out). Torriente takes a called third strike (two outs). Biz Mackey is a dangerous hitter and Gibson walks him. Dandridge sees nothing but heat and he strikes out. What an awesome display by Bob Gibson with Charleston ninety feet away and nobody out. **BB Stars 3, Cardinals 3.**

Rogan retires the first two batters in the ninth (Boyer and Simmons). Gibson is due up but Jim Bottomley (1925 Cardinals) will pinch hit. The final line for Bob Gibson is 8 IP, 9 H, 3 R, 1 HR, 6 K 2 BB. Bottomley hits a one-hopper to Warfield, who throws him out. Rogan has retired all six men he faced. **BB Stars 3, Cardinals 3.**

Jesse Haines is now pitching in the bottom of the ninth.. He falls behind Warfield 3-1 and throws a fast ball right down the middle. Warfield drills it over Musial's head. The ball is rolling all the way to the fence. Musial retrieves the ball and fires in to Frisch. Warfield ends up with a stand up triple. The infield is being brought in as is the outfield. Josh Gibson will bat for Rogan. Will they walk him? The decision is to pitch to Gibson. Haines 2-2 pitch jams Gibson and he hits a towering pop-up that Frisch (SS) takes near the pitcher's mound (one out). Cool Papa Bell is up. He is an excellent bunter. He is two for three with a walk, including a bases-empty home run off Gibson in the third. He squares to bunt and pushes it by Haines for a walk-off bunt single as Warfield slides in with the winning run.

	R	H	E	LOB
Cardinals	3	8	0	5
BB Stars	4	11	0	8

Winning Pitcher – Rogan   Losing Pitcher – Haines

The BB Stars have a commanding 4-1 series lead.

Game Six, Tuesday July 13, Busch Stadium (St. Louis), 7 pm (Day vs. Dean)

It is a warm, partly-cloudy evening. If the Cardinals do not win the remaining four games of the series, they will lose the series and more than likely miss the playoffs. There is much pressure on Dizzy Dean (1934 Cardinals). He only lasted five innings, giving up five runs (four earned) in the 5-2 loss to Bill Foster in Game Two. Dean retires the side in order (first inning).

The Cardinals get two base runners. Dahlen is thrown out stealing. Slaughter receives a two out walk but Musial grounds out.

Josh Gibson leads off the second with a home run off Dean. **BB Stars 1, Cardinals 0.**

The Cardinals get that run back in the third with one-out singles by Frisch and Slaughter (hit-and-run). With runners on first and third, Musial bounces into a force play at second as Slaughter scores (1-1). Medwick grounds out to Lloyd (SS) to end the inning. **Cardinals 1, BB Stars 1.**

In the bottom of the fourth, Keith Hernandez hits Day's first pitch, a line drive that glances off Day's glove and knocks his hat off. The ball rolls a few feet away. Hernandez is on first. Day is still on the ground; he is conscious. He finally is helped up and will walk off the field on his own power. Martin Dihigo is coming in to pitch. He will have an extended warm-up time. Dihigo pitches to Boyer, hitting a drive in the gap in left center. Bell cannot cut it off; the ball rolls to the fence. Boyer ends up on third with a stand up triple scoring Hernandez (2-1 Cardinals). Simmons hits a fly to shallow center; Bell makes the catch. Boyer stays at third. Dizzy Dean has a chance to help himself. After fouling off a couple of bunt attempts, Dizzy hits a fly ball to fairly deep center and Boyer comes in to score (credit Dean with a sac fly). Dahlen flies out to Stearnes (RF). The final line for Day is 3+ IP, 6 H, 2 R, 0 HR, 1 K, 1 BB. **Cardinals 3, BB Stars 1.**

It is up to Dean to protect this lead. In the top of the fifth, Dihigo leads off with a single to left field. Dean walks Bell, runners on first and second, none out. Lloyd bounces one to Hernandez, who fires to Dahlen (SS covering second). The relay back to first is not in time (runners first and third, one out). Charleston singles to right, Dihigo scores and Lloyd stops at second (3-2). Dean falls behind Josh Gibson 3-1 and Gibson hits a long three run home run over 400 feet to left, 5-3 BB Stars. Stearnes singles to center before Dean retires Suttles and Judy Johnson. **BB Stars 5, Cardinals 3.**

The final score is 5-3. Dean pitches one more inning (no runs). His final line is 6 IP, 8 H, 5 R, 2 HR, 5 K, 3 BB. Dihigo pitches through the eighth (5 IP, 2 H, 1 R, 0 HR, 1 K, 2 BB). Brecheen pitches three scoreless innings for the Cardinals and Richard saves the win for Dihigo.

	R	H	E	LOB
BB Stars	5	8	0	7
Cardinals	3	10	0	8

Winning Pitcher – Dihigo   Save - Richard   Losing Pitcher – Dean
The BB Stars win the series and lead the overall series, 5-1.

Game Seven, Wednesday July 14, Busch Stadium (St. Louis), 1 pm (Foster vs. Pollet)

It is a warm, partly-cloudy day; wind is blowing in. The Cardinals need to regroup and try to salvage something from this series.

Pollet, with two outs in the second, gives up three singles in a row (Johnson, Warfield, Foster) but Hafey (CF) throws out Judy Johnson at the plate to end the inning.

In the bottom of the second inning, Bottomley doubles off the wall in right. Medwick singles to left and Bottomley beats throw to the plate (1-0). Hafey pops out to Johnson. Ted Simmons strikes out into a double play (Medwick caught stealing). **Cardinals 1, BB Stars 0.**

Torriente leads off the top of the third and hits a high drive to deep center field, but Hafey runs it down (one out). Wells doubles to the wall in left center. Gibson hits a smash down the third-base line. Torre knocks it down but is unable to make a play (runners at first and third, one out). Stearnes chops one toward the hole but Bottomley makes a nice play flipping to Pollet for the out. Wells scores and Gibson moves to second (two outs). Suttles flies out to Medwick (RF). **BB Stars 1, Cardinals 1.**

In the top of the fourth with two outs and Irvin on second (single advanced on infield out) Foster gets his second hit (rarity), a single to left field, charged by Brock. He overruns the ball; Irvin scores and Foster hustles to second base. Credit Foster with a single and an RBI. He advances to second on Brock's error. Torriente hits a pop fly to shallow left field and Brock makes a great catch to end the inning. **BB Stars 2, Cardinals 1.**

In the bottom of the fourth, Foster retires Hornsby and Bottomley on routine fly balls. Medwick gets his second hit (single to left). Hafey lines one, just fair into the left field corner. Medwick is racing around third. Wells, the cut-off man fires the ball to the plate but it takes a bad hop. Gibson blocks it; Medwick slides in safely. Hafey goes to third on the throw. Foster walks Simmons. Lou Brock (1974 Cardinals) bounces out to Suttles (1B). **Cardinals 2, BB Stars 2.**

Musial has replaced Brock in left field and will bat second in the order. Boyer has replaced Torre at third base and will bat eighth.

In the bottom of the fifth inning, the Cardinals take the lead. Pollet leads off with a single to right field. Dahlen singles to left with Pollet stopping at second base. Musial drives Foster's first pitch over Torriente's head in center field; Pollet and the speedy Dahlen both score as Musial goes into second with a stand-up double (4-2). Rogan is now throwing in the bullpen. The dangerous Roger Hornsby is walked (intentionally). Frisch pinch runs for Hornsby. It is now lefty vs. lefty (Foster vs. Bottomley). Foster bears down and retires the next three batters with no further scoring (Bottomley – pop up; Medwick - K; Hafey ground out). **Cardinals 4, BB Stars 2.**

Frisch is now playing second base for the Cardinals. Pollet gives the runs right back in the sixth. Irvin singles and Judy Johnson (not a power hitter) lines one just fair over the fence in left field (4-4). Pollet retires the next three batters (including Bell who struck out batting for Foster). The final line on Foster is 5 IP, 7 H, 4 R, O HR, 3 K, 3 BB. **BB Stars 4, Cardinals 4.**

Rogan is now pitching for the BB Stars. He will bat in the lead-off spot. Bell stays in the game and replaces Torriente in center field. With two out and none on Slaughter will bat for Pollet (6 IP, 11 H, 4 R, 1 HR, 1 K, 0 BB). Slaughter bounces out Rogan to Suttles.

McDaniel is now pitching for the Cardinals in the top of the seventh. He retires the side in order.

Rogan walks Dahlen in the home half of the seventh. Musial hits what looks like a tailor-made double play ball to Wells (SS), but it takes a bad hop. Wells juggles it and both runners are safe (E-6). Frisch is up for the first time. Suttles and Johnson are in on the grass looking for the bunt. Frisch chops one to Warfield (2B), who throws him out as the runners advance (one out). Rogan walks Bottomley (intentionally) to set up a double play possibility. Rogan is high with his first two pitches. Medwick is looking for a fast ball all the way. Medwick launches one high and deep to left field; it is gone for a grand-slam home run. Rogan picks up the resin bag, then slams it to the ground. He escapes without any more damage. **Cardinals 8, BB Stars 4.**

McDaniel gives up a lead-off single in the eighth, but he retires the next three batters. The Cardinals do not score in the bottom of the eighth.

McDaniel walks Bell to start the ninth. Hrabosky warms up for the Cardinals. Lloyd bats for Rogan and flies out to Musial (LF). Wells takes a called third strike (two outs). Gibson hits McDaniel's first pitch over the fence in left field cutting, the Cardinals 'lead in half, 8-6. Hrabosky comes in to pitch to Stearnes. Hrabosky jams Stearnes, who taps one harmlessly to Bottomley, the first baseman. He fields the ball and steps on first to end the game.

	R	H	E	LOB
BB Stars	6	13	1	7
Cardinals	8	10	1	8

Winning Pitcher – McDaniel   Save – Hrabosky   Losing Pitcher - Rogan
The BB Stars lead the series, 5-2.

Game Eight, Friday July 16, Texas Arlington Stadium, 7 pm (Cooper vs. Tiant)

It is a cool, cloudy day with the wind blowing from right to left. Will we see another well-pitched game from two excellent pitchers?

We enter the top of the sixth, 0-0. The Cardinals have three singles and a walk. The only runner that reached second for the Cardinals off Tiant came in the second inning, when Leonard let Tiant's throw fly by him into the dugout for a two base error (Hernandez on second). The BB Stars have five hits and a walk off of Cooper.

Tiant creates his own trouble in the sixth by walking the first two batters (Dahlen and Schoendienst). Stan The Man Musial (1948 Cardinals) steps up to the plate and makes Tiant pay for his wildness as he jacks it over the right field-fence (3-0). Medwick grounds out to Lloyd (one out). Tiant walks Slaughter (third walk of the inning). Hilton Smith continues to warm up (began after Musial HR). Hernandez (on the hit-and-run) drives one into the gap in left center. Slaughter is being sent home; the relay from Wells is not in time (4-0). Hernandez goes to third on the throw to the plate. Smith is coming in to pitch to Ken Boyer. He pops out to Lloyd (SS). Smith walks Simmons intentionally to pitch to Cooper (ninth batter in the inning). Cooper flies out to Charleston. The final line for Tiant is 5.3 IP, 5 H, 4 R, 1 HR, 3 K, 4 BB. **Cardinals 4, BB Stars 0.**

With two out in the bottom of the sixth, Mort Cooper gives up singles to Charleston and Stearnes. The dangerous Buck Leonard is next to bat. With the count 3-2, both runners take off as Leonard lines one toward the hole on the right side. Schoendienst dives and makes a great catch to end the inning.

In the top of the eighth, the Cardinals add to their lead. With one out, Slaughter singles to left off of Hilton Smith. On the hit-and-run, Hernandez singles to right, and Slaughter advances to third base. Dandridge and Leonard are protecting against the bunt. Ken Boyer hits a high fly to Bell (CF) in medium left center field. Slaughter scores easily without a throw (sac fly). It is now 5-0. Simmons makes the third out. **Cardinals 5, BB Stars 0.**

Mort Cooper has scattered eight hits. Max Lanier and Bruce Sutter are getting ready in the Cardinals bullpen. Torriente singles to left, pinch hitting for Smith. Bell pops out to Dahlen (he replaced Frisch at SS in the seventh). Lloyd singles to center. Charleston is the next batter. Lanier, the left-hander, is ready but the decision is Cooper will pitch to Charleston. Cooper hangs a curve ball and Charleston crushes it, three run home run. The 5-run lead is now two runs. Lanier replaces Cooper, who has pitched another great game for the Cardinals (7.3 IP, 11 H, 3 R, 1 HR, 4 K, 1 BB).

Lanier retires Stearnes on a fly ball to Medwick (LF) for the second out. Suttles will pinch hit for Leonard. Bruce Sutter is now pitching for the Cardinals. Suttles hits a long drive to deep left; it is going, going, gone, home run. The Cardinal lead is now just one run, 5-4. Mackey drives one over Musial's head in center field. It bounces off the wall. Mackey, with his great speed, is into third with a stand-up triple. Hrabosky is quickly getting ready. Sutter is facing Ray Dandridge with the tying run just 90 feet away. Sutter strikes out Dandridge on a mean fork ball to end the inning. **Cardinals 5, BB Stars 4.**

Donnie Moore retires the Cardinals in order in the top of the ninth.

Sutter walks Allen to start the bottom of the ninth. Josh Gibson will bat for Moore. Instead of putting someone up to bunt or have Moore bunt, the BB Stars are putting up Gibson to win it with a walk-off home run. Sutter fools Gibson with a changeup. He lofts a high fly to Medwick in left field for the first out. The lefty, Hrabosky is coming in to pitch to Bell. With the change in pitchers, Bell will bat right- handed. Bell chops it toward second base; Schoendienst's only play is to first. The speedy Allen slides safely into second. Willie Wells, a right-handed batter (with power) will bat for Lloyd. Wells hits the ball on one-hop to Dahlen (SS), who fires to Hernandez (1B) to end the game.

	R	H	E	LOB
Cardinals	5	7	0	6
BB Stars	4	13	1	7

Winning Pitcher – Cooper   Save – Hrabosky   Losing Pitcher – Tiant
The BB Stars lead the series, 5-3.

Game Nine, Saturday July 17, Texas Arlington Stadium, 7 pm (B. Gibson vs. Newcombe)

It is a warm and clear day with little wind. The Cardinals behind their ace, Bob Gibson, would like to finish with a third win in a row. Game One of this series now seems so pivotal (Frisch being thrown out at home in the eleventh inning on Torriente's great catch and throw).

In the first, Frisch greets Newcombe with a single to right on the first pitch of the game. Slaughter hits one to deep right field but Stearnes tracks it down on the warning track. Frisch, who was almost to second base, has to hustle back to first base. Newcombe has a propensity to give up the long ball on occasions. He does not want to give Roger Hornsby anything on the inner half of the plate. Hornsby, one of the greatest hitters of all time (.424 in his best season of 1924), drives Newcombe's pitch on the outside corner over the fence in right field giving the Cardinals a quick 2-0 lead. Musial drives a fair ball into the right field corner; Stearnes falls down. Musial decides to try to stretch his double into a triple, but Stearnes recovers quickly, throwing a strike to Judy Johnson who tags out the sliding Musial. Medwick goes down swinging. **Cardinals 2, BB Stars 0.**

In the bottom of the first inning, a great throw by Musial cuts down Lloyd, who is trying to score from first on Charleston's double. Josh Gibson grounds out to end the inning.

In the bottom of the third inning, Bell doubles to right. With one out, Charleston singles to right, scoring the speedy Bell (2-1). Charleston moves to second on Milligan's passed ball. Bob Gibson strikes out Josh Gibson and Turkey Stearnes (both swinging). **Cardinals 2, BB Stars 1.**

In the top of the fifth, the Cardinals threaten to score off Newcombe. Singles by Torre and Milligan have runners on the corners with none out. Bob Gibson, on a suicide squeeze, pops it up; Josh Gibson makes the catch and fires to Judy Johnson (3B), doubling Torre off the bag. Frisch flies out to Bell.

In the bottom of the fifth, the BB Stars tie the game. Lloyd walks. Charleston singles to right. Lloyd stops at second. Josh Gibson singles to center, scoring Lloyd with Charleston stopping at second. Bob Gibson retires the next three batters without any more damage. **BB Stars 2, Cardinals 2.**

With one out in the top of the sixth, Newcombe has some control issues. He walks Hornsby. On the first pitch to Musial, the ball slips away from Josh Gibson (passed ball) and Hornsby moves to second. Musial is intentionally walked. Medwick pops it up in the infield (infield fly rule); Lloyd (SS) makes the catch. Newcombe walks Bottomley, loading the bases. Leon Day is warming up. Torre flies out to Cool Papa Bell.

In the bottom of the sixth, the BB Stars take the lead with an unearned run. Torre bobbles Allen's ground ball for an error to lead-off the inning. Newcombe successfully sacrifices Allen to second. Bell hits a soft line-drive single over Frisch's glove; Allen races around third to score the go-ahead run (unearned). Gibson retires Lloyd and Charleston to end the inning. **BB Stars 3, Cardinals 2.**

With one out in the top of the seventh, Schoendienst gets a pinch hit single (batting for Gibson). The final line for Bob Gibson is 6 IP, 9 H, 3 R, 2 ER, 0 HR, 4 K, 1 BB, 2 HB. Bob Gibson has pitched well in this series and so far has no decisions. Leon Day is now pitching for the BB Stars. Frisch doubles to right; Schoendienst is held at third. Slaughter is walked intentionally to pitch to Hornsby with the bases loaded (risky). Hornsby lines the first pitch into right field scoring Schoendienst and Frisch, Slaughter goes to third. Cardinals lead 4-3. Hornsby has driven in all 4 runs. Musial his a fly ball to Bell. Slaughter tags; Bell throws a strike to Josh Gibson, who tags out Slaughter for an inning-ending double play. The final line on Newcombe is 6.3 IP, 7 H, 3 R, 1 HR, 4 K, 3 BB. **Cardinals 4, BB Stars 3.**

There are defensive changes for the Cardinals in the bottom of the seventh Dahlen is now playing shortstop and he is batting ninth in the order. Frisch has moved from shortstop to second base. Haines is now pitching and he is batting third.

Haines falls behind Josh Gibson, 3-0 (not good). Josh always has the green light. There it goes, deep to left, gone. We are tied again, 4-4. Bob Gibson will get his third non-decision despite having three quality stats with an ERA of 3.00. Stearnes reaches on Dahlen's error. Suttles singles to center; Stearnes stops at second. Brecheen is warming up. Johnson hits a groundball to Dahlen, who flips to Frisch for the force. Suttles upends Frisch (no double play, one out). Stearnes moves to third. Newt Allen is up. He hits a high fly ball to shallow right field. Slaughter makes the catch. Stearnes bluffs dashing for home. Slaughter fires to Bottomley (cutoff man). There are now two outs. Buck Leonard is announced to bat for Day. The Lefty, Harry The Cat Brecheen, is coming in to pitch. Monte Irvin will now bat for Leonard. Irvin hits it on a one-hop to Dahlen, who flips to Frisch, forcing Johnson to end the inning. **BB Stars 4, Cardinals 4.**

J. R. Richard is now pitching for the BB Stars in the top of the eighth inning. Joe Medwick doubles off the wall in left. Bottomley and Torre both strike out. Ted Simmons bats for Milligan. He lines the first pitch into right field toward the line; Stearnes got a good break on the ball. He dives and makes a great catch, saving a run.

Defensive changes for the Cardinals (in the eighth) - Hernandez is now playing first base. Boyer is at third base. Simmons is catching. Brecheen has a very easy one, two, three eighth. We head to the ninth tied 4-4.

It is the top of the ninth inning. Dahlen fouls out to Josh Gibson (one out). Frisch chops one down to Johnson but he drops the ball, no play (E5). On the first pitch to Slaughter, Frisch steals second base. Slaughter is intentionally walked for the second consecutive plate appearance; runners are on first and second (one out). Brock pinch hits for Brecheen. Sutter is warming up to pitch the bottom of the ninth. Brock takes a called third strike (two outs, should be three). Richard is pitching to Musial. There is a base hit into right field; Frisch scores, and Slaughter ends up on third, Cardinals lead 5-4. Joe Medwick is now batting. Richard's first pitch is in the dirt and skips all the way to the back stop (wild pitch). Slaughter scores, and Musial goes to second (6-4). Medwick grounds out to Lloyd. **Cardinals 6, BB Stars 4.**

Bruce Sutter is now pitching. Josh Gibson pops one up in shallow left field; Dahlen (SS) backs up and makes the catch (one out). Stearnes bounces one up the middle, but Dahlen was playing just to the right of second base. He makes the play throwing Stearnes out (two outs). Suttles singles to center. Mackey is batting for Judy Johnson. Mackey represents the tying run. Sutter strikes him out to end the game. Cardinals win their third in a row, thanks to two unearned runs in the ninth inning.

	R	H	E	LOB
Cardinals	6	11	1	8
BB Stars	4	12	1	12

Winning Pitcher – Brecheen   Save - Sutter   Losing Pitcher – Richard
The BB Stars win the series, 5-4.

Recap of Best Season Series 8 (BB Stars vs. Cardinals)

The BB Stars finally won a series after losing three series in a row. When they won Game Six of this series, they were up five games to one. Eight of the nine games were decided by one or two runs. The BB Stars only outscored the Cardinals by two runs in the series   Chart 13-2 on page 187 has BB Stars individual/team statistics for this series. Chart 13-3 on page 188 has Cardinals individual/team statistics for this series.

The turning point of the series - Would you believe the eleventh inning of Game One? If I were a betting man the odds of Torriente making the catch were about 50-50, and the odds of him throwing out Frisch were one in five.

Hitting Star for the Cardinals - Stan Musial (1948 Cardinals)

	RS	RBI	HR	.Avg	OBP	SPct	OPS
Musial	6	9	2	.316	.421	.594	1.015

Note: Hernandez and Hornsby had higher OPS but did not create as many runs.

Best Pitcher for Cardinals – Mort Cooper (1942 Cardinals)

	G	GS	QS	CG	W-L	IP	H	HR	R/ER	ERA
M. Cooper	2	2	2	0	1-0	17	18	2	5	2.63

Note: Bob Gibson is slightly behind Cooper. He had three quality starts (no decisions) and a 3.00 ERA.

Hitting Stars for the BB Stars - Oscar Charleston and Josh Gibson

	RS	RBI	HR	.Avg	OBP	SPct	OPS
O. Charleston	5	9	3	.406	.424	.844	1.268
J. Gibson	5	10	4	.310	.333	.793	1.126

BB Stars Results vs. Cardinals 5-4, .556

Pos.	E	R	TH	PB	Hitters	G	AB	R	H	RBI	2B	3B	HR	TB	W	HB	SO	SF	SH	SB	B.AVG.	OBP	S.PCT.	OPS
LF	5	A	-1		Charleston	8	32	5	13	9	3	1	3	27	1	0	6	0	0	0	0.406	0.424	0.844	1.268
CF	8	AA	-1		CP Bell	9	38	3	10	4	2	0	1	15	4	0	3	0	0	0	0.263	0.333	0.395	0.728
OF	5	A			Stearnes	8	26	2	9	4	1	0	1	13	4	1	3	0	0	0	0.346	0.393	0.500	0.893
OF	6	B	-2		M Irwin	5	9	2	2	0	0	0	0	2	2	0	2	0	0	0	0.222	0.364	0.222	0.586
OF	6	A	-1		Torriente	5	18	2	7	1	1	0	0	6	1	0	1	0	0	0	0.389	0.421	0.333	0.754
SS	7	A			P Lloyd	8	29	4	6	1	0	0	0	7	4	0	4	0	0	1	0.207	0.303	0.241	0.544
SS	7	AA			W Wells	3	9	2	1	0	0	0	0	2	0	0	1	0	0	0	0.111	0.111	0.222	0.333
3B	7	A			J Johnson	7	18	1	6	3	1	0	1	10	2	0	2	0	0	0	0.333	0.429	0.556	0.984
3B	6	B			Dandridge	4	17	1	5	1	1	0	0	6	0	0	5	0	0	0	0.294	0.294	0.353	0.647
2B	7	A			N Allen	5	19	1	1	1	0	0	0	1	2	0	5	0	0	1	0.053	0.143	0.053	0.195
2B	7	A			F Warfield	5	16	2	4	0	0	1	0	6	0	0	5	0	0	0	0.250	0.250	0.375	0.625
1B	7	A			Suttles	8	22	3	7	1	0	1	1	12	0	0	3	0	0	0	0.318	0.318	0.545	0.864
1B	8	B			B Leonard	6	17	3	3	3	0	0	2	9	0	0	0	0	0	0	0.176	0.176	0.529	0.706
C	7	A	-2	Fr	J Gibson	8	29	5	9	10	1	0	4	23	1	0	2	0	0	2	0.310	0.333	0.793	1.126
C	6	B	-2	Aw	B Mackey	6	14	3	5	0	1	0	0	10	1	1	3	0	0	2	0.357	0.400	0.714	1.114
					pitchers	9	19	1	5	2	0	0	0	5	0	1	7	2	0	3	0.263	0.333	0.263	0.596
					TOTAL	9	337	40	94	40	13	3	13	156	20	3	46	2	2	3	0.279	0.325	0.463	0.788

Fat.	H	WP	E	R	Pitchers	G	GS	QS	CG	S	W	L	IP	H	SO	BB	HB	HR	R	ER	ERA
10/L	Vg	N	9	B	BJ Rogan	3	3	0	0	0	1	1	1	8	3	3	0	1	5	4	4.50
9/L	Ex	R	7	B	B Foster	2	2	1	0	0	0	1	0	13	5	4	5	0	6	6	4.15
10/L	Vg	NL	8	B	L Day	3	2	1	0	0	0	0	12.7	17	6	3	0	0	5	5	3.55
10/L	Av	NL	7	B	M Dihigo	2	0	0	0	0	0	0	6	5	1	3	0	0	5	5	7.50
8/L	Md	R	8	C	S Paige	1	1	0	0	0	0	1	6	4	2	1	0	0	0	0	0.00
L/9	Vg	R	8	A	H Smith	2	0	0	0	0	0	0	3.7	3	1	2	0	0	1	1	2.45
9/L	Av	R	9	A	Newcombe	2	2	1	0	0	0	0	13.3	15	6	4	0	2	6	6	4.05
10/L	Ex	NL	8	D	L Tiant	2	2	1	0	0	0	1	13.3	12	10	6	1	1	6	6	4.05
9	Av	N	5	C	JR Richard	4	0	0	0	0	1	2	7	7	9	2	0	1	4	4	1.29
Long	Md	NL	4	B	D Moore	2	0	0	0	0	0	0	3	1	1	1	0	0	0	0	0.00
					TOTAL	23	9	5	0	0	2	5	4	85	83	43	27	2	5	38	34	3.60

Chart 13-2 – BB Stars Statistics for this series

Cardinals Best Season Series vs. BB All-Stars 4.5, .444

Team	Year	WS Hitters	G	AB	R	H	RBI	2B	3B	HR	TB	W	HB	SO	SF	SH	SB	B.AVG	OBP	S.PCT	OPS
St. Louis (N)	1942	37 E.Slaughter	9	30	4	6	2	0	1	1	9	4	0	3	0	0	0	0.200	0.294	0.300	0.594
St. Louis (N)	1948	46 S. Musial	9	32	6	10	9	3	0	2	19	6	0	0	0	0	0	0.313	0.421	0.594	1.015
St. Louis (N)	1937	40 J. Medwick	9	38	2	6	5	1	0	1	10	0	0	7	0	0	0	0.158	0.158	0.263	0.421
St. Louis (N)	1929	22 C. Hafey	4	10	2	4	1	2	0	0	6	0	0	0	0	0	0	0.400	0.400	0.600	1.000
St. Louis (N)	1974	22 L. Brock	5	5	0	1	0	0	0	0	1	0	0	1	0	0	2	0.200	0.200	0.200	0.400
Chicago (N)	1894	21 B. Dahlen	8	20	3	4	0	1	1	0	4	2	0	1	0	0	0	0.200	0.273	0.200	0.473
St. Louis (N)	1927	34 F. Frisch	9	33	6	6	1	0	1	0	9	1	0	2	1	0	2	0.182	0.250	0.273	0.523
St. Louis (N)	1960	31 K. Boyer	9	23	1	5	4	1	2	0	10	0	0	4	1	0	0	0.217	0.217	0.435	0.652
St. Louis (N)	1971	41 J. Torre	4	11	1	3	2	0	0	0	3	0	0	0	0	0	0	0.273	0.273	0.273	0.545
St. Louis (N)	1924	38 R. Hornsby	7	19	3	8	5	0	0	1	11	4	0	3	0	0	0	0.421	0.522	0.579	1.101
St. Louis (N)	1953	27 Schoendi'st	5	10	2	2	0	0	1	0	2	1	0	0	0	0	0	0.200	0.273	0.200	0.473
St. Louis (N)	1979	29 Hernandez	7	22	3	11	3	2	1	1	15	1	0	2	0	0	0	0.500	0.522	0.682	1.204
St. Louis (N)	1925	27 Bottomley	8	18	3	3	1	1	0	0	5	2	0	3	0	0	0	0.167	0.250	0.278	0.528
St. Louis (N)	1978	30 T. Simmons	8	18	1	7	3	3	1	1	13	6	0	1	0	0	0	0.389	0.542	0.722	1.264
St. Louis (N)	1889	17 J. Milligan	5	14	0	3	1	1	0	0	4	0	0	3	0	1	0	0.214	0.214	0.286	0.500
		Pitchers	9	20	1	3	0	0	0	0	3	0	0	10	1	1	2	0.150	0.150	0.150	0.300
		Total		327	38	83	37	15	6	5	125	27	2	43	2		2	0.254	0.315	0.382	0.697

Team	Year	WS Pitchers	G	GS	QS	CG	S	W	L	IP	H	SO	BB	HB	HR	R	ER	ERA
St. Louis	1968	36 B. Gibson	3	3	3	3	0	0	0	21	24	14	5	3	2	8	7	3.00
St. Louis	1934	37 D. Dean	2	2	0	0	0	0	0	11	15	10	5	0	4	10	9	7.36
St. Louis	1946	27 H. Pollet	2	2	2	0	0	0	0	11	17	3	5	2	2	9	9	7.36
St. Louis	1942	29 M. Cooper	2	2	2	2	0	0	1	17	18	9	2	2	2	5	5	2.63
St. Louis	1943	23 M. Lanier	3	0	0	0	0	0	0	2.3	1	1	1	1	0	0	0	0.00
St. Louis	1927	28 J. Haines	4	0	0	0	0	0	1	4	4	1	0	0	1	3	3	6.75
St. Louis (N)	1960	25 L. McDaniel	4	0	0	0	0	1	1	6.3	6	6	0	0	1	3	3	4.27
St. Louis (N)	1948	27 H. Brecheen	3	0	0	0	0	1	1	4.7	0	1	1	1	0	0	0	0.00
St. Louis	1975	19 A. Hrabosky	4	0	0	0	0	1	0	3	2	0	0	0	0	1	1	3.00
St. Louis	1984	23 B. Sutter	4	0	0	0	0	1	0	4	7	1	1	1	1	3	3	6.75
		TOTAL	31	9	5	5	0	4	4	84.3	94	46	20		13	40	38	4.06

Chart 13-3 – Cardinals statistics for this series

Chapter 14

Best Season Nine Game Series 9 -
BB Stars vs. Tigers

Tigers Roster Review

EIGHTY PERCENT OF THE ROSTER are made up of Detroit Tigers. Twenty percent of the roster are free agents.. See the Tigers Roster (Chart 14-1 on page 190).

Offensive Leaders (Tigers) Ranked by OPS

Player	OBP	SPct	OPS	R +	RBI -	HR =	NR
N. Cash	.488	.662	1.150	119	132	41	210
B. Joyce	.482	.648	1.130	103	89	17	175
H. Heilmann	.480	.632	1.112	121	115	18	218
H. Greenberg	.433	.670	1.103	129	150	41	238
T. Cobb	.467	.621	1.088	147	127	8	266
C. Gehringer	.431	.555	.987	144	116	15	225
A. Kaline	.425	.546	.971	121	102	27	196
S. Crawford	. .438	.526	.964	109	115	7	217
W. Cooper	.336	.586	.922	79	122	35	166
R. York	.366	.527	.893	90	118	34	174

The following players would be base-stealing threats – T. Cobb 83, and S. Crawford 37 (numbers listed SB for their best season).

Tigers Roster Best Season Series vs. BB All-Stars

Team	Year	WS Hitters	G	AB	R	H	RBI	2B	3B	HR	TB	W	HB	SO	SF	SH	SB	B.AVG.	OBP	S.PCT.	OPS
Detroit	1911	47 T. Cobb	146	591	147	248	127	47	24	8	367	44	8	19	-	-	83	0.420	0.467	0.621	1.088
Detroit	1923	35 Heilmann	144	524	121	211	115	44	11	18	331	74	5	40	-	-	8	0.403	0.480	0.632	1.112
Detroit	1940	31 Greenberg	148	573	129	195	150	50	8	41	384	93	1	75	-	-	6	0.340	0.433	0.670	1.103
Detroit	1911	32 S. Crawford	146	574	109	217	115	36	14	7	302	61	0	30	-	-	37	0.378	0.438	0.526	0.964
Detroit	1955	31 A. Kaline	152	588	121	200	102	24	8	27	321	82	5	57	-	-	6	0.340	0.425	0.546	0.971
Detroit	1984	24 C. Lemon	141	509	77	146	76	34	6	20	252	51	7	83	-	-	5	0.287	0.360	0.495	0.855
New York N	1916	25 Fletcher	133	500	53	143	66	23	8	3	191	13	14	36	-	-	15	0.286	0.323	0.382	0.705
New York N	1929	23 T. Jackson	149	551	92	162	94	21	12	21	270	64	0	56	-	-	10	0.294	0.367	0.490	0.857
Detroit	1949	24 G. Kell	134	522	97	179	59	38	9	3	244	71	1	13	-	-	7	0.343	0.423	0.467	0.890
Washington	1894	18 B. Joyce	99	355	103	126	89	25	14	17	230	87	0	33	-	-	21	0.355	0.482	0.648	1.130
Detroit	1936	34 Gehringer	154	641	144	227	116	60	12	15	356	83	4	13	-	-	4	0.354	0.431	0.555	0.987
Detroit	1961	42 N. Cash	159	535	119	193	132	22	8	41	354	124	9	85	-	-	11	0.361	0.488	0.662	1.150
Detroit	1943	26 R. York	155	571	90	155	118	22	11	34	301	84	1	88	-	-	5	0.271	0.366	0.527	0.893
Detroit	1968	35 B. Freehan	155	540	73	142	84	24	2	25	245	65	24	64	-	-	0	0.263	0.367	0.454	0.821
New York N	1947	23 W. Cooper	140	515	79	157	122	24	8	35	302	24	0	26	-	-	2	0.305	0.336	0.586	0.922

Team	Year	WS Pitchers	G	GS	QS	CG	S	W	L	IP	H	SO	BB	HB	HR	R	ER	ERA
Detroit	1945	38 Newhouser	40	36	-	29	2	25	9	313	239	212	110	-	5	-	-	1.80
Detroit	1968	33 D. McLain	41	41	-	28	0	31	6	336	241	280	63	-	31	-	-	1.96
Detroit	1971	29 M. Lolich	45	45	-	29	0	25	14	376	336	308	92	-	36	-	-	2.92
Detroit	1944	42 D. Trout	49	40	-	33	0	27	14	352	314	144	83	-	9	-	-	2.11
Detroit	1976	27 M. Fidrych	31	29	-	24	0	19	9	250	217	97	53	-	12	-	-	2.33
Detroit	1936	26 T. Bridges	39	38	-	26	0	23	11	295	289	175	115	-	21	-	-	3.60
Detroit	1934	28 S. Rowe	45	30	-	20	1	24	8	266	259	149	81	-	12	-	-	3.45
Boston	1897	41 K. Nichols	46	40	-	37	3	31	11	368	362	127	68	-	9	-	-	2.64
Detroit	1973	31 J. Hiller	65	0	-	0	38	10	5	125	89	124	39	-	7	-	-	1.44
Detroit	1984	24 Hernandez	80	0	-	0	32	9	3	140	96	112	36	-	6	-	-	1.92

Chart 14-1 – Tigers Best Season Roster

Fielding Leaders	Pos	Range	Error	Throwing
T. Cobb	C/RF	AA	4	-2
C. Lemon	CF	AA	9	+1
A. Kaline	RF	A	6	-2
H. Heilmann	RF	B	4	-1
H. Greenberg	LF	B	2	-1

For outfielders - range (AA is best) and throwing (-4 is exceptional, -3 is excellent, -2 is very good) are most important. Error rating (10 is best, 1 is poor) is not as critical as infielders because outfielders normally do not make as many errors.

T. Jackson	SS	AA+	9	-
A. Fletcher	SS	AA	4	-
C. Gehringer	2B	AA+	6	-
R. York	1B	AA	7	-
N. Cash	1B	A	7	-
R. Kell	3B	B	10	-

For infielders, range (AA is best), + increase in DPs because of excellent pivot, error rating is as important as range for an infielder (10 is excellent, 1 is poor).

Catcher Throwing - Freehan has a very good throwing arm (-2) and Cooper is below average (+1). Freehan will probably be a late inning replacement.

Pitcher Hold Rating - Nichols and Lolich have excellent hold ratings; McLain and Hiller are very good; the rest of the staff is average except for Newhouser and Hernandez, who are both mediocre at holding runners.

Pitching - This is a solid pitching staff with an excellent bullpen (Hiller and Hernandez).

Game One, Sunday July 18, Tiger Stadium (Detroit), 1 pm (B. Foster vs. H. Newhouser)

It is hot and cloudy with no wind. The left-handed Tiger pitcher, Hal Newhouser (1945 Tigers, 25-9, 1.80 ERA), escapes a mini-jam in the top of the first. Bell singles to center and steals second on the first pitch to Willie Wells. Bell moves to third on a slowly hit ground ball to Kell (3B), who guns down Wells with York (1B) making a good pick and stretch (one out). The BB Stars have a runner 90 feet away from home plate with the big guns coming to the plate (Charleston, Gibson and hopefully Suttles). Newhouser strikes Charleston out (looking) and Gibson (swinging at a nasty curve in the dirt).

Bill Foster was a great pitcher with the Chicago American Giants (1920s-30s). He had a winning percentage of nearly .700 during his ten years with the

Giants (managed by his half-brother, Rube). His winning percentage in exhibition games vs. Major League Stars was .600+. Bill has a blazing fast ball which he mixes artfully with a variety of breaking and off speed pitches. **Note:** The source of information in the above paragraph is NegroLeagueBaseball.com.

Things do not start well for Foster. Ty Cobb (1911 Tigers) hits a drive that Cool Papa Bell gets to quickly, but he drops the ball (a very rare occurrence). Cobb slides into second base on the two-base error. Harry Heilmann (1923 Tigers) hits a one-hopper to Dandridge (3B), he looks Cobb back to second and throws out Heilmann (one out). Foster walks the dangerous Charlie Gehringer (1936 Tigers). This brings up one of the Tigers' greatest run producers, Hank Greenberg (150 RBIs with 1940 Tigers). Foster falls behind Greenberg (2-0) and throws a fast ball with a little extra on it. Greenberg times his swing perfectly and slams one, high and deep to left field. Charleston (LF) turns, looks up and watches the ball land in the upper-deck for a 3-run home run, Tigers lead 3-0. Foster retires York on a ground ball to Dandridge and George Kell on another deep drive to left that Charleston takes on the warning track. **Tigers 3, BB Stars 0.**

Newhouser breezes through the second and third innings (only an Irvin single).

In the bottom of the third with one out, the Tigers add to their lead. Heilmann doubles into the left- field corner. Gehringer walks (second time). Greenberg steps to the plate (three run HR in the first inning). Greenberg lines a gapper to the wall in left center, Bell retrieves it as two more Tiger runners cross the plate (5-0). Greenberg 5, I mean, Tigers 5, BB Stars 0. Foster walks York before settling down to retire Kell and Jackson. **Tigers 5, BB Stars 0.**

Neither team scores in the fourth. Hilton Smith is warming up for the BB Stars and will probably come in to pitch in the bottom of the fifth (Foster is due up third, top of fifth).

Dandridge leads off, in the top of the fifth, by reaching base on York's error. Warfield strikes out (one out); Lloyd pinch hits for Foster (4 IP, 4 H, 5 R, 4 ER, 1 HR, 1 K, 3 BB). Lloyd flies out to Cobb (CF). This should have been the third out. Bell singles to center; Dandridge stops at second. Wells hits one into the gap and Cobb chases it down. Dandridge scores; the speedy Bell races around third. Cobb makes a perfect throw to the plate and Freehan tags out the sliding Bell. Trailing 5-0, Bell made a bad decision with Cobb in center field. **Tigers 5, BB Stars 1.**

Hilton Smith will face the destructive duo (Gehringer and Greenberg) to start the fifth. The destruction continues. Gehringer singles to right, followed by a line drive into the lower deck in left field (HR – Greenberg, RBIs six and seven). Smith escapes without any further damage (with one out, error by Warfield is followed by a double play). **Tigers 7, BB Stars 1.**

The Tigers score a single run in the seventh (Gehringer 2 for 2 and 2 walks scores his fourth run on Kell single) and three runs in the eighth off Martin Dihigo (RBI single by Heilmann and a 2-run single by Charlie Gehringer. **Tigers 11, BB Stars 1.**

Newhouser faces just three batters in the ninth (single, double play, and ground out).

Newhouser did the pitching (9 IP, 6 H, 1 R, 0 ER, 0 HR, 8 K, 2 BB). Below is the combined offense for Gehringer and Greenberg:

AB	R	H	RBI	B.Avg.	OBP	S. Pct.	OPS
8	6	6	9	.750	.800	1.625	2.425

This was a great way to start against the BB Stars. Do not even begin to think that they are intimidated by this awesome Tiger win.

	R	H	E	LOB
BB Stars	1	6	2	5
Tigers	11	13	1	6

Winning Pitcher – Newhouser   Losing Pitcher – Foster
The Tigers lead the series, 1-0.

Game Two, Monday July 19, Tiger Stadium (Detroit), 1 pm (B. J. Rogan vs. D. McLain)

It is a warm, clear day with the wind blowing out (toward the fences). Wilber Bullet Joe Rogan pitched his first season with the Kansas City Monarchs in 1920 (the inaugural year of the Negro National League). He has a blazing fast ball. He is also a great hitter. He was with the Monarchs 17 years as a player and a manager. **Note:** Rogan's information source is NegroLeague-Baseball.com.

In the bottom of the third, the Tigers pick up where they left off yesterday. Cobb singles to center, then steals second and takes third when Mackey's throw goes into center field (E2). Crawford singles to center; Cobb scores first run (1-0). Rogan walks Cash (1961 Tigers, 1.150 OPS). Greenberg is up with two men on. He launches another blast to deep left; if it stays fair, it is gone. It is a fair ball, 3-run home run for Greenberg (4-0). Joyce (1894 Washington) hits a triple over Bell's head in center. Newcombe is throwing in the bullpen. Gehringer singles to center, scoring Joyce (5-0). The first six batters have reached base off Rogan, this inning. He retires the next three batters. **Tigers 5, BB Stars 0.**

McLain is hit very hard in the fourth but another base running mistake in addition to balls ending up caught on the warning track and the score remains 5-0.

In the BB Stars' fifth inning with one out, Rogan is due up. He is an excellent hitter and he has retired six in arrow. He bats for himself and gets his second hit. Rogan is not a good base runner. Singles by Bell and Lloyd load the bases. Rogan is not fast enough to try to score. Oscar Charleston has a chance to get the BB Stars back in the game. Cash is not holding the runner at first with the bases loaded. He is back deep, near the foul line. Charleston hits it hard to Cash's right. Cash spears it and fires to Fletcher (SS) for one. Fletcher jumps to avoid a take-out slide by Lloyd and fires back to Cash who has raced to the bag, double play. Charleston is out by an eyelash, side retired.

Rogan retires the side in order in the fifth. **Tigers 5, BB Stars 0.**

With one out in the top of the sixth, Torriente slaps one to the left side and Fletcher (SS) bobbles the ball for an error. Mackey hits the ball to deep center, but Cobb runs it down (two outs). Torriente stays at first. McLain hits Judy Johnson with the pitch (runners on first and second). Newt Allen singles through the box into center field and Torriente races home with the BB Stars first run (unearned, 5-1). Johnson goes to third. Stearnes will pinch hit for Rogan. McLain has struggled but comes up with the big out when he needs it. Stearnes flies out to Crawford in right field to end the inning. In six innings the BB Stars have stranded eight runners. The final line on Rogan is 5 IP, 5 H, 5 R, 1 HR, 2 K, 2 BB. **Tigers 5, BB Stars 1.**

In the bottom of the sixth, Newcombe is now pitching for the BB Stars and he retires the Tigers in order.

With one out in the top of the seventh, McLain gives up back-to-back singles to Lloyd and Charleston (runners on first and second). Leonard takes a called third strike (two outs). Torriente hits the ball hard but it is right at the second baseman, Gehringer to end the inning (BB Stars 11 hits, 10 men left on base through seven innings).

In the bottom of the seventh, Fletcher doubles into the gap in right center. McLain will bat for himself. He is a tough competitor and the Tigers are sticking with him for now. McLain tops one up the third-base line but Dandridge cannot make the play (E5), runners on first and third. Donnie Moore is warming up. Johnson (3B) and Leonard (1B) are playing in for a possible bunt with Cobb at the plate. Cobb bounces one to Allen (2B) and he flips to Lloyd for the force on McLain as Fletcher scores the sixth run for the Tigers. Cobb breaks for second on the first pitch to Crawford and Mackey throws to Lloyd, who tags Cobb for the second out. Crawford singles to right. Cash hits a ground ball to Allen's right; he back-hands it and shovels the ball to Lloyd at second for the force to end the inning. **Tigers 6, BB Stars 1.**

The Tigers are making defensive changes to start the eighth inning. York is now playing first base and will bat second. George Kell will play third and bat third. Kaline will replace Crawford in right field and bat fifth. Tommy Bridges and Kid Nichols are warming up for the Tigers.

Mackey leads off with a single to left field. Johnson hits a slow chopper to Kell; his only play is to first base (one out) and Mackey goes to second. Allen lines a base hit into right center and Mackey scores (6-2). That was the thirteenth hit off McLain and Bridges is being brought in from the Tiger bullpen.

Irvin is pinch hitting for Newcombe. Bridges jams him, and Irvin pops out to Fletcher (SS) for the second out. Bell singles through the left side as Allen stops at second. Lloyd lines a base hit to right, Allen scores and Bell stops at second (6-3). The final line for McLain is 7.3 IP, 13 H, 3 R, 2 ER, 0 HR, 4 K, 0 BB, 1 HB. Nichols replaces Bridges for the Tigers. Charleston grounds out to Fletcher to end the inning. **Tigers 6, BB Stars 3.**

Donnie Moore is now pitching for the BB Stars in the bottom of the eighth. He retires the Tigers in order.

John Hiller is warming up for the Tigers. Nichols retires Leonard on a ground ball to Gehringer to start the ninth inning (one out). Torriente and Mackey get back-to-back singles, putting runners on first and second. Josh Gibson (representing the tying run) will bat for Judy Johnson. Hiller is now pitching for Tigers. Gibson hits a soft line drive to left field; Greenberg races in, but he drops the ball (E7) and the bases are loaded. Allen lines a single to left; Torriente scores (6-4) and the bases remain loaded. Mule Suttles pinch hits for Moore, and the Tigers play Suttles to pull. Greenberg (LF) is playing Suttles toward the line. Suttles lines one to left center; Greenberg gets a late break, Cobb is too far away and it falls in. Greenberg knocks it down. Mackey and Gibson score to tie the game 6-6. Allen is trying to score from first; the relay from Kell to Freehan and Allen is out. Suttles is on second, two outs. Cool Papa Bell is now batting; he hits a drive to deep center. Cobb was playing shallow and has a long run; he cannot reach it. The ball rolls to the wall. Stearnes has scored the go-ahead run, and Bell ends up on third. These BB Stars are relentless. If you make a mistake, they usually make you pay. When the BB stars get twenty hits, and the Tigers make three errors and misplay a fly ball, the Tigers should not expect to win. It is hard to believe it is only 7-6. Lloyd strikes out to end the top of the ninth. **BB Stars 7, Tigers 6.**

The following changes are made by the BB Stars. J. R. Richard is now pitching, and he is batting second. Wells is playing shortstop and will bat fourth. Dandridge is playing third, batting fifth. Gibson remains in the game as the catcher. Suttles remains in the game and is playing first base.

Freehan flies out to Bell (one out). Fletcher singles to center field. Heilmann is batting for Hiller and goes down swinging (two outs). Cobb lofts a fly ball to shallow center; Bell comes in and makes the catch. The BB Stars even the series (1-1) with a great come from behind win. The BB Stars' bullpen did a great job (4 IP, 1R). The Tigers bullpen and its defense were not up to the task.

	R	H	E	LOB
BB Stars	7	20	2	13
Tigers	6	8	3	4

Winning Pitcher – Moore   Save – Richard   Losing Pitcher – Hiller
The series is even, 1-1.

Game Three, Tuesday July 20, Tiger Stadium (Detroit), 7 pm (S. Paige vs. M. Lolich)

It is a warm, cloudy evening with the wind blowing out. Mickey Lolich is one of the greatest left-handed pitchers in Tiger history. In 1971 he started 45 games, completed 29 with a 25-14 record, 2.92 ERA. He is facing Satchel Paige, who is to Negro League baseball what Babe Ruth was to Major League baseball. Combining great showmanship with his remarkable skills, Paige is recognized by one great baseball historian (Bill James) as the second-greatest pitcher[1] of all time behind Walter "Big Train" Johnson (Washington Senators). Satchel Paige is the first free agent[2] of baseball. Many times he left his contracted team to play for more money (some times for a day, a weekend, a month, a whole season). In 1948[3], Paige (age 42) joined the Cleveland Indians in July and finished with a 6-1 record during the heat of the pennant race. His performance contributed significantly to the Indians reaching the World Series. The Indians beat the Boston Braves, four games to two. The Indians have not won a World Series since 1948 (63 years and counting).

Records are incomplete but it is believed that Paige had over 300 shutouts and more than 1500 wins in his career (vs. all opponents). **Note:** The above data on Satchel Paige's career is from NegroLeagueBaseball.com.

In the bottom of the second, the Tigers get an unearned run off of Paige (two singles around an error by Wells, Cooper RBI single). **Tigers 1, BB Stars 0.**

In the bottom of the third, the Tigers bat around against the great Satchel Paige. Cobb singles to center. While standing on the rubber, Paige drops the ball. It is a balk and Cobb goes to second. Paige is mediocre when it comes to holding runners; Cobb steals third. Heilmann lays down a great squeeze bunt to score Cobb as Heilmann is thrown out (Suttles to Warfield). Cash singles to center. Greenberg hits his fourth home run of the series (4-0). Leon Day begins to warm up in the BB bullpen. Joyce grounds out to Warfield (2B) for the second out. Gehringer hits a home run into the lower deck in right field. Travis Jackson singles to right. Walker Cooper (free agent, 1947 Giants) triples over Bell to bring in the fifth run of the inning (6-0). Lolich strikes out. **Tigers 6, BB Stars 0.**

With one out in the top of the fourth, the BB Stars put five singles together (Suttles, Irvin, Dandridge, Warfield and Charleston pinch hitting for Paige). The result is only two runs and the bases left loaded. **Tigers 6, BB Stars 2.**

In the bottom of the fifth inning (Leon Day is pitching his second inning of relief), the Tigers squeeze another run home (Joyce single, stolen base, wild pitch and Jackson squeeze bunt). **Tigers 7, BB Stars 2.**

In the top of the sixth inning the BB Stars, with one out, threaten to score. Warfield singles to center. Allen pinch hits for Day and walks. Lolich retires Bell and Lloyd to end the threat. Lolich actually retires the last eleven BB Stars in a row.

Bill Freehan, who went in defensively for Cooper in the top of the eighth, ends the scoring with a home run off Hilton Smith in the bottom of the eighth. The final line for Lolich is 9 IP, 9 H, 2 R, 0 HR, 7 K, 1 BB.

	R	H	E	LOB
BB Stars	2	9	1	9
Tigers	8	13	1	4

Winning Pitcher – Lolich Losing Pitcher – Paige

The Tigers lead the series, 2-1.

Game Four, Wednesday July 21, Tiger Stadium (Detroit), 7 pm (L. Tiant vs. D. Trout)

It is a warm, partly cloudy day with the wind blowing from home plate to center field. Dizzy Trout had a great season in 1944 with the Tigers (25-14 with 33 complete games and an ERA of 2.11; he earned 42 win shares).

The BB Stars with one out in the first inning, score the first run. Lloyd triples over Cobb's head in center field. Lloyd scores when Fletcher robs Charleston with a great play in back of second on a ground ball up the middle and throws the runner out at first. Gibson grounds out to Gehringer (2B). **BB Stars 1, Tigers 0.**

In the top of the third, the BB Stars add to their lead. Newt Allen doubles into the gap in right center. Tiant strikes out after failing to sacrifice Allen to third. Bell lines a 2-run home run into the lower deck in right field (3-0). Lloyd singles to left. Charleston singles to center with Lloyd racing to third. Gibson hits into a force play (64) as Lloyd scores (4-0). Stearnes doubles off the wall in center. Cobb fields it and quickly throws to Gehringer, cutoff man, who fires to the plate but too late as Gibson slides in with the fifth run. Stearnes advances to third on the throw home. Leonard flies out to Crawford (RF). **BB Stars 5, Tigers 0.**

Tiant (free agent 1968 Indians) shuts out Tigers through the first four innings. In 1968, the year of the pitcher, Denny McLain of the Tigers won 31 games while Luis Tiant led the American League with a 1.60 ERA and gave up fewer than six hits/game.

Trout settles down and blanks the BB Stars in the fourth and fifth innings.

Through the first four innings, Tiant had given up only a two-out single to Cash in the fourth. In the bottom of the fifth, Gehringer opens the inning with a walk. George Kell (1949 batting champion by less than a point over Ted Williams) triples off the wall in center, driving in Gehringer (5-1). Tiant walks Freehan. Travis Jackson forces Freehan at second (Lloyd-Allen) as Kell scores (5-2). Jackson (SS) enters the game in the top of the fifth when Bell spikes Fletcher (Bell thrown out stealing). Joyce pinch-hits for Trout (5 IP, 6 H, 5 R, 1 HR, 1 K, 1 BB). Joyce hits one to deep center; Bell goes back to the warning track and makes the catch (two outs). Cobb singles to right with Jackson stopping at second base. Crawford lines a single to center, scoring Jackson and sending Cobb to third (5-3). Day is warming up for the BB Stars and School Boy Rowe (1934 Tigers) is warming up for the Tigers. Cash lines out to Leonard. **BB Stars 5, Tigers 3.**

Rowe is now pitching for the Tigers. Despite giving up a lead-off double to Josh Gibson in the sixth, he retires the next three batters without a run. Tiant rebounds with a one, two, three sixth inning.

In the seventh, Newt Allen singles to center. Tiant successfully sacrifices Allen to second. Bell singles to center, scoring Allen (6-3). Lloyd singles up the middle and Bell races to third. Rowe strikes out Charleston and Gibson to end the inning. **BB Stars 6, Tigers 3.**

Tiant retires the first two batters in the seventh. Rudy York (1943 Tigers) hits a home run just inside the left-field foul pole (6-4), batting for Rowe. Cobb triples over Bell's head. Tiant retires Crawford on a routine fly ball to Bell. **BB Stars 6, Tigers 4.**

In the top of the eighth, Kid Nichols (1897 Boston) is now pitching and he is batting second. Al Kaline is now in right field batting ninth. With two outs, Leonard is on first (single). Allen singles past Nichols into centerfield. Leonard stops at second. Biz Mackey pinch hits for Tiant (7 IP, 6H, 4 R, 1 HR, 2 K, 2 BB). Mackey singles to center, Leonard scores and Allen goes over to third (7-4). Bell forces Mackey at second to end the inning. **BB Stars 7, Tigers 4.**

In the bottom of the eighth, Leon Day is now pitching. He gets in a jam. He walks Cash. Greenberg flies out to Charleston (LF). Gehringer doubles (runners on second and third). Kell flies out to Stearnes in shallow right field; runners hold. Day strikes out Freehan (looking).

In the top of the ninth with one out, Charleston triples and Gibson is walked intentionally. Stearnes flies out to Kaline in deep right, scoring Charleston (sac fly, Stearnes). Leonard walks and Johnson strikes out. **BB Stars 8, Tigers 4.**

Suttles (1B) and Johnson (3B) are in defensively for the bottom of the ninth. Jackson doubles into left-field corner. Kaline singles to center, with Jackson stopping at third. J. R. Richard is now pitching. Cobb singles to center, scoring Jackson; Kaline stops at second (8-5). Heilmann bats for Nichols. He lines one to right field; Stearnes comes in and makes a shoe string catch. Stearnes fires to first to try to double off Cobb, but the throw is a little late. Richard walks Cash to load the bases. Greenberg represents the potential winning run at the plate with only one out. He hits a drive to deep left but Charleston has room to make the catch as Kaline trots home with the sixth Tiger run and Cobb hustles to third (sac fly for Greenberg). Richard jams Gehringer, who pops it up to Newt Allen for the final out.

	R	H	E	LOB
BB Stars	8	14	0	8
Tigers	6	10	0	8

Winning Pitcher – Tiant   Save – Richard   Losing Pitcher – Trout
The series is tied, 2-2.

Game Five, Friday July 23, Jack Murphy Stadium (San Diego), 7 pm (M. Fidrych vs. B. Foster)

It is a beautiful night for baseball. The BB Stars will be the home team for the remaining five games of the series in this beautiful baseball stadium. The park favors pitchers slightly.

Foster strikes out Cobb (looking) to start the game. Cobb is ejected after vehemently disputing the call. Lemon replaces him in center field. Gehringer chases Stearnes to the warning track for the second out. Kaline flies out to Charleston.

In the bottom of the first, Fidrych gives up three hits but no runs (Lemon threw out Bell trying to go from first to third on a single).

In the bottom of the fourth with one out, Stearnes doubles off the wall in right. Suttles follows with a single to center that scores Stearnes (1-0). **BB Stars 1, Tigers 0.**

In the top of the sixth, Heilmann pinch hits for Fidrych (5 IP, 7 H, 1 R, 0 HR, 4 K, 1 BB) and flies out to Bell (CF). Gehringer singles to left with two outs but Kaline fans to end the inning. Foster and BB Stars cling to 1-run lead (1-0).

In the bottom of the sixth, the Tigers do a double switch. Heilmann stays in the game in right field. Bridges will bat fourth and replaces Fidrych on the mound. Josh Gibson greets Tommy Bridges (1936 Tigers) with a long home run to straight-away center (2-0). Turkey Stearnes flies out to Heilmann on the warning track (one out). Suttles and Judy Johnson ground out. **BB Stars 2, Tigers 0.**

In the top of the seventh, Hank Greenberg hits his fifth home run of the series to lead-off the inning (2-1). Kell slaps a one-out single to right, but Foster retires Travis Jackson (fly out) and Walker Cooper (infield fly). **BB Stars 2, Tigers 1.**

Newt Allen leads off the bottom of the seventh with a single to center. Cristobal Torriente will pinch hit for Bill Foster, who pitched a great game (7 IP, 6 H, 1 R, 1 HR, 3 K, O BB). Willie Hernandez, a left-hander, replaces Bridges. On the first pitch, Allen takes off for second. He beats Cooper's throw, stolen base. Torriente flies out to Greenberg (LF). Hernandez gets Bell to pop out to Gehringer (2B) and Lloyd to ground out to Gehringer.

Hilton Smith is now pitching for the BB Stars in the top of the eighth. He retires the first two Tiger batters before Gehringer homers over the right-field fence to tie the game, 2-2. Joyce bats for Bridges and flies out to Stearnes (RF). **Tigers 2, BB Stars 2.**

In the bottom of the eighth, the left-hander, John Hiller, is now pitching for the Tigers. Hiller walks Charleston on four pitches. Gibson hits a slow-chopper to Travis Jackson who throws him out while Charleston advances to second. Stearnes flies out to Greenberg (LF). Suttles lines a base hit to center and Charleston races around third. Lemon's throw is late and up the first base line as Charleston slides in with the tie-breaking run (3-2). If Ty Cobb was in center, Charleston more than likely would have stayed at third (Lemon's throwing arm is below average, Cobb's arm is excellent). Judy Johnson takes a called third strike. **BB Stars 3, Tigers 2.**

Hank Greenberg has been a terror through the first five games. In the top of the ninth inning, he continues his unbelievable performance with a long drive down the left field line, high above the foul pole. The third-base umpire signals fair ball tying the score, 3-3. The BB Stars cannot believe the call. Charleston and Johnson are screaming at the third base umpire. Gibson and Smith are in an animated discussion with the home plate umpire. Black Ball manager Bob May throws his hat in disgust, kicks the third base bag as he chews out the third base umpire, Kenny Bean. Manager May has been ejected as Bean walks away. Hilton Smith retires the next three batters. Greenberg has 6 HRs and 15 RBIs in five games. What a performance. **Tigers 3, BB Stars 3.**

Hiller starts out the bottom of the ninth by striking out Newt Allen on a pitch in the dirt. Monte Irvin, batting for Hilton Smith, flies out to Lemon (CF). Cool Papa Bell lines a double into the left field corner. Wells pinch hits for Lloyd. Hiller will intentionally walk him to pitch to the left-handed batting but dangerous Oscar Charleston. The count goes to 2-2. Hiller fires a fast ball on the inner part of the plate but Charleston adjusts and hits a "seeing-eye" ground ball between York and Gehringer. The speedy Bell races around third and scores, standing up. The BB Stars have a "walk off" win!

	R	H	E	LOB
Tigers	3	8	0	4
BB Stars	4	12	0	9

Winning Pitcher – H. Smith   Losing Pitcher – Hiller
The BB Stars lead the series, 3-2.

Game Six, Saturday July 24, Jack Murphy Stadium (San Diego), 1 pm (Newhouser vs. Rogan)

It is a beautiful day for baseball, warm and clear. It is scoreless as Hank Greenberg leads off the top of the second inning. Greenberg lines the ball off the center-field wall as Bell stumbles. The ball is chased down by Torriente (RF). Greenberg goes into third base, standing up with a triple. Rogan's first pitch to Heilmann bounces off Gibson's glove and goes to the back stop, Greenberg trots in with Tiger's first run. Gibson is charged with a passed ball. Heilmann hits a one-hopper to Dandridge but he bobbles the ball for an error. Gehringer singles up the middle as Heilmann stops at second. Rogan's first pitch to Freehan is way outside and skips to the backstop as both runners advance to second and third (wild pitch).

With the count 1-1 on Freehan, Rogan bounces a pitch in the dirt that scoots through Gibson's legs for Rogan's second wild pitch scoring Heilmann and sending Gehringer to third (2-0). Freehan hits one to deep short that Wells backhands. Wells throws out Freehan as Gehringer scores the third run of the inning. Travis Jackson doubles to right center. Dihigo is warming up for the BB Stars. Newhouser flies out to Bell (CF) for the second out (should have been three). Joyce singles to center field as Jackson scores the fourth run of the inning (the second unearned run of the inning). Cobb singles to right and Joyce dashes to third. On the first pitch to Cash, Cobb steals second. Cash is the ninth batter of the inning and he grounds out to Suttles. **Tigers 4, BB Stars 0.**

In the bottom of the second the BB Stars put pressure on Newhouser when Suttles singles and Wells doubles to put runners on second and third with none out. Newhouser escapes by giving up one run on Warfield's infield out. **Tigers 4, BB Stars 1.**

In the top of the fifth, the Tigers add to their lead. With one out, Cobb reaches on an error by Wells. Cobb steals second. Cash beats out a slow-roller to Suttles, and the runners are at first and third. Greenberg hits a high fly to left center. Bell makes the catch but Cobb scores easily (5-1). The Tigers now have scored three unearned runs. Heilmann hits into a force to end the inning. **Tigers 5, BB Stars 1.**

In the top of the seventh with one out, Joyce triples off the center-field wall and he scores on a Cobb sac fly. Cash strikes out. **Tigers 6, BB Stars 1.**

Newhouser retires the first two batters in the bottom of the seventh. Biz Mackey pinch hits for Rogan and singles to center. The final line on Rogan is 7 IP, 7 H, 6 R, 3 ER, 0 HR, 5 K, 0 BB, 2 WP. Newhouser walks Bell and Torriente to load the bases. Kid Nichols is warming up. Gibson lines one into the gap; Greenberg cannot reach it. Two runs are in, Torriente is heading home and Greenberg's throw is not in time. Gibson moves to third on the throw (6-4). Newhouser gets Turkey Stearnes to bounce out to Gehringer (2B). **Tigers 6, BB Stars 4.**

Newcombe is now pitching for the BB Stars in the top of the eighth. He retires the first two batters. Gehringer lines one into the gap in right center; Bell cuts it off. Gehringer will try to stretch a single into a double, but Bell's throw is on the money and Gehringer is out to end the inning.

The Tigers make three defensive changes in the bottom of the eighth. Kell replaces Joyce at third. York replaces Cash at first and Kaline replaces Heilmann in right field. Newhouser is still pitching for Detroit. Nichols and Hernandez are warming up for the Tigers. Newhouser gets Suttles to foul out to York (one out). Willie Wells gets his third hit, a line drive home run over the left field fence. Kid Nichols replaces Newhouser (7.3 IP, 8 H, 5 ER, 1 HR, 5 K, 4 BB). Leonard bats for Dandridge and pops out to York. Allen bats for Warfield and grounds out to Gehringer. **Tigers 6, BB Stars 5.**

For the BB Stars, Johnson is now playing third base and Allen is at second base. Newcombe gives up two-out single to Kid Nichols in the ninth and gets Kell to foul out to Gibson.

Leading off the bottom of the ninth, Charleston will pinch hit for Newcombe. He walks. Willie Hernandez replaces Nichols. Bell hits a ground ball to Kell (3B), who throws to Gehringer for one. But the relay to first is not in time to get Bell. On the hit-and-run, Torriente swings and misses. The throw to Jackson covering second is not in time; Bell has a stolen base. The tying run is on second, the fastest player on the BB Stars, Cool Papa Bell. Torriente takes a called third strike. It is up to Josh Gibson. Hernandez jams Gibson and he bounces one weakly to the shortstop. Jackson throws him out to end the game. This was a game the BB Stars gave away.

	R	H	E	LOB
Tigers	6	9	0	4
BB Stars	5	8	2	7

Winning Pitcher – Newhouser   Save W. Hernandez   Losing Pitcher – Rogan
The series is tied, 3-3.

Game Seven, Sunday July 25, Jack Murphy Stadium (San Diego), 1 pm (McLain vs. Paige)

The Tigers strike quickly on this warm, cloudy day. Cobb singles to right and then steals second. Sam Crawford hits one over Bell's head for a triple. Paige retires the next three batters, leaving Crawford stranded on third (Joyce strikes out, Greenberg bounces out to third and Cash flies to right). **Tigers 1, BB Stars 0.**

In the top of the second, the Tigers get to Satchel again. Gehringer singles up the middle. Cooper flies out to Charleston (one out). Fletcher (free agent SS, 1916 Giants) doubles into right center on the hit-and-run, and Gehringer scores (2-0). Paige strikes out McLain and Cobb. **Tigers 2, BB Stars 0.**

McLain retires the first 13 batters he faces. With one out in the fifth, Buck Leonard homers over the right-field fence. Biz Mackey flies out to left (two outs). Judy Johnson doubles off the fence in left center. Newt Allen goes with the fast ball on the outside corner and hits it over the left-field fence, just inside the foul pole. Paige strikes out. **BB Stars 3, Tigers 2.**

Satchel Paige retires 11 in a row (fourth through seventh); the score remains 3-2 going into the bottom of the seventh. With one out, Leonard triples into the right-field corner off McLain. The Tigers bring the infield in. Mackey hits a fly to deep center; Leonard tags and scores the fourth run for the BB Stars (sac fly). Judy Johnson tops one in front of the plate and Cooper throws him out. **BB Stars 4, Tigers 2.**

In the top of the eighth, Heilmann pinch hits for McLain (7 IP, 5 H, 4 R, 2 HR, 6 K, 0 BB). Willie Hernandez and School Boy Rowe are warming up for the Tigers. Heilmann lines a single to center field. Cobb bounces out to second on the hit-and-run. Heilmann moves to second. Crawford drops a bloop single in front of Bell (CF); Heilmann holds at third base. Bill Joyce steps up to the plate, and the tying runs are on base. J. R. Richard is throwing in the bullpen for the BB Stars. Paige goes to 3 and 2 with Joyce. Paige fires just above the knees, and Joyce drives it to deep center. Bell leaps, but he cannot get it. The ball hits the base of the wall and bounces away from Bell. Heilmann scores. Crawford is being waved around third and he scores the tying run. Bell throws to third as Joyce slides into third with a triple. Satchel stands on the mound with his hands on his hips. Joyce won that battle with a good piece of hitting. With Greenberg at the plate, will BB Stars walk him intentionally? The decision is to bring the infield in and pitch to the hitting star of the series. Greenberg hits a bouncer to short; Lloyd charges, fields the ball and throws in one motion. Joyce who broke when the ball was hit slides and avoids the tag; he is safe. Tigers lead 5-4. Paige retires the next two batters to end the inning. **Tigers 5, BB Stars 4.**

In the bottom of the eighth, Willie Hernandez is now pitching for the Tigers and batting fifth. Freehan is now catching and batting second. Kaline is in right field, batting third. Kell is playing third and batting seventh. York is playing first base and batting ninth. Hernandez retires Allen on a ground ball to Fletcher. Gibson, batting for Paige, flies to right (two outs). Bell singles to left. With Lloyd batting, Bell is thrown out stealing (2-6).

J. R. Richard keeps the Tigers scoreless in the top of the ninth.

Lloyd leads off the bottom of the ninth with a single to right. Charleston lines a single to center; Lloyd stops at second (none out). Stearnes flies out to left (one out). With the count 1 ball and 2 strikes to Suttles (pinch hitting for Leonard), Hernandez uncorks a wild pitch; runners advance to second and third. The tying run is on third and the winning run is on second. Suttles goes down swinging on a pitch out of the strike zone (two outs). Mackey hits one a one-hopper to Gehringer, who throws him out.

	R	H	E	LOB
Tigers	5	10	0	4
BB Stars	4	8	0	2

Winning Pitcher – McLain   Save – Hernandez   Losing Pitcher – Paige
The Tigers lead the series, 4-3.

Game Eight, Monday July 26, Jack Murphy Stadium (San Diego), 7 pm (Lolich Vs. Tiant)

The Tigers threaten to score in the first. With two outs, Cobb is on second (single) and Cash is on first (walk) with Hank Greenberg stepping to the plate. In the first seven games, Greenberg has 17 RBIs. Luis Tiant does not want to walk him. He also does not want to give Greenberg a fat pitch. The count goes to 2-2 and Tiant tempts Greenberg with a fast ball just off the outside corner. Greenberg goes with the pitch and hits a high fly to right field and Irvin makes the catch to end the inning.

In the bottom of the first, Lolich retires Cool Papa Bell on a deep fly ball to Cobb (one out). Willie Wells goes down swinging on a nasty curve ball in the dirt (two outs). Lolich then gives up a single to Charleston, walks Gibson,

RBI single to Suttles, RBI single to Irvin, 2 run-double to Dandridge and walks Warfield. Lolich finally strikes out Tiant. **BB Stars 4, Tigers 0.**

After four innings the score is still 4-0 and the Tigers have no hits and three walks since the first off Tiant. Tiant retires the side in order in the fifth (including Crawford, who grounds out pinch hitting for Lolich (4 IP, 5 H, 4 R, 0 HR, 8 K, 2 BB). Lolich retires 10 of the last 11 batters he faces with 7 strikeouts.

School Boy Rowe replaces Lolich in the fifth inning. He escapes a one-out bases loaded jam by striking out pinch hitter Turkey Stearnes (batting for Irvin) and getting Ray Dandridge to line out to Travis Jackson (SS).

In the meantime, Tiant retires the side in order in the sixth and seventh innings (ten batters in a row). He has given up one hit, a single by Ty Cobb in the first inning.

The BB Stars quickly ice this game in the bottom of the seventh. Wells leads off with a single to left field. Charleston walks. Josh Gibson smashes a long 3-run home run over the wall in left. Rowe retires the next three batters. **BB Stars 7, Tigers 0.**

In the top of the eighth with one out George Kell singles, batting for Rowe. Tiant retires Joyce and Cobb to end the inning.

Tommy Bridges comes in to pitch the bottom of the eighth for the Tigers and retires the side in order.

The Tigers finally get on the board in the ninth but it is too little, too late. With one out, Cash walks. Greenberg triples for his 18th RBI of the series. Gehringer reaches on an error by Warfield as Greenberg scores the Tigers' second run. Freehan goes down swinging and Jackson hits into a force play to end the game. The final line for Luis Tiant is 9 IP, 3 H, 2 R, 0 HR, 8 K, 5 BB.

	R	H	E	LOB
Tigers	2	3	0	6
BB Stars	7	9	1	6

Winning Pitcher – Tiant   Losing Pitcher – Lolich

The series is now tied 4-4.

Game Nine, Tuesday July 27, Jack Murphy Stadium (San Diego), 7 pm (Trout vs. Foster)

It is another great night for baseball, cool and clear with little wind. It is another Game Nine with the series tied 4-4. This is the sixth series (out of nine) tied going into the final game. It will be the seventh series to end up with one team 5-4 and the other 4-5. In Series 6, the Phillies led five games to three, but the BB Stars won Game Nine.

Left-hander Bill Foster pitched a strong Game Five with no decision (7 IP, 6 H, 1 R) in a game the BB Stars won in the bottom of the ninth, 4-3. His opponent, Dizzy Trout, lost Game Four, 8- 6, with a four run third inning leading to his demise (5 IP, 6 H, 5 R, 1 HR).

With two outs in the bottom of the second inning, Judy Johnson hits a line drive HR over the left- field wall. **BB Stars 1, Tigers 0.**

Foster has retired the first nine Tiger hitters over the first three innings

In the bottom of the third, Trout becomes unglued (just like Game Four). The pitcher, Bill Foster, singles to left field. Bell takes a called third strike (one out). Lloyd lines a single to right with Foster stopping at second. Charleston hits a ground ball to York (1B), who throws to second. York forces Lloyd, who takes out Jackson (SS). There are two outs with runners on first and third. Gibson singles up the middle into center field scoring Foster. Charleston stops at second as Cobb fields the ball quickly. Cobb throws the ball to second, trying to catch Charleston making the turn (2-0). Buck Leonard lines a base hit to center, scoring Charleston with Gibson stopping at second (3-0). Fidrych begins to throw in the Tigers' bullpen. Trout tries to sneak a fast ball on the inside corner to Torriente, but he jacks it over the fence in right field for a 3-run home run (6-0). Dizzy Trout stands dejectedly on the mound as Torriente rounds the bases. Trout strikes out Johnson to end the disastrous third inning. **BB Stars 6, Tigers 0.**

Ty Cobb triples to center to start the fourth inning. He scores the Tigers first run as Gehringer grounds out to Newt Allen (2B). Kaline and Greenberg also ground out to end the inning. **BB Stars 6, Tigers 1.**

In the bottom of the fourth, the Tigers do a double switch. Fidrych replaces Trout and will bat third. Heilmann is batting ninth and has replaced Kaline in right field. The final line on Trout is 3 IP, 6 H, 6 R, 2 HR, 4 K, 1 BB.

In the bottom of the fifth inning the BB Stars add to their lead. Charleston walks and Gibson hits a home run to left. **BB Stars 8, Tigers 1.**

In the bottom of the seventh, Kid Nichols is now pitching for the Tigers. With two outs Torriente singles and Johnson moves him to third with a single to right. Allen flies out, ending the threat.

Suttles has replaced Leonard at first base for the BB Stars to start the eighth. The Tigers finally get to Foster. He walks Jackson and Heilmann. Leon Day is warming up for the BB Stars. Cobb singles to right to load the bases. Gehringer hits one up the middle that Foster cannot get; it trickles into center field, scoring two runs and Cobb racing to third. Leon Day is coming in to pitch. Norm Cash will pinch hit for Nichols; Cash hits one on the ground to Suttles' right. He grabs it and underhands to Day, covering first as

Cobb scores the third run of the inning and Gehringer moves to second (one out). Greenberg grounds out to Lloyd (SS) for the second out; Gehringer stays at second base. York hits one deep to left center, but Cool Papa Bell runs it down to end the inning (great catch). The final line for Foster is 7+ IP, 5 H, 4 R, 0 HR, 3 K, 3 BB. **BB Stars 8, Tigers 4.**

In the bottom of the eighth, John Hiller, the fourth Tiger pitcher gives up a one-out single to Bell (three hits and a walk in five plate appearances) but gives up no further runs.

Leon Day closes out the Tigers in the ninth with only a one-out walk to Freehan. The BB Stars have now won their second series in a row and their sixth series out of nine played, so far.

	R	H	E	LOB
Tigers	4	5	0	6
BB Stars	8	14	0	7

Winning Pitcher – Foster   Save – Day   Losing Pitcher – Trout
The BB Stars win the series, 5-4.

Recap of Best Season Series 9 (BB Stars vs. Tigers)

The BB Stars win their second series in a row. They have now won six of nine series (45-36, .556). After three games, the Tigers were up two games to one and had outscored the BB Stars, 25-10. Hank Greenberg had 4 home runs, 12 RBIs. Chart 14-2 on page 209 has BB Stars individual/team statistics for this series. Chart 14-3 on page 210 has Tigers individual/team statistics for this series.

The turning point of the series - I believe the turning point was actually in Game Two. The Tigers had a 5-0 lead after five innings. Greenberg's 3-run HR was the key blow in a five-run third inning off Bullet Joe Rogan. Denny McLain was in trouble in every inning. The BB Stars had eight hits but hit into two double plays and left six men on base through the first five innings. They get an unearned run in the sixth, but the Tigers add another run in the seventh to make the score 6-1. The BB Stars have 11 hits and a hits batsman. They have now stranded 10 men. McLain is still pitching.

In the eighth inning, the BB Stars finally chase McLain. It takes two relief pitchers to close out the inning. The BB Stars get two runs and four more hits, but the Tigers still lead 6-3 (the BB Stars have stranded 12 runners). In the 4-run ninth that gives the BB Stars the lead (7-6), the offensive star of the Series, Hank Greenberg makes two bad plays in left field. He drops a fly ball (error) and gets a slow break on a ball hit into the gap (Suttles double) that looked like he should have been able to catch for the third out with the score

6-4. Both runners score to tie the game. Bell triples to score Suttles (7-6). The Tigers fail to score in the bottom of the ninth and the series is tied 1-1. If the Tigers held on to win this game, they would have been up three games to none with their impressive 8-2 win in Game Three. It is ironic that Hank Greenberg could be considered the goat in the series because of his defensive lapses in Game Two.

Hitting Stars for the Tigers

	RS	RBI	HR	.Avg	OBP	SPct	OPS
Greenberg	8	18	6	.294	.351	.971	1.326
Gehringer	10	9	2	.441	.486	.676	1.162
Cobb	8	3	0	.353	.371	.471	.842

Note: Cobb had five stolen bases (team had eight).

Best Pitcher for Tigers –

	G	GS	QS	CG	W-L	IP	H	HR	R/ER	ERA
H. Newhouser	2	2	2	0	2-0	16.3	14	1	6-5	2.80

Note: W. Hernandez had two saves and a 0.00 ERA in three games (4 IP).

Hitting Stars for the BB Stars - Josh Gibson, Mule Suttles and Pop Lloyd

	RS	RBI	HR	.Avg	OBP	SPct	OPS
J. Gibson	7	11	3	.310	.375	.690	1.065
M. Suttles	4	5	0	.455	.455	.500	.955
P. Lloyd	2	1	0	.480	.500	.560	1.040

Note: Eleven of the 15 non-pitchers batted .294 and above. The team had a batting average of .310.

Best Pitcher for the BB Stars–

	G	GS	QS	CG	W-L	IP	H	HR	R/ER	ERA
L. Tiant	2	2	1	1	2-0	16	9	1	6	3.38

J. R. Richard relieved in three games and saved all three games with an 0.00 ERA in three innings pitched.

BB Stars Results vs. Tigers 5-4, .556

Pos.	E	R	TH	PB	Hitters	G	AB	R	H	RBI	2B	3B	HR	TB	W	HB	SO	SF	SH	SB	B.AVG.	OBP	S.PCT.	OPS
LF	5	A	-1		Charleston	9	29	6	9	2	1	1	0	12	5	0	5	0	0	0	0.310	0.412	0.414	0.826
CF	8	AA	-1		CP Bell	9	41	3	14	4	1	1	1	20	3	0	3	1	0	3	0.341	0.386	0.488	0.874
OF	5	A	-1		Stearnes	7	23	1	2	2	2	0	0	4	0	0	4	1	0	0	0.087	0.087	0.174	0.261
OF	6	B	-2		M Irvin	5	12	2	3	1	0	0	0	3	0	0	3	0	0	0	0.250	0.250	0.500	0.500
OF	6	A	-1		Torriente	5	13	4	4	3	0	0	1	7	3	0	1	0	0	0	0.308	0.438	0.538	0.976
SS	7	A			P Lloyd	6	25	2	12	1	0	1	0	14	1	0	0	0	0	0	0.480	0.500	0.560	1.060
SS	7	AA			W Wells	6	16	2	6	2	2	0	1	11	1	0	2	0	0	0	0.375	0.412	0.688	1.099
3B	7	A			J Johnson	7	14	2	6	1	3	0	1	12	1	1	3	0	0	0	0.429	0.500	0.857	1.357
3B	6	B			Dandridge	6	17	1	2	3	1	0	0	3	1	0	6	0	0	0	0.118	0.167	0.176	0.343
2B	7	A			N Allen	8	22	4	8	5	1	0	1	12	0	0	4	0	0	1	0.364	0.364	0.545	0.909
2B	7	A			F Warfield	4	13	0	3	2	1	0	0	3	1	0	4	0	0	0	0.231	0.286	0.231	0.516
1B	7	A			Suttles	9	22	4	10	5	0	0	0	11	0	0	5	0	0	0	0.455	0.455	0.500	0.955
1B	8	B			B Leonard	5	17	4	5	2	1	0	1	10	1	0	8	0	0	0	0.294	0.333	0.588	0.922
C	7	A	-2	Fr	J Gibson	9	29	7	9	11	2	0	3	20	3	0	2	0	2	0	0.310	0.375	0.690	1.065
C	6	B	-2	Av	B Mackey	6	11	3	4	2	0	0	0	4	0	0	1	0	1	0	0.364	0.364	0.364	0.727
					pitchers	9	20	1	3	0	0	0	0	3	0	0	10	0	1	0	0.150	0.150	0.150	0.300
					TOTAL	9	324	46	100	46	14	4	9	149	20	1	63	2	4	4	0.309	0.351	0.460	0.811

Fat.	H	WP	E	R	Pitchers	G	GS	OS	CG	S	W	L	IP	H	SO	BB	HR	R	ER	ERA
10/L	Vg	N	9	B	BJ Rogan	2	2	1	0	0	0	0	12	12	7	2	1	11	8	6.00
9/L	Ex	R	7	B	B Foster	3	3	1	0	0	0	1	18	15	7	6	2	10	9	4.50
10/L	Vg	NL	8	B	L Day	3	0	0	0	1	1	0	5	5	5	2	0	3	3	5.40
10/L	Av	NL	7	B	M Dihigo	1	0	0	0	1	0	0	1	3	2	3	0	3	3	27.00
8/L	Md	R	8	C	S Paige	2	2	0	0	0	0	1	11	17	8	0	2	11	10	8.18
L/9	Vg	R	8	A	H Smith	3	0	0	0	0	0	1	8	11	0	0	4	6	6	6.75
9/L	Av	R	9	A	Newcombe	2	0	1	0	1	1	0	4	4	10	0	0	1	1	2.25
10/L	Ex	NL	8	D	L Tiant	2	2	0	1	0	2	0	16	9	1	7	1	6	6	3.38
9	Av	N	5	C	J R Richard	3	0	0	0	1	1	0	3	3	0	1	0	0	0	0.00
Long	Md	NL	4	B	D Moore	1	0	0	0	0	0	1	1	0	0	0	0	0	0	0.00
					TOTAL	22	9	3	1	4	5	4	79	79	40	21	10	51	46	5.24

Chart 14-2 – BB Stars Statistics for this series

Tigers Best Season Series vs. BB All-Stars 4.5, .444

Team	Year	WS Hitters	G	AB	R	H	RBI	2B	3B	HR	TB	W	HB	SO	SF	SH	SB	B.AVG.	OBP	S.PCT.	OPS
Detroit	1911	47 T. Cobb	9	34	8	12	3	2	1	0	16	1	0	2	1	0	5	0.353	0.371	0.471	0.842
Detroit	1923	35 Heilmann	8	20	4	3	1	1	0	0	4	3	0	2	0	1	0	0.150	0.480	0.200	0.680
Detroit	1940	31 Greenberg	9	34	8	10	18	1	2	6	33	3	0	3	2	0	0	0.294	0.351	0.971	1.322
Detroit	1911	32 S. Crawford	4	13	2	6	3	1	1	0	9	0	0	1	0	0	0	0.462	0.462	0.692	1.154
Detroit	1955	31 A. Kaline	8	8	1	2	1	0	0	0	2	0	0	2	0	0	0	0.250	0.250	0.250	0.500
Detroit	1984	24 C. Lemon	1	3	0	0	0	0	0	0	0	0	0	0	0	0	0	0.000	0.000	0.000	0.000
New York N	1916	25 Fletcher	4	10	1	3	1	2	0	0	5	0	0	4	0	0	0	0.300	0.300	0.500	0.800
New York N	1929	23 T. Jackson	7	26	5	6	2	3	0	0	9	1	0	0	0	1	0	0.231	0.259	0.346	0.605
Detroit	1949	24 G. Kell	9	19	4	5	2	2	1	0	9	0	0	3	0	0	1	0.263	0.263	0.474	0.737
Washington	1894	18 B. Joyce	7	20	4	6	3	0	0	2	12	1	0	3	0	0	1	0.300	0.333	0.600	0.933
Detroit	1936	34 Gehringer	9	34	10	15	9	2	2	2	23	3	0	4	0	0	0	0.441	0.486	0.676	1.163
Detroit	1961	42 N. Cash	7	20	3	3	1	0	0	0	3	6	0	3	0	0	0	0.150	0.346	0.150	0.496
Detroit	1943	26 R. York	8	14	1	2	1	0	0	1	5	1	0	6	0	0	0	0.143	0.200	0.357	0.557
Detroit	1968	35 B. Freehan	8	22	2	1	2	0	0	1	4	3	0	0	0	0	1	0.045	0.16	0.182	0.342
New York N	1947	23 W. Cooper	3	9	0	2	0	2	0	0	4	0	0	5	0	0	0	0.222	0.222	0.444	0.667
		Pitchers	9	21	1	2	2	0	1	0	4	0	0	5	0	0	1	0.095	0.095	0.190	0.190
		Total	9	307	51	79	50	11	10	10	140	20	0	40	3	2	8	0.257	0.303	0.456	0.759

Team	Year	WS Pitchers	G	GS	OS	CG	S	W	L	IP	H	SO	BB	HB	HR	R	ER	ERA
Detroit	1945	38 Newhouser	2	2	1	1	0	0	2	16.3	14	13	6	1	0	6	5	2.76
Detroit	1968	33 D. McLain	2	2	1	0	0	0	1	14.3	18	10	3	0	2	7	6	3.77
Detroit	1971	29 M. Lolich	2	2	1	1	0	0	1	13	13	15	3	0	0	6	6	4.15
Detroit	1944	42 D. Trout	2	2	0	0	0	0	0	13	12	5	2	0	3	11	11	12.38
Detroit	1976	27 M. Fidrych	2	1	0	1	0	0	0	8	8	7	2	0	0	3	3	3.38
Detroit	1936	26 T. Bridges	3	0	0	0	0	0	0	2.3	5	4	0	0	1	1	1	3.86
Detroit	1934	28 S. Rowe	2	0	0	0	0	0	0	4.3	8	8	2	0	1	4	4	7.20
Boston	1897	41 K. Nichols	4	0	0	0	0	0	0	3.3	7	7	3	0	0	4	4	8.31
Detroit	1973	31 J. Hiller	3	0	0	0	2	2	0	3.3	3	4	2	0	0	4	2	5.45
Detroit	1984	24 Hernandez	3	0	0	0	0	0	0	3	3	2	0	0	0	0	0	0.00
		TOTAL	25	9	3	3	2	2	4	78.7	100	63	20	1	9	46	42	4.81

Chart 14-3 – Tigers statistics for this series

Chapter 15

Best Season Nine Game Series 10 - BB Stars vs. Cubs

Cubs Roster Review

EIGHTY-EIGHT PERCENT OF THE ROSTER are made up of Chicago Cubs. Twelve percent of the roster are free agents. See the Cubs Roster (Chart 15-1 on page 212).

Offensive Leaders (Cubs) Ranked by OPS

Player	OBP	SPct	OPS	R +	RBI -	HR =	NR
H. Wilson	.454	.723	1.177	146	190	56	280
E. Delehanty	.461	.582	1.043	135	137	9	263
G. Hartnett	.404	.630	1.032	84	122	37	169
B. Williams	.403	.606	1.010	95	122	37	180
P. Browning	.458	.547	1.005	137	50	4	183
E. Banks	.370	.614	.984	119	129	47	201
H. Zimmerman	.412	.571	.983	95	99	14	208
R. Santo	.401	.564	.965	94	114	30	178
F. Carroll	.471	.484	.955	80	51	2	129
B. Nicholson	.384	.531	.915	95	128	34	194

The following players would be base-stealing threats – P. Browning 103, F. Chance 57, E. Delehanty and J. Tinker with 30 (numbers listed SB for their best season).

CubsRoster Best Season Series vs. BB All-Stars

Team	Year	WS	Hitters	G	AB	R	H	RBI	2B	3B	HR	TB	W	HB	SO	SF	SH	SB	B.AVG.	OBP	S.PCT.	OPS
Chicago N	1972	32	B. Williams	150	574	95	191	122	34	6	37	348	62	6	59	-	-	3	0.333	0.403	0.606	1.010
Chicago N	1930	35	H. Wilson	155	585	146	208	190	35	6	56	423	105	1	84	-	-	3	0.356	0.454	0.723	1.177
Philadelphia	1899	41	Delehanty	146	581	135	238	137	55	9	9	338	55	0	18	-	-	30	0.410	0.461	0.582	1.042
Louisville	1887	30	Browning	134	547	137	220	50	35	16	4	299	55	1	35	-	-	103	0.402	0.458	0.547	1.004
Chicago N	1943	31	Nicholson	154	608	95	188	128	30	9	29	323	71	3	86	-	-	4	0.309	0.384	0.531	0.915
Chicago N	1958	31	E. Banks	154	617	119	193	129	23	11	47	379	52	4	87	-	-	4	0.313	0.370	0.614	0.984
Chicago N	1908	32	J. Tinker	157	548	67	146	68	22	14	6	214	32	3	32	-	-	30	0.266	0.310	0.391	0.701
Chicago N	1964	36	R. Santo	161	592	94	185	114	33	13	30	334	86	2	96	-	-	3	0.313	0.401	0.564	0.966
Chicago N	1945	34	S. Hack	150	597	110	193	43	29	7	2	242	99	1	30	-	-	12	0.323	0.420	0.405	0.826
Chicago N	1912	34	Zimmerman	145	557	95	207	99	41	14	14	318	38	0	60	-	-	23	0.372	0.412	0.571	0.983
Chicago N	1935	32	B. Herman	154	666	113	227	83	57	6	7	317	42	3	29	-	-	6	0.341	0.383	0.476	0.859
Chicago N	1913	20	J. Evers	136	446	81	127	49	20	5	3	166	50	3	14	-	-	11	0.285	0.361	0.372	0.733
Chicago N	1906	35	F. Chance	136	474	103	151	71	24	10	3	204	70	4	29	-	-	57	0.319	0.411	0.430	0.841
Chicago N	1930	29	G. Hartnett	141	508	84	172	122	31	3	37	320	55	4	62	-	-	0	0.339	0.404	0.630	1.034
Pittsburgh	1889	23	F. Carroll	91	318	80	105	51	21	11	2	154	85	0	26	-	-	19	0.330	0.471	0.484	0.956

Team	Year	WS	Pitchers	G	GS	OS	CG	S	W	L	IP	H	SO	BB	HB	HR	R	ER	ERA
Chicago N	1906	35	T. F. Brown	36	32	-	27	3	26	6	277	198	144	61	-	1	-	-	1.03
Chicago N	1906	24	J. Pfiester	31	28	-	20	0	20	8	195	143	90	63	-	3	-	-	1.15
Chicago N	1902	32	J. Taylor	36	33	-	33	1	23	11	325	271	83	43	-	2	-	-	1.33
Chicago N	1971	37	F. Jenkins	39	39	-	30	0	24	13	325	304	263	37	-	29	-	-	2.77
Chicago N	1952	23	B. Rush	34	32	-	17	0	17	13	250	205	157	81	-	14	-	-	2.69
Chicago N	1977	26	Reuschel	39	37	-	8	1	20	10	252	233	166	74	-	13	-	-	2.79
Chicago N	1932	31	Warneke	35	32	-	25	0	22	6	277	247	106	64	-	12	-	-	2.37
Chicago N	1918	28	H. Vaughn	35	33	-	27	0	22	10	290	216	148	76	-	4	-	-	1.73
Chicago N	1909	30	O. Overall	38	32	-	23	3	20	11	285	204	205	80	-	1	-	-	1.42
Chicago N	1906	23	E. Reulbach	33	24	-	20	3	19	4	218	129	160	92	-	2	-	-	1.65
Chicago N	1964	25	L. Jackson	40	38	-	19	0	24	11	298	265	148	58	-	17	-	-	3.14

Chart 15-1 – Cubs Best Season Roster

Fielding Leaders	Pos	Range	Error	Throwing
E. Delehanty	LF	B	7	-1
B. Nicholson	RF	B	7	-1
B. Williams	LF	B	6	-1
P. Browning	CF	B	5	0
H. Wilson	CF	C	3	-1

Outfield defense is not a strong suit for the Cubs.

For outfielders - range (AA is best) and throwing (-4 is exceptional, -3 is excellent, -2 is very good) are most important. Error rating (10 is best, 1 is poor) is not as critical as infielders because outfielders normally do not make as many errors.

S. Hack	3B	AA	10	-
R. Santo	3B	AA	8	-
J. Tinker	SS	AA+	8	-
J. Evers	2B	AA+	4	-
B. Herman	2B	AA+	4	-
F. Chance	1B	B	8	
E. Banks	SS	B+	6	
H. Zimmerman	1B	B	4	

The Cubs infield is strong defensively.

For infielders, range (AA is best), + increase in DPs because of excellent pivot, error rating is as important as range for an infielder (10 is excellent, 1 is poor).

Catcher Throwing - Hartnett has an above average throwing arm (-1) and Carroll is average (0).

Pitcher Hold Rating - Brown and Vaughn have excellent hold ratings; Overall, Jenkins, Taylor, Jackson, and Pfiester are very good; the rest of the staff is average.

Pitching - This is a good pitching staff.

Game One, Thursday July 29, Wrigley Field (Chicago), 1 pm (S. Paige vs. T. F. Brown)

It is a warm, partly cloudy day with little wind. In the bottom of the second inning, the Cubs draw first blood. Hack Wilson doubles into the left-field corner. Nicholson bounces out to Allen (2B) as Wilson advances to third base. Gabby Hartnett hits a drive to left center. Oscar Charleston makes the catch as Wilson scores on the sac fly. **Cubs 1, BB Stars 0.**

In the top of the fifth with two out, the BB Stars tie the score on Bell's single to right field, which scores Allen who had doubled. Bell is then thrown out trying to steal second with Lloyd at the plate. **BB Stars 1, Cubs 1.**

In the bottom of the fifth inning, Hartnett leads off with a walk. Ernie Banks flies out to Charleston (LF) near the warning track (one out). Johnny Evers doubles into the right field corner. The plodding Hartnett stops at third. Three Finger Brown lays down a great squeeze bunt to score Hartnett and move Evers to third (Johnson – Allen for second out). Hack grounds out, Allen (2B) to Leonard (1B). **Cubs 2, BB Stars 1.**

In the top of the seventh, the BB Stars tie the game. Brown walks Judy Johnson to start the inning. Allen chops one down the first base line that Chance grabs and flips to Brown, covering to just nip the speedy Allen (one out) as Johnson moves into scoring position. Cristobal Torriente will bat for Paige. The final line for Paige is 6 IP, 4 H, 2 R, 0 HR, 1 K, 1 BB. Torriente bloops one into shallow center field for a base hit as Johnson comes around to score the tying run (2-2). Brown, with a great move to first, picks Torriente off base (two outs). Bell singles to center. Lou Warneke is warming up for the Cubs and Donnie Moore is warming up for the BB Stars. Lloyd slaps a hit-and-run single in to left and Bell beats the throw to third. Brown jams Charleston and gets him to pop out to Chance (1B). Charleston flips his bat in disgust. **BB Stars 2, Cubs 2.**

Donnie Moore is in to pitch for the BB Stars in the bottom of the seventh inning. With two outs, Evers singles to right field. Ed Delehanty bats for Brown (7 IP, 8 H, 2 R, 0 HR, 2 K, 2 BB) and he pops out to Allen (2B).

Warneke is now pitching for the Cubs (top of eighth). He gives up a one-out double to Stearnes, but gets Leonard to ground out to Evers (2B) with Stearnes going to third base. Warneke strikes out Johnson on a high fast ball.

In the bottom of the eighth, the Cubs have the top of the order coming up. Moore strikes out Hack on a hard slider (down and in). Chance walks on four pitches. The BB Stars are expecting a hit-and-run. Moore's first pitch is way inside. Gibson fires the ball to Leonard and picks Chance off base (great play). Billy Williams fouls out to Buck Leonard (1B).

In the top of the ninth of Game One, the score is tied 2-2. How many times have the BB Stars turned a close game, their way, in the late innings? The Cubs need to win Game One.

Allen pops out to Banks (SS). Irvin bats for Moore and grounds out (Banks to Chance). Bell walks and takes second when Warneke's first pitch to Lloyd is a wild pitch. Lloyd bounces out to Evers (4-3) to end the inning.

Hilton Smith pitches in the bottom of the ninth, and he retires the Cubs, one-two-three.

In the top of the tenth, Browning has replaced Wilson in center field for the Cubs. Charleston leads off with a single to center field. The Cubs have double-barreled action in the bullpen (Vaughn-L, Overall-R). Warneke retires the dangerous Josh Gibson on a routine fly ball to Browning (CF). Vaughn is coming in to pitch to the left-handed Stearnes, who tops the ball to the right side. Chance (1B) bare hands the ball and flips to Vaughn covering first (two outs). Charleston moves into scoring position. Suttles is announced to pinch hit for Leonard. Overall replaces Vaughn to pitch to the right-handed Suttles. Overall strikes out Suttles (looking) to end the inning.

In the bottom of the tenth inning, Banks flies out to Bell (CF). Herman bats for Evers and he flies out to Bell, also (two outs). Zimmerman will pinch hit for Overall. Zim singles to center. Hack hits a deep drive to center field; Bell is back on the warning track and catches the ball at the fence. Hack was about 3-5 feet from ending this game. **Cubs 2, BB Stars 2.**

In the top of the eleventh inning, Ed Reulbach is now pitching for the Cubs. The score has been tied 2-2 since the seventh inning. Reulbach strikes out Johnson (looking). Allen singles to left field. Biz Mackey is batting for Hilton Smith. Mackey gets a base hit up the middle. Browning charges the ball as Allen races around to third.

With runners on first and third and Cool Papa Bell at the plate, the Cubs pull Hack (3B) and Chance (1B) in, looking for the bunt. As Bell squares to bunt, Hack and Chance charge. Bell bunts the ball on one-hop to Chance, who fires to Hartnett. He has the plate blocked and he tags out Allen (two outs). Lloyd grounds out to Herman, ending the inning.

Rogan is now pitching for the BB Stars in the bottom of the eleventh. He retires Cubs 2, 3 and 4 hitters (Chance, Williams and Browning) as we move on to the twelfth inning. The Cubs have been held scoreless for the last six innings (five of the innings by three pitchers out of the bullpen).

The twelfth inning is a nightmare for the Cubs and their fans. Charleston leads off with a triple over Browning's head in center. Gibson and Stearnes are both walked intentionally. The infielders are moved in to the edge of the infield grass. The outfielders are playing in a few steps Suttles chops one to short, Banks charges the ball and fires to Hartnett but the speedy Charleston beats the throw (3-2). It goes as a fielder's choice (Suttles is not credited with a hit). The bases are still loaded (none out). Johnson tops the ball toward third; Hack charges and throws to the plate. It is not in time (4-2). It is another fielder's choice.

The count goes to 3-2 on Newt Allen; Reulbach's next pitch is low, ball four, forcing in another run (5-2). Rogan, the pitcher, is coming up. There are still no outs; three runs are in and the bases are still loaded. Rush is warming up. Rogan hits a ground ball to Herman, who fires to Hartnett (at the plate) for the first out. Suttles takes Hartnett out with a hard slide, so there is no chance to double up Rogan. Reulbach's first pitch to Bell is way inside and it hits him (HB) forcing in the fourth run of the inning.

Rush is now pitching. The BB Stars now lead 6-2. The bases are loaded with still only one out. Lloyd lines a single to left, scoring Allen with the fifth run of the inning. The bases remain loaded. Rush is now pitching to Charleston, batting for the second time in the inning. He uncorks a wild pitch, scoring Rogan with the sixth run of the inning (only two hits in the inning). Runners are on second and third base. Charleston is intentionally walked (third free pass of the inning) as Josh Gibson comes to the plate (eleventh batter of the inning). Gibson hits a fly ball to Browning in center field. Bell is tagging at third. Browning makes the catch and throws a perfect strike to Hartnett who nails Bell for a double play to end the nightmare. **BB Stars 8, Cubs 2.**

The Cubs do string together three hits to score a run off Rogan but they lose a tough opening game in twelve innings.

12 Innings	R	H	E	LOB
BB Stars	8	14	1	15
Cubs	3	9	1	7

Winning Pitcher – Rogan   Losing Pitcher – Reulbach

The BB Stars lead the series, 1-0.

Game Two, Friday July 30, Wrigley Field (Chicago), 1 pm (L. Day vs. Pfeister)

It is a warm, clear, windless day, perfect for baseball. With two outs, Gibson doubles into the left-field corner. Stearnes lines a single to center as Gibson scores. Suttles flies out to Delehanty (LF). **BB Stars 1, Cubs 0.**

In the bottom of the first inning, Ed Delehanty singles to right. Herman grounds a hit-and-run single up the middle, with Delehanty coasting into third. Zimmerman flies out to Bell in shallow center (runners hold). Hack Wilson takes a called third strike (two outs). Santo booms a blast over Bell's head into the ivy for a 2-run triple. Nicholson grounds out to Warfield. **Cubs 2, BB Stars 1.**

Pfiester struggles in the second. With two outs, Warfield triples off the wall in center. The BB Stars excel at scoring runs with two outs and no runners on base. Leon Day singles to left, tying the score. Bell triples off the tip of Hack Wilson's glove in centerfield, scoring Day. Wells walks as Overall begins to throw in the Cubs' bullpen. Gibson forces Wells at second. **BB Stars 3, Cubs 2.**

In the top of the fourth, Pfiester retires the first two batters (again). He hits Bell with a pitch. Wells lines a home run to left, and Gibson doubles to left center. Stearnes grounds out to Herman (2B). In the first four innings,

Pfiester has retired the first two batters every inning. However, after two outs, he has given up 5 runs, eight hits (2 doubles, 2 triples, HR), a walk, and a hit batsman. **BB Stars 5, Cubs 2.**

In the bottom of the fourth, the Cubs get one run back (Santo triple, Banks sac fly). **BB Stars 5, Cubs 3.**

Pfiester retires the BB Stars in the fifth, his last inning (5 IP, 9 H, 5 R, 4 K, 1 HR, 1 BB, 1 HB). There is no more scoring. Leon Day throws a complete game (9 IP, 8 H, 3 R, 0 HR, 2 K, 2 BB).

	R	H	E	LOB
BB Stars	5	12	0	10
Cubs	3	8	1	5

Winning Pitcher – Day   Losing Pitcher – Pfiester
The BB Stars lead the series, 2-0.

Game Three, Saturday July 31, Comiskey Park (Chicago), 1 pm (F. Jenkins vs. B. Foster)

The Cubs score in five of the first six innings. In the meantime, Ferguson Jenkins blanks the BB Stars on two hits through six innings. In the first inning, Zimmerman homers. In the third inning, Zimmerman's two-out single scores Delehanty (double). Wilson doubles in Zimmerman (3-0). Four solo HRs over the next three innings (Banks in the fourth and sixth, Zimmerman in the fifth, and Nicholson in the sixth) give the Cubs a 7-0 lead.

Foster's final line is 6 IP, 8 H, 7 R, 5 HR, 5 K 1 BB.

The BB Stars finally score four runs off Jenkins in the ninth inning. Biz Mackey's three run home run is the key blow.

	R	H	E	LOB
Cubs	7	9	0	3
BB Stars	4	9	0	4

Winning Pitcher – Jenkins   Losing Pitcher – Foster
The BB Stars lead the series, 2-1.

Game Four, Sunday August 1, Comiskey Park (Chicago), 1 pm (J. Taylor vs. L. Tiant)

It is a warm, partly cloudy day with the wind blowing out, an ideal day for hitting. In the bottom of the first inning with two outs, the BB Stars score three runs on five hits off Jack Taylor. Stearnes' 2-run triple was the key blow. **BB Stars 3, Cubs 0.**

In the bottom of the third inning, Taylor does not retire a batter. Stearnes and Leonard lead-off, hitting back-to-back triples. Dandridge singles in the fifth run and Taylor's final line is 2+ IP, 8 H, 5, R, 2 K, 2 BB. With two outs and the bases loaded, Charleston doubles in two more runs off Hippo Vaughn. Bell is thrown out at the plate to end the inning. **BB Stars 7, Cubs 0.**

In the top of the fourth, Gabby Hartnett hits a 3-run HR to close the gap. **BB Stars 7, Cubs 3.**

In the bottom of the fifth inning, the BB Stars score three runs off Bob Rush. Charleston's 2-run HR is the key blow. Charleston is 3 for 3 with a walk, 2 runs scored, and 4 RBIs. **BB Stars 10, Cubs 3.**

The Cubs chase Tiant in the sixth (Billy Williams HR, Wilson double, Nicholson single and advances to second on Bell's error). Rogan gives up singles to Hartnett and Evers before Ernie Banks hits a 3-run HR to close the gap to 10-9. The final line for Tiant is 5+ IP, 8 H, 6 R, 2 HR, 7 K, 0 BB. The Cubs are done scoring. **BB Stars 10, Cubs 9.**

The BB Stars add a single run off Warneke in the sixth. **BB Stars 11, Cubs 9.**

In the bottom of the eighth, the BB Stars score four more runs off Reuschel and Overall. Torriente's 3-run HR is the key blow. **BB Stars 15, Cubs 9.**

	R	H	E	LOB
Cubs	9	14	1	5
BB Stars	15	20	0	7

Winning Pitcher – Tiant Losing Pitcher – Taylor
The BB Stars lead the series, 3-1.

Game Five, Monday Aug. 2, Wrigley Field (Chicago), 1 pm (S. Paige vs. T. F. Brown)

Thunderstorms precede the game and the field will be wet in the early innings. This is a critical game for the Cubs and their starting pitcher, Three Finger Brown. The Cubs trail three games to one and it could very well have been reversed. Both Paige and Brown had quality starts in Game One, which the BB Stars won in 12 innings with a 6-run explosion in the twelfth with just two hits.

Brown and Paige are dueling again. It is 0-0 in the middle of the fifth inning. Brown has given up five hits (three in the third inning but a double play helped keep runs off the board). Paige has given up just one hit (Brown single in the third inning). He retires the first two batters in the fifth inning. Joe Tinker (batting eighth) triples over Bell's head in center field. Three Finger Brown lines a base hit to right field, giving the Cubs the lead. Delehanty singles to center and Brown stops at second. Chance grounds out to Lloyd (SS). **Cubs 1, BB Stars 0.**

With one out in the sixth, Oscar Charleston ties the game with a long home run over the right-field wall. **BB Stars 1, Cubs 1.**

In the top of the seventh inning, the BB Stars take the lead. Buck Leonard leads off and bloops one into shallow right field near the foul line. Evers and Williams get there at the same time and collide. The ball rolls into foul territory. Chance, the Cubs first baseman, picks it up and throws to second base but Leonard slides in with a double. Time is called. Evers is standing and rubbing his left shoulder that collided with Billy Williams chin. Williams is helped off the field. Evers stays in the game and Nicholson is now playing right field. Johnson bounces out to Tinker (SS); Leonard stays at second. Warfield walks. Brown is not happy about walking the number eight hitter (runners on first and second).

Cristobal Torriente will bat for Paige (6 IP, 5 H, 1 R, 0 HR, 3 K, 1 BB). Torriente bloops one into shallow center and it drops in front of Hack Wilson for a base hit. Leonard has to hold up at third base because he did not know whether Wilson might catch it. Wilson does not have great range. Cool Papa Bell (CF) for the BB Stars would have caught it.

Speaking of Cool Papa, he steps to the plate with the bases loaded and one out. The Cubs are looking for the bunt (Santo and Chance are in on the grass). Bell drops down a great bunt. Santo fields it, and his only play is to first base. He just does get Bell (Evers covering first). Lloyd strikes out swinging. **BB Stars 2, Cubs 1.**

Hilton Smith is now pitching for the BB Stars. Evers leads off the bottom of the seventh with a base hit to left field that Charleston misplays, and Evers hustles into second base (hit and error). Tinker moves Evers over to third with a good sacrifice bunt (Smith to Warfield covering first). With Tinker on third, Brown will bat (very good bunter). Brown is 2 for 2 and drove in the Cubs only run. He drops a bunt 3-4 feet up the first base line. Tinker races home. The catcher, Gibson, throws out Brown (Warfield covering first). Three Finger Brown is doing everything he can to keep the Cubs in the game. Delehanty walks, but Hilton Smith picks him off first to end the inning. **Cubs 2, BB Stars 2.**

Brown strikes out Charleston (looking) to start the eighth inning. It was a mean curve ball at the knees. Brown falls behind the dangerous Josh Gibson, 2-0. Brown tries to jam Gibson, but the ball drifts toward the center of the plate and Gibson jumps on it. He hits a rope over Wilson's head that rolls to the wall. Gibson goes into third, standing up with a one-out triple. The dangerous left-handed Turkey Stearnes steps to the plate. The decision is to pitch to Stearnes and go for the strike out. The other option would have been to walk Stearnes and pitch to Leonard, trying to get the double play. The infield is pulled in for a play at the plate. The count goes to 2-2 and Stearnes muscles a curve ball to right center. Nicholson (replaced injured Williams, seventh) makes the catch. His throw home is not in time as Gibson scores the go-ahead run (sac fly for Stearnes). Leonard flies out to Wilson. **BB Stars 3, Cubs 2.**

The Cubs' only base runner in the last two innings is Nicholson who reaches on an error by Leonard (1B). The final line for Smith is 3 IP, 1 H, 1 R, 0 ER, 3 K, 1 BB. The final line for Brown is 9 IP, 9 H, 3 R, 1 HR, 4 K, 2 BB. When your starting pitcher pitches a complete game and holds the BB Stars to three runs and he drives in two runs, you have to win those games. The Cubs did not.

	R	H	E	LOB
BB Stars	3	9	2	6
Cubs	2	6	0	6

Winning Pitcher – H. Smith   Losing Pitcher – T. F. Brown
The BB Stars lead the series, 4-1.

Game Six, Tuesday August 3, Wrigley Field (Chicago), 1 pm (Day vs. Pfeister)

It is a hot cloudy day with little wind. In the bottom of the second, Nicholson doubles into the ivy in right center field. Zimmerman grounds a single into center field and Nicholson scores the Cubs first run. **Cubs 1, BB Stars 0.**

In the top of the third inning with two outs, the BB Stars score with speed at the top of the order. Bell slaps one through the left side for a single. With Wells at the plate, Bell gets a great jump and steals second. Wells lines a base hit to left. Bell, who has a great lead-off on second, scores easily. Gibson pops out to Hack (3B). **BB Stars 1, Cubs 1.**

Pfeister has pitched a gritty seven innings. Hack Wilson will bat for Pfeister to lead-off the bottom of the seventh. Pfeister's final line is 7 IP, 5 H, 1 R, 0 HR, 3 K, 5 BB. The BB Stars had 10 base runners (two were erased in double plays), and seven runners were left on base. Wilson takes Day deep with a home run to left field. Day's trouble is just beginning. Browning singles to left. Day then walks Carroll and Delehanty. The bases are loaded (none out). Newcombe is warming up for the BB Stars. The Cubs have double-barrel action (Warneke, R and Overall, R). Banks drops a soft line-drive into left center that chases home two more runs (4-1). It also chases Day to the shower. Newcombe is now pitching. In the seventh, Day faced five batters and retired none. Nicholson doubles off Newcombe into the gap in right center, scoring Delehanty and sending Banks to third. Zimmerman is given an intentional pass to reload the bases and there are still none out. Newcombe gets Hack to fly out to Bell in shallow center; runners hold (one out). Herman goes down swinging (two outs). Pinch hitter Hack Wilson, who led off the inning with a home run, ends the inning by fouling out to Gibson behind the plate. The final line for Day is 6+ IP, 9 H, 5 R, 1 HR, 4 K, 4 BB. **Cubs 5, BB Stars 1.**

Lou Warneke had an adventure. In the eighth, he gave up lead-off singles to Gibson and Stearnes but got pinch hitter Oscar Charleston (batting for Irvin) to foul out to Hack (3B) and Suttles to rap into a 6-4-3 double play. In the ninth, with two outs, he gave up three successive singles (one run) and then Overall came in to strike out Josh Gibson (swinging) to end the game.

	R	H	E	LOB
BB Stars	2	10	0	10
Cubs	5	10	0	10

Winning Pitcher – Pfeister   Save – Overall   Losing Pitcher – Day

The BB Stars lead the series, 4-2.

Game Seven, Wednesday Aug. 4, Comiskey Park (Chicago), 7 pm (Jenkins vs. Foster)

Jenkins goes into the bottom of the third, 0-0. He gives up a lead-off single to Foster (not known for his hitting skills). That is a bad sign. Bell takes a Jenkins' fast ball and puts it in the right-field seats, home run. Pop Lloyd follows with another home run just over the fence near the foul pole. Charleston singles into right field. Suttles strikes out (looking). Stearnes hits it over Williams head in right, scoring Charleston. Stearnes gets greedy and Williams guns him down trying to stretch a double into a triple. Mackey goes down swinging. **BB Stars 4, Cubs 0.**

In the fourth, with two outs and Allen on second (double), Bell triples in the BB Stars fifth run. Hippo Vaughn is ready. When Jenkins walks Lloyd, Vaughn relieves Jenkins. Vaughn strikes out Charleston to end the inning. The final line for Jenkins is 3.7 IP, 9 H, 5 R, 2 HR, 3 K, 1 BB. **BB Stars 5, Cubs 0.**

In the meantime, Foster has blanked the Cubs through five innings on two hits. In the bottom of the fifth, Suttles leads off with a double. Stearnes booms a triple off the center-field wall (6-0). Mackey grounds out to short, but Stearnes holds at third. Larry Jackson relieves Vaughn. Judy Johnson greets Jackson with a double off the left-field wall scoring Stearnes. **BB Stars 7, Cubs 0.**

The score remains 7-0 until the eighth, when the Cubs finally break through Foster with three hits and their only run. Herman doubles in Santo, who doubles to lead-off the inning. Pinch hitter Browning beats out an infield hit, but Delehanty flies out to end the threat. **BB Stars 7, Cubs 1.**

In the top of the ninth, Foster retires the Cubs in order. Foster's final line is 9 IP, 5 H, 1 R, 0 HR, 2 K, 0 BB.

	R	H	E	LOB
Cubs	1	5	0	3
BB Stars	7	13	1	6

Winning Pitcher – Foster.   Losing Pitcher – Jenkins
The BB Stars lead the series, 5-2.

Game Eight, Thursday, August 5, Comiskey Park (Chicago), 7 pm (Overall vs. Dihigo)

It is a beautiful night for baseball, clear with little wind. The Cubs cannot win the series but winning the final two games would lessen the pain. Martin Dihigo is getting a spot starting assignment for the BB Stars. Stan Hack starts things off with a double in the gap (right center). Chance slaps a single to right and Hack comes around to score. With the lefty Billy Williams at the plate, Chance takes off for second base but Gibson throws him out. Williams flies out to deep right field (Stearnes makes the catch). Hack Wilson flies out to Bell (CF). **Cubs 1, BB Stars 0.**

With two outs in the bottom of the first, Charleston homers to right off Overall. **BB Stars 1, Cubs 1.**

The Cubs get four singles in the top of the third but only one run because of a double play (Billy Williams RBI single). In the bottom of the third, the BB Stars get three singles for the tying run (RBI single for Stearnes). **BB Stars 2, Cubs 2.**

The Cubs chase Dihigo in the fourth. Nicholson goes down swinging to start the inning (one out). Dihigo walks Carroll and Evers. Tinker bangs one up the middle (Dihigo might have deflected it) into center field. Carroll scores and Tinker moves to third. Overall drops down a suicide squeeze bunt that scores Evers and moves Tinker to second. Overall is thrown out, Dihigo to Warfield (covering first). The Cubs lead 4-2 with two outs. Luis Tiant is warming up for the BB Stars. Hack lines a single to left and Tinker scores the third run of the inning (5-2). Chance bloops a single over the shortstop, Lloyd; Hack takes the turn at second and holds. Tiant replaces Dihigo. Billy

Williams hits Tiant's first pitch to deep right field. Stearnes races back and catches the ball before bouncing off the right-field wall. The final line for Dihigo is 3.7 IP, 9 H, 5 R, 0 HR, 1 K, 2 BB. **Cubs 5, BB Stars 2.**

With two outs in the bottom of the fourth, Newt Allen (pinch hitting for Tiant), triples off the centerfield wall. Torriente singles to center, scoring Allen. Lloyd forces Torriente at second base. **Cubs 5, BB Stars 3.**

Hilton Smith is now pitching for the BB Stars to start the fifth inning. He walks Hack Wilson but retires the next three hitters.

In the bottom of the fifth inning, Charleston singles between first and second into right field. Gibson flies out to Nicholson (LF). Stearnes and Leonard hit back to back home runs to give the BB Stars their first lead of the game, 6-5. Jack Taylor is now pitching for the Cubs. The Cubs do a double switch; Taylor will bat seventh. Herman replaces Evers (2B) and will bat ninth. The final line for Overall is 4.3 IP, 12 H, 6 R, 3 HR, 2 K, 0 BB. Dandridge greets Taylor with a base hit to left field. Warfield fouls out to the catcher (Carroll). Hilton Smith singles to center with Dandridge stopping at second. Torriente singles to center (sixth hit of the inning), but Wilson makes a perfect throw to Carroll at the plate to nail Dandridge for the third out. **BB Stars 6, Cubs 5.**

Smith gives up a single to Herman but Cubs do not score in sixth.

In the bottom of the sixth, the BB Stars keep on the attack. Lloyd and Charleston open the inning with back-to-back singles (runners on first and second). Josh Gibson bounces out to Herman at second with the runners advancing to second and third (one out). The Cubs decide to walk Stearnes intentionally to load the bases and set up a possible double play. Leonard, however, has other ideas and lines the ball over Chance's head into the right-field corner to score two runs and put runners on second and third (8-5). Warneke is now pitching for the Cubs. Taylor did not solve the black ball offense. Hack (3B) and Chance (1B) move in, looking for the bunt. Dandridge shows bunt and then tries to slap the ball past Hack, who knocks it down. Hack throws out Dandridge, but Stearnes scores the ninth run. Warfield pops out to Herman (2B) to end the inning. **BB Stars 9, Cubs 5.**

The Cubs are done. Smith blanks them for three more innings. The BB Stars do not score anymore, either. The finally line for Hilton Smith (in relief) is 5 IP, 2 H, 0 R, 2 K, 1 BB.

	R	H	E	LOB
Cubs	5	11	0	7
BB Stars	9	18	0	8

Winning Pitcher – H. Smith   Losing Pitcher – Overall
The BB Stars lead the series, 6-2.

Game Nine, Friday Aug. 6, Wrigley Field (Chicago), 1 pm (Paige vs. Brown)

It is a warm, clear, windy day with the wind blowing out. Three Finger Brown has pitched well in this series. However, the BB Stars start with four singles in their first five batters. They lead 1-0 and have the bases loaded, with Biz Mackey coming to the plate. Brown needs a double-play ball. His pitches have been up in the strike zone. His first pitch to Mackey is drilled to deep center; Wilson gets a late break. The ball lands on the warning track. Three runs score and Mackey is standing on third with a triple (4-0). Judy Johnson hits a fly ball to Wilson and he drops it. Mackey races home with the fifth run (credit Johnson with a sac fly and Wilson with an error). Allen pops out and Paige strikes out. **BB Stars 5, Cubs 0.**

In the third, the BB Stars continue to pound Brown. The key blow is a two-run double by Judy Johnson. A third run scores on a ground out. Brown is done after three innings; his final line is 3 IP, 8 H, 8 R, 0 HR, 3 K, 2 BB. **BB Stars 8. Cubs 0.**

Paige has retired the first eight Cubs when Billy Williams pinch hits for Brown. Williams hits a routine fly ball to Bell (CF) to end the inning (nine in a row for Paige).

Larry Jackson pitches the fourth through sixth innings for the Cubs. He gives up the final four runs in the sixth (Mackey and Johnson each have 4 RBIs). **BB Stars 12, Cubs 0.**

Through five innings, Paige has given up one hit. In the sixth, he walks two before giving up a three-run home run to Wilson. **BB Stars 12, Cubs 3.**

Reulbach and Taylor finish up the pitching for the Cubs. Wilson hits a bases-empty home run off Paige in the eighth to finish the scoring. **BB Stars 12, Cubs 4.**

Torriente bats for Paige in the ninth. Paige's final line is 8 IP, 5 H, 4 R, 2 HR, 7 K, 2 BB.

The BB Stars do a double switch. Torriente replaces Charleston (LF), and Rogan is in to mop up in the ninth. The BB Stars never let up on the Cubs. Like the White Sox, the Cubs lose seven of nine.

	R	H	E	LOB
BB Stars	12	16	0	9
Cubs	4	6	1	4

Winning Pitcher – Paige   Losing Pitcher – Brown
The BB Stars win the series, 7-2.

Recap of Best Season Series 10 (BB Stars vs. Cubs)

The BB Stars win their third series in a row. They have now won seven of ten series (52-38, .578). Losing the first game in 12 innings and getting to within a run in Game Four (9-10) and losing were too much for the Cubs to overcome. The crusher was losing Game Five, 3-2. The two quality starts from Three Finger were lost. After five games the Cubs were down 4-1 and could have been up 3-2. . Chart 15-2 on page 226 has BB Stars individual/team statistics for this series. Chart 15-3 on page 227 has Cubs individual/team statistics for this series.

BB Stars Results vs. Cubs 7-2, .778

Pos.	E	TH	PB	Hitters	G	AB	R	H	RBI	2B	3B	HR	TB	W	HB	SO	SF	SH	SB	B.AVG.	OBP	S.PCT.	OPS
LF	5 A	-1		Charleston	8	34	11	16	7	3	1	3	30	2	0	3	0	1	0	0	.471	.500	.882	1.382
CF	8 AA	-1		CP Bell	8	35	5	12	7	0	2	1	19	4	2	5	0	1	2	0	.343	.439	.543	.982
OF	5 A	-1		Stearnes	8	30	6	13	9	3	3	1	25	3	0	2	1	0	0	0	.433	.485	.833	1.318
OF	6 B	-2		M Irwin	5	14	0	4	0	1	0	0	5	2	0	2	0	0	0	0	.286	.375	.357	.732
OF	6 A	-1		Torriente	6	13	3	8	7	1	1	1	11	0	0	2	0	0	0	0	.615	.615	.846	1.462
SS	7 A			P Lloyd	7	28	5	12	3	1	1	1	16	2	0	4	0	0	0	0	.429	.467	.571	1.038
SS	7 AA			W Wells	3	15	2	4	4	0	0	0	7	1	0	3	0	0	0	0	.267	.313	.467	.779
3B	7 A			J Johnson	6	22	3	3	4	6	1	0	4	4	0	3	1	0	0	0	.136	.269	.182	.451
3B	6 B			Dandridge	3	13	2	6	2	0	0	0	8	0	0	1	0	0	0	0	.462	.462	.615	1.077
2B	7 A			N Allen	6	23	7	8	4	3	1	0	13	2	0	1	0	0	0	0	.348	.400	.565	.965
2B	7 A			F Warfield	4	13	1	1	0	0	1	0	3	2	0	2	0	0	0	0	.077	.200	.231	.431
1B	7 A			Suttles	5	18	4	6	1	0	0	0	8	2	0	3	0	0	0	0	.333	.400	.444	.844
1B	8 B			B Leonard	5	21	5	9	4	2	2	1	18	2	0	4	0	0	0	0	.429	.429	.857	1.286
C	7 A	-2	Fr	J Gibson	6	28	4	9	0	3	1	0	14	3	0	2	0	0	0	0	.321	.387	.500	.887
C	6 B	-2	Aw	B Mackey	5	14	4	4	7	0	0	1	9	1	0	0	0	0	0	0	.286	.333	.643	.976
				pitchers	9	27	4	6	2	0	0	0	6	0	0	10	0	0	0	2	.222	.222	.222	.444
				TOTAL	9	348	65	121	63	19	13	10	196	28	2	44	2	1	2	2	.348	.399	.563	.963

Fat.	H	WP	E	R	Pitchers	G	GS	QS	CG	S	W	L	IP	H	SO	BB	HB	HR	R	ER	ERA
10/L	Vg	N	9 B		BJ Rogan	3	3	0	0	0	0	1	6	9	4	1	0	1	4	4	6.00
9/L	Ex	R	7 B		B Foster	2	2	1	0	0	0	1	15	13	6	1	0	5	8	8	4.80
10/L	Vg	NL	8 B		L Day	2	2	1	0	0	0	1	15	17	6	6	0	1	8	8	4.80
10/L	Aw	NL	7 B		M Dihigo	2	1	0	0	0	0	0	4.7	9	4	2	0	0	5	5	9.64
8/L	Md	R	8 C		S Paige	3	3	0	0	0	1	0	20	14	11	4	2	2	7	7	3.15
L/9	Vg	R	8 A		H Smith	3	0	0	0	0	0	2	10	4	6	6	0	4	1	0	0.00
9/L	Aw	R	9 A		Newcombe	2	0	0	0	0	0	0	4	2	4	2	1	0	0	0	0.00
10/L	Ex	NL	8 D		L Tiant	2	1	0	0	0	0	1	5.3	8	7	0	0	0	6	6	10.13
9	Aw	N	5 C		J R Richard	1	0	0	0	0	0	0	2	1	1	1	0	0	0	0	0.00
Long	Md	NL	4 B		D Moore	1	0	0	0	0	0	0	2	1	1	0	1	0	0	0	0.00
					TOTAL	21	9	5	2	0	7	2	83	78	49	17	0	11	39	38	4.12

Chart 15-2 – BB Stars Statistics for this series

Cubs Best Season Series vs. BB All-Stars 2-7, .222

Team	Year	WS	Hitters	G	AB	R	H	RBI	2B	3B	HR	TB	W	HB	SO	SF	SH	SB	B.AVG.	OBP	S.PCT.	OPS
Chicago N	1972	32	B. Williams	6	23	2	4	2	2	0	1	7	0	0	2	0	0	0	.174	.174	.304	.478
Chicago N	1930	35	H. Wilson	9	33	5	10	6	3	0	3	22	2	0	6	0	0	0	.303	.343	.667	1.010
Philadelphia	1899	41	Delehanty	7	24	3	6	0	2	0	0	8	3	0	3	0	0	0	.250	.333	.333	.667
Louisville	1887	30	Browning	7	10	1	2	0	0	0	0	2	0	0	0	0	0	0	.200	.200	.200	.400
Chicago N	1943	31	Nicholson	8	30	3	7	3	2	0	1	12	1	0	7	0	0	0	.233	.258	.400	.658
Chicago N	1958	31	E. Banks	8	26	3	7	9	0	0	3	16	0	1	6	0	0	0	.269	.269	.615	.885
Chicago N	1908	32	J. Tinker	3	8	2	3	1	1	1	0	5	1	0	1	0	1	0	.375	.375	.625	1.000
Chicago N	1964	36	R. Santo	6	19	2	4	2	0	3	0	11	1	0	2	0	0	0	.211	.250	.579	.829
Chicago N	1945	34	S. Hack	6	20	2	4	1	1	0	0	5	2	0	3	0	0	0	.200	.273	.250	.523
Chicago N	1912	34	Zimmerman	8	21	4	8	4	0	1	2	16	2	0	2	0	0	0	.381	.435	.762	1.197
Chicago N	1935	32	B. Herman	8	24	1	6	1	2	0	0	8	0	0	3	0	0	0	.250	.250	.333	.583
Chicago N	1913	20	J. Evers	4	11	2	4	0	1	0	0	5	1	0	1	0	0	0	.364	.417	.455	.871
Chicago N	1906	35	F. Chance	7	19	1	4	1	0	0	0	4	1	0	2	0	0	0	.211	.250	.211	.461
Chicago N	1930	29	G. Hartnett	6	21	4	4	5	0	0	1	8	2	0	2	1	0	0	.190	.261	.381	.642
Pittsburgh	1889	23	F. Carroll	4	12	2	3	1	0	0	0	3	2	0	5	0	0	0	.167	.286	.250	.536
			Pitchers	9	13	1	3	4	0	0	0	3	0	0	4	1	4	0	.231	.231	.231	.462
			TOTAL	9	314	39	78	39	14	5	11	135	17	0	49	2	5	0	.248	.287	.430	.717

Team	Year	WS	Pitchers	G	GS	QS	CG	S	W	L	IP	H	SO	BB	HB	HR	R	ER	ERA
Chicago N	1906	35	T. F. Brown	3	3	2	2	1	0	0	19	25	9	6	0	1	13	13	6.16
Chicago N	1906	24	J. Pfiester	2	2	1	1	0	1	1	12	14	7	6	1	1	6	6	4.50
Chicago N	1902	32	J. Taylor	3	1	0	0	0	0	1	5	16	3	3	0	0	8	8	14.40
Chicago N	1971	37	F. Jenkins	2	2	1	1	1	0	1	12.7	18	8	2	0	3	9	9	6.38
Chicago N	1952	23	B. Rush	2	0	0	0	0	0	0	1.7	5	1	2	0	0	3	3	15.88
Chicago N	1977	26	Reuschel	2	0	0	0	0	0	0	2.7	4	2	1	0	0	3	3	10.11
Chicago N	1932	31	Warneke	4	0	0	0	0	0	0	7.7	8	1	1	0	0	2	2	2.35
Chicago N	1918	28	H. Vaughn	4	0	0	0	0	0	0	4	5	2	2	0	0	4	4	9.00
Chicago N	1909	30	O. Overall	6	1	0	0	0	1	0	8.1	15	2	6	0	4	7	7	7.56
Chicago N	1906	23	E. Reulbach	2	0	0	0	0	0	0	4.3	4	3	3	1	0	6	6	12.47
Chicago N	1964	25	L. Jackson	2	0	0	0	1	0	0	3.7	8	2	2	0	1	4	4	9.81
			TOTAL*	9	9	4	2	2	2	2	81	122	44	28	2	10	65	65	7.22

* Eleven pitchers shared ten roster positions.

Chart 15-3 – Cubs statistics for this series

The turning point of the series - The Cubs never seemed to get the big hit and their pitchers frequently did not get the big out.

- Game One - The BB Stars definitely had more opportunities. They had men on base every inning but the third. The BB Stars left 15 men on base. The twelfth inning for the BB Stars had two base runners just beat the throw to the plate on squeeze bunts. Four more runs scored with a bases- loaded walk, a hit batsman, a single and a wild pitch.
- Game Two – Jack Pfeister (Cub's starting pitcher) in three separate innings (1, 2 and 4) retired the first two batters of the inning. The BB Stars scored all of their five runs in those three innings. They won 5-3.
- Game Four - In the first inning, Jack Taylor retired the first two batters. The BB Stars scored three runs (single, single, triple and a single). The Cubs fell behind 7-0. Gabby Hartnett hit a 3-run home run for the Cubs in the fourth inning (7-3). Bob Rush (Cubs third pitcher of the game) had two out and no one on base in the bottom of the fifth inning. Bell singled, stole second. Lloyd singled and Bell scored. Charleston hit a two run home run (10-3). The Cubs scored six runs in the sixth inning and trailed 10-9. In the bottom of the eighth, Reuschel (the Cubs fifth pitcher) retired the first two batters, then he gave up three consecutive singles for one run. Overall (the sixth Cubs pitcher) gave up a pinch hit 3-run home run to Torriente. The BB Stars led 15-9 (ten runs score after two outs, none on situations during the game).
- Game Five - The Cubs could not get a timely hit and lose 3-2.
- Game Eight - The Cubs led 5-2 in the middle of the fourth. With two outs, none on, Allen pinch hit triple (batting for Tiant), Bell drove in Allen with a single (5-3). In the fifth inning, the BB Stars got the clutch hits (Stearnes two run home run tied the game and Leonard followed with another home run. It was 6-5 BB Stars. They went on to win, 9-5.

Hitting Stars for the BB Stars

	RS	RBI	HR	.Avg	OBP	SPct	OPS
Charleston	11	7	3	.471	.500	.887	1.387
Stearnes	6	9	1	.433	.493	.833	1.326
Torriente	3	7	1	.615	.615	.818	1.433
Team	65	64	10	.348	.399	.563	.962

Best Pitcher for the BB Stars

	G	GS	GF	S	W-L	IP	H	HR	R/ER	ERA
H. Smith	3	0	2	0	2-0	10	4	0	1-0	0.00

.

Hitting Stars for the Cubs

	RS	RBI	HR	.Avg	OBP	SPct	OPS
H. Zimmerman	4	4	2	.381	.435	.762	1.197
H. Wilson	5	6	3	.303	.343	.667	1.010
E. Banks	3	9	3	.269	.269	.615	.884

Note: Two home runs and four RBIs for Hack Wilson came in Game Nine when Cubs trailed 12-0.

Chapter 16

Dominating Performances
(Series 1 through Series 10)

WE HAVE NOW COMPLETED 10 of the 15 nine-game Best Season Series, or 90 games of the 135 regular season games (does not include 2 fifteen-game All-Star Series and the six-team playoff).

The BB Stars won the first four series (Braves/Pirates, Browns/Orioles, White Sox and Reds), lost the next three series in a row (Senators/Twins, Phillies and Indians), and finished the first 90 games winning the final three series (Cardinals, Tigers and Cubs).

Below are the dominating performances of the first ten series (90 games).

Dominating Hitting Performances

OPS Leaders		OBP	S. Pct.	OPS	Team/Series
1.	O. Charleston	.448	1.000	1.448	BB/4
2.	T. Kluszewski	.500	.931	1.431	Rds/4
3.	O. Charleston	.500	.887	1.387	BB/10
4.	N. Allen	.481	.880	1.361	BB/6
5.	H. Greenberg	.351	.971	1.322	Tig/9
6.	N. Allen	.542	.773	1.316	BB/2
7.	G. Sisler	.500	.806	1.306	BO/2
8.	O. Charleston	.424	.844	1.268	BB/8
9.	T. Stearnes	.346	.920	1.266	BB/7
10.	T. Simmons	.542	.722	1.264	Card/8

Net Run Leaders	RS	RBI	HR	NR	Team/Series
1. H. Greenberg	8	18	6	20	Tig/9
2. C. Gehringer	10	9	2	17	Tig/9
3. R. Ashburn	10	6	0	16	Ph/6
4. J. Morgan	7	11	3	15	Rds/4
5. J. Gibson	7	11	3	15	BB/9
6. O. Charleston	11	7	3	15	BB/10
7. O. Charleston	8	11	5	14	BB/4
8. T. Kluszewski	10	8	4	14	Rds/4
9. T. Stearnes	6	9	1	14	BB/10
10. C. P. Bell	8	6	1	13	BB/4
11. P. Lloyd	9	5	1	13	BB/4
12. S. Musial	6	9	2	13	Card/8

Offensive Summary - The OPS leaders were spread out over seven of the ten series. Oscar Charleston made the Top Ten three times, with two of the top three OPS performances. Newt Allen of the BB Stars was listed twice (a surprise). Hank Greenberg (Tigers) - was the Net Runs Leader with 20 net runs (8 runs scored, 18 RBIs, 6 HRs). Greenberg's team mate, Charlie Gehringer, was second with 17 Net Runs (10 Runs Scored, 9 RBIs and 2 HRs). Oscar Charleston was on the list twice. Five of the twelve players were from the high scoring Reds/BB Stars Series. The BB Stars scored 75 runs (8.4 runs/gm), and the Reds scored 65 runs (7.2 runs/gm) in that explosive, offensive series.

Dominating Pitching Performances

Pitchers	QS	CG	W-L	IP	H	SO	BB	ERA	Tm/Series
1. B J Rogan	1	1	2-0	19.7	8	5	4	0.46	BB/1
2. L. Day	2	2	2-0	18	10	4	5-1*	1.00	BB/5
3. E. Walsh	3	1	1-0	24	22	8	1	1.50	WS/3
4. B. Foster	2	1	1-0	16.3	10	5	7	1.65	BB/7
5. C. Hendrix	2	1	1-1	16	13	6	3	1.69	BO/2
6. R. Roberts	2	0	2-0	15	12	10	4-2*	1.80	Ph/6
7. L. Day	2	1	1-1	16.3	13	9	6	2.20	BB/1
8. S. Paige	2	2	2-0	23	18	24	2	2.35	BB/1
9. W. Johnson	3	1	1-0	27	25	23	4-1*	2.57	Sen/5
10. M. Cooper	2	0	1-0	17	18	9	2	2.65	Card/8
11. S. Paige	3	1	1-0	22	14	13	3	2.86	BB/2

Summary - *The second number is Hit Batsmen.

In Series Five, Walter Johnson was in four games (all won by the Sen-Twins). He out pitched Satchel Paige in two of the three games he started.

They both left the 1-1 game in the late innings. In the fourth game, Johnson came on in the eighth inning and saved the game.

Three of the top eleven performances were with three quality starts out of three starts (Paige-Series 2; Walsh-Series 3 and Johnson-Series 5).

In addition to his quality start, Bullet Joe Rogan won the 19 inning game by pitching shut-out ball for 8.7 innings in relief.

Chapter 17

Review of Playoff Contenders (through Series 10)

Who qualifies for the post-season playoffs?

- The BB Stars are an automatic entry for one of the six positions.
- The five Best Season teams based on winning percentage in the nine-game series. Run differential will be the tie-breaker.

What is the format for playoffs?

- The first and second seed draw a bye for the "best of five" quarter final round.
- The winners of the quarter final round play the #1 and #2 seed. With the highest seed position playing #1 seed in a "best of seven" series and the other quarterfinal winner plays #2 seed, also in a "best of seven" series.
- The two winners play in the finals, also "best of seven" with the lowest seed having home field advantage.

What teams currently are in the lead for the playoffs?

Team		W	L	Pct.	Runs	OR	Differential
1.	BB Stars	52	38	.578	NR	NR	NR
2.	Phillies	5	4	.556	46	44	+2
3.	Indians	5	4	.556	43	50	-7
4.	Senators	5	4	.556	34	43	-9
5.	Tigers	4	5	.444	51	46	+5
6.	Browns/Orioles	4	5	.444	41	37	+4

What teams have been eliminated?

- Cardinals (4-5, .444, -2)
- Braves/Pirates (4-5. ,444, -4)
- Reds (3-6, .333, -13)
- White Sox (2-7, .286, -17)
- Cubs (2-7, .286, -26)

What teams have yet to play (next book, *Best Season – The Challenging Finish*)?

- Athletics
- Giants
- Yankees
- Dodgers
- Red Sox

The 5 nine-game series remaining (45 games) will be very tough for the BB Stars. I believe a minimum of three of these teams will knock out current leaders. All five of these teams could make the playoff. The Yankees should end up as the #1 seed. The Athletics and Dodgers would be my other two picks. Giants and Red Sox are dark horses to make playoffs. Any of the teams that make this post-season playoff could win it all. I believe the Yankees will play the BB Stars for the Championship and win it in seven games.

Chapter 18

Preview of Series 11-15 (Games 91-135)

Series 11 - Athletics - This will be a great series. The Athletics were strong in the dead ball era (1900-1919), the offensive era (late 20s and early 30s) and finally in the period 1969-1974. The line-up will be tough from top to bottom. The defense will be excellent and the pitching will be solid. Athletics should be a playoff team (seed 1-3). See Offensive Leaders Ranking at the end of the chapter. The following Athletics are in the Top 12 Offensive Leaders (4- Jimmy Foxx; 7- Al Simmons; 8 - Napoleon Lajoie).

Series 12 – Giants - This features the #3 (Willie Mays) and the #4 (Oscar Charleston) of Bill James Top 100 Baseball Players of All Time. Could these two players be the key? The Giants also have Bill Terry and Johnny Mize sharing first base and Mel Ott in right field with Bobby Bonds as a back-up. The pitching of Mathewson, Hubbell, Marichal and the great free agent from the Mets, Tom Seaver will be the key pitchers. The Giants will be fighting for one of the final three seeds (4-6). At the end of the chapter Terry (#10), Dunlap (#11) and Mays (#12) are the final three players in the Offensive Leaders Ranking (based on their OPS).

Series 13 – Yankees - This is the series everyone will be waiting for – Best Season Yankees vs. the BB Stars. At the end of the chapter, four of the first nine Offensive Leaders (in remaining five series) by OPS are Ruth (#1) with a 1.358 OPS in 1921; Gehrig (#3) with a 1.240 OPS in 1927; Mantle (#6) with a 1.172 OPS in 1956, and Joe DiMaggio (#9) with a 1.083 OPS in 1941. Add other Hall of Famers – Berra and Dickey (catcher), Lazzeri (2B), and Combs (OF) plus Rizzuto (SS), Nettles (3B) and Maris (OF) and your offense is outstanding. Four lefties lead the staff (Ford, Gomez, Guidry and Lyle). This could be the battle for #1 seed in the playoffs.

Series 14 – Dodgers – Free agent, Hugh Duffy (1894 BostonN) will be one of the keys to the Dodgers making the playoffs. He has the fifth best OPS (1.199) on the five remaining teams. He batted .440 in 1894 (highest batting average in Major League baseball history). He will lead-off, followed by Jackie Robinson, Duke Snider, Hodges and Camilli platooning at first, Reese and Wills at short, Cey (3B), Campanella will catch, Guerrero will be in left field. Drysdale, Koufax, Sutton and John will lead staff. The Dodgers are not a lock to make the playoffs, however. Do they have enough offense?

Series 15 – Red Sox – Being originally from Boston, I saved Ted Williams and my favorite team, the Red Sox, until the end. They are my dark horse candidate to make the playoffs. Ted Williams has the second highest OPS behind Ruth on the remaining five franchises. Williams' OPS is 1.286 (1941). Tris Speaker will bat lead-off and play center field (1.031 OPS in 1912). There are some great Red Sox infielders and outfielders that will need to share playing time-Yaz and free agent, Brouthers (1892 Brooklyn) will be at 1B. Doerr, Pesky, Petrocelli, Stephens and Jimmy Collins are the other infielders. In the outfield, Rice, Lynn, Evans and Hooper will share responsibilities and pinch hitting duties. Schang and R. Ferrell will catch. Young, Wood, Ruth and Parnell will lead pitching staff. Ellis Kinder and Dick Radatz will do a great job as closers. I expect the Red Sox to win four of nine and possibly five games and maybe sneak into the final six (playoffs).

Offensive Leaders Ranking (Athletics, Giants, Yankees, Dodgers, and Red Sox)

#	Player	OBP	SPct	OPS	R +	RBI -	HR	=NR
1.	B. Ruth	.512	.846	1.358	177	171	59	289
2.	T. Williams	.551	.735	1.286	135	120	37	218
3.	L. Gehrig	.474	.765	1.240	149	175	47	277
4.	J. Foxx	.469	.749	1.218	151	169	58	262
5.	H. Duffy*	.505	.694	1.199	161	145	18	288
6.	M. Mantle	.467	.705	1.172	132	130	52	210
7.	A. Simmons	.423	.708	1.131	152	165	36	278
8.	N. Lajoie	.455	.642	1.097	145	125	14	256
9.	J. DiMaggio	.440	.643	1.083	122	125	30	217
10.	B. Terry	.452	.619	1.071	139	129	23	245
11.	F. Dunlap*	.449	.621	1.070	160	82	8	234
12.	W. Mays	.404	.659	1.063	123	127	51	199

* Free agent

Chapter 19

Preview of the 2 Fifteen-Game All-Star Series

First 15-Game All-Star Series (21-man rosters) - This interlude will come after completion of the 15 nine-game series (135 games). The BB Stars and the Major League Stars will each carry six pitchers. The venue is to highlight five key periods of a regular baseball season. They are Opening Day, Memorial Day weekend with a traditional doubleheader, Independence Day (July 4 doubleheader), Labor Day doubleheader, and the end of the season weekend. Each of these five periods of the season would have three games. Since they are spread out, we can have the best pitchers start five games (Walter Johnson vs. Satchel Paige will be five of the match ups).

The Opening Day Weekend will be played in Sportsman's Park, St. Louis (BB Stars, home team). Memorial Day Weekend will be in Comiskey Park, Chicago (ML Stars, home team). Games Two and Three are a Memorial Day doubleheader. The third three-game series (Independence Day) will be played in Forbes Field, Pittsburgh (BB Stars home team). Games Two and Three will be a July 4 doubleheader. The Labor Day weekend will consist of a single game on Sunday with a doubleheader on Monday. The ML Stars will host (home team) this series in Shibe Park, Philadelphia. The final series will be the final weekend of the season. The series will be played in Yankee Stadium with the BB Stars the home team for Games One and Three of the series. The ML Stars will be the home team for the second game of series.

California Winter League Fifteen-Game All-Star Series (25-man rosters) – Winter ball in California for black and white ball players from the Majors, Minors, Negro League, and semi-pro players was very special. Our final 25-man roster, fifteen-game All-Star Series will be like the California Winter League. It will be played over a seventeen-day period in five different parks and cities after the six team playoff.

1. Candlestick Park, San Francisco (BB Stars are home team).
2. Oakland Alameda Stadium (ML Stars are home team).
3. Dodger Stadium, Los Angeles (BB Stars are home team).
4. Anaheim Stadium (ML Stars are home team).
5. Jack Murphy Stadium, San Diego (BB Stars home team for Game One; ML Stars home team for Games Two and Three).

Chapter 20

Statistical Summary of The First 90 Games

Black Ball All Stars – Key Hitting Stats (ranked by OPS)

Player	AB	R	H	RBI	HR	BAvg	OBP	SPct	OPS
W. Wells	147	27	50	29	7	.340	.390	.639*	1.029*
M. Suttles	230	47	78	39	14	.339	.367	.622	.989
O. Charleston	320	52*	97	55*	19*	.303	.355	.572	.927
C. Torriente	161	32	57	25	4	.354	.399*	.509	.908
J. Gibson	269	42	79	47	18	.294	.324	.580	.904
T. Stearnes	257	32	57	55*	13	.276	.295	.572	.867
B. Mackey	152	16	55	25	2	.362*	.382	.480	.862
P. Lloyd	266	40	93	24	2	.350	.395	.455	.850
C. P. Bell	349*	46	112*	38	6	.321	.381	.438	.840
N. Allen	216	37	67	25	4	.312	.357	.460	.817
M. Irvin	113	15	30	15	4	.265	.336	.442	.778
B. Leonard	163	22	43	21	5	.264	.277	.491	.768
J. Johnson	187	26	49	23	5	.262	.324	,428	.751
F. Warfield	129	17	33	12	0	.256	.329	.395	.724
R. Dandridge	167	14	40	15	1	.240	.262	.293	.555
Pitchers	232	17	54	22	0	.233	.243	.246	.489
Total	**3369**	**483**	**1011**	**470**	**104**	**.300**	**.341**	**.484**	**.825**

- The black ball offense is excellent. Left-handed pitchers do not do well against this team, and right-handed pitchers do not do much better. They average 5.4 runs/game. When an opponent scores 4 or less runs/game, the BB Stars are 38-9, .809 winning pct.

Below are BB Stars key pitching stats (ranked by ERA)

Pitcher	G	CG	S	W-L	IP	H	SO	BB-hb	HR	ERA
Richard**	28	1	8*	2-5	55.0	43	57	18-0	3	1.96*
S. Paige	25	6*	0	8-6	164.7*	140*	129*	21-0	16*	3.33
L. Day	24	4	3	7-3	111.3	110	45	35-2*	4	3.72
B. Foster	25	2	0	8-3	125.0	114	55	31-1	16*	3.89
L. Tiant**	17	2	2	6-3	87.7	77	71	24-1	8	3.90
H. Smith	33*	0	2	7-7	57.7	69	28	10-0	6	4.53
D. Moore**	17	0	2	2-2	23.0	23	11	3-0	6	4.70
B J Rogan	25	3	1	8-6	107.3	104	45	34-2	10	4.96
Newcombe**	13	0	0	1-0*	48.7	54	24	12-0	7	5.36
M. Dihigo	17	0	0	2-3	44.7	53	27	22-0	5	6.85
Totals	90	18	18	52-38	824.7	787	491	211-7	81	4.08
Free Agents**	-	3	12	11-10	214.4	197	163	57-1	24	3.82
Non- F A	-	15	6	41-28	610.3	590	328	154-6	57	4.17

The Free Agents have contributed to the success of the BB Stars. J. R. Richard has done an excellent job in relief. His one start in his home park, the Astrodome, was phenomenal. He struck out 17 White Sox in his complete game win.

BB Stars Opponent All-Stars – Key Hitting Stats (ranked by OPS)

Team	AB	R	H	RBI	HR	BAvg	OBP	SPct	OPS
Reds	343*	62*	98*	60*	17*	.286*	.316*	.510*	.826*
Tigers	308	51	79	49	10	.256	.302	.455	.757
Phillies	314	46	80	45	8	.255	.310	.417	.727
Cubs	314	39	78	39	11	.248	.287	.430	.717
Cardinals	327	38	83	37	5	.253	.314	.381	.695
Indians	326	43	79	43	8	.242	.308	.380	.688
Brwn/Orioles	316	41	82	38	8	.259	.282	.405	.687
SenTwins	306	34	74	34	5	.241	.295	.350	.645
Brav/Pirates	335	39	76	37	8	.227	.281	.358	.639
White Sox	288	22	59	20	1	.205	.252	.272	.524
Total	3177	415	788	402	81	.248	.295	.398	.693

- The Reds were the best hitting opponents of the BB Stars in all categories by a wide margin. They were 3-6 (W-L) because of a 7.78 ERA (worst ERA).
- The White Sox ranked first in ERA with 3.55. Their record was 2-7 because they hit .205 with 22 runs, 1 home run and a deplorable OPS of .524.

BB Opponent Key Pitching Stats (ranked by ERA)

Team	G	CG	Sv	W-L	IP	H	SO	W-hb	HR	ERA
White Sox	9	1	0	2-7	78.7	98	46	11-3*	10	3.55*
Brns/Orioles	9	3*	1	4-5	80.3	87	44	15-1	8	3.92
Cardinals	9	0	4*	4-5	84.3	94	46	20-3	13	4.06
SenTwins	9	1	1	5-4*	83.0	107	61	16-1	7*	4.12
Brav/Pirates	9	0	2	4-5	89.0*	105	56	16-0	13	4.45
Phillies	9	0	3	5-4*	79.0	84*	57	25-0	10	4.56
Indians	9	0	3	5-4*	85.3	96	56	20-1	11	4.75
Tigers	9	2	2	4-5	78.7	100	63*	20-1	9	4.80
Cubs	9	2	1	2-7	81.0	121	44	28-2	10	7.22
Reds	9	0	2	3-6	81.0	119	45	21-0	13	7.78
Totals	**90**	**9**	**19**	**38-52**	**820.3**	**1011**	**518**	**192-12**	**104**	**4.92**

It is ironic that the lowest ERA of an opponent team is the White Sox (3.55), when they posted the worst record (2-7) tie with their cross-town rivals, the Cubs. The team offense and team defense were atrocious in their series.

Baseball Definitions

APPENDIX ONE IS NOT MEANT to be a complete listing of baseball definitions. The primary purpose is to define the categories on the Roster Charts and The Roster Reviews before each series. I will begin with the baseball definitions on the Black Ball and Opponent's Rosters. 80% of the definitions are the same and will be done under Common Roster Definitions.

Black Ball Roster - Hitters - There are some differences between the Black Ball Roster and the opponent rosters. The difference (definition wise) will be the segment of the roster to the left of the **Hitters** which has to do with their fielding capabilities.

- **Position** - This defines the primary position of the player (catcher, shortstop etc.).
- **E (error)** – The error rating of the player is from 10 (few errors) to 1 (many errors).
- **R (range)** – AA is excellent range which takes away opponent's hits. A player with C or D range gives up many more hits.
- **TH (throwing)** - Throwing ratings are for outfielders and catchers only. A (-) minus rating is good it decreases base runners chance of successfully advancing to another base. A (+) rating for a throwing arm improves the opponent's base running capability.
- **PB (passed ball)** - This rating is for catchers only. A passed ball is when the catcher allows a pitched ball to go by him and base runner (s)

advance a base. An excellent rating means less passed balls. A poor rating means more passed balls.

162 Games - For the Black Ball Roster only, we took their data and projected what they would do as individuals playing a 162 game schedule (equating it to today's Major League regular season schedule). For example, Josh Gibson (hitter) based on the data we had in 1993, he would hit 44 home runs in a season if he played 162 games.

Black Ball Roster – Pitchers - There are some differences between the Black Ball Roster and the opponent rosters. The difference (definition wise) will be the segment of the roster to the left of **Pitchers** which has to do with their pitching/fielding capabilities.

- **Fat. (fatigue)** – This is an indicator of what inning a pitcher would begin to experience fatigue if he has allowed eight opponents to get on base. If the pitcher also has an L symbol or Long, he can be used in long relief of more than two innings.
- **H (hold rating)** – This reflects the pitcher's ability to hold runners. A pitcher with an excellent hold rating will be tougher to steal a base against, also he has a higher probability of a successful pick-off play (pitcher, for example, throws over to first base and the runner is tagged out before he can return successfully to the base). A pitcher with a mediocre or poor hold rating will have more opponent base runners successfully steal a base.
- **WP (wild pitch rating)** - A pitcher with an excellent wild pitch rating will not throw many pitches past his catcher. A pitcher with a poor rating will throw more pitches past his catcher with men on base allowing the base runners to advance a base.

162 Games - For the BB Stars' pitchers, the statistical data is different for the original six pitchers and the four free agent pitchers. The statistics for the original six BB Stars' pitchers are projected for a 162 game season. Pitchers are not like non-pitchers. Pitchers do not play every day, therefore, their projections reflect less games played than non-pitchers. The "free agent" pitchers' statistics are their actual statistics for their "Best Season".

Opponent Roster (Hitters and Pitchers) – On the Opponent Rosters, the information to the left of the player's name is A) the Major League team he was on for his "Best Season", B) the year of his "Best Season" and C) the Win Shares (WS) he earned with that specific team for that specific year. The player's statistics to the right of his name are his actual statistics for his "Best Season". Remember the BB Stars' Roster statistics are a projection of what they would have done if they played a 162 game season.

Common Roster Definitions (Hitters) –

- **At bats (AB)** – The number of times a player or team comes to bat during a game, series or season (defined period of time) not including walks (base on balls), hit batsman (hit by pitch), sacrifice hits (sacrifice bunts) or sacrifice flies or catcher interference.
- **Runs scored (R)** – The number of times the player or team scores (moves around the bases to home plate which is where they started) for a specific time period (game, series, season or career).
- **Hits (H)** – The number of times a player or team reaches base on a ball that is hit (with bat) except for plays the official scorer (official person who records every play of the game on a score sheet) determines the fielder should have made the play but did not (error).
- **Runs Batted In (RBI)** – The number of times the hitter (batter) or team is credited with an RBI when their offensive action results in their team scoring a run (R). If it is determined the run scored because of a fielder's error (E), do not credit the hitter (batter) or team with an RBI.
- **Double (2B)** – The number of times a hitter (batter) or team reaches second base on their hit (not a fielding error).
- **Triple (3B)** – The number of times a hitter (batter) or team reaches third base on their hit.
- **Home Run (HR)** – the number of times a hitter (batter) or team circles the bases (first, second, third and home) on their hit. 99 % of home runs are hit over the fence or wall (left field foul pole to right field foul pole). Any ball that goes over the fence or wall that hits a foul pole is a fair ball. I know what you are going to ask me – "Why aren't the poles called fair poles?" That is a great question! I do not know the answer.
- **Total Bases (TB)** – The number of total bases the hitter or team has for all of his hits. Below is a simple chart that shows total bases by type of hit.

Hit (H)	Total Bases (TB)
Single	One (1)
Double	Two (2)
Triple	Three (3)
Home Run	Four (4)

If a player has three hits – a single (1 TB), a double (2 TB) and a home run (4 TB), the player has seven total bases (TB).

- **Strike Outs (SO)** – The number of times the hitter (batter) or team has made an out without hitting a fair ball or hitting a foul ball caught by an opponent before ball touches the ground or another object. It takes three strikes for a strike out. A strike can be called (hitter does not swing at pitch but the umpire says the ball was in the strike zone). The strike zone is the width of home plate (seventeen inches) between the hitter's knees and armpits. A swinging strike means the hitter (batter) swung at the ball and missed or hit the ball into foul territory. With two strikes, a hitter (batter) can foul off pitches and it is not a strike out. A foul tip (ball nicks bat) caught by the catcher on the third strike is a strike out.
- **Base on Balls or Walk (BB)** – The number of times the hitter (batter) or team reaches base because the pitcher has thrown four balls out of the strike zone and the hitter did not swing at these pitches.
- **Hit Batsman (HB)** – The number of times the hitter (batter) or team reaches first base because the pitcher hit batter with a pitch.
- **Sacrifice Fly (SF)** – The number of times the hitter (batter) or team hits a ball (with less than two outs) that is caught by a fielder before the ball touches the ground and a runner (teammate of hitter) on third base, leaves the base after the catch and safely crosses home plate, **credit** the hitter (batter) or team with a sacrifice fly (SF) and a run batted in (RBI)..
- **Sacrifice Hit (SH)** – The number of times the hitter (batter) or team with less than two outs, bunts (not a swing but a push with the bat) the ball (usually travels less than thirty feet) to advance runners. Credit the hitter (batter) or team with a sacrifice hit when he successfully advances the runner. If the hitter (batter) safely reaches first (not because of fielder error), credit the hitter (batter) with a single and not a sacrifice hit.
- **Stolen Base (SB)** – The number of times a runner on first, second or third base successfully runs to the next base (steals the base) while the pitcher is throwing the baseball to the batter and the batter does not hit the ball.
- **Batting Average (B. Avg.)** – It is a calculation (hits divided by at bats). For example, a hitter has 100 at bats (AB) with 31 hits (H). 31 divided by 100 (carried three places) is .310 (batting average).
- **On Base Percentage (OBP)** - It is a calculation (hits, base on balls and hit batsman divided by hits, base on balls, hit batsman and at bats. See example below:

AB	H	BB	HB	
100	31	6	1	(38 divided by 107 = .355).

- **Slugging Percentage (S. Pct.)** – It is a calculation (total bases divided by at bats). Example, the player with 31 hits in 100 at bats has 21 singles, 4 doubles, 2 triples and 4 home runs.

Type of hit	Hits	Total Bases
Singles (1)	21	21
Doubles (2)	4	8
Triples (3)	2	6
Home Runs (4)	4	16
Total	31	51

The player's slugging percentage is .510 (51 TB divided by 100 AB).

- **On Base Percentage + Slugging Percentage = OPS** – In today's baseball world, OPS is the key number when it comes to evaluating a player or a team's offensive efficiency. Let us look at the ficticious player in the examples above.

OBP	+	S.Pct.	=	OPS
.355		.510		.865

An .865 OPS is good but not great for an individual. It would be an excellent OPS for a team.

Miscellaneous Offensive/Defensive Definitions

- **Batting Order** – This definition is the same as "line up". The manager of each team submits this document to the home plate umpire before the beginning of the game. The manager lists the nine players who will bat in chronological order with their position in the field listed beside their name.
- **Designated Hitter (DH)** – A hitter who replaces the pitcher in the "line up" or "batting order". Since 1973, the American League has used a designated hitter for the pitcher. The National League still lets the pitcher bat for himself. In the "Best Season" competition, a designated hitter is not used.
- **Fielder's Choice (FC)** – When runners are on base and the batter hits a ground ball to an infielder, the player or fielder has a choice as to which base runner or the batter to throw out at a specific base, if an attempt is made to throw out a base runner (not the batter running to first base) and the batter reaches first base, he is not credited with a hit. He reached base on a fielder's choice (FC).
- **Force Out** – When a base runner is thrown out at a base that he is forced to run to (for example, the base runner is on first base, the batter hits the ball on the ground. The runner on first base must attempt to go to second base because the batter is running to first base). On a force play, the defensive player does not have to tag the base runner, he can step on the base before base runner gets to the base.
- **Line Up** – Before the game the manager of each team submits a line up (batting order) from one through nine which also lists the position (in the field) for each of these players (pitcher, catcher, first baseman, second baseman, third baseman, shortstop, left fielder, center fielder and right fielder).
- **Left On Base (LOB)** - This is the number of runners a team leaves on base over a specific period of time (inning, game, series, etc.) An example - When an inning ends for a team (they make three outs), how many runners were on base when they made their third out?
- **Net Runs** – It is a calculation (runs scored + runs batted in – home runs = net runs). It reflects the player or team ability to produce runs.
- **Pinch Hitter (PH)** – A player who comes off the bench to bat for a player in the line up. The player being pinched hit for may not re-enter the game.
- **Pinch Runner (PR)** – A player who comes off the bench to run for a base runner (on first, second or third base). The player being pinched run for may not re-enter the game.

- **Yard** – It is another term for Home Run.

Common Roster Definitions (Pitchers) – The pitching definitions focu
data found in charts through out the book.
- **Games (G)** – The number of games the pitcher or team's pitc
  pitched in for a specific period of time (series, season or career).
- **Games Started (GS)** – The number of games started by a pitche
  pitching staff over a given time period (series, season or career).
- **Quality Starts (QS)** – The following chart defines quality starts
  pitcher needs to pitch six innings (minimum) as a starter.

Innings pitched	Earned runs (or less)
6	3
7	3
8	4
9	4

- **Complete Games (CG)** – The number of games the pitcher who s
  the game, finishes it. Today (twenty-first century), it is rare to
  pitchers who complete more than 10 % of their starts. In the late n
  teenth century and early twentieth century 75 % or more of the ga
  were complete games.
- **Saves (S)** – The number of games the relief pitcher (of the win
  team) who finishes the game meets the falling qualifications, credit
  with a Save.
  1. He pitches three or more innings and he is not the winning pitc
  2. The tying run is on base, at bat or on deck when he enters the ga

- **Pitching Wins (W)** – The number of games won by the pitche
  team over a specific period of time (series, season or career).
- **Pitching Losses (L)** – The number of games lost by the pitche
  team over a specific period of time.
- **Winning Percentage** – This is a calculation (wins divided by
  decisions of wins and losses). For example, a pitcher or team
  seven games and loses three games, their winning percentage is .70
  divided by 10).
- **Innings Pitched** – The number of innings pitched by the pitche
  pitching staff for a specific period of time (game, series, season
  career). Innings pitched can be a whole inning (example, 8) or if
  pitcher begins an inning and retires no one it would be recorded a
  (pitched in ninth inning but retired no batters in ninth inning)
  pitcher retires one batter in his ninth inning it would be 8.3 inn
  pitched. If pitcher retired two batters in his ninth inning it woul
  8.7 innings pitched.

- **Hits (H)** – This is the number of hits allowed by the pitcher or pitching staff over a specific time period (game, series, season or career).
- **Strike Outs (SO)** – The number of strike outs by this pitcher or pitching staff over a specific time period (game, series, season or career).
- **Walks or Base on Balls (BB)** – The number of walks (BB) by the pitcher or pitching staff over a specific time period.
- **Hit Batsman (HB)** – The number of batters hit by pitch (HB) by this pitcher or pitching staff over a specific time period.
- **Home Runs (HR)** – The number of home runs allowed by this pitcher or pitching staff over a specific period of time.
- **Runs Allowed (R)** – The total number of runs allowed by this pitcher or pitching staff over a specific period of time.
- **Earned Runs Allowed (ER)** – The total number of earned runs allowed by a pitcher or pitching staff over a specific time period. Earned runs do not include runs allowed due to defensive lapses (errors or passed balls). Runs allowed because the pitcher threw a wild pitch are earned runs because it was the pitching failure that allowed the run. If the pitcher makes a fielding error (wild throw or misplay fielding a ball), the runs allowed because of his fielding error would be unearned.
- **Earned Run Average (ERA)** – This is a calculation to reflect the number of **earned runs** a pitcher or pitching staff would give up in nine innings (normal complete game). The formula is earned runs (ER) times nine divided by innings pitched. Example, the pitcher gives up six earned runs in thirteen innings pitched. His ERA is 4.15 (6 ER x 9 or 54 divided by 13 IP).

Series Results – Using modified Roster Charts for the BB Stars and the Opponents, you post their actual results (Hitting and Pitching) at the end of the chapter for each nine game series.

Fielding Definitions – The fielding segment of definitions will be limited. The Black Ball Roster Review section (Chapter One) and the Opponent Roster Reviews for the ten series in this book will be the primary fielding information for each team.

- **Fielding positions by the numbers**
  1. **Pitcher**
  2. **Catcher**
  3. **First Baseman**
  4. **Second Baseman**
  5. **Third Baseman**
  6. **Shortstop**
  7. **Left Fielder**
  8. **Center Fielder**
  9. **Right Fielder**

- **Defensive Substitution** – Some players have superior offensive skills but are weak defensively (poor or average range; prone to making errors; an outfielder or catcher with average or below average throwing arm). If your team is leading in the seventh inning or later, defensive substitution is highly recommended. If it is earlier in the game and your team is leading by four or more runs, make defensive substitutions earlier.
- **Double Switch** – With no designated hitter (DH) in the "Best Season" competition, the double switch is used frequently. For example, your pitcher is due to lead off the next inning. The pitcher gets in trouble and as the manager you decide to make a pitching change. The relief pitcher you are bringing in, you would like to pitch a couple of innings. Make a double switch. The team's number eight hitter is the team's shortstop and he made the final out in the previous inning. Bring the new pitcher in to the game and have him bat in the eighth spot. The new shortstop will lead off batting in the ninth position.

Summary – As stated at the beginning of Appendix One on Baseball Definitions, there was no intent to have this be a comprehensive appendix on baseball definitions. It was an overview to help readers grasp all the baseball information (primarily on all the charts that summarize how exceptional all of these 400 players were and how well they actually performed in this "Best Season" competition). The author is assuming that the reader has basic knowledge on the game of baseball..

Creation of Player Card Set [1993]

1. Enough players for sixteen 25 man baseball rosters, so customers could form leagues.
2. Rosters need to be balanced (as best we could) as follows:
   - 10 pitchers/team (160)
   - 2 catchers (32)
   - 2 first basemen (32)
   - 2 second basemen (32)
   - 2 third base men (32)
   - 2 shortstops (32)
   - 5 outfielders (80)
   - 25 total players/team roster
3. Player selection (approximate)
   - 100% of HOF players (185)
   - another 115 career players
   - another 100+ players with their **Best Season** only
4. HOF/Career players (2 cards/player)
   - HOF/Career card (average stats/season)
   - Best Season (all 400+ players)
   - Best Season card set (stats 20-25% above average)
5. Included in set
   - 40+ players from 1880s-1890s
   - 21 players from Negro Leagues
6. Not included in set
   - Active players as of 1992 season
   - Without knowing it, we eliminated all potential steroid users

Acknowledgements

THIS PROJECT HAS HONORED AND blessed me, so much. There have been so many people encouraging me with this project (even strangers). If I leave anyone off this list, please forgive me.

I want to thank God, the Father for honoring me with this assignment. I want to thank God, the Son. Jesus walked with me every step of the way. I want to thank God the Holy Spirit, who continued to nudge me and share His Wisdom to show me the way and open all the doors according to His Timing, not mine.

Then I want to thank my best friend, my wife of forty-five plus years, Michele. I have always had a problem with my priorities. My passion for baseball and baseball board games has too often come before God, Michele, family and everything else in my life. Michele has been very patient with me. She has always encouraged me as well as our children to pursue our dreams. Often the pursuit of my dreams hinders Michele in pursuing her own dreams. She was the reason Pursue the Pennant survived in 1990-91.

Back in 1993, my right hand man at Pursue the Pennant, Jon Dunkle, did most of the hard work in the creation of our 416 player Hall of Fame/All Time All Star Card Set (including 21 players from the Black Ball Era or Negro Leagues). Jon made the decision to increase the number of players (in the card set) from the Negro Leagues. As of 1993, there were nine Negro League players in the National Baseball Hall of Fame. Jon made the decision to expand the players in the card set from the Negro Leagues to twenty one players with a balance by playing position. He did this so our customers would have the option to have a Black Ball Era (Negro League) team to compete against Major League players. I believe this was part of God's Plan for me. Eighteen years after the creation of this card set, I began my research (playing games) with these great Black Ball Stars (my team name for them) playing the Best Season of the Best Players (1880s-1980s). Thank you, Jon.

I want to thank our son, Derek May for the work he did at Pursue the Pennant as well as his assistance to help me with Microsoft Word (in writing the book) and the converting of Microsoft Excel spreadsheets to jpg charts for book.

In 2002, when I was pursuing another baseball project (Baseball Fans Unite – International). This nonprofit organization was to help fans to have a voice in the Major League Baseball labor negotiations. I met Dr. Ray Doswell at the Negro League Baseball Museum in Kansas City. I was in town on business and he gave me a personal tour of the museum. In fact, The Lord honored me when I arrived at the museum. Buck O'Neill, the former all star first baseman for the Kansas City Monarchs (Negro Leagues) was just leaving and we had a chance to exchange greetings. I believe he was 90 years young at the time. Meeting Dr. Doswell (Executive Director of the NLBM) in 2002 was a move of God. He knew I would need Dr. Doswell in 2010.

In 2002, I had the opportunity to talk on the phone with one of my favorite baseball analysts, Tim Kurkjian of ESPN. Once again, God had given me a key baseball contact which was important in the writing of my book in 2011-2012.

In the fall of 2010, as I began to do my research (organize tournaments to utilize the 1993 PTP HOF card set and play the games) I contacted Dr. Doswell and Tim Kurkjian to share my excitement of using the twenty one Black Ball Stars as they played Major League players. The Lord had revealed to me the possibility of an article or book to honor these twenty-one Black Ball All Stars as they played the great players over 100 years of Major League Baseball history. The feedback from both of these men was very encouraging. Dr. Doswell put me in contact with Dr. Leslie Heaphy (the person who honored me by writing the foreword for this book). Dr. Heaphy is the Detail Editor of Black Ball Journal. She thought my writing project had merit. She encouraged me to attend the Lester Malloy Negro League Baseball Conference (Indianapolis, July 2011). This conference would be attended by nearly 100 baseball historians, who like myself, they are members of The Society of American Baseball Research (SABR).

In addition to Dr. Doswell and Tim Kurkjian, there was a family member who is very knowledgeable about baseball. Kenny Bean is our son-in-law. He has been playing Fantasy Baseball for years. He plays on two softball teams and he umpires. I wanted his opinion on my initial writing. He enthusiastically responded that I was on target. I respect Kenny's feedback as much as any baseball expert.

Our other son-in-law, Heath Lockhart is a very creative individual. His company created my business card and brochure "Honoring Black Ball". Both were extremely well done. They were very useful to me at the July Conference.

In early July 2011, I had the honor and privilege to take my nine year old grandson, Caleb Lockhart to meet Monte Irvin, ninety-two year old former Negro League (Newark Eagles) and Major League (New York Giants) Hall of Fame ballplayer. It was a wonderful experience. He was so kind and gracious. He repeated how much the Negro League ball players just "loved to play ball". He made it very clear, they knew they could play competitive ball with the best of Major League baseball. Monte Irvin was a further inspiration to me to want to honor him and these other great men. Monte Irvin is one of the twenty one players participating in the competition.

The Lester Malloy Negro League Conference was a key to my moving forward with my writing project. If these baseball historians were concerned about my potential book because it would be historical fiction, I would have had second thoughts about moving forward. This is the major reason I wanted a quality brochure to help tell my story of why I planned to write a book to honor these star ball players from the black ball (Negro League) era.

Dr. Leslie Heaphy was very excited about my project. Michael Haupert (a baseball historian, writer and Professor of Economics at the University of Wisconsin-Lacrosse) was excited about what I was trying to accomplish through the book. Note: In December 2011, Michael encouraged me to break my potential 500-600 page book in to two books (thank you Michael).

The feedback I received was very encouraging. Larry Lester and Dick Clark (SABR Negro League co-chairman) were very supportive also. Two former Negro League players, "Jumping Johnny" Wilson and Al Spearman wished me well with the writing.

In October 2011, I met Bill Blair in Dallas Texas. He was a former pitcher for the Indianapolis Clowns (1946-1951) when the Negro Leagues were on their last legs (Major League Baseball team owners were signing all the great Negro League players). Bill helped me to be on "Talking Sports" with Roger B. Brown. This provided me with an opportunity to reach the African-American community and tell them about my future book to "honor black ball".

Also, my pastor and men's group at church provided me a forum for an informal presentation which sharpened my skills for a presentation to the Rockwall Noon Rotary Club. The presentation (in early November) to this group of 100 + business men and women gave me further confidence that my writing about honoring players of the Negro Leagues would play to a wider audience.

Also in November 2011, Paul Rogers III (Dallas Chapter President, SABR) invited me to speak at the monthly chapter meeting of local baseball historians. It was another fun night with baseball historian enthusiasts.

Baseball historians, Bill James and Mark Amour have had a profound impact on my book. I have enjoyed Bill James as a writer since the 1990s. Without Bill James and some of the other pioneers of finding new ways to measure baseball by the numbers, there would be no "Money Ball". Mark Armour used Bill James groundbreaking "Win Shares" book to show conclusively the impact of integration on improved play on the field. Mark Armour alludes to the fact there must have been Willie Mays/Frank Robinson like ball players in the Negro Leagues (Paige, Gibson, Charleston etc.), too bad we have no way to honor them. How about *The Best Season – The First 90 Games,* followed by *The Best Season – The Challenging Finish?*

Thanks to Pat in the National Baseball Hall of Fame Photo Archives Department for helping me to access their Buck Leonard action photo for the cover of my first book.

When Michael Haupert suggested I split my book in two, I was 98% of the way done with half my book. I began to look in to the possibility of self-publishing my book. When I completed my research of self publishing companies, Dog Ear Publishing came out on top. Thank you, Mark Jackson and your great team.

Two of our close friends from church are Julie and Mark Atwood. Julie is an author of some wonderful books. Mark, her husband helps Julie self-publish her books. Before I sent my manuscript to Dog Ear Publishing, Julie edited my entire manuscript.

Mark gave me insight to the self publishing process. Thank you Julie and Mark for all of your help and your words of encouragement.

I want to add my special thanks to all of my family, our church family and friends for their prayer support and encouragement.

Bob May
March 2012

End Notes

Introduction

1. Gordon Company Productions, Phil Alden Robinson Film, *Field of Dreams,* based on the book *Shoeless Joe* by W. P. Kinsella, Universal City Studios, 1989.
2. Bill James and Jim Henzler (Stats Inc.), *Win Shares,* STATS Publishing, a division of Sports Teams Analysis and Tracking Systems, Inc. March 2002; copyright 2002 by Bill James and STATS, Inc.
3. Bill James, *The New Bill James Historical Baseball Abstract,* Free Press, a division of Simon and Schuster, Inc., 1230 Avenue of the Americas, New York, NY 10020, copyright 2001 by Bill James. First Free Press trade paperback edition published 2003.
4. Mark Armour, Baseball Biography Project, *MLB Integration, 1947-1986.* This article was originally published as *The Effects of Integration* in Jim Charlton (Editor), Baseball Research Journal 36 (SABR 2007).
5. Bill James, *The New Bill James Historical Baseball Abstract,* First Free Press trade paperback edition, 2003 (pages 358-368).
6. Kevin Czerwinski, *Finishing What He Started,* MLB.com, September 2006.
7. Kadir Nelson (words and paintings by), *We Are The Ship,* The Story of Negro League Baseball, 2008, First Inning, pages 2-3, , published by Jump at the Son/Hyperion Books for Children, an imprint of Disney Book Group.

Chapter 1 – Black Ball Player Biographies/Roster

1. There were three website resources used for the twenty-one Black Ball Players Biographies.
   - Negro League Baseball.com
   - NLPA.com (Negro League Players Association)
   - BaseballHall.org (National Baseball Hall of Fame).
2. .Bill James, *The New Bill James Baseball Abstract*, First Free Press paperback edition (2003), pages 358-368.
3. BaseballHall.org/members/Lloyd (bio), quote from Hall of Fame Short-stop, Honus Wagner.
4. NegroLeagueBaseball.com, click on "Negro League Players", click on " James Cool Papa Bell", see notes (first paragraph) for story from Satchel Paige on Bell's speed.
5. *Total Baseball,* edited by John Thorn and Pete Palmer with Michael Gershman, Third Edition (1993), copyright *Total Baseball* (1993), data from Part Two – The Annual Record.
   - National League, 1956 (Page 2036) for Newcombe.
   - American League, 1968 (Page 2061) for Tiant.
   - National League, 1979 (Page 2082) for Richard.
   - American League, 1985 (Page 2095) for Moore.

Publisher of Total Baseball is Harper Perrenial (1993).

Chapter 9 – Best Season Nine-Game Series 4 - BB Stars vs.Reds

1. Bill James, *Bill James Historical Baseball Abstract,* First Free Press Paperback Edition (2003), see page 893.

Chapter 14 – Best Season Nine-Game Series 4 - BB Stars vs Tigers

1. Bill James, *Bill James Historical Baseball Abstract,* First Free Press Paperback Edition (2003), see page 193.
2. Larry Tye, *Satchel,* Random House Trade Paperback Edition (2010), Copyright by Larry Tye (2009), free agency (pages 195, 269 and 289).
3. Larry Tye, *Satchel,* Random House Trade Paperback Edition (2010), Copyright by Larry Tye (2009), 1948, Cleveland Indians (pages 204-219).

Bibliography

Unpublished Sources

- Blair, Bill, publisher of The Elite weekly newspaper, Dallas TX. Former Negro League player, interviewd October, 2011.
- Clark, Dick, co-chair of Society for American Baseball Research-Negro League Committee, discussed project in July 2011.
- Doswell, Ray, Executive Director, Negro League Baseball Museum, received input at various times in late 2010 and throughout 2011.
- Haupert, Michael, Professor of Economics, Wisconsin-Lacrosse University and a baseball historian encouraged me to write in July 2011. In December 2011, he suggested splitting my original manuscript in half (one book became two books).
- Heaphy, Leslie, Detail Editor for Black Ball, A Journal of the Negro Leagues. She originally suggested I attend Lester Malloy Negro League Conference in July 2011. She wrote the Foreword to the book.
- Irvin, Monte, member of the National Baseball Hall of Fame, former player for the Negro League Newark Eagles and the Major League New York Giants, interviewd in July 2011.
- Kurkjian, Tim, baseball analyst (ESPN) provided positive feedback on excerpts from manuscript.
- Lester, Larry, co-chair of Society for American Baseball Research Negro League Committee, discussed project in July 2011.
- Rogers,lll, Paul, Professor of Law at Southern Methodist University as well as the SABR Chapter President for DFW region. He asked me to speak at the November 2011 Chapter Meeting about this writing project.

- Spearman, Al, former pitcher for the Chicago American Giants, who spent an hour on the phone (August 2011) sharing about his life in the Negro Leagues and the minor leagues.
- Wilson, Johnny, former player in the Negro Leagues and a star with the Harlem Globetrotters professional basketball team. Interviewed him in July 2011.

Published Resources

- Armour, Mark, Baseball Biography Project, *MLB Integration, 1947-1986.* This article was originally published as *The Effects of Integration* in Jim Charlton (Editor), Baseball Research Journal 36 (SABR 2007).
- Cieslinki, Mike, Copyright of Pursue the Pennant Baseball Board Game (1985).
- Czerwinski, Kevin, *Finishing what he started,* MLB.Com.
- Henzler, Jim and James, Bill, *Win Shares,* STATS Publishing, a division of Sports Teams Analysis and Tracking Systems, Inc. March 2002; copyright 2002 by Bill James and STATS, Inc.
- James, Bill, *The New Bill James Historical Baseball Abstract,* Free Press, a division of Simon and Schuster, Inc., 1230 Avenue of the Americas, New York, NY 10020, copyright 2001 by Bill James. First Free Press trade paperback edition published 2003.
- Nelson, Kadir, words and paintings by, *We Are The Ship,* The Story of Negro League Baseball, 2008, published by Jump at the Son/Hyperion Books for Children, an imprint of Disney Book Group.
- Palmer, Pete and Thorn, John with Gershwin, Michael, Third Edition (1993), copyright *Total Baseball* (1993), published by HarperPerennial, a division of HarperCollinsPublishers.
- Tye, Larry, *Satchel,* Random House Trade Paperback Edition (2010), Copyright by Larry Tye (2009)

Broadcasts

- Gordon Company Productions, Phil Alden Robinson Film, *Field of Dreams,* based on the book *Shoeless Joe* by W. P. Kinsella, Universal City Studios, 1989.

Websites

- *www.BaseballHall.org,* information accessed February 2012.
- *www.NegroLeagueBaseball.com,* information accessed February 2012.
- *www.nlpa.com,* information accessed February 2012.

Recommended Reading – Black Ball Era

- Gay, Timothy, *Satch, Dizzy and Rapid Robert,* the wild saga of interracial baseball before Jackie Robinson, Simon and Schuster Paperback (2011), copyright by Timothy Gay (2010).

- Nelson, Kadir, words and paintings by, *We Are The Ship,* The Story of Negro League Baseball, 2008, published by Jump at the Son/Hyperion Books for Children, an imprint of Disney Book Group.

- Peterson, Robert, *Only The Ball Was White,* a history of legendary black players and all-black professional teams, Oxford University Press, copyright by Robert Peterson (1970).

- Tye, Larry, *Satchel,* the life and times of an American Legend, Random House Trade Paperback Edition (2010), Copyright by Larry Tye (2009)

About the Author

The Best Season – The First Ninety Games
Honoring Black Ball through baseball game simulation.

Bob May (author) – Bob has been a passionate baseball fan all his life. He has 55 years of experience in playing the best baseball board game simulations. He believes that sophisticated baseball board game simulations are an excellent way to measure performance across eras without losing the play-by-play experience of being at the park and making each managerial decision.

In 1987, Bob purchased a Pursue the Pennant baseball board game. He was so pleased with the "on the field" realism (player's statistics reflecting ball park factors) within two years he became an invested partner in the company. He became President. In 1993, he led his management team in the creation of the player card set with 416 great players from the 1880s to the 1980s, including twenty-one players from the Black Ball Era (segregated Negro Leagues). Eighteen years later (2010) his research (which led to this book) began.

This is Bob's first book. There is a second book to come, *The Best Season –The Challenging Finish,* which will complete the 165 games + playoffs.

In the summer of 2011, Bob was sharing his baseball book writing project with a pastor friend of his. The pastor said with a smile "Isn't it nice when God lets us play in our own sandbox?" Bob believes that these books can help to bring us closer and to be more respectful of one another. It is time we begin to honor one another. Bob knows that God has definitely honored him by giving him a purpose to write these books.

Made in United States
North Haven, CT
22 February 2023

33031810R00148